Transitional Objects and Potential Spaces:

Literary Uses of D. W. WINNICOTT

PSYCHOANALYSIS AND CULTURE

Arnold M. Cooper and Steven Marcus, Editors

Also by Peter L. Rudnytsky

Freud and Oedipus (1987)

Ed., Ivan L. Rudnytsky, *Essays in Modern Ukrainian History* (1988)

Ed., *The Persistence of Myth: Psychoanalytic and Structuralist Perspectives* (1988)

Ed. (with Marie-Rose Logan), *Contending Kingdoms: Historical, Psychological, and Feminist Approaches to the Literature of Sixteenth-Century England and France* (1990)

The Psychoanalytic Vocation: Rank, Winnicott, and the Legacy of Freud (1991)

Introduction for Otto Rank, *The Incest Theme in Literature and Legend* (1992)

Ed. (with Ellen Handler Spitz), *Freud and Forbidden Knowledge* (1993)

Transitional Objects and Potential Spaces:

Literary Uses of
D. W. WINNICOTT

EDITED BY PETER L. RUDNYTSKY

COLUMBIA UNIVERSITY PRESS
New York

Columbia University Press
New York   Chichester, West Sussex
Copyright © 1993 Columbia University Press
All rights reserved

Library of Congress Cataloging-in-Publication Data

Transitional objects and potential spaces: literary uses of D. W.
Winnicott / edited by Peter L. Rudnytsky.
p.   cm. —(Psychoanalysis and culture)
Collection of previously published articles, 1952–1989.
Includes bibliographical references and index.
ISBN 0–231–07572–3 (alk. paper)
1. Criticism.
2. Object relations (Psychoanalysis) in literature.
3. Winnicott, D. W. (Donald Woods), 1896–1971—Influences.
I. Rudnytsky, Peter L.   II. Series.
PN98.P75 T 73   1993
801′.95—dc20
92-43907
CIP

⊗

Printed in the United States of America
c 10 9 8 7 6 5 4 3 2 1

In Memory of Madeleine Davis

Contents

Acknowledgments

I am grateful to Jennifer Crewe of Columbia University Press for her support of this project and to the contributors for their cooperation. I wish to thank the editors and publishers who have allowed me to reprint the papers gathered here, especially David Tuckett of the *International Review of Psycho-Analysis*. The book is dedicated to the memory of one who embodied the spirit of Winnicott's teachings and unstintingly promoted the dissemination and understanding of his work.

Permission to reprint the previously published papers in this volume has been graciously granted by the following: D. W. Winnicott, "The Location of Cultural Experience," in *Playing and Reality* (London: Tavistock, 1971), by Mark Paterson and Associates and by Tavistock Publications; Marion Milner, "The Role of Illusion in Symbol Formation," in M. Klein, P. Heimann, and R. E. Money-Kyrle, eds., *New Directions in Psycho-Analysis,* (New York: Basic Books, 1955), originally published as "Aspects of Symbolism in Comprehension of the Not-Self," *International Journal of Psycho-Analysis* 33 (1952), copyright © Institute of Psycho-Analysis, by David Tuckett; Christopher Bollas, "The Aesthetic Moment and the Search for Transformation," *The Annual of Psychoanalysis* 6 (1978), by Jerome A. Winer, M.D.;

Murray Schwartz, "Where Is Literature?" *College English* 36 (1975), by the National Council of Teachers of English; Albert D. Hutter, "Poetry in Psychoanalysis: Hopkins, Rosetti, Winnicott," *International Review of Psycho-Analysis* 63 (1982), copyright © Institute of Psycho-Analysis, by David Tuckett; Madelon Sprengnether, "Ghost Writing: A Meditation on Literary Criticism as Narrative," in J. Reppen and M. Charney, eds., *The Psychoanalytic Study of Literature*, (Hillsdale, N.J.: Analytic Press, 1985), by Analytic Press; David Willbern, "Phantasmagoric *Macbeth*," *English Literary Renaissance* 16 (1986), by Arthur F. Kinney; Antoinette B. Dauber, "Thomas Traherne and the Poetics of Object Relations," *Criticism* 23 (1981), by Wayne State University Press; John Turner, "Wordsworth and Winnicott in the Area of Play," *International Journal of Psycho-Analysis* 15 (1988), copyright © Institute of Psycho-Analysis, by David Tuckett; David Holbrook, "Lawrence's False Solution," originally published as "The Fiery Hill: *Lady Chatterley's Lover*," in *The Quest for Love* (London: Methuen, 1964), by David Holbrook; Richard Poirier, "Frost, Winnicott, Burke," *Raritan* 2 (1982), by Richard Poirier; Patrick J. Casement, "Samuel Beckett's Relationship to His Mother-Tongue," *International Review of Psycho-Analysis* 9 (1982), copyright © Institute of Psycho-Analysis, by David Tuckett; Brooke Hopkins, "Jesus and Object-Use," *International Review of Psycho-Analysis* 16 (1989), copyright © Institute of Psycho-Analysis, by David Tuckett; and Ellen Handler Spitz, "Picturing the Child's Inner World of Fantasy: On the Dialectic between Image and Word," *The Psychoanalytic Study of the Child* 43 (1988), Yale University Press.

Introduction

PETER L. RUDNYTSKY

*Der Mensch spielt nur, wo er in
voller Bedeutung des Worts Mensch
ist, und er ist nur da ganz Mensch,
wo er spielt.*   —Schiller

As the foremost representative of the British Independent tradition of object relations theory, D. W. Winnicott (1896–1971) is increasingly acknowledged to be one of the most important figures in psychoanalysis since Freud. His work has had an immense impact in Great Britain not only on his professional colleagues but also on the culture at large (where his renown as a pediatrician can be compared to that of Dr. Benjamin Spock in the United States) and has influenced the thought and practice of analysts throughout the world. Strikingly, however, even today Winnicott's ideas remain comparatively unknown among those in the universities—mainly, but not exclusively, literary scholars—who are drawn to psychoanalysis and employ it in their own work. This is true in Britain as well as the United States, for in both countries the perspective on psychoanalysis adopted by most academics has been filtered through the French postmodernist lens of Jacques Lacan, rather than the humanist lens of the English Winnicott. There must be ten literary critics conversant with Lacan's *Écrits* for every one who has read Winnicott's *Playing and Reality*. It is not necessary to polarize Lacan and Winnicott into diametrically opposed alternatives to deplore this state of affairs and to surmise that those whose knowledge of psychoanalysis is confined to books might have something to learn from the esteem in which Winnicott is held by practicing analysts.

Winnicott's neglect by literary scholars is all the more surprising since Independent object relations theory can claim to offer the first satisfactory psychoanalytic account of aesthetics. Freud and his early disciples such as Otto Rank ultimately viewed the work of art as the disguised transformation of a masturbation fantasy (Rudnytsky 1992). Melanie Klein and her followers added a consideration of the role played by destructive and reparative impulses in artistic creation, but this rival species of object relations theory still treats the work of art as a derivative of forces that in themselves are not aesthetic. Within the framework of American ego psychology, Ernst Kris formulated the idea of "regression in the service of the ego" (1952:243–64), a valuable contribution to the understanding of creativity, but one that remains hobbled by the limitations of Freud's structural theory, with its lack of a superordinate concept of self. Lacanians have purloined many specific texts to impressive effect, but their model of the three registers—the Imaginary, the Symbolic, and the Real—does not appear to yield a comprehensive metapsychology of art.

Each of the three phrases that form the title and subtitle of this volume contains a term pivotal to Winnicott's thought; taken together they epitomize his psychoanalytic aesthetics. *Transitional objects,* his best-known concept (put forward in a paper published in 1953), are the ubiquitous first possessions of infants and young children—a blanket, teddy bear, or doll—that belong at once to them and to the outside world. The intermediate quality of transitional objects between fantasy and reality foreshadows that of works of art, which likewise partake simultaneously of reality and illusion. In "The Location of Cultural Experience" (1967), reprinted in this volume, Winnicott named this third area between complete subjectivity and complete objectivity, in which play and aesthetic experience can occur, *potential space.* This space originally both joins and separates a mother and baby. Although Winnicott always speaks of potential *space* in the singular, since it constitutes a conceptual rather than an empirical realm, I have deliberately employed the plural form to evoke the uniqueness of every relationship between two human beings or between a work of art and its critics. The last of these concepts (not advanced until 1969) is the *use of an object.* By "use" Winnicott means the venting of destructive impulses, and an object (or person) must be able to survive an individual's destructive attacks if it is to be placed in the sphere of external reality. This difficult idea attests to the abiding influence on Winnicott's thinking of Klein, to whose party in the British Psycho-Analytical Society he belonged before joining what became known as the Middle Group.

Uniquely among psychoanalytic approaches to art, Winnicott's respects art's integrity as an autonomous human activity, while continuing to insist on its infantile origins. He derives art from *play,* a child's state of relaxed absorption made possible by its mother's unobtrusive presence, which differs from masturbation in that it terminates if somatic urges become too insistent. At first the mother (or other primary caregiver) must endow her infant with the capacity for illusion by making her love (metonymically represented by the breast) available on demand, but she must then also accustom the infant to disillusionment by gradual failures of empathy. Art provides a lifelong refuge to which we can turn as we negotiate our precarious oscillations between illusion and reality. Art, like play, must be situated in both a *temporal* and a *spatial* dimension, as Winnicott does with his concepts of transitional objects and potential space. His emphasis on destructiveness as a means of creating externality preserves an instinctual element in the equation, and he recognizes that sexual fantasies also haunt the theater of the mind, although they do not form its ultimate ground.

Even with respect to psychoanalytic colleagues, Winnicott rarely acknowledged intellectual debts, preferring to follow his idiosyncratic line of development and to derive inspiration from his clinical work. Strikingly, he never quotes Freud's dictum in "Creative Writers and Day-Dreaming" that "the opposite of play is not what is serious but what is real" (1908:144), though it hovers subliminally in the title of *Playing and Reality.* Still less did Winnicott define himself in relation to philosophical or literary history. Despite his lack of a scholarly temperament, Winnicott's ideas possess illustrious antecedents. His contention that art occurs in an autonomous domain and cannot be reduced to sublimation converges with Kant's theory of the *disinterestedness* of aesthetic experience in *The Critique of Judgment* (1790). According to Kant, whereas "the delight which we connect with the representation of the real existence of an object is called interest" and thus "always involves a reference to the faculty of desire," aesthetic judgments are disinterested because they are not "concerned in the real existence of the thing" (42–43). Both Kant and Winnicott exempt aesthetic experience from reality-testing, and Winnicott (1963) explains the freedom from desire in disinterestedness by suggesting that children's play arises in response not to the libidinally exciting "object-mother" but to the quietly supportive "environmental-mother." Kant leads directly to Schiller, who in *Letters on the Aesthetic Education of Man* (1795) defined play as the highest expression of human freedom. Winnicott never alludes to Schiller's theory of play, but he remains the latter's lineal descendant.

It must be acknowledged that the German idealists have fallen into disfavor in contemporary criticism. Above all, the concept of disinterestedness affronts politically oriented postmodernists, who insist that art is always contaminated by ideology and hence devoid of transcendence. The legacy of Kant and Schiller, moreover, passes through Coleridge's theory of imagination into New Criticism whose presiding genius was T. S. Eliot which dominated Anglo-American literary study during the 1950s and 1960s but has subsequently been widely condemned for using formalism to promote a reactionary cultural and political agenda.

Although the challenge to the Kantian tradition has been salutary, Winnicott points the way to a counterstatement. In the introduction to *Playing and Reality* he announces that his contribution is "to ask for a paradox to be accepted and tolerated and respected, and for it not to be resolved"; the notion that cultural experience takes place in an "intermediate area," he adds, "appears in full force in the work characteristic of the so-called metaphysical poets (Donne, etc.)" (1971:xi–xii). Like the New Critics, he esteems paradox as a trope of the imagination and invokes metaphysical poetry as a touchstone. Despite the right-wing leanings of Eliot and many American New Critics, a reverence for paradox cannot be correlated with any particular political position, though it does imply a subordination of politics to aesthetics, an inherently conservative tendency. A capacity to tolerate paradox simply enables one to see life from more than one point of view and therefore combats dogmatism in any form. Winnicott himself was an ardent democrat and socially progressive. His devotion to paradox exemplifies Keats's definition of Negative Capability as a willingness to remain in "uncertainties, Mysteries, doubts, without any irritable reaching after fact & reason" (Rollins 1972:193).

That aesthetic experience constitutes a unique realm governed by its own laws was first grasped by Aristotle in the *Poetics* when he remarked that human beings take pleasure in the representation of painful events in tragedy, whereas the same events would cause suffering in real life. Kant builds on Aristotle by grounding the distinction between aesthetic and nonaesthetic experience in terms of the response elicited. As Murray Krieger explains: "What would characterize the experience as aesthetic rather than either cognitive or moral would be its self-sufficiency, its capacity to trap us within itself, to keep us from moving beyond it to further knowledge or to practical effects" (1976:11).

In my view, the category of the aesthetic remains indispensable despite the recent challenges that have been mounted against it. No theory of art can be sustained that does not take into account the human capacity to entertain illusions and distinguish them from reality. The crucial test of whether an object or experience is aesthetic, however, lies neither in its intrinsic nature nor solely in the state of mind of the person who confronts it, but in the relation between the two. In "The Role of Illusion in Symbol Formation," included in this volume, Marion Milner highlights the concept of a *frame,* which "marks off the different kind of reality within it from that which is outside it." A frame, like the aesthetic realm it demarcates, can be defined only pragmatically and in certain mystical moments may even seem to enclose the great Globe itself. Like the temporal and spatial boundaries necessary to do analysis or teaching, the frame around a work of art transports the beholder into a realm in which life appears under the aegis of contemplation rather than action.

Object relations psychoanalysis vindicates the Aristotelian and Kantian tradition by drawing attention to the infantile origins of aesthetic experience. In "The Aesthetic Moment and the Search for Transformation," also included in this volume, Christopher Bollas traces the "deep rapport between subject and object" in epiphanic moments to the "first human aesthetic" of maternal care. Bollas goes beyond Winnicott by deriving the transitional object from the mother's function as a *transformational object* for the infant. The mother transforms the infant through her unique way of holding, handling, and feeding it, and these existential memories of our earliest self-states, Bollas contends, are reenacted when the "beseeching subject" seeks in works of art "an experience where the unintegrations of self find integrations through the form."

Read in conjunction with *Playing and Reality* as a whole, the three papers by Winnicott, Milner, and Bollas in this volume lay the foundation for an object relations aesthetics. The papers are closely interconnected. Winnicott and Milner used each other as sounding boards and developed their ideas in tandem during the 1950s and 1960s; Bollas acknowledges his indebtedness to Milner. "The Location of Cultural Experience" shows how radical a thinker Winnicott became in his final years. He embraces the outlook of W. R. D. Fairbairn, the intellectual architect of object relations theory, from whom he had formerly distanced himself, and criticizes drive theory because it is a capacity for "total experience" and "not instinctual satisfaction that makes a baby begin to be." He urges psychoanalysts "to tackle the question of *what life itself is about*" and concludes by affirming that the formation of potential space depends on "experience that leads to trust," and "can be looked upon as sacred." Without recourse to religion, Winnicott restores a transcendent dimension to cultural experiences, "which provide the continuity in the human race" across generations and begin in children's play.

For Milner, as for Winnicott, art "provides a method, in adult life, for reproducing states that are part of everyday experience in healthy infancy." Her emphasis on *healthy* infancy typifies the Independent tradition, as does her recognition that emotional growth depends on a "capacity in the environment" to meet the child's needs. Milner tactfully qualifies both Ernest Jones's classic Freudian theory of symbolism as the result of sexual repression and Klein's exclusive concentration on anxiety and destructiveness by pointing out that a capacity for prelogical thinking is integral to developing "a creative relation to the world." Milner interweaves aesthetic and psychoanalytic theory by presenting a case history, for which she has a special gift, and adduces the literary examples of Traherne and Wordsworth, writers taken up in detail by other contributors to this volume.

Although one of Bollas's earliest papers, "The Aesthetic Moment and the Search for Transformation" shows why he is the most creative and original thinker of the post-Winnicottian generation. Like Milner, he brings compelling clinical material to bear on the search for the transformational object but is equally at home in literature. He cites the example of Ishmael smitten by the portrait of a whale in Melville's *Moby-Dick* to illustrate how, if a person's language has been dissociated from feeling, an aesthetic moment may occur "when he faces a formidable and confusing external object that establishes an internal confusion in the subject." This search on the part of schizoid individuals, not for integration but for an objective correlative to their "internal confusion," helps to explain the alienating effect of much modern art. According to Bollas, "we learn the grammar of our being before we grasp the rules of our language." Language succeeds the mother as a transformational object informed by one's personal aesthetic. Understanding in verbal communication occurs when a listener's empathic response produces a "symmetry with the environment," on the model of a mother who alters the environment to make it "symmetrical" to her infant's need. Bollas thus subsumes a theory of language, the alpha and omega for Lacanians, within an object relations framework, which recognizes that nonverbal affects precede linguistic representations.

The remaining three papers in the first part, "The Analytic Frame," extend the implications of Winnicott's ideas in important ways. In "Where Is Literature?" Murray Schwartz argues that literary criticism "originates in our personal experiences of individual works" and answers the question posed in his title by situating literature in the potential space between inner and outer reality. Schwartz's awareness of the need to reconcile subjective and objective realms leads him to call for a mode of reading that strives "to play at resymbolizing the work of art in terms of our own identities *and* to test this process against the historically given aspects of the work." Albert D. Hutter, both a practicing analyst and a literary critic, melds his two fields of expertise in "Poetry in Psychoanalysis: Hopkins, Rossetti, Winnicott." Probing the literary allusions of a patient in a clinical vignette from *Playing and Reality*, Hutter urges that "like poetry, the analytic experience works when it is perceived neither as something done *to* the patient nor as something done *by* the analyst," but rather as a process unfolding in a shared potential space. In his approach to literature, Hutter, like Schwartz, seeks to "combine subjective response and our attempts to be objective about a text." Madelon Sprengnether's "Ghost Writing: A Meditation on Literary Criticism as Narrative" movingly recounts her evolution, under Winnicott's tutelage, from denial to acceptance of "the shapes of my desire revealed in my critical writing." Sprengnether discovers in her young daughter's responses to the mysteries of life a prototype for her own unconsciously motivated critical endeavors. By making contact with her personal vulnerabilities, Sprengnether attains her acutest insights into literary texts and becomes herself an inspiration to other psychoanalytic critics.

Whereas the papers in part one stake out general theoretical positions, those in "Literary Objects" deploy Winnicott in the reading of specific authors and texts. I have arranged the contributions in chronological order of the writers discussed—from Shakespeare to Beckett—to evoke a Winnicottian canon, though by no means an exclusive one. At the heart of David Willbern's profound and wide-ranging "Phantasmagoric *Macbeth*" is the suggestion that "Shakespeare provides his audience with a framed potential space wherein he presents a character, Macbeth, for whom such a space is closed off." Willbern compares Lady Macbeth's mysterious child to the dagger hallucinated by Macbeth as "an *extradramatic* apparition, a transitional phenomenon proffered to us, the audience, as our own quandary," which "compels us to share Macbeth's epistemological and psychological disorientations." He thus radically transforms the received understanding of the most vexing critical questions that have arisen concerning this tragedy.

Since Milner cites Traherne and Wordsworth, and Wordsworth's preoccupation with infancy in his poetry is indebted to Traherne's, it is appropriate that these two writers should be the subjects of the ensuing essays. Antoinette B. Dauber's "Thomas Traherne and the Poetics of Object Relations" attributes Traherne's uniqueness among seventeenth-century English poets to his rejection of the "psychological consensus" concerning the playthings that compensate the young soul for its separation from God. Whereas Henry Vaughan "gratefully receives the consolation of the transitional object as a divine gift," Traherne "blames such attractive objects for the loss of the first bliss." In a scholarly and historically responsible fashion, Dauber at once elucidates Traherne's vision and demonstrates the convergence between his religious preoccupations and contemporary object relations theory. John Turner's magisterial "Wordsworth and Winnicott in the Area of Play" compresses a book into article form. He first describes "the necessity for paradox" to Wordsworth's project in the "Immortality Ode," then connects paradox to the theme of "betrayal of central trust" in Wordsworth's poetry as a whole and explores the "culture of subjectivity" in Romanticism generally, goes on to situate Winnicott's fascination with play and paradox in the context of "a social as well as intellectual history of the idea of illusion from the Romantic age onward," and finally offers some caveats concerning this bourgeois tradition. For all Winnicott's strengths, Turner admonishes, those who are "looking for a language with which to explore injustice" will turn to his writings in vain because his account of culture ignores the "social, economic, and political relations" that shape subjectivity.

The remaining three papers in "Literary Objects" stand out for the distinctiveness of their individual perspectives. A pupil and successor of F. R. Leavis at Downing College, Cambridge, David Holbrook, who knew Winnicott personally, brings a moral sensibility to bear on his assessment of "Lawrence's False Solution." Although Lawrence has roots in a tradition of spiritual discipline going back to John Bunyan, which accepts that "there are values and truths greater than the individual such as may be found in love and personal relationship, or in a sense of life's continuity that transcends mere personal existence," Holbrook holds that in *Lady Chatterley's Lover* Lawrence betrays these ideals in favor of a misogynistic and ultimately dehumanizing glorification of sex. He traces Lawrence's creative impasse to his disturbed relationship with his mother. Holbrook's reading is a powerful one, and his humanism reflects an important facet of Winnicott's legacy.

Richard Poirier, one of America's most eminent critics, adds a stylish American canvas to the gallery of English portraits. His "Frost, Winnicott, Burke" juxtaposes Winnicott's theories, Frost's poetry, and the Emersonian meditations of Kenneth Burke. Taking for granted that Frost's genius needs to be understood "in the aspect of childhood," Poirier highlights his "conflicts of self-identification" to argue that he does not regard words as the referential signs of things, but things as the opaque signs of words. A variant of Winnicott's paradox concerning transitional objects, which are at once subjective and objective, this inversion leads Poirier to the deconstructionist conclusion—the antithesis of Holbrook's Leavisite solemnity—that Frost "is essentially unknowable and unfindable" and that "there is in his poetry a true absence of self."

With Christopher Bollas, Patrick Casement is the most distinguished member of his generation of the Middle Group in the British Psycho-Analytical Society. His books carry forward the tradition of brilliant clinical writing for which the Independents have long been renowned. "Samuel Beckett's Relationship to His Mother-Tongue" is a foray into applied psychoanalysis that further expands the cultural and theoretical horizons of this volume. Drawing on biographical evidence, Casement proposes that Beckett's abandonment of English in favor of French as his literary language "expressed his need to escape from his turbulent relationship with his mother." Only after her death in 1950 did Beckett begin to translate his French writings into English. The retreat into French, Casement surmises, afforded Beckett a sort of affectless potential space in which he could "attempt to state his darkest thoughts without actually confronting the inner sphere in which these thoughts were located." The autobiographical resonances of many passages in Beckett's fiction can be clearly heard thanks to Casement's sensitive analysis.

Neither clinical nor literary, the four papers gathered in the final part, "Cultural Fields," cast a Winnicottian searchlight over a wide range of phenomena. Brooke Hopkins's "Jesus and Object-Use: A Winnicottian Account of the Resurrection Myth" expounds the central article of Christian faith by means of Winnicott's idea that an object becomes real for an individual by surviving the destructive attacks directed against it in fantasy. Hopkins does not disparage religion but rather makes it possible to understand its power in psychological terms. Hopkins's analysis has the elegance of simplicity; it will permanently alter the reader's understanding of Christianity. Whereas Hopkins examines culture in its most sophisticated manifestation, Ellen Handler Spitz returns to its developmental origins in "Picturing the Child's Inner World of Fantasy: On the Dialectic Between Image and Word." She takes up children's picturebooks, specifically Maurice Sendak's *Where the Wild Things Are*. Picturebooks are among children's first artifacts, and, Spitz notes, they are intended to facilitate "those unheralded but cataclysmic moments in childhood when gaps between the world of image and verbal language are being negotiated." As in the resurrection myth, or artistic masterpieces for adults, the picturebook allows the child to make regressive contact with its "wild things" or destructive fantasies, while providing a holding environment—ranging from the containers of form and convention to literally the parent's lap—to ensure that "there will be a safe return to reality." Synthesizing Klein and Winnicott, Spitz honors the psychoanalytic commitment to childhood in practice as well as theory.

An opposition between what is seen and what is heard likewise informs Claire Kahane's "Gender and Voice in Transitional Phenomena." Without denying Winnicott's greatness, Kahane mounts a sophisticated feminist critique of his limitations. She echoes John Turner in arguing that Winnicott overlooks the ways that culture "not only holds but *captures* both mother and infant within its prevailing symbolic network of representations constructed according to the norms of a masculine subject." Kahane thus aligns herself with the political postmodernists who reject the concept of disinterestedness because aesthetic experience is always tainted by ideology. I have upheld the contrary view, but her rejoinder is a necessary one that enhances this collection. Kahane instances the photographic self-portraits of Cindy Sherman as commentaries on how inauthentically women are represented in contemporary culture; her contrast between visual and acoustic mirrors draws on the influential work of Julia Kristeva. The final essay, Anne M. Wyatt-Brown's "From the Clinic to the Classroom: D. W. Winnicott, James Britton, and the Revolution in Writing Theory," seizes on the fact that James Britton, one of the leading composition theorists of our time, was Winnicott's brother-in-law to probe their intellectual affinities. Endorsing Winnicott's beliefs about "the collaborative nature of learning," Britton has increasingly put faith in "the innate creativity of children" and encouraged teachers to adopt an attitude of "friendly but detached observation" with students as they learn to write. Like the clinic, then, the classroom can be a holding environment and "a new testing ground" for Winnicott's principles.

Any theoretical commitment—even to psychoanalysis—entails the attempt to find reasons to justify one's most deeply felt intuitions about the nature of human life. Thus, one's choice of intellectual heroes, and of a philosophical outlook, is susceptible only to a limited degree to logical argument. Lacan and Winnicott concur that human subjectivity is constituted by a process of mirroring or reflection, but whereas Lacan concludes that the ego is permanently estranged from itself, Winnicott affirms that this process enables the individual "to posit an existence of the self" (1971:64). Whether the glass (or mirror) is half full or half empty depends on one's point of view. Postmodernism, in both its deconstructionist and political guises, has had its heyday, and many people are seeking a new synthesis. For those who wager that life is more than the trace, Winnicott and object relations psychoanalysis will be indispensable.

If, as I have intimated, Winnicott's ideas have been unduly neglected by scholars in the humanities, the essays in the present volume testify eloquently that this neglect has been far from complete. By making available a sampling of the superlative work in literary and cultural criticism that Winnicott has already inspired, I hope to stimulate the appetite for more. As psychoanalysis enters its second century, let the dialogue continue.

REFERENCES

Freud, S. 1908. "Creative Writers and Day-Dreaming." In vol. 9 of *The Standard Edition of the Complete Psychological Works*, pp. 142–53. Edited and translated by J. Strachey et al. 24 vols. London: Hogarth Press, 1953–74.

Kant, I. 1790. *The Critique of Judgment*. Translated by J. C. Meredith. Oxford: Clarendon Press, 1980.

Krieger, M. 1976. *Theory of Criticism: A Tradition and Its System*. Baltimore: Johns Hopkins University Press.

Kris, E. 1952. *Psychoanalytic Explorations in Art*. New York: International Universities Press.

Rollins, H. E., ed. 1972. *The Letters of John Keats*. Vol. 1. Cambridge: Harvard University Press.

Rudnytsky, P. L. 1992. Introduction to O. Rank, *The Incest Theme in Litera-*

ture and Legend, pp. xi–xxxv. Translated by G. C. Richter. Baltimore: Johns Hopkins University Press.

Winnicott, D. W. 1953. "Transitional Objects and Transitional Phenomena." In Winnicott 1971, pp. 1–25.

———. 1963. "The Development of the Capacity for Concern." In *The Maturational Processes and the Facilitating Environment: Studies in the Theory of Emotional Development,* pp. 73–82. New York: International Universities Press; 1965; London: Hogarth Press, 1965.

———. 1969. "The Use of an Object and Relating Through Identifications." In Winnicott 1971, pp. 86–94.

———. [1971] 1984. *Playing and Reality.* New York: Basic Books; London: Tavistock.

Part One

THE
ANALYTIC
FRAME

1

The Location of
Cultural Experience

D. W. WINNICOTT

On the seashore of endless worlds,
children play.   —Tagore

In this paper I wish to develop the theme that I stated briefly on
the occasion of the Banquet organized by the British Psycho-Analytical
Society to mark the completion of the *Standard Edition* of Freud's
works (London; October 8, 1966). In my attempt to pay tribute to
James Strachey I said:

> Freud did not have a place in his topography of the mind for the
> experience of things cultural. He gave new value to inner psychic
> reality, and from this came a new value for things that are actual and
> truly external. Freud used the word "sublimation" to point the way
> to a place where cultural experience is meaningful, but perhaps he
> did not get so far as to tell us where in the mind cultural experience
> is.

Now I want to enlarge this idea and make an attempt at a positive
statement that can be critically examined. I shall use my own language.

The quotation from Tagore has always intrigued me. In my adoles-
cence I had no idea what it could mean, but it found a place in me, and
its imprint has not faded.

When I first became a Freudian I *knew* what it meant. The sea and the shore represented endless intercourse between man and woman, and the child emerged from this union to have a brief moment before becoming in turn adult or parent. Then, as a student of unconscious symbolism, I *knew* (one always *knows*) that the sea is the mother, and onto the seashore the child is born. Babies come up out of the sea and are spewed out upon the land, like Jonah from the whale. So now the seashore was the mother's body, after the child is born and the mother and the now viable baby are getting to know each other.

Then I began to see that this employs a sophisticated concept of the parent-infant relationship and that there could be an unsophisticated infantile point of view, a different one from that of the mother or the observer, and that this infant's viewpoint could be profitably examined. For a long time my mind remained in a state of not-knowing, this state crystallizing into my formulation of the transitional phenomena. In the interim I played about with the concept of "mental representations" and with the description of these in terms of objects and phenomena located in the personal psychic reality, felt to be inside; also, I followed the effects of the operation of the mental mechanisms of projection and introjection. I realized, however, that *play is in fact neither a matter of inner psychic reality nor a matter of external reality.*

Now I have come to the subject-matter of this paper, and to the question: *if play is neither inside nor outside, where is it?* I was near to the idea that I express here in my paper "The Capacity to Be Alone" (1958), in which I said that, at first, the child is alone only in the presence of someone. In that paper I did not develop the idea of the common ground in this relationship between the child and the some-one.

My patients (especially when regressive and dependent in the trans-ference or transference dreams) have taught me how to find an answer to the question: where is play? I wish to condense what I have learned in my psychoanalytic work into a theoretical statement.

I have claimed that when we witness an infant's employment of a transitional object, the first not-me possession, we are witnessing both the child's first use of a symbol and the first experience of play. An essential part of my formulation of transitional phenomena is that we agree never to make the challenge to the baby: did you create this object, or did you find it conveniently lying around? That is to say, an essential feature of transitional phenomena and objects is a quality in our attitude when we observe them.

The object is a symbol of the union of the baby and the mother (or part of the mother). This symbol can be located. It is at the place in space and time where and when the mother is in transition from being (in the baby's mind) merged in with the infant and alternatively being experienced as an object to be perceived rather than conceived of. The use of an object symbolizes the union of two now separate things, baby and mother, *at the point in time and space of the initiation of their state of separateness.*[1]

A complication exists right from the very beginning of any consideration of this idea, in that it is necessary to postulate that if the use of the object by the baby builds up into anything (i.e., is more than an activity that might be found even in a baby born with no brain), then there must be the beginning of the setting up in the infant's mind or personal psychic reality of an image of the object. But the mental representation in the inner world is kept significant, or the imago in the inner world is kept alive, by the reinforcement given through the availability of the external separated-off and actual mother, along with her technique of child care.

It is perhaps worthwhile trying to formulate this in a way that gives the time factor due weight. The feeling of the mother's existence lasts x minutes. If the mother is away more than x minutes, then the imago fades, and along with this the baby's capacity to use the symbol of the union ceases. The baby is distressed, but this distress is soon *mended* because the mother returns in $x+y$ minutes. In $x+y$ minutes the baby has not become altered. But in $x+y+z$ minutes the baby has become *traumatized*. In $x+y+z$ minutes the mother's return does not mend the baby's altered state. Trauma implies that the baby has experienced a break in life's continuity, so that primitive defenses now become organized to defend against a repetition of "unthinkable anxiety" or a return of the acute confusional state that belongs to disintegration of nascent ego structure.

We must assume that the vast majority of babies never experience the $x+y+z$ quantity of deprivation. This means that the majority of children do not carry around with them for life the knowledge from experience of having been mad. Madness here simply means a *breakup* of whatever may exist at the time of *a personal continuity of existence.* After "recovery" from $x+y+z$ deprivation a baby has to start again, permanently deprived of the root that could provide *continuity with the personal beginning.* This implies the existence of a memory system and an organization of memories.

By contrast, from the effects of $x+y+z$ degree of deprivation, babies are constantly being *cured* by the mother's localized spoiling that mends the ego structure. This mending of the ego structure reestablishes the baby's capacity to use a symbol of union; the baby then comes once more to allow and even to benefit from separation. *This is the place that I have set out to examine,* the separation that is not a separation but a form of union.[2]

It was at an important point in the phase of development of these ideas in me in the early forties that Marion Milner (in conversation) was able to convey to me the tremendous significance that there can be in the interplay of the edges of two curtains, or of the surface of a jug that is placed in front of another jug (cf. Milner 1969).

It is to be noted that the phenomena that I am describing have no climax. This distinguishes them from phenomena that have instinctual backing, where the orgiastic element plays an essential part, and where satisfactions are closely linked with climax.

But these phenomena that have reality in the area whose existence I am postulating belong to *the experience* of relating to objects. One can think of the "electricity" that seems to generate in meaningful or intimate contact, that is a feature, for instance, when two people are in love. These phenomena of the play area have infinite variability, contrasting with the relative stereotypy of phenomena that relate either to personal body functioning or to environmental actuality.

Psychoanalysts who have rightly emphasized the significance of instinctual experience and of reactions to frustration have failed to state with comparable clearness or conviction the tremendous intensity of these nonclimactic experiences that are called playing. Starting as we do from psychoneurotic illness and with ego defenses related to anxiety that arises out of the instinctual life, we tend to think of health in terms of the state of ego defenses. We say it is healthy when these defenses are not rigid, etc. But we seldom reach the point at which we can start to describe what life is like apart from illness or absence of illness.

That is to say, we have yet to tackle the question of *what life itself is about.* Our psychotic patients force us to give attention to this sort of basic problem. We now see that it is not instinctual satisfaction that makes a baby begin to be, to feel that life is real, to find life worth living. In fact, instinctual gratifications start off as part-functions and they become *seductions* unless based on a well-established capacity in the individual person for total experience, and for experience in the area of transitional phenomena. It is the self that must precede the self's use of instinct; the rider must ride the horse, not be run away with. I could use Buffon's saying: "Le style est l'homme même." When one speaks of a man, one speaks of him *along with* the summation of his cultural experiences. The whole forms a unit.

I have used the term *cultural experience* as an extension of the idea of transitional phenomena and of play without being certain that I can define the word "culture." The accent indeed is on experience. In using the word "culture," I am thinking of the inherited tradition. I am thinking of something that is in the common pool of humanity, into which individuals and groups of people may contribute, and from which we may all draw *if we have somewhere to put what we find.*

There is a dependence here on some kind of recording method. No doubt a very great deal was lost of the early civilizations, but in the myths that were a product of oral tradition there could be said to be a cultural pool giving the history of human culture spanning six thousand years. This history through myth persists to the present time in spite of the efforts of historians to be objective, which they can never be, though they must try.

Perhaps I have said enough to show both what I know and what I do not know about the meaning of the word "culture." It interests me, however, as a side issue, that in any cultural field *it is not possible to be original except on a basis of tradition.* Conversely, no one in the line of cultural contributors repeats except as a deliberate quotation, and the unforgivable sin in the cultural field is plagiarism. The interplay between originality and the acceptance of tradition as the basis for inventiveness seems to me to be just one more example, and a very exciting one, of the interplay between separateness and union.

I must pursue a little further the topic in terms of the baby's very early experiences, when the various capacities are being initiated, made ontogenetically possible because of the mother's extremely sensitive adaptation to the needs of her baby, based on her identification with the baby. (I refer to the stages of growth before the baby has acquired mental mechanisms that do soon become available for the organizing of complex defenses. I repeat here: a human infant must travel some distance from early experiences in order to have the maturity to be deep.)

This theory does not affect what we have come to believe in respect of the etiology of psychoneurosis, or the treatment of patients who are psychoneurotic; nor does it clash with Freud's structural theory of the mind in terms of ego, id, superego. What I say does affect our view of the question: what is life about? You may cure your patient and not know what it is that makes him or her go on living. It is of first importance for us to acknowledge openly that absence of psychoneurotic illness may be health, but it is not life. Psychotic patients who are all the time hovering between living and not living force us to look at this problem, one that really belongs *not to psychoneurotics but to all human beings*. I am claiming that these same phenomena that are life and death to our schizoid or borderline patients appear in our cultural experiences. It is these cultural experiences that provide the continuity in the human race that transcends personal existence. I am assuming that cultural experiences are in direct continuity with play, the play of those who have not yet heard of games.

Main Thesis

Here, then, is my main statement. I am claiming:

1. The place where cultural experience is located is in the *potential space* between the individual and the environment (originally the object). The same can be said of playing. Cultural experience begins with creative living first manifested in play.

2. For every individual the use of this space is determined by *life experiences* that take place at the early stages of the individual's existence.

3. From the beginning the baby has maximally intense experiences *in the potential space between the subjective object and the object objectively perceived,* between me-extensions and the not-me. This potential space is at the interplay between there being nothing but me and there being objects and phenomena outside omnipotent control.

4. Every baby has his or her own favorable or unfavorable experience here. Dependence is maximal. The potential space happens only *in relation to a feeling of confidence* on the part of the baby—that is, confidence related to the dependability of the mother-figure or environmental elements, confidence being the evidence of dependability that is becoming introjected.

5. In order to study the play and then the cultural life of the individual, one must study the fate of the potential space between any one baby and the human (and therefore fallible) mother-figure who is essentially adaptive because of love.

It will be seen that if this area is to be thought of as part of the ego organization, here is a part of the ego that is not a body-ego, that is not founded on the pattern of body *functioning* but is founded on body *experiences.* These experiences belong to object-relating of a nonorgiastic kind, or to what can be called ego-relatedness, at the place where it can be said that *continuity* is giving place to *contiguity.*

Continuing Argument

This statement makes necessary an examination of the fate of this potential space, which may or may not come into prominence as a vital area in the mental life of the developing person.

What happens if the mother is able to start on a graduated failure of adaptation from a position of adapting fully? This is the crux of the matter, and the problem needs study because it affects our technique as analysts when we have patients who are regressed in the sense of being dependent. In the average good experience in this field of management (that starts so early, and that starts and starts again), the baby finds intense, even agonizing, pleasure associated with imaginative play. There is no set game, so everything is creative, and although playing is part of object-relating, whatever happens is personal to the baby. Everything physical is imaginatively elaborated, is invested with a first-time-ever quality. Can I say that this is the meaning intended for the word "cathect"?

I can see that I am in the territory of Fairbairn's (1941) concept of "object-seeking" (as opposed to "satisfaction-seeking").

As observers we note that everything in the play has been done before, has been felt before, has been smelt before, and where there appear specific symbols of the union of baby and mother (transitional objects) these very objects have been adopted, not created. Yet *for the baby* (if the mother can supply the right conditions) every detail of the baby's life is an example of creative living. Every object is a "found" object. Given the chance, the baby begins to live creatively, and to use actual objects to be creative into and with. If the baby is not given this chance, then there is no area in which the baby may have play, or may have cultural experience; then it follows that there is no link with the cultural inheritance, and there will be no contribution to the cultural pool.

The "deprived child" is notoriously restless and unable to play, and has an impoverishment of capacity to experience in the cultural field. This observation leads to a study of the effect of deprivation at the time of the loss of what has become accepted as reliable. A study of the effects of loss at any early stage involves us in looking at this intermediate area, or potential space between subject and object. Failure of dependability or loss of object means to the child a loss of the play area, and loss of meaningful symbol. In favorable circumstances the potential space becomes filled with the products of the baby's own creative imagination. In unfavorable circumstances the creative use of objects is missing or relatively uncertain. I have described elsewhere (Winnicott 1960) the way in which the defense of the compliant false self appears, with the hiding of the true self that has the potential for creative use of objects.

There is, in cases of premature failure of environmental reliability, an alternative danger, which is that this potential space may become filled with what is injected into it from someone other than the baby. It seems that whatever is in this space that comes from someone else is persecutory material, and the baby has no means of rejecting it. Analysts need to beware lest they create a feeling of confidence and an intermediate area in which play can take place and then inject into this area or inflate it with interpretations that in effect are from their own creative imaginations.

Fred Plaut, a Jungian analyst, has written a paper (1966) from which I quote:

> The capacity to form images and to use these constructively by recombination into new patterns is—unlike dreams or fantasies— dependent on the individual's ability to trust.

The word *trust* in this context shows an understanding of what I mean by the building up of confidence based on experience, at the time of maximal dependence, before the enjoyment and employment of separation and independence.

I suggest that the time has come for psychoanalytic theory to pay tribute to this *third area,* that of cultural experience which is a derivative of play. Psychotics insist on our knowing about it, and it is of great importance in our assessment of the lives rather than the health of human beings. (The other two areas are inner or personal psychic reality and the actual world with the individual living in it.)

Summary

I have tried to draw attention to the importance both in theory and in practice of a third area, that of play, which expands into creative living and into the whole cultural life of man. This third area has been contrasted with inner or personal psychic reality and with the actual world in which the individual lives, which can be objectively perceived.

I have located this important area of *experience* in the potential space between the individual and the environment, that which initially both joins and separates the baby and the mother when the mother's love, displayed or made manifest as human reliability, does in fact give the baby a sense of trust or of confidence in the environmental factor.

Attention is drawn to the fact that this potential space is a highly variable factor (from individual to individual), whereas the two other locations—personal or psychic reality and the actual world—are relatively constant, one being biologically determined and the other being common property.

The potential space between baby and mother, between child and family, between individual and society or the world, depends on experience that leads to trust. It can be looked upon as sacred to the individual in that it is here that the individual experiences creative living.

By contrast, exploitation of this area leads to a pathological condition in which the individual is cluttered up with persecutory elements of which he has no means of ridding himself.

It may perhaps be seen from this how important it can be for the analyst to recognize the existence of this place, the only place where play can start, a place that is at the continuity-contiguity moment, where transitional phenomena originate.

My hope is that I have begun to answer my own question: where is cultural experience located?

NOTES

1. It is necessary to simplify matters by referring to the use of objects, but the title of my original paper was "Transitional Objects and Transitional Phenomena" (1953).

2. Merrell Middlemore (1941) saw the infinite richness in the intertwined techniques of the nursing couple. She was near what I am attempting to state here. Rich material exists for us to observe and enjoy in this field of the bodily relationship that may (though it may not) exist between baby and mother, especially if in making our observations (whether direct or in psychoanalysis) we are not simply thinking in terms of oral erotism with satisfaction or frustration, etc.

See also Hoffer (1949, 1950).

REFERENCES

Fairbairn, W. R. D. 1941. "A Revised Psychopathology of the Psychoses and Psychoneuroses." *International Journal of Psycho-Analysis*, vol. 22.

Hoffer, W. 1949. "Mouth, Hand, and Ego-Integration." *Psychoanalytic Study of the Child*, vols. 3 / 4.

———. 1950. "Development of the Body Ego." *Psychoanalytic Study of the Child*, vol. 5.

Middlemore, M. P. 1941. *The Nursing Couple*. London: Hamish Hamilton Medical Books.

Milner, M. 1969. *The Hands of the Living God*. London: Hogarth Press.

Plaut, F. 1966. "Reflections about Not Being Able to Imagine." *Journal of Analytical Psychology*, vol. 11.

Winnicott, D. W. 1953. "Transitional Objects and Transitional Phenomena." In *Collected Papers: Through Paediatrics to Psycho-Analysis*. London: Tavistock, 1958.

———. 1958. "The Capacity to Be Alone." In *The Maturational Processes and the Facilitating Environment: Studies in the Theory of Emotional Development*. New York: International Universities Press, 1965; London: Hogarth Press, 1965.

———. 1960. "Ego Distortion in Terms of True and False Self." In Winnicott, *The Maturational Processes and the Facilitating Environment*.

2

The Role of Illusion in Symbol Formation

MARION MILNER

Psychoanalytic Concepts of the Two Functions of the Symbol

Much has been written by psychoanalysts on the process by which the infant's interest is transferred from an original primary object to a secondary one. The process is described as depending upon the identification of the primary object with another that is in reality different from it but emotionally is felt to be the same. Ernest Jones and Melanie Klein in particular, following up Freud's formulations, write about this transference of interest as being due to conflict with forces forbidding the interest in the original object, as well as to the actual loss of the original object. Jones, in his paper "The Theory of Symbolism" (1916), emphasizes the aspects of this prohibition which are to do with the forces that keep society together as a whole. Melanie Klein, in various papers, describes also the aspect of it that keeps the individual together as a whole; she maintains it is the fear of our own aggression toward our original objects that makes us so dread their retaliation that we transfer our interest to less attacked and so less frightening substitutes. Jones also describes how the transfer of interest is due not only to social prohibition and frustration and the wish to escape from the immanent frustrated mouth, penis, vagina, and their retaliating counterparts but also to the need to endow the external world with something of the self and so make it familiar and understandable.

The identification of one object with another is described as the forerunner of symbolism, and Melanie Klein, both in her paper "Infant Analysis" (1923) and in the "The Importance of Symbol Formation in the Development of the Ego" (1930), says that symbolism is the basis of all talents. Jones describes this identification as a process of symbolic equivalence through which progress to sublimation is achieved, but adds that symbolism itself, in the sense in which he uses the word, is a bar to progress. Leaving aside for a moment this difference over the use of the word *symbol*, there is one point about wording which, I feel, requires comment. Jones describes the process of identification that underlies symbol formation as being not only the result of the forbidding forces but also a result of the need to establish a relation to reality. He says that this process arises from the desire to deal with reality in the easiest possible way, from "the desire for ease and pleasure struggling with the demand of necessity." It seems to me that this way of putting it is liable to lead to misunderstanding. The phrase "desire for ease and pleasure" set against the "demand of necessity" gives the impression that this desire is something that we could, if we were sufficiently strong-minded, do without. The phrase reflects perhaps a certain puritanism which is liable to appear in psychoanalytic writing. Do we really mean that it is only the desire for ease and pleasure, and not necessity, that drives us to identify one thing with another which is in fact not the same? Are we not rather driven by the internal necessity for inner organization, pattern, coherence, the basic need to discover identity in difference without which experience becomes chaos? Actually I think Jones himself implies such an idea when he says that this confounding of one thing with another, this not discriminating, is also the basis of generalization; and he indicates the positive aspect of this failure to discriminate, in relation to discovery of the real world, when he says: "there opens up the possibility . . . of a theory of scientific discovery, inventions, etc., for psychologically this consists in an overcoming of the resistances that normally prevent regression towards the infantile unconscious tendency to note identity in differences." This was written in 1916. In 1951 Herbert Read wrote: "The first perceptions of what is novel in any science tend to assume the form of metaphors—the first stages of science are poetic."

Jones quotes Rank and Sachs when they make a distinction between the primary process of identification which underlies symbolism and symbolism itself. He quotes their description of how the original function (demonstrable in the history of civilization) of the identification underlying symbolism was a means of adaptation to reality, but that it "becomes superfluous and sinks to the mere significance of a symbol as soon as this task of adaptation has been accomplished." He quotes their description of a symbol as the "unconscious precipitate of primitive means of adaptation to reality that have become superfluous and useless, a sort of lumber room of civilization to which the adult readily flees in states of reduced or deficient capacity for adaptation to reality, in order to regain his old long-forgotten playthings of childhood." But they add the significant remark that what later generations know and regard only as a symbol had in earlier stages of mental life full and real meaning and value.

Jones goes on to quote Rank's and Sachs's statement that symbol formation is a regressive phenomenon and that it is most plainly seen in civilized man, in conditions where conscious adaptation to reality is either restricted, as in religious or artistic ecstasy, or completely abrogated, as in dreams and mental disorders. Here it seems to me that a valuable link has been made between symbolism and ecstasy, but the context in which these two ideas have been brought together leaves out, in respect of the arts, what Jones has described in respect of scientific invention: that is, that it may be a regression in order to take a step forward. Thus Rank's and Sachs's statement does not draw attention to the possibility that some form of artistic ecstasy may be an essential phase in adaptation to reality, since it may mark the creative moment in which new and vital identifications are established. In fact Rank and Sachs do not here allow for the possibility that truth underlies the much quoted aphorism that Art creates Nature; and so also they miss the chance of indicating an underlying relation between art and science.[1]

I think some of the difficulty arises here from lack of a sufficiently clear distinction between the two uses of the process that has been given the name of symbolization. Fenichel (1946) has made this distinction more clear. He says: "In adults a conscious idea may be used as a symbol for the purpose of hiding an objectionable unconscious idea; the idea of a penis may be represented by a snake, an ape, a hat, an airplane, if the idea of penis is objectionable. The distinct idea of a penis had been grasped but rejected." But he then goes on to say that symbolic thinking is also a part of the primal prelogical thinking and adds:

archaic symbolism as a part of prelogical thinking and distortion by means of representing a repressed idea through a conscious symbol are not the same. Whereas in distortion the idea of penis is avoided through disguising it by the idea of snake, in prelogical thinking penis and snake are *one and the same;* that is, they are perceived by a common conception: the sight of the snake provokes penis emotions; and this fact is later utilized when the conscious idea of snake replaces the unconscious one of penis. (Italics added)

A distinction between two uses of the word *symbol* has also been described by a nonanalyst. Herbert Read (1950) says:

But there is a very general distinction to be made between those uses of the word which on the one hand retain the sense of a throwing together of tangible, visible objects, with each other or with some immaterial or abstract notion, and those uses which on the other hand imply no such initial separation, but rather treat the symbol as an integral or original form of expression. A word itself may be a symbol in this sense, and language a system of symbols.

The similarity between this second use of the word *symbol* and Fenichel's second use of it is clear, although Read says earlier that he feels that it is a pity that he and analysts have to use the same word to describe different things.

Illusion and Fusion

It is the use of symbolism as part of what Fenichel calls prelogical thinking that I wish to discuss here. In particular I wish to consider what are the conditions under which the primary and the secondary object are fused and felt as one and the same. I want to study both the emotional state of the person experiencing this fusion and what conditions in the environment might facilitate or interfere with it; in fact, to study something of the internal and external conditions that make it possible to find the familiar in the unfamiliar—which, incidentally, Wordsworth (1798) said is the whole of the poet's business.

When considering what concepts are available as tools for thinking about this process of fusion or identification, the concept of fantasy is obviously essential, since it is only in fantasy that two dissimilar objects are fused into one. But this concept is not quite specific enough to cover the phenomenon; the word *illusion* is also needed because this word does imply that there is a relation to an external object of feeling, even though a fantastic one, since the person producing the fusion believes that the secondary object *is* the primary one. In order to come to understand more about the meaning of the word *illusion,* I found it was useful to consider its role in a work of art. I had already, when trying to study some of the psychological factors that facilitate or impede the painting of pictures,[2] become interested in the part played by the frame. The frame marks off the different kind of reality that is within it from that which is outside it; but a temporal spatial frame also marks off the special kind of reality of a psychoanalytic session. And in psychoanalysis it is the existence of this frame that makes possible the full development of that creative illusion that analysts call the transference. Also the central idea underlying psychoanalytic technique is that it is by means of this illusion that a better adaptation to the world outside is ultimately developed. It seemed to me that the full implications of this idea for analytic theory had still to be worked out, especially in connection with the role of symbolism in the analytic relationship.

In considering the dynamics of the process the concept of anxiety is clearly needed. Melanie Klein has laid great stress on the fact that it is dread of the original object itself, as well as the loss of it, that leads to the search for a substitute. But there is also a word needed for the emotional experience of finding the substitute, and it is here that the word *ecstasy* may be useful.

There is also another ordinary English word, not often used in psychoanalytic literature, except to talk about perversion, or lack of it, in neurotic states, and that is the word *concentration.* I wish to bring it in here because, in analyzing children, I have found myself continually noticing the varying moods or quality of concentration shown by the children and have tried to understand the relation of these variations to the kind of material produced. These observations have not been confined to the analytic situation; I have often noticed, when in contact with children playing, that there occurs now and then a particular type of absorption in what they are doing, which gives the impression that something of great importance is going on. Before becoming an analyst I used to wonder what a child, if he or she had sufficient power of expression, would say about these moods, how the child would describe them from inside. When I became an analyst I began to guess that the children were in fact trying to tell me, in their own way, what it does feel like. And I thought I recognized the nature of these communications the more easily because I had already tried for myself, introspectively, to find ways of describing such states, most particularly in connection with the kinds of concentration that produce a good or a bad drawing.

Before going on to present and discuss some clinical material, there is one other concept that I think needs clarifying, and that is the meaning of the term "primary object." Earlier psychoanalytic discussions of symbol formation most often emphasized the child's attempts to find substitutes for those original objects of interest that are the parents' organs. But some also emphasized the aspect of the child's attempts to find his or her own organs and their functioning in every object. In more recent work these two views tend to be combined, and the idea develops that the primary "object" that the infant seeks to find again is a fusion of self and object, it is mouth and breast felt as fused into one. Thus the concept of fusion is present, both in the primary situation, between self and object, and in the secondary one, between the new situation and the old one.

Case Material: A Game of War Between Two Villages

Moments when the original "poet" in each of us created the outside world for us, by finding the familiar in the unfamiliar, are perhaps forgotten by most people; or else they are guarded in some secret place of memory because they were too much like visitations of the gods to be mixed with everyday thinking. But in autobiographies some do dare to tell, and often in poetry. Perhaps, in ordinary life, it is good teachers who are most aware of these moments, from outside, since it is their job to provide the conditions under which they can occur, so to stage-manage the situation that imagination catches fire and a whole subject or skill lights up with significance. But it is in the analytic situation that this process can be studied from inside and outside at the same time. So now I will present some material from child analysis which seems to me to be offering data about the nature of the process.

The patient is a boy of eleven who was suffering from a loss of talent for school work. During his first school years, from four to six, he had been remarkably interested and successful and always top of his form; but he had gradually come to find himself very near the bottom, and at times had been totally unable to get himself to school at all.

The particular play that I wish to discuss had been preceded by a long period in which all the toys had been set out in the form of a village, full of people and animals; the boy would then bomb the village by dropping balls of burning paper upon it, my role being to play the part of the villagers, and try to save all the toys from actual destruction.

The rules of the game were such that this was often very difficult, so that gradually more and more of the toys were burned, and from time to time I had replaced them by new ones. (This boy had, in fact, lived through part of the blitz on London and had started this play some time after my own house had been damaged by blast; and he had shown delayed interest in the extent of the damage when he came to my house for his analysis.)

In the session that I have chosen to describe, he begins by saying that we are to have two villages and a war between them, but that the war is not to begin at once. My village is to be made up of all the people and animals and houses; his of toy trucks, cars, etc., and "lots of junk and oddments to exchange," though I am to have some odd-ments as well. He begins by sending along a truck from his village with half a gun in it and takes various things in exchange. He then brings a test tube and exchanges it for a number of objects, including a little bowl, bits of metal, a ladder, etc. When I comment on the amount taken in exchange he says: "Yes, the test tube is equal to a lot," but on the return journey to his own village he adds: "I think those people were a bit odd, I don't think I like those people much, I think I will give them just a little time bomb." So he takes back his test tube, sticks some matches in it, and drops it over my village. He then drops a whole box of matches on my village and says the villagers have to find it and put it out before it explodes. But then I have to come and bomb his village, and when I drop a flare, instead of putting it out he adds fuel to it. Then he says: "You have got to bring all your people over to my village, the war is over." I have to bring the animals and people over in trucks, but at once he says they must go back because they all have to watch the burning of the whole stack of match boxes (which he has bought with his own money). He makes me stand back from the blaze, and shows great pleasure.

He now decides that his "people" (empty trucks) are to call on mine; his are explorers and mine are to think his are gods. The trucks arrive, my people have to be frightened. He tells me to make them say something; so I make the policeman ask what they want; but he replies: "You've forgotten, they think it's gods." He now borrows the "Mrs. Noah" figure from my village and stands her in one of his trucks. Then, in a godlike voice, he commands that the villagers go into their houses and prepare food.[3] It is now the end of the session and while I am beginning to tidy up he plays with some melting wax, humming to himself the hymn-tune "Praise, my soul, the King of Heaven." He smears some wax on both my thumbs and says he is double-jointed, and asks if I am too.

At first I saw this material in terms of his bisexual conflict, and I tried to interpret it in that way. I told him that I thought the war between the two villages was expressing his feeling that I, as the mother, the woman, have all the human values, while he has only the mechanical ones. This interpretation linked with earlier material in which he had spent weeks making Meccano models with sets that he brought to the session, and had continually shown me the models illustrated in the handbook, assuring me that "You can make *anything* with Meccano"; but this play had stopped suddenly after he had tried to make a mechanical man, as specified in the book, and it had failed to work (i.e., move). And I had told him then how disappointed he was that he could not make a live baby out of his Meccano. So, in this village play, I pointed out how he had now attempted some rearrangement and exchange in which I was to be given some of the maleness (gun and test tube), and he was to have something of the femaleness (ending up with getting the "Mrs. Noah" figure). I explained also how this compromise had not entirely worked, since jealousy had broken through, as was shown in his attempt to justify his impending envious attacks by saying "I don't like these people"; that is to say "I am not guilty because they are bad anyway, so it doesn't matter hurting them." Also I told him that by burning his own village he was not only punishing himself, but at the same time expressing (externalizing) the state of anxiety in which he felt full of explosive feces that might at any moment blow up his own body; and added that he had returned to the attempt to avoid the cause of jealousy by trying to mitigate the absoluteness of his split between "mechanized" male and "human" female. I suggested that he was trying to tell me how he could not stand the empty, depersonalized gods (trucks), so effected a compromise by borrowing the good mother figure to fill the empty truck. I pointed out how, after this, he could tell me that he was double-jointed; that is, he combined both positions, and he hoped I could too.

In the next session immediately following this one, he spent the whole hour mending his satchel, a job that he said ordinarily his mother would do for him. Here I interpreted that the two villages were also mother and father, and that he felt he had succeeded in bringing them together inside him.

Certainly he did seem to be working out his conflicts about the relation between father and mother, both internally and externally, and trying to find ways of dealing with his jealousy and envy of his mother in what Melanie Klein (1928) has called the "femininity phase." Considered in this light, his mechanized village then also stood for his feeling about his school. For at this time he was constantly complaining how utterly uninteresting and boring his school work was, and he frequently brought material to do with waste lands and desert places: this being in marked contrast with the early school years during which he had been interested and successful. Thus one way of trying to describe the situation was in terms of the idea that the school, the place in which he must seek knowledge, had become too much identified with the destroyed mother's body, so that it had indeed become a desert; for the game of attacking and burning the village had been played throughout the period of his most acute school difficulties. But at the same time it was also too much identified with the desired mother's body, for such material certainly also pointed to intense conflict in the direct Oedipus situation, as well as in the "femininity phase"; and for a long time it had seemed to me that the school difficulty was being presented largely in these terms. Thus the entry into the world of knowledge and school work seemed to be identified with the entry into the mother's body, an undertaking at once demanded by the schoolmaster-father figure but forbidden under threat of castration by the sexual rival father. In fact one could describe the situation here in terms of the use of symbolism as a defense and say that because the school had become the symbol of the forbidden mother's body this was then a bar to progress.

The defense against the anxiety aroused by this symbolic identification took the form of a reversal of roles in his play with me; he himself became the sadistic punishing schoolmaster, and I had to be the bad pupil. For days, and sometimes weeks, I had to play the role of the persecuted schoolboy: I was set long monotonous tasks, my efforts were treated with scorn, I was forbidden to talk and made to write out "lines" if I did; and if I did not comply with these demands, then he wanted to cane me. (When asked if he were really treated as badly as this at school he always said "no"; he certainly was never caned, and the school, though of the conventional pattern, did try most generously to adapt to his difficulties.) Clearly then there was a great amount of resentment and fear to be worked through in the Oedipus situation, but I did not feel this was the only reason for the persistence of this type of play. It was other aspects of the material which finally led me to see the problem as also something to do with difficulties in establishing the relation to external reality as such.

One of these was the fact that he frequently adopted a particularly bullying tone when talking to me, even when he was not playing the schoolmaster game, but he always dropped this tone as soon as he began imaginative play with the toys. This observation suggested that perhaps this boy could drop the hectoring tone, during this kind of play, because it was a situation in which he could have a different kind of relation to external reality, by means of the toys; he could do what he liked with them, and yet they were outside him. He nearly always began the session with the bullying tone and insistence that I was not ready for him at the right time, whatever the actual time of starting; but as soon as he had settled down to using the toys as a pliable medium, external to himself, but not insisting on their own separate objective existence, then apparently he could treat me with friendliness and consideration, and even accept real frustration from me.

The Receptive Role of the Toys

This observation set me wondering about the exact function of this relation to the toys, and in what terms it could be discussed. I noticed how, on days when he did play with the toys, there seemed to develop a relationship between him and them that reminded me of the process I had myself tried to observe introspectively when doing "free" drawings (1950). I thought there was perhaps something useful to be said about the actual process of playing with the toys as compared with, on the one hand, pure day-dreaming, and on the other, direct expedient muscular activity directed toward a living object. In the play with the toys there was something halfway between day-dreaming and purposeful instinctive or expedient action. As soon as he moved a toy in response to some wish or fantasy then the play-village was different, and the new sight set off a new set of possibilities; just as in free imaginative drawing, the sight of a mark made on the paper provokes new associations, the line as it were answers back and functions as a very primitive type of external object.

About two months after the war-of-the-villages play something occurred that seemed to offer a further clue as to what was happening when he played with the toys; for the bullying tone suddenly vanished for four days, beginning with a day when he told me about something that had happened at school which clearly gave him great pleasure. For many weeks before he had been intensely preoccupied with a photography club that he and his particular friends had organized in their out-of-school hours; now he reported that their form master had given him permission to hold their meetings in school, during a time set aside for special activities, and had even given them a little room in which to work.

This sudden disappearance of his dictatorship attitude gave me the idea that the fact of his spontaneously created activity being incorporated in the framework of the school routine was a fulfilling, in external life, of the solution foreshadowed in the war-between-the-villages play. What he had felt to be the mechanized, soulless world of school had now seemed to him to have become humanized, by the taking into its empty trucks of a bit of himself, something that he had created. But what was particularly interesting was the fact that he had only been able to respond to the school's gesture at this particular moment; for there had been many efforts on their part to help him before this, such as special coaching after his continual absences. One could of course say that it was because of the strength of his own aggression and his anxiety about it that he had not been able to make more use of the help offered; but it seemed to me that these earlier efforts on the part of the school had not had more apparent effect also because they had not taken the particular form of the incorporation of, acceptance of, a bit of his own spontaneous creation. Now the school, by being receptive, by being in-giving as well as out-giving, had shown itself capable of good mothering; it was a male world that had become more like his mother, who had in fact been a very good mother. Much earlier he had foreshadowed this same need by one of his rare dreams, in which his mother had been present at school in his Latin class (Latin being the bugbear of his school subjects).

This view of the meaning of the villages play as partly to do with problems of this boy's whole relation to what was, for him, the unmitigated not-me-ness of his school life threw light on one of the elements in the original situation when his difficulties first became apparent. Not only had his father been called away to the war just at the time when his baby brother had been born and when London was being bombed, but he had also lost his most valued toy, a woolly rabbit. As the analysis advanced I had come to realize how significant this loss had been, for it became more clear that one of my main roles in the transference was to be the lost rabbit. He so often treated me as totally his own to do what he liked with, as though I were dirt, his dirt, or as a tool, an extension of his own hand. (He had never been a thumb sucker.) If I was not free the moment he arrived, even though he was often thirty minutes early, I was reprimanded or threatened with punishment for being late. In fact it certainly did seem that for a very long time he did need to have the illusion that I was part of himself.

Play and the Boundary Between Inner and Outer

Here I tried to review the various psychoanalytic concepts of mechanisms that can be forerunners of or defenses against object relations, and to see which might be useful to explain what was happening. Certainly he split himself and put the bad bit of himself into me when he punished me as the pupil. Certainly he used threatening words that were intended to enter into me and cow me into doing what he wanted and being his slave. Certainly he tried to make me play the role of the all-gratifying idealized fantasy object; he once told me that he did feel himself quite special and that the frustrating things that happened to other people would not happen to him. I thought this did mean that he felt at times that he had this marvelous object inside him which would protect and gratify him. And this linked with the fact that he would sometimes hum hymn tunes, such as "Praise, my soul, the King of Heaven," although he explicitly expressed great scorn for religion. Certainly also he found it very difficult to maintain the idea of my separate identity; in his demands he continually denied the existence of my other patients or any family ties. The way he behaved could also be described by saying that he kept me inside him, since he continually used to insist that I knew what he had been doing or was going to do, when I had in fact no possible means of knowing. Yet I did not feel that these ways of talking about what happened were entirely adequate; for all of them take for granted the idea of a clear boundary—if I am felt to be inside him then he has a boundary, and the same if a bit of him is felt to be projected into me.

But there was much material in this analysis to do with burning, boiling down, and melting, which seemed to me to express the idea of the obliteration of boundaries. And I had a growing amount of evidence, both from clinical material and introspective study of problems in painting, that the variations in the feeling of the existence or nonexistence of the body boundary are themselves very important. In this connection Clifford Scott (1949) restates Winnicott's view (1945, 1948) about how a good mother allows the child to fuse its predisposition to hallucinate a good situation with the earliest sensations of a good situation. Scott then describes this as an "oscillation between the illusion of union and the fact of contact, which is another way of describing the discovery of an interface, a boundary, or a place of contact, and perhaps at the same time is another way of describing the discovery of 'the me' and 'the you.' " He goes on to say, "But I think only a partial picture of union and contact is given by discussing the good situation. Equally important is the evil union and the evil contact and the discovery of the evil me and the evil you."[4] He also talks of the extremes of the states in which all discriminations and interfaces are destroyed as in what he calls "cosmic bliss" and "catastrophic chaos." And these extremes relate, I think, to behaviorist observations that can be made, both in and out of analysis, of the variations of facial expression between extreme beauty and extreme ugliness. I had, for instance, a child patient of six who would at times show an extremely seraphic face, and it occurred in connection with great concentration on the use or lack of use of outline in painting. I also observed a schizophrenic patient (adult) who would at times have moments of startling physical beauty counterbalanced by moments of something startlingly repellent.

One could certainly think of this phenomenon in terms of complete union with a marvelous or atrocious inner object, with the obliteration of inner boundaries between the ego and the incorporated object. But there was also the question of where the actual body boundary was felt to be. Did it mean that the skin was felt to include the whole world and therefore in a sense was denied altogether? Certainly the introspective quality of what have been called oceanic states seems to include this feeling, as does also the catastrophic chaos that Scott refers to. For the schizophrenic patient described above constantly complained that she could not get the world outside her and that this, rather than being a source of bliss, was agony to her. Certainly there is very much here that I do not understand. Also the whole question of beauty appearing in analysis, perceived by the analyst either as a varying physical quality of the patient or as a quality of the material, has not been much discussed in the literature, though Ella Sharpe (1937) does mention dreams that the patient describes as beautiful. When perceived by the analyst it can clearly be described in terms of the countertransference, and used, just as any other aspect of the countertransference can be used (Heimann 1950), as part of the analytic data. Thus in trying to understand all that this boy was trying to show me I had to take into account the fact that at times there was a quality in his play which I can only describe as beautiful—occasions when it was he who did the stage managing, and it was my imagination that caught fire. It was in fact play with light and fire. He would close the shutters of the room and insist that it be lit only by candlelight, sometimes a dozen candles arranged in patterns or all grouped together in a solid block. And then he would make what he called furnaces, with a very careful choice of what ingredients should make the fire, including dried leaves from special plants in my garden; and sometimes all the ingredients had to be put in a metal cup on the electric fire and stirred continuously, all this carried out in the half darkness of candlelight. And often there had to be a sacrifice, a lead soldier had to be added to the fire, and this figure was spoken of either as the victim or the sacrifice. In fact, all this type of play had a dramatic ritual quality comparable to the fertility rites described by Frazer in primitive societies. And this effect was the more striking because this boy's conscious interests were entirely conventional for his age; he was absorbed in Meccano and model railways.

Aesthetic Experience and the Merging of the Boundary

The fact that in this type of material the boy's play nearly became "a play," in that there was a sense of pattern and dramatic form in what he produced, leads to many questions about the relation of a work of art to analytic work, which are not relevant here. But the particular point I wish to select for further consideration is that he seemed to me to be trying to express the idea of integration, in a variety of different ways. Thus the fire seemed to be here not only a destructive fire but also the fire of Eros; and not only the figurative expression of his own passionate body feelings, not only the fantasy representative of the wish for passionate union with the external object but also a way of representing the inner fire of concentration. The process in which interest is withdrawn temporarily from the external world so that the inner work of integration can be carried out was, I think, shown by the boiling or melting down of the various ingredients in what he called "the fire cup" to make a new whole. And the sacrifice of the toy soldier by melting it down both expressed the wish to get rid of a bad internal object, particularly the cramping and cruel aspect of his superego, and also his sense of the need to absorb his inner objects into his ego and so modify them. But in addition to this I think it represented his feeling of the need to be able, at times, to transcend the commonsense ego; for common sense was very strong in him, his conscious attitude was one of feet firmly planted on the ground. For instance, when he did tell a dream, which was rarely, he usually apologized if it was at all nonsensical. And formerly also this boy had told me that he was "no good at art," and he was extremely tentative in any attempts at drawing. But later this changed. For he told me one day, with pride, that he was good at both science and art, which he felt was not very usual among his schoolfellows, though he was still inclined to be apologetic about his aesthetic experiences. When he told me of the delight he took in the colors of the various crystals he had studied in his chemistry he added, "It's childish to like them so much."

Although an important factor in this development of his capacity to feel himself "good at art" was his growing belief in his power to restore his injured objects, this is not the aspect of the material that I wish to discuss here; for I am concentrating on the earlier problem of establishing object relationships at all, rather than on the restoration of the injured object once it is established. Granted that these two are mutually interdependent and that anxiety in the one phase can cause regression to the earlier one, there is still much to be said about the earlier phase as such. Thus a central idea began to emerge about what this boy was trying to tell me; it was the idea that the basic identifications which make it possible to find new objects, to find the familiar in the unfamiliar, require an ability to tolerate a temporary loss of sense of self, a temporary giving up of the discriminating ego, which stands apart and tries to see things objectively and rationally and without emotional coloring. It perhaps requires a state of mind that has been described by Bernard Berenson (1950) as "the aesthetic moment."

> In visual art the aesthetic moment is that fleeting instant, so brief as to be almost timeless, when the spectator is at one with the work of art he is looking at, or with actuality of any kind that the spectator himself sees in terms of art, as form and color. He ceases to be his ordinary self, and the picture or building, statue, landscape, or aesthetic actuality is no longer outside himself. The two become one entity; time and space are abolished and the spectator is possessed by one awareness. When he recovers workaday consciousness it is as if he had been initiated into illuminating, formative mysteries.

Now I think it is possible to add something to my attempts to describe what happened in this boy during the play when his whole behavior to me changed, and to link this with what an artist or a poet does. For observations in analysis suggest that experiences of the kind described by Berenson are not confined to the contemplation of works of art, but that art provides a method, in adult life, for reproducing states that are part of everyday experience in healthy infancy. Sometimes poets have explicitly related such states to their early experience: for instance, Traherne, and also Wordsworth, in his note on "Intimations of Immortality from Recollections of Early Childhood." Thus Wordsworth says that as a child he was unable to think of external things as having external existence, he communed with all he saw as something not apart from but inherent in his own immaterial nature; when going to school he would often grasp at a wall to recall himself from the abyss of idealism. I suggest that it is useful, in child analysis, to look out for the ways in which the child may be trying to express such experiences, when he has not yet sufficient command of words to tell what he feels, directly, but can only use words or whatever other media the playroom offers him, figuratively: for instance, as this child used candlelight and fire and the activities of melting and burning, as well as the actual toys. And I think it may be useful also to bear in mind that if, when talking about this state, one uses only those concepts, such as introjection and projection, which presuppose the existence of the organism within its boundaries in a world of other organisms within boundaries, one may perhaps distort one's perception of the phenomenon. Thus it is important not to forget the obvious fact that we know the boundaries exist but the child does not; in the primal state, it is only gradually and intermittently that he discovers them; and on the way to this he uses play. Later, he keeps his perception of the world from becoming fixed, and no longer capable of growth, by using art, either as artist or as audience; and he may also use psychoanalysis. For, as Rank (1932) says, art and play both link the world of "subjective unreality" and "objective reality," harmoniously fusing the edges but not confusing them. So the developing human being becomes able deliberately to allow illusions about what he is seeing to occur; he allows himself to experience, within the enclosed space-time of the drama or the picture or the story or the analytic hour, a transcending of that commonsense perception that would see a picture as only an attempt at photography, or the analyst as only a present-day person.

The Need for a Medium Between the Self-Created and External Realities

What I want to suggest here is that these states are a necessary phase in the development of object relationships and that the understanding of their function gives a meaning to the phrase "Art creates Nature." In this connection a later phase in the transference phenomena shown by this boy is relevant. It was after he had become deeply interested in chemistry that there occurred in analysis, for several weeks, a repeated catechism. He would say "What is your name?" and I would have to say "What is my name?" Then he would answer with the name of some chemical, and I would say "What is there about that?" And he would answer "It's lovely stuff, I've made it!"; and sometimes he would give me the name of the chemical, which is used as a water-softener.

Here then is the link with the artist's use of his medium, what the *Concise Oxford Dictionary* defines as an "intervening substance through which impressions are conveyed to the senses"; and this pliable stuff that can be made to take the shape of one's fantasies can include the "stuff" of sound and breath, which becomes our speech. (This boy would sometimes tell me that I was a gas, or that he was going to dissolve me down or evaporate me till I became one.) So it seemed that he had become able to use both me and the playroom equipment as this intervening pliable substance; he had become able to do with these what Caudwell (1937) says the poet does with words, when he uses them to give the organism an appetitive interest in external reality, when he makes the earth become charged with affective coloring and glow with a strange emotional fire.

As regards the use of the medium of speech,[5] there was a stage, after the war-of-the-villages play, when it was very difficult to get this boy to talk. He would play, but silently, and when he did talk, it was always to try and teach me something; sometimes it was the language of chemistry, which he knew and I did not. And this I think expressed the need of the artist in him (and also the scientist, for he soon became determined to make science his career) to have a bit of his own experience incorporated in the social world, just as he had been able to have his own club incorporated in the world of school. For, as Caudwell points out, the artist is acutely aware of the discrepancy between, on the one hand, all the ways of expressing feeling that are provided by the current development of speech and art, in our particular culture and epoch; and, on the other hand, our changing experiences that are continually outstripping the available means of expression. Thus the artist wishes to cast his private experiences in such form that they will be incorporated in the social world of art and so lessen the discrepancy. Caudwell points out that it is not only the artist who feels this discrepancy and not only the discrepancy between feeling and current forms of expression of it; it is also the scientist, in respect not of feeling but of perception and currently accepted ways of formulating it, currently accepted views of "reality," who wishes to contribute something of his (or her) own to the changing symbols of science. Perhaps even he must do this if the already discovered symbols are to become fully significant for him.

Effects of Premature Loss of Belief in the Self-Created Reality

The phenomenon of treating the world as one's own creation is mentioned by Fenichel. He says:

> There always remain certain traces of the original objectless condition, or at least a longing for it ("oceanic feeling"). Introjection is an attempt to make parts of the external world flow into the ego. Projection, by putting unpleasant sensations into the external world, also attempts to reverse the separation of ego from non-ego.

And he goes on to refer to the child who "when playing hide-and-seek closes his eyes and believes he now cannot be seen." Fenichel then says, "The archaic animistic conception of the world which is based on a confusion of ego and non-ego is thus illustrated."

Although there are differences of opinion about what he calls here "the original objectless condition," about whether or not there is some primitive object relation from the very beginning, which alternates with the "objectless" or fused condition, I think Fenichel's description is valuable. The example of the child playing hide-and-seek vividly shows the belief in a self-created reality, just as analytical material shows related phenomena such as the child's belief that when he opens his eyes and sees the world, he thereby creates it, he feels it is the lovely (or horrible) stuff that he has made.

The idea that these states of illusion of oneness are perhaps a recurrently necessary phase in the continued growth of the sense of twoness leads to a further question: What happens when they are prevented from occurring with sufficient frequency or at the right moments?

This boy had had in general a very good home and been much loved. But he had suffered very early environmental thwartings in the feeding situation. In the early weeks of his life his mother had had too little milk, and the nurse had been in the habit of not getting the supplementary feed ready in time, so that he had had to wait to finish his meal and had shown great distress: an experience that was relived in the transference, when whatever time I was ready for him, he always said I was too late.

Although it is obvious that a child must suffer frustration, there is still something to be said about the way in which it should occur and the timing of it. I suggest that if, through the pressure of unsatisfied need, the child has to become aware of his separate identity too soon or too continually, then either the illusion of union can be what Scott calls catastrophic chaos rather than cosmic bliss, or the illusion is given up and premature ego-development may occur; then separateness and the demands of necessity may be apparently accepted, but necessity becomes a cage rather than something to be cooperated with for the freeing of further powers. With this boy it was clear how the imposed necessities, regulations, and non-self-chosen tasks of a conventional school had provided a setting for a repetition of his first difficulties in relation to the environment. In fact he often told me what his ideal school would be like, and it amounted to being taught by a method very like what modern educationists call the project method.

If one asks the question, what factors play an essential part in the process of coming to recognize a world that is outside oneself, not one's own creation, there is one that I think has not been much stressed in the literature. Thus, in addition to the physical facts of the repeated bodily experiences of being separated from the loved object, and being together with it, and the repeated physical experiences of interchange with the not-self world, breathing, feeding, eliminating: in addition to the gradually growing capacity to tolerate the difference between the feeling of oneness, of being united with everything, and the feeling of twoness, of self and object, there is the factor of a capacity in the environment. It is the capacity of the environment to foster this growth, by providing conditions in which a recurrent partial return to the feeling of being one is possible; and I suggest that the environment does this by the recurrent providing of a framed space and time and a pliable medium, so that, on occasions, it will not be necessary for self-preservation's sake to distinguish clearly between inner and outer, self and not-self. I wish to suggest that it was his need for this capacity in the environment that my patient was telling me about in his village play, when he said there was to be a war, "but not yet." It was as if he were saying that the true battle with the environment, the creative struggle of interacting opposites, could not begin, or be effectively continued, until there had also been established his right to a recurrent merging of the opposites. And until this was established necessity was indeed a mechanized god, whose service was not freedom but a colorless slavery.

Looked at in this way the boy's remark, "I don't like those people," was not only due to a denial of an uprush of feared uncontrollable jealousy and envy, it represented also the reenactment of a memory or memories of a near breakdown of relationship to the outside world. It was the memory, I suggest, of actual experience of a too sudden breaking in on the illusion of oneness, an intrusion that had had the effect of preventing the emergence from primary narcissism occurring gradually in the child's own time. But it represented also a later situation; for the premature ego-development, referred to by Melanie Klein as inhibiting the development of symbolization (or, in Jones's terms, of symbolic equivalents), was also brought about by the impingement of the war. For the sake of self-preservation, it had been necessary for him continually and clearly to distinguish between external and internal reality, to attend to the real qualities of the symbol too soon. Thus it was reported to me that this boy had shown remarkable fortitude when, with his father away in the navy, he and his baby brother and mother had lived through the blitz on London. And also, later on, his reports indicated that he was very self-controlled in school, in that situation where self-preservation demands a fairly continual hold upon objectivity, since day-dreaming and treating the external world as part of one's dream are not easily tolerated by schoolmasters. But the fact that this amount of objectivity was only achieved at a fairly high cost in anxiety was shown in his analysis, for at one time he was continually punishing me for imagined lapses into forgetfulness, inattention, unpunctuality. It was only later that he was able to tell me about what he now called his absentmindedness, in a tolerant way and without anxiety.

Implications for Technique

The considerations I have tried to formulate here are not only matters for theory, they have direct bearings upon technique. With this boy there was always the question of whether to emphasize, in interpreting, the projection mechanisms and persecutory defenses and to interpret the aggression as such; but when I did this the aggression did not seem to lessen, and I was sometimes in despair at its quite implacable quality. At times he treated me as if I were like the man in the Bible from whom a devil was driven out, but into whom seven more came, so that he went on attacking me with almost the fervor of a holy war. But when I began to think along the lines described above, even though I knew that I was not succeeding in putting these ideas clearly into words in my interpretations, the aggression did begin to lessen, and the continual battle over the time of the beginning of each session disappeared. Of course I may be mistaken in thinking that the change in the boy's behavior, which accompanied the change in my idea of the problem, was a matter of cause and effect, since the issue is very complicated and brings in many debatable questions of theory. But I think it was significant that, near the end of his analysis, this boy told me that when he was grown up and earning his own living he would give me a papier-mâché chemical clock, which would keep perfect time and would be his own invention. He said it would be of papier-mâché because I had an ornament, a little Indian dog, made of this, and also I remembered how he himself had tried, during his play with me, to make papier-mâché bowls, but unsuccessfully. Granted that the idea of the giving of the clock stood for many things, including returning to me the restored breast and restored penis, and also represented his gratitude for the recovery of his own potency, I thought he was telling me something else as well. I thought that the malleability of the papier-mâché provided him with a way of expressing how he felt about part of the curative factor in his analysis. It was his way of saying how, in the setting of the analytic playroom, he had been able to find a bit of the external world that was malleable; he had found that it was safe to treat it as a bit of himself, and so had let it serve as a bridge between inner and outer. And it was through this, I suggest, as well as through the interpretations I had given about the content of his wishes toward outer and inner objects, that he had become able to accept the real qualities of externality, objective time standing as the chief representative of these. And in those phases when he could not make this bridge—because the fact that I had to work to a timetable forced on him an objective reality that he was not yet ready for—then I became merely the gap into which he projected all his "bad" wishes, or internal objects representing these. When he could not feel that he had "made" me, that I was his lovely stuff, then I was the opposite, not only bad but also alien, and bad because alien; so I became the receptacle for all that he felt was alien to his ego in himself, all the "devil" parts of himself that he was frightened of and so had to repudiate. It seemed as if it was only by being able, again and again, to experience the illusion that I was part of himself, fused with the goodness that he could conceive of internally, that he became able to tolerate a goodness that was not his own creation and to allow me goodness independently. Exactly how an infant does come to tolerate a goodness that is recognized to exist independently of himself seems to me to have not yet been entirely satisfactorily explained, though the factor of the relief obtained from giving up the illusion of omnipotence is mentioned in the literature and was clearly apparent in this boy. The repeated discovery that I went on being friendly and remained unhurt by him, in spite of the continual attacks on me, certainly played a very important part. For instance, there was another ritual catechism which would begin with "Why are you a fool?" and I had to say, "Why am I a fool?" Then he would answer, "Because I say so." Clearly if he had to feel that all the foolishness of adults was his doing, as well as their goodness, then he was going to bear a heavy burden. But I think he could not proceed to the stage of experiencing the relief of disillusion until he had also had sufficient time both to experience and to become conscious of the previous stage; he had to become aware that he was experiencing the stage of fusion before he could reach the relief of defusion. And it was only when he could become conscious of the relief of defusion that we were then able to reach his depression about injuries that he had felt he was responsible for, both internally and externally, in his family situation and in relation to me.

On looking back it seems to me that the greatest progress in his analysis came when I, on the basis of the above considerations, was able to deal with the negative countertransference. At first, without really being aware of it, I had taken for granted the view of infantile omnipotence which is described by Fenichel:

> Yet even after speech, logic, and the reality principle have been established we find that prelogical thinking is still in operation and even beyond the role it plays in states of ego regression or as a form of purposeful distortion. It no longer fulfills, it is true, the function of preparing for future actions but becomes, rather, a *substitute* for unpleasant reality.

I had accepted this view but had grown rather tired of being continually treated by this boy as his gas, his breath, his feces, and had wondered how long the working through of this phase would take. But when I began to suspect that Fenichel was wrong here, and that this prelogical fusion of subject and object does continue to have a function of preparing for future action, when I began to see and to interpret, as far as I could, that this use of me might be not only a defensive regression but an essential recurrent phase in the development of a creative relation to the world, then the whole character of the analysis changed; the boy then gradually became able to allow the external object, represented by me, to exist in its own right.

Caudwell says that the artist and the scientist

> are men who acquire a special experience of life—affective with the artist, perceptual with the scientist—which negates the common ego

or the common social world, and therefore requires refashioning of these worlds to include the new experience.

This boy had, I think, indicated the nature of this process by his reaction to the school's refashioning of a tiny bit of itself and its routines. For this had happened in response to the vividness of his belief in the validity of his own experience, a vividness that also had contributed to a refashioning in me of some of my analytic ideas.

Conclusion

On the basis of the study of such material as I have described here, and also from my own experiments in painting, I came to see the pertinence of Melanie Klein's statement that symbolization is the basis of all talents; that is, that it is the basis of those skills by which we relate ourselves to the world around us. To try to restrict the meaning of the word *symbolization,* as some writers tend to do, to the use of the symbol for purposes of distortion may have the advantage of simplification, but it has other disadvantages. One of these is that it causes unnecessary confusion when one tries to communicate with workers in related disciplines, such as epistemology, aesthetics, and the philosophy of science; it interferes with what might be a valuable collaboration in the work of clarifying some of the obscure issues about the nature of thought. This isolation of psychoanalysis, by its terminology, from related fields may not have been a disadvantage in the early days of the struggle to establish analytic concepts in their own right, but now such isolation, can, I think, lead to an impoverishment of our own thinking.

Another advantage of not limiting the meaning of the word *symbol* to a defensive function would be a clarification of theory by bringing it more in line with our practice. The analytic rule that the patient shall try to put all that he is aware of into words does seem to me to imply a belief in the importance of symbolization for maturity as well as for infancy; it implies the recognition that words are in fact symbols by means of which the world is comprehended. Thus in the daily battle with our patients over the transference, we are asking them to accept a symbolic relation to the analyst instead of a literal one, to accept the symbolism of speech and talking about their wants rather than taking action to satisfy them directly. And, as all analytic experience shows, it is when the patient becomes able to talk about all that he is aware of, when he *can* follow the analytic rule, then in fact he becomes able to relate himself more adequately to the world outside. As he becomes able to tolerate more fully the difference between the symbolic reality of the analytic relationship and the literal reality of libidinal satisfaction outside the frame of the session, then he becomes better.

Postscript

After completing this paper I began the analysis of another child, also aged eleven, who presented a somewhat similar problem of persistence in what looked like aggressive attacks. This child, a girl, fervently and defiantly scribbled over every surface she could find. Although it looked as if it were done in anger, interpretation in terms of aggression only led to increase in the defiance. In fact, the apparent defiance did not change until I began to guess that the trouble was less to do with feces given in anger and meant to express anger than with feces given in love and meant to express love. In this sense it was a battle over how she was to communicate her love, a battle over what kind of medium she was going to use for the language of love. So intense were her feelings about this that, after the first two days of analysis, she did not speak to me again (except when outside the playroom) for six months, although she would often write down what she wanted to say. Gradually I had come to look at the scribbling in the following way: by refusing to discriminate and claiming the right to scribble over everything, she was trying to deny the discrepancy between the feeling and the expression of it; by denying completely my right to protect any of my property from defacement she was even trying to win me over to her original belief that when she gave her messes lovingly they were literally as lovely as the feelings she had in the giving of them. In terms of the theory of symbolism, she was struggling with the problem of the identity of the symbol and the thing symbolized, in the particular case of bodily excretions as symbols for psychic and psychosomatic experiences. She was also struggling with the very early problem of coming to discriminate not only between the lovely feelings in giving the mess and the mess itself but also between the product and the organ that made it.

When I began to consider what she was doing in these terms, I also became able to see the boy's battle of the villages in a wider perspective. Both children were struggling with the problem of how to communicate the ecstasies of loving, as well as the agonies; and the boy's "lovely stuff" was certainly both the lovely stuff of his lovely dreams *and* his lovely sensations which, at one level, he could only think of in terms of "lovely" feces. The phrase "denial by idealization" is familiar, but the denial here is, I suggest, in the nature of the mess, not in the nature of the psychic experience of which it is the symbol. For this is the maximum experience of joy, ecstasy, which is a psychic fact, a capacity for heavenly or godlike experience possessed by everyone. The psychic agony came, and the anger, when this boy had to face the fact that there was discrepancy between the objective qualities of his messes—that is, how they looked to other people—and his subjective evaluation of them as actually being the same as the godlike experiences. Thus both children were struggling with the agony of disillusion in giving up their belief that everyone must see in their dirt what they see in it: "my people" are to see his empty trucks and "think it's gods." In fact, he is saying what the poet Yeats said: "Tread softly, because you tread on my dreams."

But was this struggle to make me see as they saw in essence any different from the artist's struggle to communicate his private vision? I have suggested that both the artist and the scientist are more acutely aware than the "average" man of the inadequacies of what Caudwell calls "the common ego," the commonly accepted body of knowledge and ways of thinking about and expressing experience, more sensitive to the gap between what can be talked about and the actuality of experience. If this is true, then it is also true to say that what is in the beginning only a subjective private vision can become, to future generations, objectivity. Thus the battle between the villages seemed to me to be not only a symbolic dramatization of the battle of love and hate, the struggle with ambivalence toward the object, but also a genuine work of dramatic art in which the actual process by which the world is created, for all of us, is poetically represented.

The battle over communicating the private vision, when the battle-ground is the evaluation of the body products, has a peculiar poignancy. In challenging the accepted objective view and claiming the right to make others share their vision, there is a danger that is perhaps the sticking point in the development of many who would otherwise be creative people. For to win this battle, when fought on this field, would mean to seduce the world to madness, to denial of the difference between cleanliness and dirt, organization and chaos. Thus in one sense the battle is a very practical one; it is over what is a suitable and convenient stuff for symbols to be made of; but at the same time it is also a battle over the painful recognition that, if the lovely stuff is to convey the lovely feelings, there must be work done on the material.

NOTES

1. Rank, in his later work, does in fact take a much wider view of the function of art.

2. This study was published under the pseudonym "Joanna Field" (1950).

3. I have had to omit some of the play in the middle of the session for reasons of space. It was connected with the theme of the previous months, in which there had been only one village, which he had continually bombed and burned. I had interpreted it as partly an attempt to gain reassurance about his attacks on his mother's body, by acting them out in this comparatively harmless way and with my approval; I had also linked it with the aggression he had actually shown when his mother was pregnant.

4. Winnicott, in a private communication, states that he does not entirely agree with Scott's restatement of his view, as quoted above. He adds the following modification:

"I agree with Scott's comment only if he is looking back at early infancy, starting from the adult (or child). Regression is a painful and precarious business partly because the individual regressing goes back with experiences of forward emotional development and with more or less knowledge in his pocket. For the person regressed there must be a denial of 'evil union' and of 'evil me' and 'evil you' when an 'ideal union' between 'good self' and 'good mother' is being lived (in the highly specialized therapeutic environment provided, or in the insane state).

"This begs the whole question, however, of the earliest stages of an individual's emotional development studied there and then. For an infant, at the start, there is no good or bad, only a not yet de-fused object. One could think of separation as the cause of the first *idea* of union; before this there's union but no *idea* of union, and here the terms good and bad have no function. For union of this kind, so important for the founding of the mental health of the individual, the mother's active adaptation is an absolute necessity, an active adaptation to the infant's needs which can only come about through the mother's devotion to the infant.

"Less than good-enough adaptation on the part of a mother to her infant's needs at this very early stage leads (it seems to me) to the premature ego-development, the precocious abandonment of illusion of which M. Milner writes in this paper."

5. Unfortunately I was not able, before writing this paper, to read S. Langer's (1942) detailed discussion of the nature and function of symbolism, as it was not yet published in England and I could not obtain a copy. Had I been able to obtain the book in time I would have made specific reference to some of Langer's statements about speech and symbolism. Particularly relevant to my problem is her emphasis on the advantages of small sounds made with part of one's own body as a medium for symbol formation. One of these advantages is the intrinsic unimportance, in their own right, of these sounds.

This relates to my point about the effectiveness of the toys as a medium for thought and communication being due to their pliability; that is, that their real qualities are unimportant for practical expedient living, so they can be given arbitrary or conventional meanings and thus be used as a language. I would also like to have elaborated on the relation of Langer's conception of the function of symbols to Jung's (1933) and to have considered the bearing of both on the material presented here.

REFERENCES

Berenson, B. 1950. *Aesthetics and History*. London: Constable.

Caudwell, C. 1937. *Illusion and Reality*. London: Lawrence and Wishart.

Fenichel, O. 1946. *The Psycho-Analytic Theory of Neurosis*. London: Kegan Paul.

Heimann, P. 1950. "On Counter Transference." *International Journal of Psycho-Analysis*, vol. 31.

Jones, E. [1916] 1948. "The Theory of Symbolism." In *Papers on Psycho-Analysis*. London: Bailliére, Tindall, and Cox.

Jung, C. 1933. *Psychological Types*. London: Kegan Paul; Princeton: Princeton University Press, 1971 (vol. 6 in Jung, *Collected Works*).

Klein, M. [1923] 1948. "Infant Analysis." In *Contributions to Psycho-Analysis, 1921–45*. London: Hogarth Press.

———. [1928] 1948. "Early Stages of the Oedipus Conflict." In *Contributions to Psycho-Analysis, 1921–45*.

———. [1930] 1948. "The Importance of Symbol Formation in the Development of the Ego." In *Contributions to Psycho-Analysis, 1921–45*.

Langer, S. 1942. *Philosophy in a New Key*. Cambridge, Mass.: Harvard University Press.

Milner, M. [J. Field]. 1950. *On Not Being Able to Paint*. London: Heinemann; New York: International Universities Press, 1957.

Rank, O. 1932. *Art and Artist*. New York: Knopf.

Read, H. 1951. *Art and the Evolution of Man*. London: Freedom Press.

———. 1951. "Psycho-Analysis and the Problem of Aesthetic Value." *International Journal of Psycho-Analysis*, vol. 32.

Scott, W. C. M. 1949. "The Body Scheme in Psychotherapy." *British Journal of Medical Psychology*, vol. 22.

Sharpe, E. 1937. *Dream Analysis*. London: Hogarth Press.

Winnicott, D. W. 1945. "Primitive Emotional Development." *International Journal of Psycho-Analysis*, vol. 26.

———. 1948. "Pediatrics and Psychiatry." *British Journal of Medical Psychology*, vol. 22.

Wordsworth, W. 1798. Preface to *Lyrical Ballads*.

3

The Aesthetic Moment and the Search for Transformation

CHRISTOPHER BOLLAS

The aesthetic experience occurs as *moment*.[1] Eliseo Vivas describes it as "rapt, intransitive attention" (quoted in Krieger 1976:11). Murray Krieger writes: "What would characterize the experience as aesthetic rather than either cognitive or moral would be its self sufficiency, its capacity to trap us within itself, to keep us from moving beyond it to further knowledge or to practical efforts" (11). A spell that holds self and other in symmetry and solitude, time crystallizes into space, providing a rendezvous of self and other (text, composition, painting) that actualizes deep rapport between subject and object. The aesthetic moment constitutes this deep rapport between subject and object and provides the person with a generative illusion of fitting with an object, evoking an existential memory. Existential, as opposed to cognitive, memory is conveyed not through visual or abstract thinking, but through the affects of being. Such moments feel familiar, uncanny, sacred, reverential, and outside cognitive coherence. They are registered through an experience of being, rather than mind, because the epistemology of the aesthetic moment is prior to representational cognition

Readers of Marion Milner's work (1955) will notice how my work is derivative of her own. I would like to acknowledge this debt.

and speaks that part of us where the experience of rapport with the other was the essence of being. Indeed, the aesthetic induces an existential recollection of the time when communicating took place solely through the illusion of deep rapport of subject and object. Being-with, as dialogue, is the communicating of the infant with the mother, where the mother's task is to provide the infant with an experience of continuity of being. Her handling and the infant's state of being are prior to the infant's processing his existence through mentation.[2]

The mother's idiom of care and the infant's experience of this handling is the first human aesthetic. It is the most profound occasion where the content of the self is formed and transformed by the environment. The uncanny pleasure of being held by a poem, a composition, a painting, or, for that matter, any object rests on those moments (they are moment as the infant cannot link them with cognition) when the infant's internal world is partly given form by the mother. This first human aesthetic informs the development of personal character (the utterance of self through the manner of being rather than the representations of the mind) and will predispose all future aesthetic experiences that place the person in subjective rapport with an object. As I will argue that each aesthetic experience is transformational, the search for what Krieger terms the "aesthetic object" is a quest for what we may call a transformational object. The transformational object promises to the beseeching subject an experience where the unintegrations of self find integrations through the form provided by the transformational object. As the mother is the first transformational object, and her style of mothering the paradigm of transformation for her child, I will explore the terms of this aesthetic before linking it to literary aesthetics and psychoanalysis.

The self is born into the care of a maternal environment. Depending on whose representation of the person's subjective experience of infancy we read, we either focus on the person's capacities (development of cognition, motility, adaptive defenses, ego capacities), his incapacities (inherent deprivation of being an infant due to psychic conflicts), or both. No doubt the infant has an internal structural tendency at this point of being, as Piaget argues, but without a facilitative mother, as Winnicott stresses, the infant's nascent ego capacities will suffer, perhaps irreparably. This is objective evidence. My focus is on the infant's subjective experience of the mother, as he is objectively aware neither of his own ego capacities nor of the mother's logic of care. He experiences distress and the dissolving of distress through the apparitional-like presence of mother. Agony of hunger, moment of emptiness, is transformed by mother's milk into an experience of fullness. This is a primary transformation: emptiness, agony, rage, become fullness and contentedness. The aesthetics of this experience is the particular way the mother meets the infant's need, the manner in which she transforms his internal and external realities. Alongside the infant's subjective experience of being transformed is the reality that he is being transformed according to the mother's aesthetic. I believe that he will eventually incorporate the food, the new experience (fullness), and the aesthetic of handling. The baby takes in not only the contents of the mother's communications but the form of her utterances, and, since in the beginning of life handling of the infant is the primary mode of communicating, I maintain that the internalization of the mother's form (her aesthetic) is prior to the internalization of her verbal messages. Indeed, I believe Gregory Bateson's notion of the double bind, where message is contradicted by mode of delivery or vice versa, is a conflict between the form as utterance and the speech as message. The infant is caught between two mutually contradictory experiences.

The mother conveys her aesthetic by her style of being with the infant through inactive presence, feeding, diaper changing, soothing, and playing, and it is that which constitutes the phenomenology of her transformation of the infant's being. With a "good-enough mother," as Winnicott (1965:145) puts it, a tradition of generative transformations of internal and external realities is established. Continuity of being is maintained. Winnicott, a psychoanalyst, writes that this experience takes place in what he terms a "facilitating environment" (223), the mother's system of care that protects the infant from either internal or external impingement. The infant is primarily protected against impingements that lead him to substitute being taken care of with precocious mental processes that interrupt and dissolve being with mentation and vigilance. Murray Krieger, a literary critic, frames a similar space when he describes the aesthetic experience. "I have tried to establish, then, that to the degree that an experience is functioning in the aesthetic mode, we find ourselves locked within it, freely and yet in a controlled way playing among its surfaces and its depths" (1976:12). Like Winnicott's facilitating environment, Krieger's "aesthetic mode" holds the self within an experience, of reverie or rapport, that does not stimulate the self into thought. Naturally, thinking does not disappear, but the subjective experience is that thinking is *out there,* in the mother; it is the aesthetic object that is responsible for processing existence through thought and activity. Writes Krieger: "Would not such an object have, as a major objective, the need to keep us locked within it—to keep us, that is, from escaping into the world of cognitive or practical concerns?" (12). I agree with Krieger, but he avoids asking an obvious question. Where are the origins of this experience? For the aesthetic experience is not something learned by the adult, but is an existential recollection of an experience where being handled by the maternal aesthetic made thinking irrelevant to survival.

This facilitating environment or aesthetic mode places the subject before an object where the disunities of the former are given generative forms by the latter. Content and discontent of the subject as infant are externalized, mimetically, before the mother, who gives new form to the infant's experience through her aesthetic of handling.[3] Eventually, the aesthetic of handling yields to the aesthetic of language, and it is at this point that the experience of being yields and is integrated with the experience of thinking. The mother's facilitation of the word-forming experience, alongside the infant's grasp of grammatical structure, is the most significant transformation of the infant's encoded utterance. Until the grasp of the word, the infant's meaning resides only within the mother's psyche-soma. With the word, the infant has found a new transformational object, which facilitates the transition from deep enigmatic privacy toward the culture of the human village.[4]

When the transformational object passes from the mother to the mother's tongue (the word), the first human aesthetic, self to mother, passes toward the second human aesthetic: the finding of the word to speak the self. As it was mother's style of transforming the infant's being that constituted the first human aesthetic, so, too, I believe, it will be the forming of words to handle and transform the moods of the self that will frame the terms of that individual's personal aesthetic.

The first human aesthetic passes into the idiom of formal aesthetics, as the mother's aesthetic of care passes through her tongue, from cooing, mirror-uttering, singing, storytelling, and wording into the word. As we are a part of this extraordinary transition, we take the structure of the maternal aesthetic with us in several ways. Embedded in Heinz Lichtenstein's (1961)[5] notion of the identity theme is not only a thematics[6] but an aesthetics. Our internal world is transformed by the mother's unconscious desire into a primary theme of being with mother, which will print all future ways of being with the other. In an earlier paper (1974), I argued that a person's character is a subjective recollection of the person's past, printed through the person's way of being with himself and others. I would emend this point now, to argue that character is an aesthetic of being, as we have internalized, into the structure of our existence, the phenomenological reality of the maternal aesthetic. We have internalized a forming and transforming idiom as well as the thematics of mother's discourse and the fantasy world of our own making. Whenever we desired, despaired, reached toward, played, or were in rage, love, pain, or need, we were met by mother and handled according to her aesthetic. Whatever our existential critique of her aesthetic, be it generative integration into our own being, compliance followed by dissociated splitting of our true self, or defensive handling of the aesthetic (denial, splitting, repression), we mingled with this aesthetic. Indeed, the way mother handled us (either as accepting and facilitating or refusing and rigid or a mixture of both) will influence our way of handling our self. In a sense, we learn the grammar of our being before we grasp the rules of our language.

If the fate of being with a transformational other becomes an aesthetic of being, it does not preclude us from search for a new transformation. For the ego has internalized not simply an object (the mother) but a process (her aesthetic of transformation), and this process is a paradigm of subject relating to an object that transforms the subject's being. In a "good-enough" situation the mother as transformational object manipulates the environment to make it symmetrical to human need. As this experience is internalized into the structure of the ego, the self seeks transformational objects to reach relative symmetry with the environment. A person wants to express to a quizzical friend why he appears to be depressed. "Are you angry about something?," asks the friend. "No," he replies, "I'm not angry. I'm bewildered by a letter I've received." The word "anger" is not an adequate transformation of the mood to the word; it will not make the external expression generatively symmetrical with the internal impression. The word "bewildered" does, and the subject feels relieved and may be understood.

If failure occurs, let us say, at the point of acquiring the word, the word may become a meaningless expression of the child's internal world. Words may feel useless, or, if the rules of the family prohibit words that speak the mood of the self, they may feel dangerous. This foreclosure of the infant's internal life into language may facilitate the schizoid character position, where language is dissociated from feeling, and where the moods of the internal world are almost exclusively registered in the subject's way of being. True self states are manifested through the "language" of character, held within the self, whereas complaint or abstract thought representations are placed into the word. As such, the subject's internal, or private, self is continually dissociated from his executant self. An aesthetic moment for such an individual may occur when he faces a formidable and confusing external object that establishes an internal confusion in the subject, providing him with an uncanny feeling of the aweful and the familiar, an experience where this aesthetic object seems to demand resolution into clarity but threatens the self with annihilation if the subject seeks a word to speak it. An example of this aesthetic experience occurs in Herman Melville's novel *Moby-Dick,* when Ishmael is captured by the confused portrait of a whale in the Spouter Inn. It is Ishmael's captivity by the awesome representation of a large hovering mass about to impale itself on a ship that constitutes his aesthetic moment. He cannot define what he sees, though he tries to throw the experience into thought, because the experience of his captivity is outside cognitive apprehension. When he does transform this experience into a word, "whale," he can leave the painting and is released from his captivity. Because Ishmael can experience aesthetic moments—he is captured by paintings, sermons, books on whales, the whale itself, and idiomatic presences of others (Queequeg)—he dwells in the aesthetic moment with a transformational other: the object that captures and places him in a deep spell of the uncanny. As such, Ishmael reflects the creative alternative to Ahab, who scans the seas for a concrete transformational object (Moby Dick), because Ishmael occupies Melville's position—the domicile of the artist who is in the unique position to create his own aesthetic moments and find symbolic equations for psychohistorical experiences that henceforth (as text, painting) become a new reality.

A young man in psychotherapy, whom I will call Anthony, was born into a wealthy family dominated by a warm but very ambitious mother who refused to give up her active social life for the care of her new infant. She hired a nanny, and the infant was passed from one figure to another, from mother to nanny, from nanny to mother, during the first five years of his life. He is very fond of his mother, who is associated with warmth, smell, soft clothing, and tranquillity. He has no memory of his nanny. As he says: "Just a blank. I remember nothing." Now, this youth has what I believe to be an aesthetic experience that utters the terms of the first human aesthetic. As he wanders through the city, every so often he will see a young man, always in a bus or car, who is going in the opposite direction (a momentary presence) and who evokes a sudden feeling that this is the person who can "transform" him. He considers such moments to be the most glorious moments of his life, because they fill him with a "transcendental" sense of "exquisite harmony," even though these moments are followed by a sense of blankness and despair. This transformational object appears and disappears; it promises deliverance but yields absence and blankness. As Anthony has discovered in the psychotherapy, the search for this transformational object, and the phenomenology of his aesthetic experience, is an existential memory (the past called into the subject's being) of his experience of the maternal aesthetic. When he was with mother he was filled with a sense of joy; when she left him to the nanny, he felt blank and deserted.

Transformational-object seeking is an endless memorial search for something in the future that rests in the past. I believe that if we investigate many types of object relating we will discover that the subject is seeking the transformational object and aspiring to be matched in symbiotic harmony within an aesthetic frame that promises to metamorphose the self. On a transcendental plane, we believe in God, or we fall in love; on an empirical plane, we look for that ideal home, or job, or car because we hope to achieve reunion with an object that will transform our internal and external realities.

I cannot do justice to the many literary scholars who have concerned themselves with the aesthetics of literature and the location of transformation. In his early work *The Dynamics of Literary Response* (1968), Norman Holland found that the text formed and transformed itself and, subsequently, the reader. In *Poems in Persons* (Holland 1973) and *5 Readers Reading* (Holland 1975), he finds the transformation of the content of the story to lie in the reader's transformation of the text, as the reader edits the work according to the identity theme bequeathed by the reader's mother, and in harmony with his own idiom of defense and adaptation. Murray Schwartz (1975) claims that the literary experience actually lies somewhere in the "potential space" between the text and the reader. No doubt both Holland and Schwartz have struggled with the philosophical controversies of the nineteenth century over the place of the object, vis-à-vis the subject. Kant acknowledged that the object existed as a thing-in-itself, but it was outside human apprehension, as we know only the object that we create through the idiom of our own mind. Hegel's reply to Kant, however unsystematic it is, seems pertinent to my argument that the aesthetic moment is grounded in an actual experience of deep rapport of subject and object. Hegel agrees with Kant that it may be impossible to prove the existence of the object, but, he argues, it is undeniable that we have had an experience of the object and that the experience with the object has restructured our subjectivity. One of the differences between them is that Kant focuses on cognitive knowing of the object and Hegel speaks to what I term "existential knowing." Kant's thing-in-itself can never be known cognitively as it is in-itself, but only according to its effects on the mind. Hegel's object-in-itself may be outside cognition, but the experience of being-with an object, the dialectic of relating, imprints the object into the subject, registering the object in the subject's history.

Holland's interest lies primarily with the domain of literary response, and I think he would agree that he is not articulating the terms of the aesthetic experience. Although I believe that response to a situation or a text may reveal the thematics of self that Holland (1975) finds through his "Delphic Seminars,"[7] my focus is on *that unique moment* of deep subjective rapport between reader and text, or author and text. Whatever the reader's response to the content conveyed by the text, his arrest in the aesthetic is not a reflection of the content, but the way the content has been held and transformed by the poetics of the text. This may occur only occasionally. One poem out of many, perhaps; only a few moments, if any, during a novel; or possibly an entire work of literature, a symphony, a painting, a landscape. But when found, these are the "texts" we bring with us into our life. We mark them, and we return to dwell "within" them. Where I believe I converge with Holland is in the belief that the paradigm of the aesthetic experience emerges in the earliest moments of one's existence. Such an experience does not correspond, however, to the privacy of an individual's re-creation of the text, but to the moment when reader and text are arrested from the movement of their independent thematic, when the reader is captured by and held within a moment of wonder, reverie, or rapport with the text.

When the aesthetic moment captures us, as Krieger puts it, we are suddenly brought back from our idiomatic re-creation of the text's thematic into a direct experience of reverie with the form of the text. We are enraptured by a literary arrest, and we may dwell for some time with this moment. In this space, reader, text, and author are held by the poetic. After this experience, we are both released—the reader to continue to re-create the text in his own thematic image, the text to pursue its intended course.

Not surprisingly, the search for generative transformation brings many people to psychoanalysis. Because it is one of the tasks of the psychoanalyst to listen to a patient in a very special manner, and to respond, with a sense of the right moment, and through the use of the simplest words, the technique of psychoanalysis is primarily an aesthetics of care. Psychoanalysts create a poetics of interpretation (timing, spacing, wording, intoning) that delivers the content of the analyst's interpretation or silence to the patient in a manner that is symmetrical to the patient's ego capacities. The aesthetic of psychoanalysis strives to place the patient and the analyst in deep subjective rapport with one another, and this aesthetic evokes a state of being which reenacts the infant's relation to mother. So, whether the material of a session is oedipal, for example, with the analyst functioning thematically as the father, or the oedipal mother, the aesthetics of psychoanalysis, induced by the analytic technique, places the analyst in the position of the transformational object. Underlying the thematics of transference is the formal paradigm of infant-patient, emptying himself of his internal world before the mother-analyst. Indeed, I feel clinicians often confuse the thematics of the transference with the aesthetics of the transformational-object situation. Though the transference may bring forth the thematics of the infant and match the transformational relationship, this is not always the case. Clinicians speak of oedipal content with preoedipal origins or precursors when they are often describing the voice of the thematic transference (in this example oedipal) and simultaneously witnessing the utterance of the transformational-object situation (always mother to infant and infant to mother).

Creativity includes the aesthetic and the thematic. The thematic will print the subject's fantasies, reflecting his own use of the aesthetic frame that contains the thematic. Although the thematic reflects the subject's inheritance of the aesthetic frame, it becomes the idiomatic discourse of the internal world. In literature, the aesthetic frame establishes the way the writer forms and transforms the content of his text. In life, the aesthetic frame constitutes the subject's manner of holding and transforming internal and external realities. In literature, the aesthetic frame is the poetic of the text; in life, it is the aesthetics of being.

NOTES

1. I am primarily concerned with *moment* as an occasion when time becomes a space for the subject. We are stopped, held, in reverie, to be released, eventually back into time proper. I believe such moments may occur within the reading of a text, or a poem, or during the experience of hearing an entire reading of a text or a symphony.

2. Mentation is thought processing, whether organized or disorganized, conscious or unconscious.

3. Though the maternal aesthetic originates, quite obviously, from the mother, it becomes a mutual experience as infant and mother find new modes of fitting with one another.

4. The word is both transformational (as it gives form to content) and transitional, in Winnicott's sense, as it facilitates the infant's departure from the secret culture of mother-child to the social world where there are new symbolic equations to print the experience of living.

5. Lichtenstein argues that each person's mother imprints on the infant a theme of identity, inevitably reflecting the mother's unconscious use of her infant.

6. The thematic prints the subject's experience of the aesthetic and, as such, contains the subject's projections. We could find, as Holland (1973) does, an identity theme within the thematic of the text, but, unfortunately, that is only one of the hundreds of ideas uttered as thematic. Though a writer may alter his style, each work is managed by its aesthetic frame: the phenomenology of its transformation of the thematic.

7. Seminars in which readers share their reactions to the text and their re-creations of one another's re-creations of the text, yielding the identity themes of the participants.

REFERENCES

Bollas, C. 1974. "Character: The Language of Self." *International Journal of Psychoanalytic Psychotherapy* 3(4):397–418.

Holland, N. 1968. *The Dynamics of Literary Response.* New York: Oxford University Press.

———. 1973. *Poems in Persons: An Introduction to the Psychoanalysis of Literature.* New York: Norton.

———. 1975. *5 Readers Reading.* New Haven: Yale University Press.

Holland, N., and M. Schwartz. 1975. "The Delphi Seminar." *College English* 36(7):789–800.

Krieger, M. 1976. *Theory of Criticism.* Baltimore: Johns Hopkins University Press.

Lichtenstein, H. 1961. "Identity and Sexuality: A Study of Their Interrelationship in Man." *Journal of the American Psychoanalytic Association* 9:179–260.

Milner, M. 1957. "The Role of Illusion in Symbol Formation." In M. Klein, ed., *New Directions in Psychoanalysis*, pp. 82–108. New York: Basic Books.

Piaget, J. 1951. *Play, Dreams, and Imitation in Childhood.* New York: Norton.

Schwartz, M. 1975. "Where Is Literature?" *College English* 36(7):756–65.

Winnicott, D. W. 1965. *The Maturational Processes and the Facilitating Environment: Studies in the Theory of Emotional Development.* New York: International Universities Press; London: Hogarth Press.

4

Where Is Literature?

MURRAY M. SCHWARTZ

I

Without Contraries is no progression. —William Blake

All criticism of literature originates in our personal experiences of individual works, and all criticism is a transformation of those experiences. This seems obvious, yet, implicitly or explicitly, it is the most frequently denied or avoided aspect of the professional study of literature. Indeed, the current crop of critical self-examinations of literary study yields a rich display of professional avoidance techniques. Professional self-justification seems to have become a pursuit of impersonal contexts or, in one jargon, "pretexts" for the interpretation of the texts that matter to individual critics. The texts and contexts vary but the pursuit remains constant: justification of intellectual activity that interprets literature justifies literature as an object, declares it an autonomous body of works to be studied. This endeavor seems curiously paradoxical, like pulling oneself by one's own bootstraps. Actually, the trick involved is simple, since the category "literature" is never questioned; it is *assumed* to exist in itself, and only the context or "pretext" for its interpretation is changed.

In the professional recruitment of new contexts, no extraliterary categories escape being drafted. Marxist, phenomenological, structuralist, and psychoanalytic concepts all find themselves serving one or another methodology, and it is not uncommon to find students resisting not only a particular critical context but the very endeavor in which their teachers seem so energetically engaged. They seem to suffer a poverty of riches, an array of choices so extensive and sophisticated that in the act of choosing more seems lost than gained, as if the choice of a critical methodology were equivalent to being absorbed and delimited by it. Such absorption seems ambivalently desired, and it is not uncommon (for me) to find students, during doctoral exams, trying somewhat desperately to speak three critical languages at once in a futile attempt to compromise with the apparent demands of professional identities. I often find myself imagining these students in analogy with those "schizophrenics" whose identities represent the painfully unresolved contradictions disavowed by the members of their families.[1] Such an extreme analogy fits my own mental style, but I think it also speaks to the real condition of students attempting to avoid the professional identity diffusion they perceive as the actual condition of their teachers as a group. Occasionally, the opposite strategy occurs, a refusal to generalize in the language of any methodology, as if to say, "A plague on all your houses."

Broadly speaking, students are required to adopt or submit to a critical methodology that claims objectivity for itself, objectivity *aside from* the students' own experience of the works to be interpreted. Northrop Frye gives us the most blatant articulation of this critical piety in his essay, "The Critical Path" (1970). In asserting that "the critic should see literature as, like a science, a unified coherent and autonomous created form," he does more than verbalize a widely held position; he also transforms his *personal* requirement into a moral imperative ("the critic *should* see"), for he has told us just one page before, "*I wanted* a historical approach to literature, but an approach that would be or include a genuine history of literature, and not the assimilating of literature to some other kind of history." In this movement from "I wanted" to "the critic should," Frye exposes the central transformation of the personal into the impersonal and the collective that defines critical activity *for him.* Yet the transformation is not acknowledged. *I* find it there in his essay even as he denies the very existence of his and my inner worlds or personal styles. Listen for yourself: "There are two worlds for man: one is the environment of nature and existing society, which is presented to man as a datum and is first of all to be studied; and the other is the world he wants to live in, the civilization he accepts as an ideal and tries to realize."

Such thinking is profoundly dualistic in the sense that it presupposes the Cartesian splitting of subject and object, places "man" on one side and "nature" and "society" on the other. Nature and society are to be studied; they are *given* objects ("man" is imagined passively), their otherness assumed. Such splitting can yield a rich topography of myths organizing the data of "nature" and "society," but Frye's critical methodology operates at an intellectualized remove from the affective sources of our organizing powers themselves. He assumes (even after his brilliant encounter with Blake) that the external reality of the natural and social worlds is categorically separate from the perceiving personality. Is not an obsession with the ideal, the "autonomous created form," an understandable component of this style of thought? If we think of ourselves simply as students of "objective" data "presented" to us (by whom?) from without, then the distance between the real and the ideal becomes simply a way of conceptualizing an unbridgable gap between desire and its object. Frye's categories make concrete social action a function of manipulating external structures alone. For all his capacity to map past myths of concern, the role of *our* psyches in creating and re-creating those myths even as we map them remains inaccessible to our understanding in Frye's objectification of the critical task.

Frye's style of objectification is widely shared but also widely criticized. Geoffrey Hartman (1970), recalling the external sources of our emotional experience of literature, says of Frye: "Where in this description are the qualities of storytelling that actually involve us—tone, rhythm, humor, surprises, and displacements?" And George Levine (1972) goes even further in his rejection of Frye's idealism, to the place, in fact, where I want to go in this essay, to "the reality of human motives and activities": "It is preoccupation with the ideal that injures Frye's argument, for it lacks a sense of the reality of human motives and activities, governed not by strange mythic powers, intellectual ideals, feelings in a vacuum, but by complicated and unsystematic structures of human relation, greed, lusts for power, love, self-deception, psychoses, neuroses, hungers, hopes, pains, etc."

These critics of Frye share with me and with many of the students I know a strong desire to impart our experiences of literature without abandoning the possibility of formal knowledge or criticism and without relegating these things to the realm of "professional" activity. When students claim priority for their own responses against the "professional" demand for formalized, "objective" knowledge, I take their claim seriously, not in the sense that it would enthrone a cacophony of "gut" expressions in the place of true authority, but in the invitation it seems to contain for me as a teacher to imagine ways in which the experience of literature can be acknowledged *and* transformed into shared cognitions and recognitions. The concepts I need in order to answer that invitation cannot come from a place in which literature is merely an "object" of study. The orientation cannot come from any methodology that avoids or denies the personal origin of the criticism it makes possible.

To respond to this invitation—which comes from myself as well as from my students—I have been studying psychoanalytic theory and practicing psychoanalytic criticism for a number of years. Could I not find in psychoanalysis the one methodology that speaks to and systematically explores what is most personal in our lives? Was not psychoanalysis the only methodology that had its origins in self-analysis? Did not this methodology provide a way of bridging the gap between myself (and my students' selves) and the otherness of the literary work so highly valued as "other" by rival methodologies? Is there not in psychoanalysis a dialectical model different from the dualisms represented by Frye, and different also from those ideologies, like Marxism, that function dialectically in their formal procedures but exclude the immediate experience of the work of art? In short, was there not a way in psychoanalytic psychology of imagining a union of person and profession, private and public identities?

In the search for a model that can reconcile continuity and discontinuity, one's self in the environment and one's self in opposition to the environment, we find that much psychoanalytic writing offers the same kind of duality that structures the thinking of professional literary critics. The person or the work of literature to be analyzed becomes an "object" in the same way that nature and existing society are data for Frye. Psychoanalysis, too, has its Cartesian limitations. For all the richness of analogues that aspects of psychoanalytic theory offer the literary critic for explicating the structure of relationships in individual works or classes of works, there is a psychoanalytic "disinterestedness" that corresponds to the denial of the critic's subjectivity in other methodologies—structuralist, Marxist, etc. Frye's style of objectification is analogous to what Sedgwick (1972) has called "the purely exterior medical sociology" of psychiatry. It is this "medical" psychology that leads literary critics to psychoanalyze literary works in terms of the fiction that characters are real people who can be classified in the way psychiatric disorders are classified, the "hysteric character," the "anal character," and so on. Sedgwick opposes to this exterior model the views of the "immanentist critics of psychiatry," represented most intensively by R. D. Laing, those who propound a nominalist attitude toward all classification of disease. In their views all categories of psychic phenomena are seen as functional for those who cling to them, and the central function usually turns out to be a form of social control.

Roland Barthes (1963) has clarified the opposition between "external" models and "immanentist" models in literary criticism, and his descriptions give me a way of posing the problem of literature's location. Psychoanalytic criticism, he tells us, is congruent with all other forms of interpretive criticism in that it posits "an *elsewhere* of the work," locates the significance of the work outside itself, for example, in the biography of the author. In his words:

> psychoanalytic criticism is still a psychology, it postulates an *elsewhere* of the work (the writer's childhood), a secret of the author, a substance to be deciphered, which remains the human soul, even at the price of a new vocabulary: better a psychopathology of the writer than no psychology at all. By coordinating the details of a work with the details of a life, psychoanalytic criticism continues to practice an aesthetic of motivations entirely based on a relation of exteriority: it is because Racine himself was an orphan that there are so many fathers in his plays; biographical transcendence is saved: there are, there will always be writers' lives to "excavate."

"Immanent analysis," on the other hand, would refer the work to nothing outside itself, would "function in a realm purely internal to the work." Such an approach is phenomenological or thematic or structural in its formal procedures, and its validity is confirmed by its ability, somehow, to explain "the power of astonishment" the work supposedly contains.

Barthes' description of "external" models applies to almost all the criticism I know, and what I find limited in the description is also what I find limited in the criticism. The "elsewhere" posited is granted the status of a *causal agent:* "because Racine himself was an orphan." Racine's orphanage has been made the source and progenitor of his work, the child has become the father of the man once more. We may as well say that the birth of Shakespeare's brother Gilbert two years after him explains why conflict between brothers is so pervasive a motif in his works. By such maneuvers, all such criticism, psychoanalytic or not, seems to need to authorize its interpretations anywhere but in the person of the critic, even when it avoids the reductive, "nothing but" strategy of some early psychoanalytic thought. Yet even if the psychoanalytic criticism Barthes is describing succeeded in encompassing the multiple motivations of any literary product, it would not meet his objection, for an overdetermined work still remains an "elsewhere" pretending to explain an experience I or you have in reading the work. The problem lies in attempting to account for our experiences without accounting for ourselves—our feelings, ideas, and ways of organizing the world we perceive—in those experiences.

Barthes' "immanent analysis" poses the same problem, for the experience of a literary work cannot be explained by any amount of phenomenological, thematic, or structural elucidation located "in" the work "out there." To move from such an elucidation to an interpretation of the work is not like elucidating the internal dynamics of an engine to decide what makes it run. Even in saying that Shakespeare's plays are organized by actual or symbolic conflicts between brothers I have made a choice that depends on my own experience of his plays, and if I go on to say that these conflicts account for the power of the plays, I have made a statement about my own relation to the plays, which may or may not be yours. As long as the *process* of interpretation—the choices of themes, feelings, personal relationships, etc.— occurs only "in" the *product* to be interpreted, in the work considered as an object whose power to evoke responses is purely internal to itself, the "power of astonishment" or any other power attributed to the work will remain a mystery. Frye, Barthes, and the adherents of a medical model of psychoanalysis have this in common: they all remain constrained by what Alfred North Whitehead called the "fallacy of misplaced concreteness": either to posit an "elsewhere" outside the work of literature or to posit the work itself as "elsewhere," in the world of autonomous objects.

This misplaced concreteness is evident to me even when a critic succeeds in avoiding the "anaesthetic" distance Frederick Crews (1970) has identified with Frye, for the problem I am confronting is the *relationship* inevitably present between our subjectivities and the text external to us. It is not enough to say, as Crews has, that "the proper point of vantage is neither fantasy nor facts, but the negotiating ego," be it the author's or reader's, even an emotionally open, psychoanalytically equipped reader's, if that reader remains a generalization. Even as I find Crews transcending Frye's style of impersonal categorization, I find him subscribing to a view of the other, be it author or text, independent of the actively synthesizing personalities of individual readers. Thus, he can say: "Milton's sensuality is hedged with law while Keats's is proclaimed as an imperious right, but both authors are posing ways for us to assert a measure of libidinal freedom." What if I experience Keats's sensuality as a threat to my social relationships? Am

I simply failing to achieve a proper complicity with the author? Or am I then to say, "Keats proclaims sensuality as an imperious right which we feel endangers the fabric of social relationships even as it tempts us to indulge in its beauties"? In Crews's statement, who is doing the "hedging" and "proclaiming," I wonder, the authors or Crews? His "us" still betrays to me the limitations of a model that projects all meaning into the objects found to be meaningful and assumes a proper communal response to the object. This is like pretending that there is *a* statue in the stone, if only we can chip away the cover to reveal the true body beneath.

The question remains: if not here, in my experience of it, or there, in the world of objects to be correctly read by a generalized "we," then where is literature?

II

> *The reality-principle says, if* here, *then not* there; *if inside, then not outside. The alternative to dualism is dialectics; that is to say, love—*
>
> > *Two distincts, division none:*
> > *Number there in love was slain.*
>
> *Whitehead says the reality is unification: reality is events (not things), which are prehensive unification; gathering diversities together in a unity; not simply* here, *or* there, *but a gathering of here and there (subject and object) into a unity.*
> —Norman O. Brown, *Love's Body*

To get from here to there one must make a transition. I want to move from the critical dilemmas I have briefly outlined through some aspects of contemporary psychoanalysis (equally briefly) to an answer to the question, "Where is literature?"

In his reinterpretation of Freud's "Specimen Dream," the so-called dream of "Irma," Erik Erikson (1954) has provided us with the most comprehensive dream analysis in psychoanalytic literature, and in doing so he has also provided us with a reorientation of psychoanalytic theory. Erikson goes beyond the earlier strategy of reading the dream "downward," from the manifest content to the latent dream thoughts; he grants the manifest content of the dream, the dreamer's "style of representation," a status equal with that of the repressed wish, the unconscious, infantile core of the dream. In effect, what Erikson does in his discussion of the manifest content of the dream is what literary critics do in their phenomenological and thematic analyses of texts; he formulates the temporal, spatial, and sensory configurations of the dreamer's personal style. Erikson then listens for the dreamer's (and his own) "true associations, which, unforseen and often unwelcome, make their determined entrance like a host of unsorted strangers, until they gradually become a chorus echoing a few central themes." What he seeks is not to expose a repressed infantile desire alone or to show how the dream transforms this desire into its manifest form, or even both of these. He seeks to make the thematic, structural, and infantile aspects of the dream converge in his conception of the dreamer's individual style of dreaming and living. Through this merger of methods he is able to conclude: "Dreams, then, not only fulfill naked wishes of sexual licence, of unlimited dominance and of unrestricted destructiveness. Where they work, they also lift the dreamer's isolation, appease his own conscience, and preserve his identity, each in specific and instructive ways."

This new, analytic *and* synthetic, theory of the dreaming process and product gives us one way of locating the central contribution of contemporary ego psychology, and it gives us a response to Barthes' valid criticism of the older psychoanalytic obsession with origins. What is new in Erikson's approach, in addition to the centrality of the ego as a unifying concept, is his focus on the whole person within his cultural environment. *Erikson merges the "external" model and the "immanentist" model* kept separate in schools of literary criticism, and, beyond this, he expands the region of psychoanalytic explanation. But his analysis does not, in itself, answer our question about the location of literature.

Erikson gives us some of his personal responses to Freud's dream, and he also gives us something else that a good teacher gives his students. He presents a theory of the dream process and its product in a form that openly acknowledges his own analytic and synthetic activities, so that we can be aware of his mind in interplay with Freud's throughout his essay. In doing this he has located the dream neither "here," in his own associations, nor "there," in Freud's associations. Rather, in his interpretation as a whole, I see Whitehead's "gathering of here and there (subject and object) into a unity." Without Freud's associations there would be little possibility of objective confirmation of the meanings of the dream in Freud's life, and therefore no basic theory of dreams as wish fulfillments. Without Erikson's associations there would be no effort to link the dream to Freud's cultural and social surroundings, no re-creation of the historical context of the dream within a larger psychosocial theory of dreaming that connects a conscious style with unconscious wishes. The new interpretation of the dream consists of an active interplay of Erikson's style of representation and Freud's. Each seeks our consent to the interpretation of a "specimen" dream, and each seeks to separate his own interpretive economy from what existed before him. The interplay between them thus involves an area of identification, a sharing of the desire to provide model interpretations and inclusive theoretical constructs, and the interplay also involves an area of differentiation, each of them having sought to reconceive the basic data of psychoanalysis, the words and associations of the dreamer, in his own style of understanding.

In his analysis Erikson treats the "Irma" dream as creative act analogous to a child's play or the creation of a poem. He does this by locating the dream, for himself as well as for Freud, in what D. W. Winnicott (1953; 1967) called "the vast area between objectivity and subjectivity." The actual dream could obviously never be located in this area, since it is a purely intrapsychic activity, but the dream-as-reported could be, and it is in so locating it that it *becomes* a creative act *for Erikson,* and can be *recognized* as a creative act *for Freud.* My point is that only in bringing his own sense of the creative interplay between Freud and his circumstances to bear on the dream, along with the analytic concepts that derive from that sense, could Erikson have reformed a sharable interpretive method. Rather than attempt to carve *the* perfect statue from the stone, he has shown us *his* way of finding it.

In other words, Erikson brings his own identity to the dream. The interpretation, then, does not result from the elimination of "irrelevant" subjective responses and ideas; Erikson forms an interpretation by actively mixing himself with his subject, just as Frye, Barthes, and Crews do, but with a difference. Where they implicitly deny the subjectivity of their responses by pretending to describe "objective" facts "out there," Erikson allows the process of interplay freedom of expression. The result is neither "external" nor "immanentist" alone; it is the externalization of a relationship between Erikson and Freud, self and other.

Winnicott has called the area between objectivity and subjectivity a "potential space," in which we are free to engage in active interplay between ourselves and the external world of persons and objects. You can imagine this area as bounded on one side by absolute insistence on objective perception (like Dickens's Mr. Gradgrind, we live in this terminal relation to the world when we only test reality. "Now, what I want is Facts. Teach these boys and girls nothing but Facts. . . . Plant nothing else, and root out everything else.") On the other end of this area, we have pure subjectivity (think, for example, of Shakespeare's Glendower proclaiming, "I can call spirits from the vasty deep." To which Hotspur replies, "Why, so can I, or so can any man, / But will they come when you do call for them?"). Potential space, the transitional area between last stops on the line of relatedness, is where most of us live in waking hours. "It is an area," Winnicott says, "that is not challenged, because no claim is made on its behalf except that it shall exist as a resting-place for the individual engaged in the perpetual human task of keeping inner and outer reality separate yet interrelated."

In this area we relate to the world of other people and objects by using symbols, which Winnicott calls "transitional objects," that mix *and* distinguish inner and outer realities. A child's favorite blanket or teddy bear is among the first of such symbols. It does not simply substitute for his memory of mother or her breast, although it resembles aspects of her nurturance in its texture or smell; nor does it simply function as a useful object for the child, although it gets used, say, as a covering or something to caress. The transitional object represents *both* the unity of the child and his mother (external world) *and* their separateness. In developmental terms, we create such symbols as we grow to recognize and seek satisfaction of personal needs and desires. As children we begin to live in potential space, as we learn to use the physical distance between ourselves and our mothers, as we learn to play.

All playing stems from this first interplay of ourselves and the world, in which what we conceive and what we perceive are interwoven in our experiences. Winnicott has given a name to a familiar location, yet it is one we often attempt to close off, as if a playground were usurping the territory of sober critical thought; and we do this by attempting to subtract ourselves from the matrix of our experiences (as in Frye's injunction that nature and existing society are "out there" "to be studied"), believing that the alternative is rampant subjectivity, each of us announcing the truth of his conceptions. In potential space, however, this polarization yields to the interpenetration of what is given (e.g., the material properties of objects or the historical meanings of words) with what is imagined (e.g., the personal value of objects or the private associations of language). Such a location is illusory from a strictly rational perspective, but so is being in love. We structure the world as we perceive it, and we apprehend not simply what is but also what we wish to be. Here is the psychoanalyst Arnold Modell's (1968) summary: "There is a unity between the creation of a cultural form and the creation of the image of a loved object. Both involve the interpenetration of the private with the public, conventionalized schemata; that is, the modes of loving and knowing are inseparable."

III

For nothing can be sole or whole
That has not been rent.
        —William Butler Yeats

Winnicott has defined an area of experience at the point of its inception. If it seems perverse to suggest that literature is a teddy bear, I find it enlightening to realize what they have in common, the place of their meaningful experience for us, first as children, later as adults. The concepts of potential space and transitional phenomena can restore to literary studies a full appreciation of the mediating functions of language, without instituting hierarchies of value based on the choices of a few, and without reducing linguistic mediations to mere formalisms. In this transitional area, my words and their structure are more complex than a child's, and my variations of expression, perhaps, more numerous. Still, when I speak or write I am not being "objective," but objectifying a personal style of experiencing the world, and this process of outering my experience is sharable or mysterious, sensible or opaque, only in relation to your own ways of knowing and your affective style. What we call objective is the result of a created relationship with the world, its other people and its objects. What is to be studied, then, is not the Gradgrindian Facts of "nature" or "society," or "the texts," but the more inclusive realm in which and through which both the data and ourselves are constantly interacting and recombining in new configurations. What is given (the hardness of a stone, or the meanings of words) and what is created (what the hardness says, the feelings we bring to the words) are not antagonistic but interwoven, and the critical act is not an argument but an interpretation, a coming between the opposition of subject and object, here and there, me and you.

Literature is written language located in potential space, the language *we* locate there. Since each of us lives out his or her own identity and its variations in interaction with social and historical circumstances, each of us brings to the literary transaction a unique style of attempting to unite inner and outer realities—our potential spaces and transitional objects are often shared but never identical. It is thus the function of literary studies to provide a context different from but including the intellectual and ideological formulations offered as "objective" by current methodologies. In this context we are free to play at resymbolizing the work of art in the terms of our own identities *and* to test this process against the historically given aspects of the work. I may, for example, bring intense feelings about and images of sexuality to an interpretation of "Leda and the Swan." To announce these without reference to the story of Troy would be to absorb the poem into my own subjectivity. But to speak only of Leda, Zeus, the story of Troy, even the arrangement of words on the page, would be to deny my experience of the poem. Between these two choices lies a third: to re-create the relationship between myself and the story and structure I know about and bring to my experience of the poem. Actually, the third choice does not involve a new model of interpretation; it brings the fact of my involvement into the open. The context I am describing has been here all along. It is literally the classroom, and conceptually the area in which the first world of literature—our psyches—and the second world of literature—historical reality—can safely be confused and distinguished. The third choice is the union of the other two.

NOTE

1. For a discussion of this relation between pathology and its context, see Khan (1972).

REFERENCES

Barthes, R. 1963. "The Two Criticisms." In *Critical Essays*, pp. 249–54. Translated by R. Howard. Evanston: Northwestern University Press, 1972.

Crews, F. 1970. "Anaesthetic Criticism." In F. Crews, ed., *Psychoanalysis and the Literary Process*, pp. 1–24. Cambridge, Mass.: Winthrop.

Erikson, E. H. 1954. "The Dream Specimen of Psychoanalysis." In R. P. Knight and C. R. Friedman, eds., *Psychoanalytic Psychiatry and Psychology: Clinical and Theoretical Papers,* pp. 131–70. New York: Hallmark-Hubner.

Frye, N. 1970. "The Critical Path." *Daedalus* 99:268–342.

Hartman, G. 1970. "Toward Literary History." *Daedalus* 99:354–83.

Khan, M. M. R. 1972. "Exorcism of the Intrusive Ego-Alien Factors in the Analytic Situation and Process." In P. L. Giovacchini, ed., *Tactics and Techniques in Psychoanalytic Therapy,* pp. 383–404. New York: Science House.

Levine, G. 1972. "Our Culture and Our Convictions." *Partisan Review* 39:63–79.

Modell, A. 1968. *Object Love and Reality: An Introduction to a Psychoanalytic Theory of Object Relations.* New York: International Universities Press.

Sedgwick, P. 1972. "Mental Illness IS Illness." *Salmagundi* 20:196–224.

Winnicott, D. W. 1953. "Transitional Objects and Transitional Phenomena." In Winnicott 1971, pp. 1–25.

———. 1967. "The Location of Cultural Experience." In Winnicott 1971, pp. 95–103.

———. 1971. *Playing and Reality.* New York: Basic Books; London: Tavistock, 1984.

5

Poetry in Psychoanalysis: Hopkins, Rossetti, Winnicott

ALBERT D. HUTTER

As Freud (1918) presents the case history of the Wolf Man, a strange phenomenon occurs: his relentless application of logical deduction, his minute focus on detail and its careful explanation, lead us not to certainty but to fiction. Freud endlessly replays the same events with slight alterations until we can no longer distinguish between literal event and its imagined or reconstructed variants. Starting with the patient's adult phobias and obsessions, Freud convincingly traces the Wolf Man's neurosis back to an actual primal scene—but then he proceeds to dismember his own construct: "Perhaps," he speculates, "what the child observed was not copulation between his parents but copulation between animals, which he then displaced on to his parents" (57). "The view," as he writes earlier in the same case, "that we are putting up for discussion is as follows. It maintains that scenes from early infancy, such as are brought up by an exhaustive analysis of neuroses . . . are not reproductions of real occurrences. . . . It considers them rather as products of the imagination . . . which are intended to serve as some kind of symbolic representation of real wishes and interests" (49). Not only is such a view acceptable to Freud; it also allows him to dispose of yet another attack upon his theories: "If that is so," he concludes, "we can of course spare ourselves the necessity of attributing such a surprising amount to the mental life and intellectual capacity of children of the tenderest age" (49).

In short, Freud takes up these opposing positions so effectively that he persuades us of the validity of each in turn. Peter Brooks (1979) has recently described this entire account of the primal scene fantasy in the Wolf Man case as

> one of the most daring moments of Freud's thought, and one of his most heroic gestures as a writer. He could have achieved a more coherent, finished, enclosed, and authoritative narrative. . . . Or . . . he could have struck out parts of the earlier argument, and substituted for them his later reflections. What is remarkable is that, having discovered his point of origin, that which made sense of the dream, the neurosis, and his own account of them, Freud then felt obliged to re-trace the story, offering another and much less evidential . . . kind of origin, to tell another version of the plot, and then finally leave one juxtaposed to the other, indeed one superimposed on the other as a kind of palimpsest, a layered text which offers differing versions of the same story. (78)

Such layering and contradiction is, of course, true not solely for the Wolf Man case: it characterizes Freud's career. What remains so striking as we reread Freud—reevaluating him, deconstructing him, decentering him, reappraising him—is that he has already anticipated us. He revises his theory at least three times, and most of his major works begin by challenging the limits of all that has preceded them. Freud continues to fascinate us in part because he achieves this remarkable degree of openness by the most rational methods. His insistent reasoning leads not simply to solution but always beyond, to competing narratives—"fictions" in the most positive sense of that term. And what we have come to value in Freud is a method of thought as much as the specific conclusions he reaches at different points in his career.

D. W. Winnicott develops the liberating and expansive process of psychoanalytic thinking through a more tentative, even ambiguous posture. If Freud proceeds by logic, Winnicott proceeds by paradox: "My contribution," he writes, "is to ask for a paradox to be accepted and tolerated and respected, and for it not to be resolved. By flight to split-off intellectual functioning it is possible to resolve the paradox, but the price of this is the loss of the value of the paradox itself" (1971:xii). Winnicott's writings, particularly his case histories, often have an elliptical, even disjointed quality, which in turn reflects the fragmentation of the particularly troubled patients with whom he works. Like Freud, Winnicott warrants rereading and reappraisal; in some ways, his hesitant, self-mocking conjectures are the perfect complement to Freud's tightly reasoned polemic.

Winnicott emphasizes the function of analytic silence as space, a play space for the patient's self-discovery. More specifically, two transference phenomena he frequently stresses—introjection and projection—describe a process wherein the analyst permits the patient to play creatively, to associate to and through the person of the analyst, to relate to a real object and to be created, in turn, by the analyst's understanding of the patient. Winnicott's use of the term *creative* is not a catchall for something vaguely praiseworthy; rather, the analyst, in the process of the therapy, fosters the patient's re-*creation* of self through experience and interpretation while he encourages the patient to create a more coherent self through the analytic transference.

The Winnicott case history we shall examine, like Freud's complex account of the Wolf Man, resembles fictional narrative. Our attempts to understand the various kinds of "story"—that is, the story an analyst extrapolates from the patient's fragmented, hour-by-hour story, and the story re-created by us, as readers, whether we are reading an analytic case or a work of fiction—raise problems of transference and countertransference in the telling, retelling, and hearing of such stories. These problems are often very hard to perceive and to separate (we wonder: Is this Freud's version of the patient's account, or the patient's neurotic distortion of a supposedly real event, or my reaction to Freud or his patient?), but they are essential aspects of any attempt to understand narrative and reader response. And as we learn to delineate such questions and attempt to answer them, we are also gaining more insight into the clinical context of transference and countertransference. Poetry and fiction are far more important for understanding analytic technique than their usual treatment in the field of "applied psychoanalysis" would imply. Like poetry, the analytic experience works when it is perceived neither as something done *to* the patient nor as something done *by* the analyst, but rather as something that occurs in what Winnicott would call "potential space." Winnicott's theories of this space, like his notions of "transitional objects" and "transitional phenomena," begin with his work with children. Initially, that space and those phenomena are largely nonverbal—looking, mirroring, touching, literally creating and testing a play space. But as Winnicott himself delimits a "location of cultural experience" (1971:95–103) and begins to discuss the practice of analysis within these same terms of space and transition, the activities of creation and *re*-creation take place almost exclusively through words—and silence: like the literary critic, the analyst uses language to describe language. Critics reconstitute the experience of a poem or novel much as an analyst (along with his patient) reconstructs the verbal fragments and images of an hour and the narrative fragments of a personal history.

Poetry, literature in general, and a poetic sense of language play an especially important part in psychoanalysis—more important, I suspect, than even Winnicott realizes. In *Playing and Reality,* his brief seven-page account of a patient, described as living from poem to poem like a chain smoker (62), gives us more than a glimpse of a gifted, literate patient—who uses her aesthetic gifts both to defend and to communicate—or of the remarkable skills of her therapist: it suggests as well a series of relations and correlations between poetry and the language of an analysis, between literary analysis and the activity of psychoanalysis.

Winnicott saw this patient, a woman who was apparently an art teacher, once a week for a long (two- or three-hour) session. Such a session, like the "on-demand" analyses he describes elsewhere, deviates dramatically from standard psychoanalytic technique. It is not my purpose here to evaluate the merits of such radical parameters, to determine whether this is truly an analysis at all (as opposed to an analytically informed therapy); moreover, my interests in the literary content of the clinical material may well cause me to understate issues of technique. Although I note the possible resistance in the patient's use of poetry (especially in her choice of poems and in her recitation of one of them) and concede that Winnicott's responsiveness to poetic allusion may, at times, suggest an unconscious collusion with her defenses, I am more concerned with poetry as communication. In effect, precisely because this session is so atypical and extraordinary it exposes and exaggerates technical questions—particularly of transference and countertransference—which inform all analytic work. One clinical issue that is immediately significant is Winnicott's nurturance of this patient, particularly when we later learn that this is an extra session "given to her to make up for having had to miss her usual time," one the patient felt she especially needed. Indeed, throughout the report, there are notes and asides that reveal Winnicott's readiness to break the rules. For example, he observes that "in this analysis a kettle and a gas ring, coffee, tea, and a certain kind of biscuit are reliably available," and after a particularly important interpretation the patient reaches for "some milk and asked if she could drink it." Winnicott, of course, replied, " 'Drink it up' " (61). These details point to a crucial insight that emerges for the patient during this session: she must learn how to accept her analyst's capacity to give and to feel. Since feeding is related to accepting the interpretive milk of the analyst, one of her first quoted statements is, appropriately, "some difficulty about food." In these opening remarks, she moves from books to food, and Winnicott notes that association, although he does not interpret it. The course of the entire session, however, suggests that at the start she fails to see the analyst as another person, capable of understanding and giving, so that she herself is tormented, unable to feed properly on anything, even to ingest words in books: she cannot read. Her progress through these hours will be measured by an increased capacity to "take in" the language of others, from a novel remembered to her student's postcard to the poets she cites—and finally, to Winnicott himself.

By thus skipping ahead, however, I am distorting what Winnicott first sees and the way we first experience the patient. Initially, we do not attend to her problem in relating to others because what over-whelms her is the symptom: she cannot perceive herself. Because she has no mirror, cannot allow herself a mirror in which to find herself reliably, she announces, early on: " 'I don't seem able quite to BE' " (57). But after three-quarters of an hour she becomes "occupied with watching out of the window where she was standing, seeing a sparrow pecking away at a crust, suddenly 'taking a crumb away to its nest—or somewhere,' " and this in turn suddenly reminds her of a dream. Again, the image of the sparrow, and specifically the sparrow taking a crumb back to its nest, presumably for its offspring, insistently recalls feeding; but at this point such an idea is still only barely felt and quickly dissipated ("to its nest—or somewhere"). In addition to the emotional and developmental implications of this image, it also echoes a famous passage from the correspondence of John Keats: "The setting sun will always set me to rights—or if a Sparrow come before my Window I take part in its existence and pick about the Gravel."[1] Given what we later see of this patient—her range of literary knowledge and the problem of what she will call being "negatived"—we shall connect her associations to Keats's aesthetic, particularly the idea of negative capa-bility, that state in which "man is capable of being in uncertainties, Mysteries, doubts, without any irritable reaching after fact & rea-son."[2] That aesthetic depends upon one's capacity to achieve identity by an absolute projection, to tolerate a loss of self and a loss of rationality by trusting in the capacity to re-create oneself in another character or in the environment: "That I might drink, and leave the world unseen, / And with thee fade away into the forest dim." [3] This loss is not a negation of self but an affirmation of self through an exaggerated notion of object relating. It is as if the artist in Keats facilitates a movement outside, into the potential space that is neither purely the individual's ego nor entirely external but allows for a period of "becoming" something else while remaining securely oneself. This artistic identity is presumably accepted as well by the reader of Keats, "ingested," used as a vehicle for exploring the poem and in the process expanding without relinquishing the boundaries of his or her own ego.

Our patient, however, is not thinking in these terms. Throughout Winnicott's report of the session I am never certain how much she understands of what she reads or recites. But, in effect, my judgments, like Winnicott's judgments, further complicate a process that they are also meant to illuminate. Winnicott's patient does with her poems what most of our patients do with poems or novels or, perhaps most commonly today, with films: she alludes to a work, which requires, first from her and then from her analyst, an act of interpretation. Where the analyst is familiar with the work to which the patient alludes, the patient's implied understanding of it may offer a significant approach into personality and pathology—perhaps most strikingly when the patient's "reading" of the material is partial and distorted. But "distortion" requires a judgment by the therapist of what the work is *in fact* about and how the patient's view distorts that presumably objective reading. Obviously, complete objectivity is impossible and any judgments about a work must be made with great care and an awareness of our own capacity for subjective distortions; but just as obviously, such judgments are indispensable in the course of our analytic work. For example, in evaluating the termination phase of an analysis, the therapist's sense of a changed capacity in the patient to respond to different kinds of aesthetic works (showing, for example, less defensiveness, greater empathy without an accompanying loss of identity, etc.) might well provide a fresh perspective in this most critical—and delicate— process. But the problem that the analyst confronts in weighing his taste and understanding as he evaluates the aesthetic responses of a patient is compounded for us because we are yet one step further removed: we look through two filters, not unlike a supervisor hearing an analyst reporting work with the patient who is describing a phenomenon, while we also try to look at the phenomenon itself. While it may be perilous and frustrating, this process offers us an unusually clear opportunity to understand how both analyst and patient perceive a common structure—the artwork itself.

Thus, to return to Winnicott and his patient, if her sudden reference to a sparrow reminds us of Keats, this certainly does not appear to be her own immediate association. Instead, she remembers a dream: " 'Some girl student kept bringing pictures that she had drawn. How could I tell her that these pictures show no improvement? I had thought that by letting myself be alone and meeting my depression. . . . I'd better stop watching those sparrows—I can't think' " (58).

Several aspects of this dream are worth noting. The first two sentences replicate the analytic situation with the roles reversed. Now in her own dream she is in the position of the analyst asked to judge material created and brought to her. And what she sees—what she sees finally in herself—is "no improvement." But even putting herself into this position—being another, looking back at herself, making critical judgments—all this seems intolerable, and in the report of the dream she wrenches herself from one state (outside herself) to another without transition. Hence the confusing shift to the third sentence: " 'I had thought that by letting myself be alone and meeting my depression . . .' " It is less confusing if we realize that she is talking about and trying to deal with herself, through the figure of the "girl student." This dream underscores two of the key psychodynamic issues of the session: her difficulty in seeing and accepting others and her difficulty in seeing and accepting herself, including negative aspects of herself. She remembered the dream quite suddenly as a result of momentarily getting outside of herself, looking at the sparrow and imagining what the sparrow was doing. She similarly concludes the dream by another apparent non sequitur that in fact returns her to that initial image: " 'I'd better stop watching those sparrows—I can't think.' " Watching the sparrows—that is, looking outside at other figures, projecting, identifying—all these activities are threatening and exhausting; they bring her back to her sense of her own illness, her refusal to acknowledge that illness or even her attraction toward being ill; they bring her back to a sense of her own fragile identity: " 'It's as though there isn't really a ME.' " And she remembers an " 'awful book of early teens called *Returned Empty*. That's what I feel like.' " The title of the book is striking not only because of the self-emptiness it so clearly states but also because of the implied return from some other place, the attempt to have seen oneself in and through others, which the first word suggests.

There is in fact a book called *Returned Empty*, a novel apparently intended for an adolescent audience, written in 1920 by Florence L.

Barclay. Barclay herself achieved wide popular success by virtue of combining a quasi-religious mysticism with a not-so-veiled eroticism and a remarkably direct presentation of incestuous fantasies. Her book's title refers ironically to a packing label on the parcel that delivers the novel's hero to a foundling home. The hero is named Luke Sparrow. But beyond the name itself, his peculiar sense of possessing special gifts combined with a feeling of emptiness, of nonexistence, strongly resembles the self-image of Winnicott's patient. Throughout the first half of the book Sparrow seeks something undefined but so powerfully alluring that he is compelled to wander the country and look in at domestic scenes through windows, always on the outside, until he finally finds what he is searching for: a beautiful, gray-haired, aristocratic widow, whom he first believes to be his mother. " 'I would to God you were my mother,' " he exclaims, " 'but, if that may not be, then—in Heaven's name—what are you to me?' Her voice was a paean of triumphant joy. "I am your wife.' " Luke is understandably distressed to find that he is the reincarnated husband of this ideal motherly woman, and he spends much of the rest of the novel fleeing his "wife," at least in the flesh. He even attempts to drown himself so that they will be rejoined in the presumably safe and noncorporeal world of eternal heavenly bliss.

On aesthetic grounds Winnicott's patient is perfectly justified in calling *Returned Empty* an "awful book," but it is one that bears remarkably on her own situation: the personal emptiness and sense of isolation, the fantasies of suicide, the transference and her defenses against transference feelings, especially a feared and repudiated eroticism that she transforms into a more "poetic," spiritual phenomenon. As we shall see, one movement in the course of this session is from her "aesthetic" defenses, in which she "spiritualizes" eroticism and identifies strongly with this quality in a poem by Christina Rossetti, to a more open admission of the presence of the analyst, which provokes her gratitude and her anger, as they are expressed in her references to Hopkins.

Now an hour of the session has elapsed, and the patient, writes Winnicott, "went on about the use of poetry"; she then recites Christina Rossetti's poem "Passing Away." We should again be struck with how unlike most analytic hours this is. If a patient were suddenly to begin reciting long poems we would most likely regard it as a resistance: the patient occupies the hour not with his or her words but with someone else's, perhaps revealing a difficulty in accepting silence and a need to fill the void. Based on the notes we have, Winnicott says nothing; he allows the patient to recite the poem and to move at her own pace in associating to it. But Winnicott's language at this point calls for special attention: he says the patient "recited a poem." The artificial connotation of "recited" tells us something important about the poem—or, better, about Winnicott's sense of how the patient uses the poem—even before we look at it. The stilted nature of recitation anticipates her subsequent use of the archaic expression " 'I'm *loath* to come into this room' " (italics added). She relies on the formality of language, on an artificial, external structure, in her attempt to convey her fear of genuine communication, which will in turn expose her fears about herself—that she is ill, dejected, fragmentary. Rossetti's poem presents these problems of fragmentation and despair within an extraordinarily formal, controlled medium:

Passing Away

Passing away, saith the World, passing away:
Chances, beauty, and youth, sapped day by day:
Thy life never continueth in one stay.
Is the eye waxen dim, is the dark hair changing to grey
That hath won neither laurel nor bay?
I shall clothe myself in Spring and bud in May:
Thou, root-stricken, shalt not rebuild thy decay
On my bosom for aye.
Then I answered: Yea.

Passing away, saith my Soul, passing away:
With its burden of fear and hope, of labour and play,
Hearken what the past doth witness and say:
Rust in thy gold, a moth is in thine array,
A canker is in thy bud, thy leaf must decay.
At midnight, at cockcrow, at morning, one certain day
Lo the Bridegroom shall come and shall not delay;
Watch thou and pray.
Then I answered: Yea.

Passing away, saith my God, passing away:
Winter passeth after the long delay:
New grapes on the vine, new figs on the tender spray,
Turtle calleth turtle in Heaven's May.

Though I tarry, wait for Me, trust Me, watch and pray:
Arise, come away, night is past and lo it is day,
My love, My sister, My spouse, thou shalt hear Me say.
Then I answered: Yea.

Rossetti's text seems clear enough: in the first stanza she examines the transitory nature of living in the world, where she must quickly fade into old age and then death—"Chances, beauty, and youth, sapped day by day." The world describes how it will renew itself, "I shall clothe myself in Spring and bud in May" (line 6), but the poet cannot follow suit: "Thou, root stricken, shalt not rebuild thy decay / On my bosom for aye" lines (7–8). To this, the poet can only answer "Yea," an affirmation that is an emphatic negation. In the second stanza the Soul reveals the rust hidden in gold, the moth that devours clothing, the canker in the bud, the inevitable decay of all things born. Rossetti's soul then tells her to watch for Christ, who will come "one certain day." And now her "Yea" is closer to an affirmation, a response of hope to the injunction "Watch thou and pray" (line 18). In the final stanza Christ speaks to her, reversing the sense of decay set up by the previous two stanzas, which focus on seasonal change leading to death. He reassures her that "winter passeth after the long delay: / New grapes on the vine, new figs on the tender spray." She is removed from the decay of worldly seasons into an eternal, heavenly spring; and although God's message is to urge patience and trust in waiting for Him, the effect of this stanza is as if he were already with her, so that her final "Yea" is an immediate affirmation of the intimacy of Christ speaking to her in the preceding line: "My love, My sister, My spouse" (line 25).

The poem's apparent simplicity is deceptive: it is a remarkable tour de force precisely because of its formal tightness. The same rhyme, for example, is sustained for twenty-six lines, and its introduction in the title and recurrence within lines throughout the poem exacerbates its almost claustrophobic quality. Rossetti's intention, however, seems to be not claustrophobia but freedom and affirmation, and she tries to achieve this effect by the insistence of rhyme scheme, the constriction of rhythm, which returns us to a three-beat line at the close of each stanza, and by the repetition of image and theme. Whatever our own reactions may be to this poem, Rossetti is very much in control of her medium and its effects—most strikingly in the final stanza, where a few, subtle technical shifts intensify the closeness to God at which she aims and intensify as well the resonance of that final "Yea." The repetition of words increases in these lines ("New grapes . . . new figs . . . Turtle calleth turtle") and that repetition becomes most effective in stressing the words "me" and "my." Such a stress, I suspect, first results in a sense that we are actually hearing Christ's voice in a way we do not hear the other two rhetorical speakers (the World and the Soul) and, paradoxically, also tends to fuse the poet with the speaker— Christ—of the last stanza.

The effect of such apparently deliberate confusion is one of merging: syntactically, Rossetti and Christ are married in the text; they merge and appear as one figure. In the first stanza "I" and "Thou" are very carefully opposed at the beginning of contiguous lines (6 and 7); in the second stanza the use of "thy" is insistent and distances the poem's speaker and listener from the figure of the soul, who keeps stressing *"thy* gold . . . *thine* array . . . *thy* bud . . . *thy* leaf"; but in the final stanza the one use of "thou" is late in the penultimate line, while Christ's voice rings out most clearly because of the repetition of "me" and "my" and because of the direct and intimate address in the line beginning "My love." The force of that line is exaggerated in its movement toward the final affirmation because Rossetti now chooses to skip a line. The first two stanzas each have nine lines, and each stanza finishes with two three-beat lines. In the last stanza that symmetry is deliberately broken, and we leap from God's embrace—"My love, My sister, My spouse"—to Rossetti's shorter and more direct answer.

Rossetti intends to convey and affirm a profound religious experience; and the more I work with the poem, the more I admire its technical virtuosity. Yet my first impression of the poem also persists— for me, at least, it borders on triteness. The devices that make it so remarkable technically at the same time bring it dangerously close to a sing-song, oversimplified sound and meaning. Certain images are undeniably powerful, most noticeably the image buried at the exact center of the poem, "the canker in the bud," and indeed its location and resonance may suggest that what Rossetti wants (a thorough affirmation of Christ) and what she feels (a sense of decay and unworthiness within herself) are at odds. Just as one might say of Milton's Satan, corruption in "Passing Away" is more vivid and persuasive than its opposites, goodness and salvation. I might also argue that the evocative quality of the final stanza owes much to its imitation of the Song of Songs (chapter 2):

10 My beloved spake, and said unto me, Rise up, my love, my fair
one, and come away.

11 For, lo, the winter is past, the rain is over and gone;

12 The flowers appear on the earth; the time of the singing of birds
is come, and the voice of the turtle is heard in our land;

13. . . . Arise, my love, my fair one, and come away.

And if we hear that echo of the Bible here, it speaks as well to the
power of precisely those worldly joys and beauties Rossetti seems to be
renouncing. It certainly underscores a paradox within the poem and
within its biblical source: the image of heavenly sweetness is drawn
from the transitory joys of the world, which we are meant to transcend,
if not to renounce.

Thus, to explain the poem's effect on me, I might, in various ways,
attempt to connect my own reaction to qualities I find in the poem or
in the tradition it represents, qualities that are perhaps not so obviously
under the conscious control of its author. I try to use my own sense of
the poetry as Winnicott uses his sense of his patient's language: to
express significant issues and subtle changes. But I also want to avoid
mistaking my feelings about the poem for an absolute assessment of its
merits: such rigidity of judgment in fact characterizes the problems of
this particular patient. What Winnicott aims for with his patients we
need to aim for with our reading of her recited poems: a tolerance for
paradox; an acceptance of contradiction within the poem as within the
patient and within ourselves; a sense of what the form of these words,
their ordering and relationship, may tell us in opposition to their stated
meaning.

The same formal qualities of Rossetti's work will be seen in different
ways and experienced differently by different people at different times.
How, then, does this particular patient react? She goes immediately to
the decayed center of the text and applies it to herself: " 'My life
finishes with a canker in the bud.' " This is not necessarily a misread-
ing, as we've just seen, but it does seem to be a very personal and
partial reading. We don't know whether the patient has understood
Rossetti's intention and deliberately rejected it—perhaps even sensed
an ambivalence in Rossetti which she, the patient, pronounces most
unambivalently; perhaps, given the patient's suffering, she can only
respond to those things outside herself which echo that suffering. Her
next statement, directed at Winnicott (" 'You've taken away my God!' "),
suggests that she has been responding to more than the image of
rottenness in the poem but still cannot do what Rossetti presumably

does—transcend the negative in herself and her world and find her own God. But the process of analysis makes her aware of her flight from herself and her frustrated search for a god; her awareness is enhanced by Winnicott's refusal to provide a facile substitute for God by playing at a psychoanalytic deity who makes brilliant interpretations and organizes the patient's life and thoughts for her. But the statement " 'You've taken away my God,' " like every other statement she makes that touches directly on the person of the analyst, is too perilous. After a long pause, she retreats into a combined apology and denial; and her language again uses the images of orality, although the movement is reversed, so that her earlier thoughts about eating, about food and books, about the sparrow pecking at a crust or feeding its young, are now refused: " 'I'm just spewing out on you anything that comes. I don't know what I've been talking about. I don't know . . . I dunno . . .' " (58).

The next part of the session, covered in a page and a half, exposes several significant details: her associations to painting, finger painting, and reading—all as forms of self-expression dangerous because they lead to a sense of messiness, presumably the mess she feels herself to be; Winnicott's maddening omissions of detail concerning what he calls "the original trauma" and her use of an "apt quotation from the poet Gerard Manley Hopkins" (59). A small point requires special attention. The patient, presumably referring to one of her students, says, " 'Imagine, a girl sent me a postcard from holiday,' " and Winnicott replies, " 'As if you mattered to her.' " The patient is noncommittal (" 'maybe' "), and Winnicott pursues the theme of mattering for others, perceiving one's self through others. But what I find equally significant here is the act of writing, just as at several earlier points the act of reading carried so much meaning. It is through writing that we dare to externalize and "objectify" ourselves—undoubtedly why writing is so difficult and so filled with what we loosely call "writer's block." Every time we face a blank page it is as though we face what this patient feels so exaggeratedly about herself but what all of us surely feel at one time or another: the page mirrors our own blankness, our emptiness. There is nothing left to say. Filling up that page requires a certain kind of courage, especially when it will be examined by someone else and perhaps criticized (as in this patient's dream), because beyond any immediate criticism there is always, I believe, a more fundamental fear that if the criticism goes far enough or deep enough it will uncover a vacuum. One way to protect ourselves from such a revelation is to hide behind someone else's words, or even to claim them as our own. If we define plagiarism in terms of identity, the assumption or appropriation of a false identity, then this patient may be understood as an emotional plagiarist—and such plagiarism is one issue that she resolves over the course of the session. The shift, for example, from her recitation of Rossetti to the more integrated use of Hopkins, as we shall see, suggests a larger shift from a denial of self to an acceptance of herself and her analyst.

Plagiarism, in any community that depends upon an exchange of knowledge, is the deepest betrayal of that community; it seems particularly pernicious because it destroys the reliable sense of relationship between identity and production. Winnicott himself talks about plagiarism in an aside at another point in *Playing and Reality:* "the unforgivable sin in the cultural field is plagiarism. The interplay between originality and the acceptance of tradition as the basis for inventiveness seems to me to be just one more example, and a very exciting one, of the interplay between separateness and union" (99).

Throughout the session we are discussing, the patient repeatedly crosses the boundary between finding herself in someone else's writing or experience and hiding herself behind that writing, substituting what she feels to be someone else's more authentic experience for her own fragmented or negative sense of self. She begins with a connection between eating and reading, she relies heavily on a tradition of poetry as self-expression and as a means for resolving conflict, and she makes frequent references to small acts of writing, like the girl's postcard. Then, after nearly two hours, Winnicott writes, *"the patient seemed to be in the room with me,"* a transformation demonstrated by a significant alteration in the theme of writing: now *she* can write. And although the writing is overtly negative—done in black, it is a memorial card to her birthday, her "deathday"—it confirms the change that has taken place in the session. When Winnicott says that she now seemed to be in the room with him, he is, I believe, responding to his own emotional sense—his countertransference—that she can tolerate him as a full person, "a whole object," and that she can begin to accept his generosity, his giving. She acknowledges for the first time, "as if this were her first remark to me, 'I'm glad you knew I needed this session.' " That apparently simple statement, acknowledging not just the analyst but the analyst as someone else, someone who thinks and feels and is capable of giving, comes about after many partial attempts. It is not too much of an exaggeration to say that she comes to accept Winnicott through the sparrow, through her struggle with a whole tradition of nineteenth-century poetry, through the creative acts of reading and painting and writing.

Once she can accept Winnicott as another being and acknowledge her gratitude, she can begin to work with a still more difficult problem—her anger, both at others and herself. There have already been hints of this anger—for example, in her earlier accusation that Winnicott has robbed her of her God—but she is now able to express it more directly. She begins by focusing on "specific hates" and then on herself, and through this focus she begins to write the birthday / deathday card. As a result of her anger, and, still more important, through her analyst's capacity to tolerate that anger, she becomes more and more herself, and consequently more and more a presence in the room. Finally she starts to assume one of the functions of the analyst—she herself wants to analyze the session, but she has trouble remembering exactly what was said. And then Winnicott comments:

> Here I made an interpretation: "All sorts of things happen and they wither. This is the myriad deaths you have died. But if someone is there, someone who can give you back what has happened, then the details dealt with in this way become part of you, and do not die."
> (61)

The interpretation is remarkably effective—in all that it says, in the poetry of its saying, as well as in its timing. And the patient seems to affirm its efficacy by reaching, at that point, for some milk: she is ready now to take in what Winnicott has to offer. Quite a bit later, Winnicott will use a modified line from Hopkins's "Spring and Fall: To a Young Child," but the interpretation at this point in the session seems to anticipate the essential quality of his later, deliberate use of that poem.

Hopkins was preoccupied, throughout his life and work, with an intimate experience of God that directly corresponds to a child's experience of a parent. At times, as we shall see in "Carrion Comfort," that experience is characterized by struggle, by the subjugation and resolution of rebellion. "Spring and Fall" is atypically lyrical and smooth, possibly because in this poem Hopkins portrays himself as a giving parent rather than as a struggling child: the poem reflects an ideally empathic parent, capable of sharing experience and reflecting back to the child a sense of insight and understanding. Perhaps it is also appropriate to see Hopkins in this poem as a "good analyst" as well as a "good parent," since the central experience of "Spring and Fall" is a combination of empathic understanding and interpretation—and an interpretation aimed not only at the relief of present suffering but also toward the growth of the child.

Spring and Fall
To a Young Child

Márgarét, áre you grieving
Over Goldengrove unleaving?
Leáves, líke the things of man, you
With your fresh thoughts care for, can you?
Áh! ás the heart grows older
It will come to such sights colder
By and by, nor spare a sigh
Though worlds of wanwood leafmeal lie;
And yet you *will* weep and know why.
Now no matter, child, the name:
Sórrow's springs áre the same.
Nor mouth had, no nor mind, expressed
What heart heard of, ghost guessed:
It is the blight man was born for,
It is Margaret you mourn for.

Hopkins is able to mirror back to the girl, Margaret, her sense of mourning, of the "myriad deaths" we all die, which is first perceived by her in the death of the leaves, the arrival of fall: "worlds of wanwood leafmeal." Although she mourns, the experience of sorrow is transformed into an experience of beauty and pleasure, and this happens, I believe, because we can experience in and through this poem the capacity of the parent to reflect back to the child that child's perceptions, even in death and loss; by our capacity to accept loss and to mirror that acceptance, we are, paradoxically, able to foster the reality and growth of the child's own identity.

After Winnicott's interpretation ("the myriad deaths you have died"), his patient seems to experience her own feelings more acutely, and her sobbing is accompanied by "positive feeling and activities that were of themselves evidence of her being real and living in the actual world" (61). She affirms her contact with other people, remembers significant childhood events, and returns again to her sense of her analyst. She now experiences not simply his generosity but her ability and inability to use the session, to produce, and to risk looking for herself in the words and actions and reflections of the session:

"I don't feel I've . . . I feel I've wasted this session."
(Pause.)
"I feel as though I came to meet somebody and they didn't come."

No doubt she is talking, at least in part, about herself. She is acknowledging her difficulty in accepting—tolerating—her own existence, and this is the direction Winnicott now pursues, pushing her thought further:

I said: "If you hadn't existed at all, it would have been all right."
She: "But what is so awful is existence that's negatived! . . ."

As she continues, wondering about herself and all that seems wrong with her, she returns to a sense of the other person in the room. Winnicott claims that "now a change of attitude, indicating the beginning of an acceptance of my existence," is taking place, but this is surely not the beginning. The whole session has dealt with aspects of this problem, which she can now articulate, as she does in her next remark: " 'I keep stopping you from talking!' "

Winnicott's skill is apparent in the new direction he probes in his reply: " 'You want me to talk now [meaning, among other things, you are READY for me to talk now], but you fear I might say something good.' " And she responds with another poem—now not a recitation but simply a line, rendered through her own subjective translation: "She said: 'It was in my mind: "Don't make me wish to BE!" ' That's a line of a poem by Gerard Manley Hopkins.' " Winnicott provides us, in a footnote, with a little more of the text, but the entire poem is worth examining because the struggle of Hopkins in the poem recalls this patient's struggle—in her life and within the analysis:

Carrion Comfort

Not, I'll not, carrion comfort, Despair, not feast on thee;
Not untwist—slack they may be—these last strands of man
In me ór, most weary, cry *I can no more*. I can;
Can something, hope, wish day come, not choose not to be.

But ah, but O thou terrible, why wouldst thou rude on me
Thy wring-world right foot rock? lay a lionlimb against me? scan

With darksome devouring eyes my bruisèd bones? and fan,
O in turns of tempest, me heaped there; me frantic to avoid thee and flee?

Why? That my chaff might fly; my grain lie, sheer and clear.
Nay in all that toil, that coil, since (seems) I kissed the rod,
Hand rather, my heart lo! lapped strength, stole joy, would laugh, chéer.
Cheer whom though? The hero whose heaven-handling flung me, fóot tród
Me? or me that fought him? O which one? is it each one? That night, that
    year
Of now done darkness I wretch lay wrestling with (my God!) my God.

This sonnet is one of a group known as "the terrible sonnets," reflecting a period of particular despair in Hopkins's life. Hopkins's decisions first to convert to Catholicism and then to become a priest were costly for him and for his family, and most of his subsequent career as a Jesuit priest was characterized by conflict and pain. His internal conflict often manifested itself in physical symptoms, and he died relatively young. His tightly strung, twisted, highly original, and sometimes tortured verse was itself both an expression of his inner conflict and a subject for that conflict: at various times during his priesthood he renounced the writing of poetry, and he was often frustrated and even disgusted by his attempts to express himself through words. Near the end of his life he asked his friend, Robert Bridges, to destroy his work, which Bridges happily failed to do. But in this sonnet, as in most of Hopkins's work, we can see that a central issue of the poetry is the definition of self through a deeply ambivalent relationship with the person of God. In his best, and best-known, poetry—such as this sonnet, "God's Grandeur," "The Windhover"—we see the same pattern of conflict, battle, or doubt ("Why do men then now not reck his rod?") followed by the exclamatory joy of acceptance and union with God ("Because the Holy Ghost over the bent / World broods with warm breast and with ah! bright wings").

"Carrion Comfort" opens with a negation, and that "not" implies the broader problem of "Accidie," the sin of Despair, which is the negation of the idea of God.[4] In the first quatrain Hopkins is wrestling with such despair, and he, like our patient, seems to find himself through negation: "I can . . . not choose not to be." Like our patient he, too, begins from a sense of feeding, "I'll not feast on thee," and chooses what he will take inside himself and what he will reject. In the remaining lines he turns from despair and directly engages God. Like Winnicott's patient, Hopkins defines himself by questioning the existence of another, then the meaning and intentions of that other, by testing his anger against that figure, until finally he can find himself reflected in the continued (undamaged) existence and continued acceptance of another being: in one case, the analyst; in the other, God. Why do you turn against me, he asks, and why do you contemplate my suffering? The answer is that through suffering the speaker, Hopkins, may discover himself: "That my chaff might fly; my grain lie, sheer and clear." And he speaks then of accepting God, gaining strength through God, taking God inside, for the imagery is now clearly oral: he *"lapped* strength, stole joy." But this sense of joy quickly leads him to question the meaning of the strength he has received: is it a celebration of himself, another example of his own self-importance, or is it a reflection of the glory of God? To answer the question "O which one?" he responds with a tentative answer in the form of another question "is it each one?" This notion, that strength is mutual, that indeed the process of questioning, even questioning of the most extreme and dangerous sort, will lead to a magnification both of one's self and of one's God, is central to the closing lines of the poem and to its double discovery—the parenthetical "my God!" followed by affirmation: "My God." Like Jacob wrestling with the angel, Hopkins discovers himself through grappling with God, and what began as complaint and despair—the whole process of self-doubt, of questioning—finishes as celebration.

Because this poem continues to move, to question, to double back on itself, to discover and uncover down to the final four words, I find that it more accurately reflects the change in Winnicott's patient than does Rossetti's poem of resolved religious doubts. I also find in its difficult language and complex syntax a sharper reflection of the patient's difficulty throughout the session, while the Rossetti, by contrast, seems to offer a clear, perhaps too-clear, structure and voice. Winnicott's patient has rendered the Hopkins line in terms of her continuing struggle with her own particular God, her analyst, when she exclaims: " 'Don't make me wish to BE.' " Since she is still very much engaged in the struggle that Hopkins's poem tentatively resolves, Hopkins's dense and convoluted style is especially appropriate to her own experience at this point in the session.

There is, in addition, a quality in both "Passing Away" and "Carrion Comfort" that mirrors another aspect to this session: both poems achieve closure by implying a second story or second text—the Song of

Songs in Rossetti's final stanza, the story of Jacob and the Angel in Hopkins's final line. In this way, Rossetti, as well as Hopkins, manages to end by creating a new text, a narrative that combines the ultimate authority of the Bible with the openness achieved by superimposing one narrative on another. In this sense the richness of the poetry conveys the complex feelings and thought of the patient, just as Freud's narrative technique, as it was described at the beginning of this paper, expresses the possibility of multilayered meaning: competing but complementary narratives simultaneously explicate and complicate.

After the patient offers Winnicott the line from "Carrion Comfort," she and Winnicott talk about poetry, how she uses it often and even lives through it. It is here that she is described as living "from poem to poem (like cigarette to cigarette in chain-smoking)," a simile that neatly combines the idea of feeding with language and suggests how such "word-food" may be mouthed without genuinely taking it inside, without introjecting it and making it part of oneself. She often uses poetry without fully understanding it, much as she can occupy a room with someone else without being fully present and accepting the other person. Now, however, she does seem to feel and understand this poem.

Winnicott continues by referring "to God as I AM, a useful concept when the individual cannot bear to BE" (62); she responds by likening this function of God to the function of the analyst: "someone to be there while you're playing." Later she confesses her own wish not to get well, an admission that allows Winnicott to return to the dream and constructively to employ her criticism of the girl's painting in that dream: *this negative is now positive.* They go on to distinguish between talking to oneself, which was closer to the experience of reciting the Rossetti poem, and interaction, as it occurs in their combined understanding of Hopkins. Winnicott concludes his summary of what happened in this session and the following session by stressing the patient's capacity to raise questions. Like Hopkins, this patient discovers herself and her strengths by her capacity to doubt and to question in the presence of another being. She later remarks that " 'one could postulate the existence of a ME from the question, as from the searching' " (64). In order to search she needs to feel free to "play," that is, to explore creatively the borders of her own personality and her impact on others. In another essay reprinted in *Playing and Reality,* on "The Mirror-Role of Mother and Family," Winnicott begins with the notion that the child defines itself by seeing itself reflected in the face—that is, the responsiveness—of the mother. When the mother reacts to her child, she reflects some sense of what the child experiences, and the child first learns to know itself by this mirroring activity of the mother. Later, the larger environment performs the same function for the child, and culture plays a significant role in expanding the boundaries of the child's knowledge and self-knowledge. When mothering is inadequate, the child's sense of self is thrown into doubt, along with the capacity for whole object-relations. Psychotherapy may then function as a corrective mirroring activity, working largely through words and stories. Winnicott writes:

> Psychotherapy is not making clever and apt interpretations; by and large it is a long-term giving the patient back what the patient brings. It is a complex derivative of the face that reflects what is there to be seen. I like to think of my work this way, and to think that if I do this well enough the patient will find his or her own self, and will be able to exist and to feel real. (117)

In keeping with Winnicott's own clinical spirit, let me summarize this paper by a series of tentative conclusions or interpretations.

1. Like the analytic activity described by Winnicott, our capacity to read well and interpret literature also depends upon our capacity to "play," to experiment with and interact with an object outside of the self and to use this interaction to expand the boundaries of the ego and of the cultural space that each of us creates and inhabits. Winnicott writes: "The thing about playing is always the precariousness of the interplay of personal psychic reality and the experience of control of actual objects. This is the precariousness of magic itself, magic that arises in intimacy, in a relationship that is being found to be reliable" (47).

2. The tradition of "applied psychoanalysis" does a disservice to both halves of that phrase. Literature is more than a proving ground for analytic theory, just as psychoanalytic theory is designed to do more than buttress or validate particular positions in literary theory or particular kinds of literary explanation. Most psychoanalytic readings of literary texts, or characters, or biography, as well as a good deal of literary theory that relies upon partial and often unsophisticated (or uninformed) use of clinical material, have left "applied psychoanalysis" with an unfortunate legacy of partial and reductive misreadings. Most of these misreadings—by analysts and by literary critics alike—occur because two very complex disciplines are used incompletely, without adequate knowledge either of literary history and explication, on the one hand, or of psychoanalytic theory and, more important, its clinical

practice, on the other. When Freud himself speaks of his debt to literature he is referring primarily to a debt of content. Yet it is particularly through the formal analyses of literary modes, the study of narrative or poetic structures, applied to analogous elements in psychoanalytic practice that literary studies most effectively contribute to the field of psychoanalysis. The analyst works primarily with words and stories, and his capacity to hear, understand, and play with the words and structures provided by the patient is inevitably enhanced by his capacity to read and comprehend literature. The question here is not one of training a "cultured" analyst but of integrating two closely related disciplines that both study words, images, stories.

3. The particular case I have discussed employs poetry in what we might term a *communicative space:* the various poems or lines referred to gradually form a language and a set of rules of their own. Winnicott and his patient explore their understandings of each other and of his or her role in the other's life by sharing their sense of what specific poems mean. They do not always understand the poems or lines to mean the same thing, but it is precisely in the interaction between patient and analyst that occurs over ambiguous lines, over borrowings from a poet or subjective rerenderings of a common text, that the essential space of the analysis is created and the essential interaction, the transference, can develop. One paradox that we might add to the list provided in Winnicott's text is that psychoanalytic understanding is developed through *different* readings of a *common* text, whether that text is the personality and language of the patient or something the patient is alluding to or reciting, like a poem.

4. If we apply this notion of psychoanalysis to reading literature, we should combine subjective response and our attempts to be objective about a text within a larger and paradoxical context. We acknowledge an inevitable personal distortion of any text, but we also acknowledge the legitimacy of our attempts to describe a common text. Literary critics continue to struggle with ways of simultaneously agreeing on a text and its general meanings while also tolerating and even encouraging individual, idiosyncratic response. When critics insist upon one or the other extreme—the inviolate text of New Criticism or the absolute relativity of some contemporary postmodern critics—they create a dilemma analogous to the extremes in psychoanalytic practice (either a static view of the patient-as-object or, conversely, a merging of affect by patient and analyst, a deliberate blurring of subject and object). What we require, in both criticism and analysis, is the space to move

freely between subject and object, reader and text, patient and analyst. But to read or to practice therapy with this degree of freedom we need to tolerate and develop paradox: in this case the paradox of *a subjective yet shared knowledge.*

5. Winnicott's case also raises, in passing, questions about the nature of reading and writing and related issues, like plagiarism and the question of identity. This patient demonstrates the difficulty inherent in genuine reading, the difficulty of letting go and interacting with another object implicit in that activity, and she hints at some of the special problems inherent in writing. All of us have known, I suspect, some version of writer's block. Winnicott's patient suggests that this phenomenon touches the most primitive anxieties over identity and the capacity to engage with others. And if that is so, each act of writing—indeed each act of reading—has the potential to support and foster our capacity for self-development.

NOTES

1. Letter to Bailey, November 22, 1817. *The Letters of John Keats: 1814–1821. 1:186.*
2. Letter to George and Thomas Keats, December 27?, 1817, *Letters* 1:193.
3. "Ode to a Nightingale," *Poetical Works of John Keats.*
4. Accidie is specifically described as "the state of mind [not-caring] of a monk who had mistaken his vocation." See *Encyclopaedia of Religion and Ethics,* edited by James Hastings et al. (1908–26), vol. 1.

REFERENCES

Barclay, F. L. 1920. *Returned Empty.* London and New York: G. P. Putnam.
Brooks, P. 1979. "Fictions of the Wolf Man." *Diacritics* 9:72–81.
Freud, S. 1918. *From the History of an Infantile Neurosis.* In vol. 17 of *The Standard Edition of the Complete Psychological Works.* Edited and translated by J. Strachey et al. 24 vols. London: Hogarth Press, 1953–74.
Hastings, J., et al., eds. 1908–26. *Encyclopaedia of Religion and Ethics.* New York: Scribner's.
Hopkins, G. M. 1967 (4th ed.). *The Poems of Gerard Manley Hopkins.* Edited by W. H. Gardner and N. H. MacKenzie. London: Oxford University Press.
Keats, J. 1958. *The Letters of John Keats, 1814–21.* Edited by H. E. Rollins. 2 vols. Cambridge, Mass.: Harvard University Press.

———. 1969. *The Poetical Works of John Keats.* Edited by E. H. Coleridge. London and New York: Oxford University Press.

Rossetti, C. G. 1906. *The Poetical Works of Christina Georgina Rossetti.* Edited by W. M. Rossetti. London: Macmillan.

Winnicott, D. W. 1971. *Playing and Reality.* New York: Basic Books; London: Tavistock, 1984.

6

Ghost Writing: A Meditation on Literary Criticism as Narrative

MADELON SPRENGNETHER

*And what should dream or writing
be if, as we know now, one may
dream while writing.*
　　　　　—Jacques Derrida,
　　　　　　Of Grammatology

*But poems are like dreams: in them
you put what you don't know you
know.*　　　—Adrienne Rich,
　　"When We Dead Awaken"

This is an essay about narrative, specifically the kind of narrative that we call literary criticism. It is at the same time an example of autobiographical writing and a form of storytelling, my point being that the practice of literary criticism participates in both these forms: fiction and autobiography. In order to demonstrate the interweaving of these forms, I have chosen first to examine some of my own critical writing in the light of my understanding of my concerns at the time of writing, then to consider the process of narrative formation through the efforts of my young daughter toward interpretation, and finally to discuss the "ghost" in narrative, the way in which writing is haunted by the unconscious. In telling this story I shall be re-creating in some measure the process of my own discovery: my shock at recognizing the shapes of my desire revealed in my critical writing, my fascination with my daughter's narrative constructions, which I came to see as a model for self-creation, or the creation of an ego, and my conviction finally that this ego (as Lacan has claimed) is haunted or shadowed from the moment of its creation by a kind of ghost. I see writing in this way as the product of both conscious and unconscious activity, a design inhabited by dream and desire. By opening literary criticism (a form of narrative usually excluded from such discussion) to this kind of understanding, I would hope to open it as well to a sense of movement and play.

I recognize, of course, that my own essay, as a story or a series of parables, has its own ghost, a shape of desire, apart from my stated intention, that urged it into articulation, that haunts it still at the moment of this writing. Once named, however, this ghost shifts its location, as each self-creation ceases to be true from the moment it is apprehended. This interplay—between the ego and its shadow, writing and its ghost, criticism and desire—interests me. I would like the reader to regard the essay that follows in the spirit of Montaigne, as an experiment, a trying out, a movement toward some understanding of this interplay.

Many years ago, when I was in graduate school, I began to be troubled by the sense that my critical writing bore no relation to my daily life. While I wrote cheerfully and prolifically about unities and harmonies in texts, I felt my life to be full of dissonance. The wisdom I professed in my seminar papers about human relations, and that I claimed to discover in the stories, poems, and novels I read, was nowhere evident in my relations with my family or my friends. Not knowing how to resolve the apparent split between what I said and what I did, I tried to accommodate myself to this schizoid condition. For a while this was not only possible, it was encouraged by the critical mode in which I had been trained to read: the New Criticism.

I was living, in 1964, in a fairly sheltered environment, one that permitted the exclusion of both personal and political concerns from the realm of literary interpretation. By 1968, the time at which I left graduate school, this illusion had been shattered, primarily by the pressure of the Vietnam War, a pressure that I, and the people I knew, experienced in every area of our lives. The kind of genteel separation between life and work with which I was familiar, at a time when people were marching on Washington, burning draft cards, and refusing induction orders, seemed not only impossible but absurd. I will not lay claim, however, to any sudden revelation, only to an increased awareness of the problem from which I was suffering.

Other events in my first year of teaching contributed to this awareness. In the spring of 1969, I gave birth to a daughter, whose presence in my life has altered my relation to myself and to my profession. The lines of demarcation I had drawn between my thoughts and feelings, my intellectual and emotional life, my lectures on the human condition and the nitty gritty of changing diapers, cooking, and housekeeping, began to blur, even in the absence, in those years preceding the rebirth of the women's movement, of a rhetoric in which to discuss these matters. It was in the area of teaching that I first found a language more congenial to my needs.

The books I was reading at that time were mainly about children and dealt with the relationship between learning and trust. I read Holt (1968), Kozol (1967), Dennison (1969), Herndon (1968), Kohl (1967), Erikson (1950), and Piaget (1968), and paid attention to my daughter and her apprehensions of the world, making connections where I could between these intimate contexts of learning and the ways in which my students seemed to learn. The books I was reading all dealt in some measure with the emotional climate in which learning (a seemingly abstract process) takes place. I was drawn to these texts because they offered models of interaction that included more aspects of experience than the ones with which I was familiar. While I began teaching at an opportune moment, given the amount of educational innovation which characterized that period, I was not myself a great innovator. But I did try to personalize my teaching a little, holding some classes at my house and getting to know some students as friends.

In the meantime, I was struggling to complete my dissertation, a process I found extremely painful and which was accomplished only through an enormous effort of will. Its subject matter, I now think, reflects this sense of struggle, dealing with works that pose significant barriers to form: Nashe's picaresque tale *The Unfortunate Traveller,* Sidney's mammoth and unfinished *New Arcadia,* and Spenser's meta-morphic *Faerie Queene.* In each work I argued for a concept of emergent form, an order that becomes apparent to the reader in the process of reading, out of an initial sense of disorder or fragmentation. Later I abandoned this argument, feeling uneasy about my insistence on a harmonious resolution in texts that seemed more clearly problematic. I felt I was forcing the issue, as though I were trying to fit the Renaissance back into a medieval framework.

It was in the period following the completion of my dissertation, moreover, that I experienced my most severe writing problems. The first essay I wrote for publication underwent at least five rewritings before it made any sense. Through the first three rewritings, it became progressively more incoherent: stilted, garbled, and abstract. Finally, after teaching a course on the picaresque, I was able to write my way out of this dilemma. Given my sense of internal division, it seems no accident to me now that this essay concerned problems of narration in a mode that exhibits an unstable relation between style and subject.

Nashe's picaresque narrator, I argued, remains willfully ignorant or unconscious of the increasingly violent and deterministic nature of his encounters. This stance seems designed to rescue him from despair, from the realization that, as I phrased it then, "We are all unfortunate travellers, embarked on a course of suffering, loss of liberty, and death." I did not perceive when I wrote this how much I felt drawn to such a vision and unaccountably moved by the grisly scenes of torture and execution so characteristic of this book and of Nashe's style generally. What saved me from this realization is what saves Jack from a similar awareness, a half-willed decision not to see, a fundamental evasiveness in the interests of hope. I, like Jack, relied on "wit," on all the verbal strategies at my command to distance myself from the vision of punishment that so deeply informs his world, and perhaps my own.

It was not until two essays later that I began to observe the ways in which the works I chose to write about and the problems that drew my attention reflected some of the issues with which I was wrestling personally. Not long after I started psychotherapy, I wrote again about Sidney's *New Arcadia,* focusing this time not on the triumph of order but on the convolutions of the narrative as an index of Sidney's interest in a kind of psychological fiction for which he had no adequate models. I became interested in mannerism as a style that formalizes disjunctions such as this between form and content and that raises questions of interpretation in deliberately nontransparent modes of fiction. This interest also manifested itself in a continuing fascination with Spenser's allegory, another narrative mode in which things are not what they appear to be.

The experience of psychotherapy as a reinterpretation or radical rewriting of my life contributed to my absorption with strategies of narrative duplicity or opacity. In terms of personal narrative I was dealing with a text that no longer made sense to me, one that seemed to obscure rather than to illuminate my history. In writing about *Euphues,* I found myself describing the euphuistic style as a kind of verbal camouflage, designed to protect both speaker and listener from direct understanding. It was in the course of writing this essay, moreover, that I first perceived the extent to which I was writing myself through the process of interpreting a literary work.

I had stopped in the middle of a paragraph to read over a passage that I had composed with unusual ease, when I recognized with a shock the parallel between what I had just written and a particularly painful aspect of my recent history. I was first embarrassed by this realization, then anxious that I was too revealed, that my readers would know more than I wanted them to know about me from reading this essay. Then I began to notice how few people shared my understanding about the autobiographical aspects of literary interpretation, and I felt protected by their ignorance. Also, during this period, I felt vaguely ashamed of the habit I was forming of shifting perceptions I had about my relations with people with whom I was intimate into the realm of literary understanding. Since they were my clearest insights I was not about to give them up, at the same time that the whole process somehow seemed illegitimate, or at the very least not something I should talk about.

I was still haunted by the paradigm of objectivity I had inherited from my graduate training. I needed a critical language that permitted a greater degree of latitude in discussing matters of emotional complexity. It makes sense that I should have turned at this point to psychoanalytic theory. While I had, in a nonsystematic way, read a good deal of Freud in the previous ten years, I began my serious reading of psychoanalytic theory with Winnicott. I started with *Therapeutic Consultations in Child Psychiatry* (1971b), the book that describes the squiggle game, in which child and therapist participate in the creation of an image by adding to one another's doodle marks. This game, according to Winnicott, engages the child's unconscious fantasies when he or she becomes absorbed in it to a sufficient degree. Winnicott describes this stage of absorption as something like the moment of passage from consciousness to unconsciousness we experience in going to sleep. I was struck by this description, in part because my daughter was at an age at which she voiced her fantasies as easily as her more ordinary perceptions about her world. I began to listen in.

One day, after she had gone to a three- and four-year-olds' birthday party at a fish hatchery, where each child had had the opportunity to catch a small fish, she started talking, as she was falling asleep, about what she had seen. At first she described how, after a fish was caught, the man who was helping them would clean it, slitting the fish open, and letting it bleed in the water. Then gradually, with no apparent transition, she began talking about vampires and how it is safer to kill them with a knife than with a gun because with a gun you might miss. This perception in turn led her to her final observation that if someone were to cut her open like the fish, she would die. It seemed to me at the time that I was hearing the process Winnicott described—the moment of elision between the world of reality and that of dream. My daughter was at that moment weaving the events of the day into her fantasy life in a way that amounted to an interpretation.

I became more attentive to these childish attempts at interpretation. One morning, as I was making breakfast, absently listening to her chatter, I caught the phrase "God's wife." I stopped and asked, "Does God have a wife?" "Well, yes," she said. She paused for a moment and then explained, "Because what about the queen and the baby?" I realized that the image of the queen and the baby had come from a book of mine with reproductions of illuminated manuscripts, in which Mary is depicted as the queen of heaven, holding Jesus on her lap. My daughter's assumption, from the little she had heard about God, was that he was the king of heaven and that Mary, being a queen, must be his wife, and Jesus their child. She had constructed a family image replete with sexuality, where orthodox Christianity has taken some pains to disjoin these elements. Her interpretation, on the whole, seemed the more sensible one.

I had not noticed until this point the extent to which she had become engaged in the formation of religious myth—neither my husband nor I had offered her any religious training. Some of her most profound thoughts on the subject came, I later discovered, from the movie *Jesus Christ Superstar,* which she saw with a teenage friend. What impressed her most about this film was the portrayal of the crucifixion. For weeks, she would announce solemnly, at random moments, "God died," except that her word at the time for die was "dive." At the same time, a good friend of ours that fall had died, and she would, in the same reverent tones, refer to the fact that "Paul dive" and "God dive." While she was in some sense coming to terms with the idea of death, she had not yet encountered the idea of resurrection. This concept entered her consciousness from a different direction.

One day at the beach a little boy she knew nearly drowned. By the time he was pulled out of the water, he had stopped breathing and had to be revived with mouth-to-mouth resuscitation. Later he was taken to the hospital, where he made a full recovery. My daughter was extremely impressed by this scene and for a long time afterward would talk about how when you die you are taken to the hospital where the doctors bring you back to life. She was similarly impressed for a while by the children's room of the local natural history museum, where there were many animal pelts and bones for the children to handle.

This led to another serious meditation in which she concluded (until I explained otherwise) that when people die their skins are taken off, but their faces are left on—like the animal skins she had seen at the museum. This meditation was also coupled with a reflection, drawn from a different source, that "we are all covered with blood when we are born."

Slowly I realized that the theories she had constructed were not, as I supposed, based on my attempts at realistic explanation, but rather that they were drawn from a multitude of sources, some of which were unknown to me, and that they underwent various transformations internally until they emerged in a form that bore the marks of her particular character and intelligence, as well as reflecting in some fashion the problems with which she was struggling at the time. Sometimes she would be engaged in a process of interpretation for months without my being aware of it. The most poignant example of this silent labor concerned our move from Vermont to Minnesota when she was two-and-a-half. We had, I thought, explained to her why we were moving, that we had better jobs in Minnesota and that we thought of Minneapolis as a good place to live. One day as we were driving home, she asked again why we had moved and I repeated this explanation, at which point she asked if the old home was broken.

I would be tempted to use the word "bricolage" to describe my daughter's interpretive strategies, if it did not sound as though I were attempting to raise an infant structuralist. But the word does describe something of the way in which she fashioned explanations of her world out of the random bits of information available to her, from her parents, her friends, her cultural environment. Her vocabulary is simultaneously idiosyncratic and plagiarized. Her picture of the world is a collage composed of the accidents of her gender, race, nationality, the historical moment in which she lives, and the personal histories of her parents, as well as her own. She alludes to all of these elements, embedding them in her essays toward understanding, in the way, perhaps, that a more sophisticated author such as Montaigne might allude to classical texts in his essays explaining himself and his relations to the world. For she is, of course, an author, like the small Gabrielle, in Winnicott's posthumous case study called *The Piggle* (1977), struggling to articulate her perceptions in a fashion comprehensible to herself and others.

What I have said about my daughter is no doubt obvious to psychoanalysts and to most parents. It does not seem to be as obvious to literary critics, many of whom will affirm the radical instability of

texts, while implicitly affirming the stability of their method of interpretation, seeking a metaphysical basis in the process of interpretation
which is immune from the accidents of personality. To the extent that
the deconstructionist mode is practiced in this fashion it resembles the
New Criticism in its insistence on the objectivity or impersonality of
the interpreter.

What I came to understand about my own writing (and here I mean
journal writing, notes I make to myself about teaching, poems, and
personal essays, as well as literary criticism) is that it is perhaps the
primary way I have of apprehending myself in relation to the world. By
creating a narrative, composed of elements both internal and external,
I am also creating a self, or perhaps a series of selves, since this process,
like that of psychoanalysis, is properly speaking interminable. When I
accepted this, the act of writing itself became easier for me. It also
became more revealing. I have begun to think recently, for instance,
about my obsession with interpretation itself and why it is that I first
wrote about texts that pose such obvious barriers to understanding. I
remembered that when I was in high school I loved the fiction of Henry
James because his protagonists were so often immersed in an ambiguous and confusing linguistic environment, requiring heroic efforts at
interpretation. This world seemed to me at the time to be completely
familiar and thus realistic. It felt like my family, in which indirect
discourse was the norm. I was used to translating what was said into
what was meant, assuming throughout that I was dealing with two
texts, one of which was unstated. If my taste for James has waned, it is
because of other changes in my life. The texts I am most drawn to at
any given period of my life seem to be the ones that give form and
expression to problems or issues I only dimly perceive in myself. In this
sense, they act as extended metaphors or objective correlatives, and my
engagement with them an attempt through narrative to draw into
consciousness some of the buried metaphors by which I live.

Thus literary interpretation strikes me as a refracted form of autobiography. The text of psychoanalysis itself—the product of a complex
interplay of internal and external observation, informed with metaphor—may be read in this fashion. Derrida (1978) makes this point
(among others) about Freud's *Beyond the Pleasure Principle*. By recon-
stituting the web of relations among Freud, his favorite daughter Sophie, who died shortly after the birth of her second child (Freud's
favorite grandson, who shortly thereafter also died) and the first child
Ernst, who played in earnest his game of absence and return, Derrida
reveals the melancholy undersong of this most melancholy book. Meta-

psychology for Freud reads as poetry, a shaking loose of metaphor that acts as personal narrative, no less powerful or persuasive for being so. That Derrida's essay in turn may be subjected to this kind of scrutiny has been efficiently demonstrated by Johnson (1977) in her reading of Lacan's reading of Poe.

We are by now becoming accustomed to reading Freud as a literary text. How long will it take for us to read Derrida in this fashion? To what extent does repetition compulsion, for example, characterize the career of a literary critic? Does the figure of Sophie, for instance, disappear from Derrida's text on Freud to return in the guise of Nietzsche's veiled figure of woman as truth (Derrida 1979)? Does this Sophie, related by Derrida himself to Freud's mother and by implication to the triple goddess of the essay on the three caskets, in any way resemble the forever absent mother of Rousseau (Derrida 1976)? If so, what significance could one attribute to such a pattern? What significance could one attribute to my interest in tracing such a pattern?

There is, as Johnson (1977) indicates in her discussion of frames of reference, no privileged position from which to read this series. While de Man (1971) refers to this awareness in terms of the critic's blindness, I prefer to think of it as the necessary inscription of the unintended. Literary criticism, like every other form of writing, bears its freight of unconscious meaning. The dream of total objectivity is a dream of total outsidedness, whereas the message of modern psychoanalysis is one of participation, of complicity, of the simultaneous elusiveness of boundaries and of the self. While Lacan (1977) seems engaged in guerilla warfare against the domestication of consciousness, Derrida systematically dismantles the structures of Western thought which have permitted such a cheapening of our mental life. Derrida, in particular, by "othering" writing, reveals its resonance.

It is, I believe, the necessary inscription of the unintended in any text which creates the quality of resonance, that rich wake of meaning which rocks our conscious life and disturbs us in our dreams. Passionate readers are aware of the brooding presence of certain texts in their lives, of the extent to which their lives may be organized around lines of poetry, situations in novels, characters in plays, which alter and accrue meaning through time just as the events of their childhood, altering in memory, reverberate throughout their lives. We do not distinguish, in such instances, between real and fictional events, any more than we do in our dreams.

Sodium pentothol, I am told by a forensic psychiatrist, was abandoned as a truth serum for legal purposes when it was discovered that under its influence people revealed their fantasies as readily as their actions, according them the same weight, the same validity. Harold Bloom, a reader of Blake and Hart Crane at six, once said to me that for him at that age these books constituted what was real. My daughter at age two could not distinguish between the wolf on stage in a production of *Peter and the Wolf* and a real wolf who might eat her. She finally resolved her anxiety, while watching the performance that day, still believing in the reality of the wolf, by claiming that she was too big for him to eat. Such innocence in the face of fantasy is of course dangerous, but so is the denial of dream altogether, which produces even stranger fantasies, like that of the solitary rationalist Descartes, annihilating the disappointingly fallible world from his armchair in order to reconstruct it on a basis of mental certitude. And still he couldn't be sure he wasn't dreaming.

Winnicott (1977), in his seventies, sat on the floor to play with a three-year-old child who was terrorized by her own dream creations. He attempted to enter her world in order to help her understand her own symbol-making mind, not to destroy it, but to relate it to what she already knew. The conversations between this elderly man and this little girl reveal a process of communication which, like sodium pentothol, does not respect the boundaries between fantasy and reality, in which communication on fantasy levels in particular is necessary for health, if by health we mean the capacity to live relatively comfortably with other people in the world.

Winnicott's fascination with sliding states of consciousness emerges elsewhere in his formulation of potential space as the locus of cultural activity and play (1971a). A relaxed acceptance of this condition of blurred boundaries, he would argue, is a prerequisite for artistic production. Milner (1957), in an essay dealing not with writer's block but with painter's block, talks about the inhibiting effect of fear of the unintended, of not allowing room for the expression of the unanticipated in one's work. She relates this to fear of one's own unconscious mind.

Looking back now on my own writing in graduate school and my subsequent difficulties, it seems to me that the feeling of hypocrisy from which I suffered had to do with the weight of everything I could not say, in part because of the inadequacy of my critical vocabulary but also because of my fears about myself and my dreams. I was afraid, even in an impersonally styled essay, of revealing anything but my belief in unity, harmony, and grace. To have done otherwise, at that time, would have undermined my fragile sense of self. It was a long time before I could give up my fiction of control, the illusion that there was nothing hidden either in my writing or in my life. I had to acknowledge the presence of some of the ghosts in my life before I could allow them to inhabit my writing.

I have also had to admit that I will never know them completely. While the language I invent for them allows them to speak, it is not their native tongue. They are liars and plagiarizers, borrowing my words for their existence, compulsively telling their story. To this extent, all writing is simultaneously fiction and autobiography. To accept this condition perhaps is to be able to play, in the unself-conscious world-making way that children do. The understanding of the small Gabrielle, as reported by her mother, about the voluminous notetaking activity of Winnicott during their sessions together was that he was writing his autobiography, as of course he was, reading himself through her as she through him. Gabrielle's summary of this mutually dependent and illuminating interpretive process was this: "He used to write and I used to play" (Winnicott 1977:201).

REFERENCES

de Man, P. 1971. *Blindness and Insight*. New York: Oxford University Press.

Dennison, G. 1969. *The Lives of Children*. New York: Random House.

Derrida, J. 1976. *Of Grammatology*. Translated by G. C. Spivak. Baltimore: Johns Hopkins University Press.

———. 1978. "Coming Into One's Own." *Psychoanalysis and the Question of the Text*. Edited by G. Hartman. Baltimore: Johns Hopkins University Press.

———. 1979. *Spurs: Nietzsche's Styles*. Translated by B. Harlow. Chicago: University of Chicago Press.

Erikson, E. 1950. *Childhood and Society*. New York: Norton.

Herndon, J. 1968. *The Way It Spozed to Be*. New York: Simon and Schuster.

Holt, J. 1968. *How Children Fail*. New York: Pitman.

Johnson, B. 1977. "The Frame of Reference: Poe, Lacan, Derrida." *Yale French Studies* 55 / 56:457–505.

Kohl, H. 1967. *36 Children*. New York: New American Library.

Kozol, J. 1967. *Death at an Early Age*. Boston: Houghton Mifflin.

Lacan, J. 1977. *Ecrits*. Translated by A. Sheridan. New York: Norton.

Milner, M. [J. Field]. 1950. *On Not Being Able to Paint*. London: Heinemann; New York: International Universities Press, 1957.

Piaget, J. 1968. *Six Psychological Studies*. New York: Vintage.

Winnicott, D. W. 1971a. *Playing and Reality*. New York: Basic Books; London: Tavistock, 1984.

———. 1971b. *Therapeutic Consultations in Child Psychiatry*. New York: Basic Books.

———. 1977. *The Piggle: An Account of the Psychoanalytic Treatment of a Little Girl*. Edited by I. Ramsey. New York: International Universities Press.

Part Two

LITERARY
OBJECTS

7

Phantasmagoric Macbeth

DAVID WILLBERN

*What will not a fearful man con-
ceive in the dark?*
—Robert Burton,
Anatomy of Melancholy

Imagining *Macbeth* is a bloody labor. With its oneiric style, gory
passages, and sinister issues, the play taxes imaginative conceptions
and critical perceptions. An answering criticism may require, as G.
Wilson Knight insisted, "a new logic": a perspective beyond rational
orders of causality, sequence, or choice. In place of a conventional
analysis that traversed the two-dimensional plot of the play, Knight
called for a three-dimensional mapping of its irrational dreamscape
(1949:58). In this essay I will sketch such a map, through a style of
imagining *Macbeth* that is vivid and visceral, psychoanalytic and phantasmagoric.

I begin with the still point and turning point of the play: the murder
of King Duncan. Although the event offers powerful dramatic possibilities, Shakespeare does not stage it. Among the effects of omitting this
potent scene is to displace it into fantasy—to make an audience imagine
it—and thus to expand the range of responses. What we fantasize can
be more vivid and affecting than what might be staged. To recast
Macbeth as aesthetician: "[Re]present[ed] fears are less than horrible
imaginings" (1.3.137–38).[1] As D. J. Palmer notes of the offstage regicide, "instead of distancing the deed from us, . . . the effect is to
intensify its sacrilegious horror" (1982:67). Unstaged and unseen, yet

horribly imaginable, the central regicide may affect an audience at deep psychological and emotional levels.

Psychoanalytic interpretations offer various intrafamilial reconstructions of the crime. Imagining Duncan's murder as symbolic patricide is commonplace in psychological (as well as religious and political) readings. In this case the patriarch heads a violent masculine hierarchy that excludes women: there is no queen of Scotland. Macbeth poses initially as a dutiful son who advances by the death of his own father, Sinel (*see* 1.3.71, 1.4.25). Lady Macbeth makes the patricidal analogue explicit by calling attention to the king's resemblance to her father (2.2.12–13). Duncan's actual sons flee after the murder and are blamed for the crime. Such a standard psychoanalytic reading is based on Freud's oedipal triangle, including his brief remarks about *Macbeth* (1916). In this geometry of unconscious desire, Macbeth represents the rebellious oedipal son, Duncan is the father, and the maternal angle prefigures Lady Macbeth or (via conventional symbolic characterization of a country as feminine, maternal) Scotland herself.[2]

Actual geometric figures may make these symbolic intrafamilial relations easier to imagine:

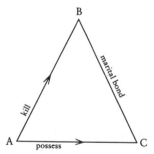

A = Macbeth
B = Duncan (as father)
C = Scotland (female)
Lady Macbeth

In this, the classic oedipal triangle, side AB indicates the patricidal wish, side AC the incestuous wish, and side BC the marital bond of husband-wife (father-mother, king-Scotland). The lines of force are unidirectional, driving the son along his one-way career.

By shifting perspective and reconfiguring the oedipal triangle, we can imagine the intrafamilial drama in another way: as symbolic matricide. Such a view focuses on Duncan's loving and generous nature and envisions his murder as an assault against maternal providence. Macbeth murders Sleep in its innocence, the agent that "knits up the ravell'd sleave of care," a bath, a balm, "great Nature's second course, / Chief nourisher in life's feast" (2.2.34–39). Duncan himself is "the spring, the head, the fountain" of his country's and his countrymen's blood. As Macbeth remarks of the king's death, "The wine of life is drawn" (2.3.95). The phrase evokes a fantastic union of murder (spilled blood) and feast (filled cup). In this reconstruction of king as mother, Duncan becomes identified with Scotland: "it weeps, it bleeds; and each new day a gash / Is added to her wounds" (4.3.41). Duncan's own "gash'd stabs look'd like a breach in nature / For ruin's wasteful entrance," and the actual instruments of entrance are "daggers / Unmannerly breech'd with gore" (2.3.113–16). Linguistic associations here suggest regicide as rape, making Macbeth's grim reference to "Tarquin's ravishing strides" suggestively apt (2.1.55). The imagistic combination of parricide and sexual assault indicates the incestuous component of matricidal fantasies.[3]

This imagined re-vision of regicide as matricide generates a more complex dynamic to which I will return. For the moment, note that the interpretation posits maternal authority as the source and target of the play's violence. While there is no queen, there are demonic emblems of female power in the witches and Lady Macbeth. Assaults on Duncan and on Lady Macduff (the only actual mother in the play) then become displaced attacks on more dangerous and less accessible maternal evils. This dynamic suggests in psychoanalytic terms a failed splitting: the division between benevolent maternal support (Duncan) and malevolent manipulation (the witches, Lady Macbeth) breaks down, so that Macbeth kills what is fair and trusts what is foul.

Geometrically this design presents mirroring images, or the reflection of a subliminal, shadowy figure:

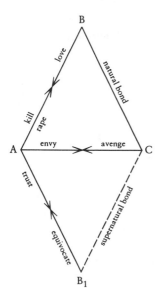

A = Macbeth
B = Duncan (mother)
B_1 = Witches / Lady Macbeth
C = Malcolm / Macduff / Banquo / Fleance

Here side AB indicates the matricidal impulse of erotic assault. Its diabolic mirror, side AB_1, suggests the bond of fatal trust. Side BC represents the natural familial bond of mother and sons (analogous to the sacral bond of king and subject), while side B_1C evokes the supernatural connection of witches and avenging children. Side AC marks a mutual contest (fraternal rivalry): as AC it indicates Macbeth's envy of his rivals and his violence toward them, while as CA it indicates their reciprocal vengeance against him.

Combining these patricidal and matricidal readings suggests King Duncan as a magical composite parent, both father and mother; his murder then becomes a complete parricide. Such a revision is appropriate to the style of splittings and recombinations inherent in the play, which can also reconstitute Macbeth and his wife as a unit (this is Freud's [1916] reading). This interpretation would stress the ambivalent androgyny of the bearded weird sisters, or Lady Macbeth's vigorous gender-straddling. Duncan's effort to idealize masculine authority and power is an attempt to subsume or repress chthonic feminine energies, which yet return in force.[4]

The most intriguing psychoanalytic reconstruction, and the most complex, is of the regicide as symbolic infanticide. In this interpretation, the king becomes a satiated then victimized infant. For instance, as Duncan prepares to visit Inverness, he savors his "plenteous joys, / Wanton in fulness," and announces that Macbeth is "full so valiant, ... I am fed; / It is a banquet to me" (1.4.33–34, 54–56). Together Duncan and Banquo describe the Macbeths' home: "This castle hath a pleasant seat; the air / Nimbly and sweetly recommends itself / Unto my gentle senses. . . . Heaven's breath / Smells wooingly here" (1.6.1–10). Their references to beds and procreant cradles and breeding impinge immediately on the entrance of Lady Macbeth, who has just warned that "the raven himself is hoarse, / That croaks the fatal entrance of Duncan / Under my battlements" (1.5.38–40). The imagery evokes a typically Shakespearean fusion of architecture and anatomy: a fusion furthered by Duncan's conversation with Banquo. Inverness is the scene of hospitality and hell, and the castle becomes (fantastically) Lady Macbeth's body, the battlements her transfigured woman's breasts.[5] The locus of gratified desire and gratuitous death is the same: a pattern repeated in Duncan's bed (the place of healing rest and fatal assault) and in the witches' cauldron (where ministry and murder coalesce).

When Banquo retires, he remarks that "the King . . . hath been in unusual pleasure . . . and shut up / In measureless content" (2.1.12–17). We can imagine the sequence: Duncan is drawn seductively into the attractive, nurturing locus of the fragrant castle, fed full to satiety, and (smiling in his sleep) brutally murdered. This event is exactly analogous to Lady Macbeth's fantasized murder of the infant at her breast, another crucial moment of gratification and violence that we do not actually see but that may arouse our imaginations to horror and disgust.

These last two reconstructions of regicide—as matricide and as infanticide—offer reciprocal perspectives on the central event of the play. We can see the core assault from both sides of the mother-infant bond: that is, the mother is murderous and the infant is victimized, *and* the mother is potentially murderous but the infant is the avenger who retaliates by killing her (or others who represent her, since Lady Macbeth dies offstage, apparently by her own hand, and the witches are beyond assault). Reciprocity turns easily into retaliation. The geometry of this design is complex, as the triangle of manifest relations is circumscribed by the arcs of supernatural bonds.

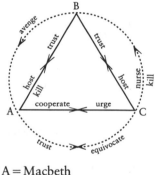

A = Macbeth
B = Duncan (infant victim)
    Avenging Infant
C = Lady Macbeth / Witches

The triangle indicates manifest motives, while the circle suggests their shadows. For example, side AC indicates the relations of Macbeth and his wife, while its shadow (arc AC) marks the pattern of his trust and the witches' "paltering." The diabolic consanguinity of Lady Macbeth and the witches is suggested by the lines of force diverging from point C. Side AB represents the relation of murderous Macbeth and victimized Duncan (imagined as infant), while arc BA traces the trajectory of revenge.

In brief, the sleeping king and the nursing infant are analogous and reciprocal. The avenging infant takes revenge for both figures. As the nursing babe is ripped untimely from his mother's breast, so the avenging son is ripped untimely from his mother's womb. Macduff's birth repeats yet survives the fatal bond of nurturance and negation that Lady Macbeth's fantasized infanticide forges. Unlike her child, who suffers traumatic disintegration, Macduff is the "child of integrity"—so-called by Malcolm, another son who is proudly "unknown to woman." As Cleanth Brooks (1947) noted, before appearing ultimately as Macduff, the avenging infant manifests itself most dramatically in the apparitions of the bloody child and the child with tree in hand, as well as the unending line of Banquo's progeny. The apparitions are ironic verification of Macbeth's fear that "Pity, like a naked, new-born babe" will disclose the crime and take up Duncan's cause.

These various associations of nursing, murder, and revenge in primitive, infantile terms may explain the curious criminal strategy of deflecting the blame for Duncan's murder by gilding the *faces* of the grooms with the king's blood. Juxtaposing such lines as "The wine of life is drawn" with the nightmarish query, "Who would have thought the old man to have so much blood in him?" suggests a phantasmagoric confluence of liquids: wine, blood, milk, gall. Fantastically, it is as though Duncan's blood is sacrificially drunk from his wound, in a ritual union of murder and feast. Hearing sacramental tones in Macbeth's speech before the murder of Duncan, Richard Ide suggests that the phrase, "The bell invites me," echoes the ritual Invitation to Holy Communion, leading to "Macbeth's crude sacrilege, the perversion of the Lord's Supper" (1975:348–49). David Barron writes that "the drink to which his wife summons him is the blood of Duncan" (1960:265). Banquo's murderer also has blood on his face, and when Macbeth stares at his friend's apparition, its head and face gashed all over, "the blood-bolter'd Banquo *smiles* upon him" (4.1.123). This smile reflects the helpless, victimized infant ("smiling in my face"), but now no longer helpless. Its potency lies in the regal lineage over which it proudly presides. It is a smile of vengeance and vindication: a smile to reciprocate and retaliate the communal but ambiguous smile of friends ("There's daggers in men's smiles") or mothers or infants. Then there is Lady Macbeth's infamous contention:

> I have given suck,
> And know how tender 'tis to love the babe that milks me:
> I would, while it was smiling in my face,

Have pluck'd my nipple from his boneless gums,

And dash'd the brains out, had I so sworn

As you have done to this.

(1.7.54–59)

This catastrophic moment of violent disruption and death is also one of loving union and nurturance. It presents the icon of Charity shattered by maternal malevolence.[6] The phrase, "while *it* was smiling in *my* face," linguistically replicates the perfect mirroring of mother and infant that founds familial harmony: it locates the infant's smile "in" the mother's face. Lady Macbeth's brutally broken nursing scene is a feast disrupted by a murder, the most vivid (or morbid) representation of a central and recurrent event in the play.[7] This catastrophic weaning conflates in a single moment a disturbance that Shakespeare had earlier separated. Juliet's Nurse recalls that her charge's weaning occurred on the very day of a memorable earthquake (*Romeo and Juliet*, 1.3.20ff.). Moreover, the Nurse's practice of putting wormwood on her nipple places poison at the source of maternal nourishment, in an analogy to Lady Macbeth's murthering ministry, or to the Captain's remark that "from the spring whence comfort seem'd to come / Discomfort swells" (*Macbeth*, 1.2.26–27). Such weaning practices were customary in Shakespeare's time, and much folklore attached to them. Robert Burton lists "Bad Nurses" as the first accidental cause of melancholy, followed by "Education," then "Terrors and Affrights" (1628: vol 1:330ff., 1:215). Beyond Renaissance beliefs in actual "engrafting" and "imprinting" (Burton's terms) of characteristics through the nurse's milk lie some home truths. Current developmental theory could well agree with Burton that "the strange imagination of a woman works effectually upon her infant." It may not be precisely that "minds are altered by milk," but they are by mothers, in the nursing relation. The chemistry is wrong but the psychology is right.[8] In psychoanalytic terms, this primal relation is a "dual unity" wherein mother and infant are bound "symbiotically" in nurturance and trust (the ideal paradigm): see Winnicott (1960) and Mahler (1975). Perversions of the dual unity afflict *Macbeth* throughout, as community degenerates into hostility: for instance, the "two spent swimmers, that do cling together / And choke their art," or Duncan's horses that turn on one another as predator and prey. Critical commentary echoes psychoanalytic terms. Stephen Booth notes that the two swimmers, "thus intertwined, become an entity in which the two independent beings are indistinguishable" (1983:99). Harry Berger stresses the "symbiotic" and "destructive" bond of the swimmers, and the equation of comrade with enemy. Moreover, his close-focus reading of Rosse's description of "Bellona's bridegroom, lapp'd in proof" offers an image of striking perception and relevance. The phrase, "Bellona's bridegroom," is paradoxical, he writes, "because the archaic goddess of war was a fierce unyielding virgin the opposite of Mars's Venus; 'lapp'd' means wrapped, swathed (like a baby?), clothed, as in a soft blanket or robe, or as in waves, but the proof is gore. The image is not only gigantic, but also erotic and infantile" (1980:13). This intimacy of care and gore recurs in the Captain's report of Macbeth's heroism. His actions demonstrate the instant transmutation of courtesy into carnage. Macbeth, "like Valour's minion,"

> carv'd out his passage,
> Till he fac'd the slave [Macdonwald];
> Which ne'er shook hands, nor bade farewell to him,
> Till he unseam'd him from the nave to the chops,
> And fix'd his head upon our battlements.
>
> (1.2.19–23)

Duncan responds to this gory tale by praising Macbeth as a "worthy gentleman," yet the Captain's allusion to true gentlemanliness (shaking hands) in the midst of war reciprocates Lady Macbeth's moment of carnage in the midst of womanly nursing. Both images present a dyad of violent community, and the bloody disruption of natural order by monstrous inhumanity.

Macbeth carving out his passage is a most suggestive image. Not merely does he hack his way through rebel soldiers to confront and unseam the merciless Macdonwald, but more generally he knifes his way to the throne and beyond. Moreover, the phrase "carv'd out his passage" evokes the mystery of Caesarean section that resonates throughout the play. Macbeth opens up Macdonwald in a grotesque parody of this procedure, as well as other surgical practices of "bleeding." He becomes both butcher and surgeon (the London Company of Barber-Surgeons had organized in the sixteenth century, under the sign of blood). What emerges from the act of unseaming Macdonwald is both Macbeth's glory and his treachery. Fantastically, one can imagine the issue of Macdonwald's Caesarean section as the avenging infant ("not of woman born") that returns to kill Macbeth. That is, Macbeth "unmans" Macdonwald by subjecting him to battlefield gynecological surgery, thus making him the fantastic origin of the agent of revenge. Shakespeare's imagery evokes still more bizarre imaginings, of Macbeth like an infant *in utero* forging his way into the world through the containing body of his source. His carved passage effects a C-section from within, incising his world from navel to neck in a simultaneous assault on and escape from the maternal matrix that holds (embraces and limits) him. This is a carnal metonymy of the whole tragedy. Macbeth carves his career in an element that ambiguously supports and surrounds him, that offers him advancement while confining him to decreasing circles of motion (like a bear at the stake). Although his emphasis differs, Barron's metaphors effectively enwomb Macbeth: "Macbeth determines to break out of his strangling situation through violence . . . and thus cut his way out of the female environment which chokes and smothers him." "He is already caught up in the witches' world. He is *cabin'd, cribb'd, confined* in the entrails of devouring woman, and must therefore cut his way out with the sword" (1970:268–69. 271; see also Watson 1984 and Hunter 1980).

The claustrophobia of cabin, crib, and confine in *Macbeth* may even allude to specific beliefs in Jacobean obstetrics, which held that a male fetus "was faster tied and bound [within the womb] then the female, because the ligaments which hold and fasten him are stronger and dryer then they that bind and support a wench" (Jacques Guillemeau, *Child-birth or, The happie deliverie of women* [London, 1612]; quoted in Fox 1979:130). Fox further notes that the "birth-strangl'd babe" whose finger the witches add to the bubbling cauldron was not an unusual phenomenon in Jacobean obstetrics: in breech-births the mother's pubic bone could constrict the infant's breathing passage (136). Barron suggests a similar point (1970:277n16). Furthermore, Caesarean section in early seventeenth-century England was literally a matricidal procedure, performed only on mothers already dead or certain to die (Schnucker 1974). So that the gruesome battlefield surgery transforms the enemy other into a woman while it murders him/her.

This paradox of advancement and restriction informs Macbeth's style of acting out his martial identity through violent aggression against others who reflect his own violence: Macdonwald, Cawdor, Banquo, Macduff. Macbeth literally and figuratively *mirrors* his antagonists by his posture of facing and imitating them, making the violent dyad an embrace of doubles. He confronts the traitor Cawdor "with self-comparisons, / Point against point, rebellious arm 'gainst arm," and he faces Macdonwald in a similar posture in which antagonists are imagistically and grammatically confused. (Shakespeare's lines do not distinguish whose point and whose arm; the pronoun in the line, "Which ne'er shook hands . . . ," is Janus-faced.) Antagonists become mirror images or doubles, enemy twins who yoke themselves in a bond both aggressive and erotic. (Coriolanus and Aufidius are the clearest instance of the tenacity and tension of this bond.)[9]

From a psychoanalytic perspective the image of rival twins represents a later manifestation of wishes and fears evoked in the early mirroring of (male) infant and (female) mother. Later reenactment in valiant violence is a paradoxical attempt at release: an aggressive "heroic" struggle against an enemy who represents an original, inexorable matrix. In Freudian terms, oedipal revenge is a repetition of oral desires and dreads. In Shakespearean terms, Coriolanus' heroic autonomy and hysterical virility are efforts to escape or transcend maternal dependence, yet at the same time they are instruments of Volumnia's wishes. The more he tries to author himself, the more he is his mother's son. No exit; only repetition. Macbeth is caught in a similar bind: as he carves his independent passage he simultaneously sinks into the controlling maternal matrix that, like the witches, both nurses and curses him. In psychoanalytic terms, violent aggression and the maintenance of difference through repeated enactments of violated union may be a defense against a basic fear of undifferentiation or the state of no-difference: for example, between rival twins, or infant and mother. This defense is doomed to endless repetition in identities that paradoxically act out autonomously yet follow an embryonic script, like the tragic careers of Coriolanus or Macbeth.

This paradoxical pathology suggests a potential hazard of the necessary reciprocity between mother and infant in human development. Identity is based on identification, but it must emerge from mimesis if genuine separateness is to develop. "The precursor of the mirror," writes D. W. Winnicott, "is the mother's face" (1967:111). At first this mirroring reflects no difference for the infant between self and other (or mouth and breast). Perfect reciprocity institutes no difference. Individuation is therefore a process of breaking out of this exact mirroring without breaking the mirror (the reflecting relationship). Winnicott terms it a gradual process of "dis-illusionment." Establishing externality or otherness requires separation, which may present itself or be perceived as deprivation or aggression. A distance must be forged, then bridged, or the infant may not establish boundaries of its own self as distinguishable from the nurturing matrix. In the Ovidian myth, Narcissus died, deprived by his own apparent abundance: "inopem me copia fecit." A persistent "no difference" psychically murders a child. The mother who mirrors her child exactly, who gratifies instantly and perfectly her infant's every need, becomes a magical provider whose effect is ironically damaging: "she is dangerous, a witch" (Winnicott 1960:151–52).

As Winnicott (1971c) describes it, the necessary distance can normally be forged by the infant's "attack" on the object (breast or mother)—an attack that represents in fantasy its destruction. When the object survives, proving that it is not vulnerable to the infant's fantasies of omnipotence, its externality becomes apparent, thereby creating a space for interrelationship between ego and object, self and other. A process of self-other differentiation can thus emerge from a moment of violence (though not necessarily anger) and can result in the beneficial "use" of the object as a distinguishable other. An example is the infant who attacks the breast, through hungry sucking or perhaps even biting, but does not injure the mother, because the infant is weak and toothless. When the mother neither retaliates nor withdraws, the breast survives the infant's "destruction" and begins to become marked off from the subject's field of self.

Lady Macbeth's imagined infant has "boneless gums," yet she reacts to its nursing with gratuitous violence, in apparent retaliation. Or, from another view, she rejects its developing identity by using it to demonstrate her own ruthlessness. Here the space of difference is not initiated by the infant nor mutually sustained by the mother but suddenly and catastrophically created by her: from mother's breast untimely ripped. This fantasy of a bloody break at the origin of relationship provides a scheme for the style of masculine identity in *Macbeth* that seeks confirmation in violence. ("What bloody man is that?") To be a man, in this tragedy's central terms, means to be bloody or bloodied. Wounds are the mark of manliness; fighting establishes virility in the face of and at the expense of a mirroring rival. At play's end, with butcher and fiend safely dispatched, this fatal ideology of masculinity persists, as Old Siward, pleased that his dead son "had his hurts before," exclaims, "Had I as many sons as I have hairs, / I would not wish them to a fairer death" (4.9.14–15). Fair is still foul, and the ironic pun ("hairs" / "heirs") emphasizes the confusions of self and other, issue and excrement (to use Shakespeare's vocabulary).

Lady Macbeth also wishes her son to death, by throwing the fantasized infant to the ground. By so doing, she cancels and tears to pieces that greatest bond of all (3.2.49). Her imagined gesture annihilates the fluid field within which human relationships emerge and develop. Her sudden rupture of that "potential space" closes the intermediate area between perfect mirroring (the magical unity of no difference) and the establishment of self-other boundaries and the lessons of difference. In Winnicott's terms (1971a), the resulting absence of a dependable "holding environment" disables normal symbolic representation or leads to an invasion of projected "persecutory material." With the ruin of this playspace and the loss of an intermediate provisional arena where things *may be* (for example, both real *and* imagined), the capacity for normal relationship suffers pathological distortion (Winnicott 1971a).

For Macbeth this space is horribly distorted. He finds no mediating ground where things *may be:* instead, things *are* and *are not* in maddening equivocation. There is no place for fantasy, no interim for the provisional play of wish and deed. As Shakespeare's Brutus puts it,

> Between the acting of a dreadful thing
> And the first motion, all the *Interim* is
> Like a phantasm, or a hideous dream.
>
> (*Julius Caesar*, 2.1.60–62)

The word *"Interim"* is capitalized and italicized in the Folio texts of this passage and *Macbeth* 1.3.154–56 (below), and nowhere else in Shakespeare:

> Think upon what has chanc'd; and at more time
> The *Interim* having weigh'd it, let us speak
> Our free hearts each to other.

Macbeth never keeps this promise to Banquo—unless murder speaks his heart. Like Macbeth, Brutus (who cannot sleep and who speaks these lines immediately after a knocking at the gate) endures the anxieties of the interim between the initial proposal ("motion") of a deed and its eventual enactment, during which interval he suffers a psychic insurrection that shakes his single state of man (Knight 1949). But even as Macbeth suffers doubts, he moves inexorably toward Duncan's bedchamber, drawn by a fantastic replica of his own dagger. For him the phantasmagoric interim displaces reality; dreams replace deliberations, and the distinction between wish and deed is blurred, then erased. The normal process of desire → interim → act (or inhibition) is distorted. Other characters in *Macbeth* endure their interims more normally. Banquo puts his uncanny experience in its proper place when he *dreams* of the three weird sisters (2.1.90) and asks the "merciful powers" to "restrain . . . the cursed thoughts that nature / Gives way to in repose" (2.1.5–7).[10] Once he begins to ponder his profit in the witches' predictions, he stops himself and says, "But hush, no more" (3.1.10). Banquo can recognize his desires yet inhibit his deeds, as can Lady Macbeth. They provide places in dream or fantasy for their dangerous wishes (such as Lady Macbeth's infanticide or her somnambulism). But Macbeth, having murdered sleep, cannot dream. Rather, he acts out his dreams in his nightmarish waking life. As a character, "Macbeth is helpless as a man in a nightmare," as Knight put it (1949:153). As a play, *Macbeth* is like a psyche turned inside out, its fantasies actualized as external events, agents, and obsessive repetitions (Lesser 1977).

The normal psychological process of admitted and inhibited fantasy is crudely yet effectively illustrated in Malcolm's long speech to Macduff, where he purportedly tests Macduff's loyalty by pretending to be more villainous than Macbeth, finally disclaiming the heinous character he constructs (4.3). Malcolm can pretend: he can out-Herod Herod and then relegate the fantasy to its proper, repudiated place. He can imaginatively inhabit the phantasmagoric interim and then inhibit its dreadful action. Anyone can do this. It is within our imaginative range to express the most vile character and most wicked act, in thoughts or words. Malcolm's speech demonstrates onstage the validity of Auden's claim that "watching *Macbeth,* every member of the audience knows that the possibility of becoming a Macbeth exists in his own nature" (1964).[11]

Macbeth, however, is not free to imagine or play himself. Compelled to enact his fantasies, he must be and do. "Strange things I have in head, that will to hand, / Which must be acted, ere they may be scann'd" (3.4.137–38). Like a hurried player he must act out his role before the script is clear to him (Egan 1968; Ide 1975). He becomes an unread but ready actor in a phantasmagoric tragedy of blood—a Jacobean adumbration of the modern theater of cruelty—wherein his actions are determined before he can reflect upon or choose them. "The theater of cruelty," writes Derrida, "is indeed a theater of dreams, but of *cruel* dreams, that is to say, absolutely necessary and determined dreams, dreams calculated and given direction" (1978:242). Once embarked on his compulsive career, Macbeth becomes even more *determined* (as both agent and victim) after he sees the apparitions. "From this moment," he swears,

> The very firstlings of my heart shall be
> The firstlings of my hand. And even now,

> To crown my thoughts with acts, be it thought and done.
>
> (4.1.146–49)

This is simple pathology: a compulsion. It signifies the closure of the interim, or of normal imaginative playspace, and its restriction to instantaneous acting-out. Francis Fergusson (1957) put it one way when he isolated the concept, "to outrun the pauser, reason," as the action or motive of the play. Norman Rabkin put it another way when he described Macbeth in "purposeless subjection to drives he does not understand and goals he does not want" (1981:103). Jerald Ramsey characterizes this design of compulsive (re)activity as Macbeth's "doom of reflex and repetition" (1973:290).

Where there is no viable potential space, then in Winnicott's terms the psychological efficacy of "transitional objects" is limited (1953). (A transitional object is an emblem of exchange in the playspace between infant and mother, such as a blanket or doll. It represents an essential con-fusion of wish and gift. The child does not ask, "Is this me or other?" nor "Did I make [wish, hallucinate] this or was it given to me?" A transitional object is both inner creation and outer presentation, with no attendant anxiety about its ontological status.) In these terms, the world of *Macbeth* becomes a field of transitional phenomena in which the hero asks the impossible question: "Is this real or am I hallucinating it?" He interrogates his own vision: "Is this a dagger which I see before me, / The handle toward my hand?" That dagger is the perfect transitional object: both there and not there, real and not real, provided and imagined, his and not his. It appears in authentic answer to his own intent, mirrors his own instrument, and then, as he watches, transforms itself from *present* replica to *future* image: it drips blood. As he shifts from subject ("I see") to object ("before me"), his description echoes this fantastic reciprocity: "the *hand*le toward my *hand*." What is without is also within, what is *not* also *is,* in an unsettling ontological equivocation. The phenomenon will not abide his question because (like Birnham Wood and the man not of woman born) it is beyond any terms he can imagine.

Macbeth seeks futilely to establish boundaries in a world where things won't stay put—like Banquo's bloody ghost that rises to unseat the king. But whereas Macbeth moves through a world and a play in which he can only *do* and not play "as if," we as audience can entertain the paradoxical nature of Macbeth's world, imagining witches, daggers, babes, and ghosts as both there and not there. They are images spawned from Macbeth's desires and dreads, *and also* from the super-natural agency of the weird sisters. For us these phenomena can be transitional, while for Macbeth they are obsessive, haunting visions. In the play of *Macbeth* Shakespeare provides his audience with a framed potential space wherein he presents a character, Macbeth, for whom such space is closed off. This suggests one feature of tragedy as a psychological genre: it can demonstrate the failure of psychic strategies (or defenses) while strengthening its audience's abilities to manage those strategies. The play of *Macbeth* occupies our own potential space (thereby filling it) with manifestations of its own violation, closure, or emptiness: it *signifies nothing* (Willbern 1980).

Of course I am projecting an audience from my own conceptions. Not all audiences are so play-full as mine, nor may they tolerate ambiguity and equivocation so eagerly. Some may wish to establish boundaries and provide answers to questions that the play leaves invit-ingly open. They want either to grasp Macbeth's dagger or blink it away.[12] Similarly, they want either to certify or reject the existence of Lady Macbeth's mysterious child. One veteran of hundreds of produc-tions of the play has no doubts on the issue. Of course Lady Macbeth has a child, he asserts, because she says so, and it's by Macbeth and not any former husband. Marvin Rosenberg continues to stage the scene in his conception, setting an actual infant on the boards, in a crib, whose timely cries and gurgles contribute momentous sound ef-fects during Lady Macbeth's speech (1982: Appendix). Fox imagines a pregnant Lady Macbeth, whose condition gradually shows by play's end (1979:132).

Rosenberg's reaching for an actual infant to match the one Lady Macbeth conjures up imitates Macbeth's reaching for his actual dagger to match the one he sees before him. Just as Macbeth's action imitates the vision (is the dagger leading him or is he projecting it in his way?), so an audience's imaginative response may realize (make real) the fantasy held out by the scene. "The bloody business informs thus" to our minds' eyes. Although I consider Rosenberg's staging unwise, his reification of a phantasm is certainly within the range of audience response to (and directors' conceptions of) the scene, as the history of ongoing debates about this and similar problems in *Macbeth* amply demonstrates. "An essential feature of transitional phenomena is a quality in our attitude when we observe them" (Winnicott 1971b:96).[13] Some audiences cannot tolerate dramatized paradoxes of transitional phenomena. As a result, their attitudes toward radically questionable plays like *Macbeth* or *Hamlet* or *Othello* may be to seek after certainties, in an apt imitation of the tragic characters' own doomed quests. Other audiences, such as the one I am projecting, are more comfortable with unanswerable questions, or recognize that wonder and worry over such questions can be part of an effective response to the play: not problems to be solved but responses to be experienced and examined.[14]

Consider the famous riddle of Lady Macbeth's child. Does she have one or not? I offer a reply if not a solution. First, the dramatic world of *Macbeth* is phantasmagorical, inhabited by witches, phantom daggers, ghosts, apparitions (*n.b.*, of children), bloodstains real and imagined. It evokes an environment where our most basic differentiations and boundaries are jeopardized by the mutual coexistence of and antagonism between such primary distinctions as "real/imagined," "inside/outside," "alive/dead," "animate/inanimate," "male/female," "fair/foul," even "day/night" ("What is the night?" asks Macbeth; his wife replies, "Almost at odds with morning, which is which" [3.4.125–26]). In brief, "nothing is but what is not"; existence is a function of impossible opposition.

In such a world of apparitions and violated boundaries, Lady Macbeth's infant may be an *extradramatic* apparition: a transitional phenomenon proffered to us, the audience, as our own quandary, just as Macbeth's dagger is held out to him. Do we accept it as real or do we reject it? Do we search for historical clues (say, in Holinshed) or do we acquiesce in the fantastic moment? Critical assessments of the actuality of the babe are well known. For my audience, the resulting dilemma of "Is it or is it not?" iterates the central question of and for this play. The question has two appropriate answers, each at odds with each. What is a reasonable response to such dramatic equivocation?[15] Rather than argue about the historical or dramatic authenticity of Lady Macbeth's child, we might take another view. "It is impenetrably ambiguous whether she means it," writes Nicholas Brooke, "let alone whether it is true or not. But as an imaginative fact that babe is certainly very vivid to us in ways that are no part of Lady Macbeth's consciousness: it takes its place, with Macbeth's naked new-born babe, and all the other babes of the play that Cleanth Brooks enumerated, in a dimension well beyond the reach of the characters" (1980:75; see also Stallybrass 1984 and Grove 1982). Such a dimension, outside consciousness and beyond its reach, might well be termed the play's "unconscious." More precisely, it is a dimension where logical questions have no force, where *is* and *is not* coexist. In Freudian terms, it is a domain of primary process representation: a field of fluid, shifting representations, where every similarity tends toward identity. Boundaries are indeterminate and unstable; images appear, disappear, and reappear; wishes and fears materialize out of thin air. Time defies temporal rules: past, present, and future cohere in an instant, or the moment of the deed subsumes all time before and after. Contradiction is merely a style of unification; denial or negation does not exist.

Various psychoanalytic terms and concepts describe such a domain, including "the unconscious," "primary process," "potential space," and "transitional phenomena." Keats's idea of "Negative Capability," whereby Shakespeare sustained his creative tension of imaginative contradiction, is applicable here, as is Stephen Booth's (1983) elaboration of that idea to include the mind of the audience, momentarily enduring perplexing experiences within the comfort of tragic form. Norman Rabkin borrowed from twentieth-century physics the concept of "complementarity" (light, for example, must sometimes be treated as a wave, sometimes as a particle; each perspective contradicts the other) as a key to Shakespeare's "dialectical dramaturgy" (1967:11). Although Rabkin usually applies the term to competing values and value-perceptions, the concept characterizes the epistemological style of *Macbeth:* the reified hallucination of the dagger exemplifies complementarity, as the *object* complements the *fantasy*. Both perspectives are valid, yet each logically invalidates the other. Or consider the directorial issue of showing or not showing a levitating dagger or a bloodied Banquo. Either choice determines an idea of the play incompatible with the other (Cartelli 1983).

Lady Macbeth's apparent infant can be seen from a similar perspective. That is, through the device of the phantom child, Shakespeare places his audience at the psychological center of *Macbeth*'s dreamscape. Lady Macbeth's infanticide generates a fantastic apparition *for the imaginations of the audience*. By so radically playing "is/is not," Shakespeare provisionally dislocates those conventional theatrical gratifications we as audience might expect. He has made the play itself equivocate, resulting potentially in a radical questioning of the status of our own response.

Shakespeare's tragedies typically encourage epistemological skepticism in his audience. The plays raise questions in order not to answer them, or to provide contradictory answers. (Is the specter of Hamlet the King a genuine ghost or the devil? Did Gertrude know of the murder? Is Prince Hamlet mad? How old is he?) *Not knowing* may then become the response-state of an audience, and dealing with the experience of not knowing and being unable to find stable answers further complicates that response. As Stanley Cavell (1979) has argued about a famous question in *Othello,* what is important is not whether the Moor's marriage to Desdemona has been consummated, but that we may doubt it, whatever the evidence. (This is an audience's version of Othello's quandary of doubt and evidence.) Similarly, the question isn't whether Lady Macbeth has a child: it's that she says she does and we may doubt it. "Doubtful it stood" (1.2.7) is a comment on more than specific questions in the play: it is a description of my projected audience's general response posture. We stand, secure, in doubt, unsure. Lady Macbeth's infant both is and is not, in a pregnant paradigm of the whole *Macbeth* experience. She is mother in surmise and in skepticism. Bradley's authoritative ruling on the question seems to me, then, exactly wrong: "Lady Macbeth's child," he asserted, "may be alive or may be dead. It may even be, or have been, her child by a former husband. . . . It may be that Macbeth had many children or that he had none. We cannot say, and it does not concern the play" (1904:40; see L. C. Knights's famous reply [1933]). Exactly the contrary. It may be all these possibilities, or none, or some. Our inability to say—our dubious stance—is a central concern of the play, because it compels us to share Macbeth's epistemological and psychological disorientations.

In this sense we can simultaneously "be" and "not be" Macbeth, sharing his vision while seeing more clearly. By such devices Shakespeare has made *Macbeth* his most boldly psychological play—even more than *A Midsummer Night's Dream* or *Hamlet* or *The Tempest.* *Macbeth* is Shakespeare's dramatic version of the dynamic relation of unconscious process to ordinary thought. In an historical period when fictions of supernatural agency (such as Fate or witches) were beginning to be challenged by emerging notions of individual pathology (consider the unstable evolution of the theology of "possession" into the psychology of "hysteria"), Shakespeare reimagined and dramatized the ambiguous interaction of fate and desire. In *Macbeth,* he merged externality and internality, not only in the paradoxes of the hero's vision (the dagger) but also in the relation of "witches" as supernatural agency and "wishes" as personal (unconscious) desire. Both represent the unknowable mystery of motivation; both situate the arena of compulsive action. *Macbeth* collocates these arenas, so that the unconscious becomes a source of (feminine) equivocation, or undifferentiation, or most properly "de-differentiation."

The idea of a "feminine" or undifferentiated unconscious is implicit in Lady Macbeth's urgent solicitation of her husband's desire. She enters the play speaking her husband's words (reading his letter): she announces what is unspoken. Hers is the voice of wishing: "Art thou afraid / To be the same in thine own act and valour / As thou art in desire?" (1.7.39–41). At one point, in an uncanny augury of de Beauvoir and Lacan, Shakespeare puts her precisely in the position of the "Other." After imagining the whirlwind vision of naked Pity, Macbeth complains:

> I have no spur
> To prick the sides of my intent, but only
> Vaulting ambition, which o'erleaps itself
> And falls on th' other—
> *Enter Lady Macbeth*
> (1.7.25–28 S.D.)

Linda Bamber argues that, unlike the other tragedies, *Macbeth* and *Coriolanus* present no genuine Other for the masculine Self. Instead, the feminine Other actually corresponds to the hero's pathological projections of her. In the absence of a real self-other dialectic, Macbeth cannot engage with a real outside world; instead he is "entirely taken up by internal dialogue" (1982:19, 93, 105).[16] I suggest a related idea: *Macbeth* manifests a fatal con-fusion between "feminine" otherness and "masculine" ambition. One controls and expresses the other, but which is which? Like the embrace of two spent swimmers, the intimate bond of (female) other and (male) desire becomes one of unstable support and struggle. It threatens to degenerate into a process of de-differentiation. Like the witches, unsexed Lady Macbeth, or unmanly Macbeth, both agencies (other and desire) are of neither gender, or of both. Complementarity here threatens to collapse into critical mass.

Lady Macbeth's consanguinity with the unconscious is of course most evident through the witches, who are the supernatural reflection and dilation of her persona. Macbeth's language actually identifies the witches with unconscious process, in imagery that characterizes as well his relation to both agencies:

> Now o'er the one half-world
> Nature seems dead, and wicked dreams abuse
> The curtain'd sleep: Witchcraft celebrates
> Pale Hecate's off'rings; and wither'd Murther, . . .
> With Tarquin's ravishing strides, towards his design

>Moves like a ghost.

>(2.1.49–56)

Macbeth's bisection of the world inscribes a geography of reciprocal hemispheres: Nature and the unnatural, day and night, life and death, waking and sleeping. Such a geography holds throughout the play, literally in terms of landscape (battlefield, castle, cave), and metaphorically in terms of surface deceit (hospitality) and subterranean desire (hostility). It takes its theological form in the re-vision of Inverness as Hell (2.3) and transforms suggestively in Donalbain's remark that "fate [is] hid in an auger-hole" (2.3.123–24). The proximity of hidden depths and prophecy ("auger" echoes "augur") becomes most evident in Shakespeare's description of the three weird sisters, their cave, and their cauldron.

What Macbeth sees in the witches' cave (4.1)—one form of the "deed without a name"—is in effect the mystery of generation, "the seeds of time" ripening into the future. He envisions the germination of others, while he himself is cut off from it. His own "doing" is an impotent de-generation that imagines the tumbling of Nature's germens; his "firstlings" will be bloody deaths. The bubbling cauldron most vividly and viscerally signifies the mixture of generativity and destruction. It is a source of energy and insight, poisonous motivation and prophetic vision; a "hell-broth" of unconscious desire; a distilled, degenerative, demonic womb. Its ingredients give a taste of its symbolic value: composed of fragments of dismembered bodies (particularly appendages), it represents a fatal maternal enclosure, or a nursery brew with an insatiable appetite:

>Witches' mummy; maw and gulf,
>Of the ravin'd salt-sea shark. . . .
>Add thereto a tiger's chaudron,
>For th' ingredience of our cauldron.

>(4.1.22–34)

Shakespeare's rhyme echoes an unconscious identity of inorganic and organic vessels, or of cauldron and womb.[17]

Beyond their location (cave) and equipment (cauldron), the witches' rhetorical and dramatic style suggests their emblematics of the unconscious. These "imperfect speakers" talk in rhyme, rhythmic repetition, alliteration; their speech is fragmented, allusive, incantatory, ritualistic;

they present themselves in an eerie song and dance (Grove 1982; Goldman 1982). The language and action of the three sisters can be imagined as an intrapsychic triadic confabulation: a primary-process conversation of separate yet unified parts (similar to Freud's model of the unconscious). Unlike their uncanny roundabout, the rest of the play is narrative and sequential—like the history play it also is. The contrast in styles is like the difference between unconscious and conscious representation, or between dreaming and waking, or primary and secondary process.[18]

The complementary figure to this "feminine" unconscious is the "masculine" desire it seems to urge and oversee. In Macbeth's tale of Witchcraft and Murther, Witchcraft presides over Murther's design. The manifest content of "wicked dreams" involves female invocation and celebration, followed by male motion and doing (imaged as Tarquin's rape). Macbeth's role in this allegory is as "wither'd Murther": *wither'd* suggests Murther's timeless age, echoes the witches ("so wither'd and so wild" [1.3.40]), and prefigures Macbeth's decline into "the sere, the yellow leaf." It also suggests his implicit impotence as a tool of supernatural agency: he thinks he is vital ("striding"), but actually he is wasted ("like a ghost").

The theme of impotence, implicit in the issue of Macbeth's childlessness, becomes most evident in the dagger scene. A Freudian interpretation of the dagger as symbolic phallus is valid, though it needs elaboration. Macbeth, who wants to "make love" to murder (3.1.123), complains that he has "no spur / To prick the sides of [his] intent." Charged by his sexually transfigured wife with being too womanly for his manly task, he confronts in the dagger an image that is simultaneously the sign of castration and the means to restore potency. To regain his masculinity, Macbeth must match the fantastic, separated dagger with his own instrument and kill Duncan. The symbolic identification of dagger with phallus further explains why the regicide is also rape, since it restores Macbeth's aggressive masculinity.

Moreover, as an emblem of Macbeth's "external" motivation the dagger represents a *split* in his consciousness, a projection of his wishes and fears. Beyond symbolizing castration or displaced potency, and equating sexuality with murder, it displays a style of representation that animates the whole play. For instance, Macbeth and his Lady are (as Freud saw) splits of a single entity, as are Lady Macbeth and the witches, or the various victimized and avenging children. The primary split between conscious and unconscious reflects that other primary (and in this play ambiguous) split—between male and female, or even between sexed and unsexed. Shakespeare has combined these divisions to suggest the interrelation of each, in an almost Freudian way (Freud 1916, 1938). That is, *Macbeth* dramatizes simultaneously a dynamic of conscious and unconscious desire *and* a dynamic of sexual difference. From the beginning of the play, unconscious forces bubble up into consciousness, blurring boundaries and distorting reality. As well, the concept of sexual division becomes obscure and mutable. The witches especially blur boundaries even as they draw them: a blend of female and male, their basic style is equivocation. From the start their language makes distinctions that do not hold: "When shall we three meet again, / In thunder, lightning, or in rain?" The nature of storms makes such a choice impossible. A diabolic Trinity, the witches represent unity and splitting simultaneously.

Splitting is perhaps Shakespeare's preeminent strategy of representation, or his favored mode of defense. It animates an early play, *The Comedy of Errors,* where it develops potentially psychotic divisions before the conventional re-pairs of comic form (Freedman 1981). It designs the tragedy of King Lear, who fractures his kingdom, his family, and his psyche in one catastrophic gesture. It inaugurates a late play, by the similar disaster of stormy separation: "We split, we split!" (*The Tempest,* 1.1.60). *Twelfth Night,* almost contemporary with the obsessively divisive *Hamlet,* presents a brief comic vision of *Macbeth*'s nightmare, in its "natural perspective, that *is and is not*" (5.1.217). In this case comedy provides rational answers to the quandary, in the image of an illusory optical device, or the ultimate solution of twinning. Equivocation becomes duplicity, and finally actual duplication. But in the tragedy of *Macbeth,* splittings are not rationally resolved, and the potentially psychotic realm of undifferentiated objects becomes real. Shakespeare dramatizes what psychoanalysis theorizes.

Not that Shakespeare was a Jacobean psychoanalyst. Still, his modes of representing human behavior reflect and elaborate concepts of contemporary analytic theory. Shakespeare's attention to human behavior, language, thought, feeling, and fantasy was as intense and insightful as Freud's, though in a different style of representation. One way to think of the relation between Shakespearean and Freudian (or psychoanalytic) representations of psychic, familial, and social structures is through the idea of "isomorphisms." When two apparently different complex structures can be mapped onto each other with close similarities in nature and function between corresponding parts, mathematicians and logicians term the structures "isomorphic."[19] It is at least metaphorically plausible to see Shakespearean drama and psychoanalytic theory as isomorphic. They are two variant literary representations of human behavior, uncannily similar when examined in relation to each other. The durable example of *Hamlet* is the most prominent demonstration of this isomorphism; I suggest *Macbeth* as another compelling instance. These plays are manifestly about psychic structure and symbolic representation; their imaginative domain is also that of psychoanalysis.

Michel Foucault, in the first volume of his *History of Sexuality*, offers a wider social analogy. He suggests that during the eighteenth and nineteenth centuries European society moved from "a *symbolics of blood* to an *analytics of sexuality*" (1978:145–50). That is, cultural "regimes of power" shifted from the evidence of sanguinity (blood-relations, inheritance, the ritual symbolism of physical violence) to the control of sexuality (procreativity, concern for human life, definitions of sexual difference). What *Macbeth* suggests is that for Shakespeare this shift was already imaginable in the early seventeenth century. He had at hand a "symbolics of blood"—his play is awash in it—but what he must invent is an "analytics of sexuality." He knew (I imagine) that the problematic issue of sexual difference underlay his play—in terms of procreativity, sterility, masculinity, and femininity—and he enacted an "analysis" of its problems through imaginative drama. As Freud often averred, analysis was available to poetry before theory found its language. In this sense, Shakespeare prefigures Freud: drama enacts what theory affirms, in an isomorphic relation.

A case in point is the doctor who observes Lady Macbeth's "slumbery agitation" in Act 5. He is looking at a dramatic enactment of "the unconscious," though he cannot quite see it. Her sleepwalking scene begins with the blood-spot and its psychological persistence ("Yet here's a spot"), translating *reality* (the stain) into its mnemonic *sign*. She enacts a mode of re-presentation whereby traces of past events return, unbidden and ineradicable. But not merely in memory: the recurrence of the past effects a fantastic alteration in her perception of reality. Macbeth sees the dagger (and follows it); Lady Macbeth sees and smells the blood-spot (and tries to remove it). Outside its normal psychic confines, memory manifests itself in her senses and on her flesh. The sign of the memory *trace* is the hallucinated *mark* of blood. Here is another emblem of the psyche turned inside out that is *Macbeth*. Lady Macbeth's compulsion recalls Macbeth's, except that she sleepwalks and curses a blood-spot, while he wades in blood. He is active, she passive. He acts out the unconscious; the unconscious acts out on her. Now split off from the demonic matrix of the witches, Lady Macbeth no longer actively manifests the unconscious but is passively subjected to it. The doctor, like a good professional, takes notes on her associations to blood, time, doing, Duncan, the Thane of Fife. But he can offer no help. He lacks a theory of hysteria: a sexualized view of the female that could address her pathology, read the language of the stain (her "thick-coming fancies"), and *analyze* her *bloody* mindedness (Foucault 1978:104; Davis 1982:20). "This disease is beyond my practice," he concludes.

> More needs she the divine than the physician. . . .
>
> My mind she has mated, and amaz'd my sight.
>
> I think, but dare not speak.
>
> (5.1.71–76)

The doctor's words recall Macbeth's circumstances, to the point of amazed sight (the witches, the dagger, Banquo's ghost), and the division between hidden thought and the audacity of expression. The doctor is also like Banquo standing before the witches, fascinated yet forbidden to interpret their mystery (1.3.46). His reference to his "mated" mind may allude to the pia mater (the membrane enveloping the brain), suggesting the subduing of the medical mind by the maternal element, and a suggestive identity between brain and womb. (In *Love's Labour's Lost,*" Holofernes describes his poetic "gift" as "begot in the ventricle of memory, nourish'd in the womb of pia mater, and delivered upon the mellowing of occasion" [4.2.65–60]).[20] Just this identity lies behind the mythology of hysteria: a displacement upward from abdomen to head that pathologizes conventional analogies between womb and psyche, or between uterine and lunatic conception. *"Hysterica passio"*—most dramatically embodied in the rising of Lear's "mother" (2.4.56–57)—represents the metaphoric relocation of unconscious psychic disorder at its imagined maternal origin. In Shakespeare similar metaphors are commonplace: from the "unborn sorrow, ripe in fortune's womb" that Richard II's queen foresees (2.2.10), to Falstaff's multitongued "womb" that speaks his name (2 *Henry IV*, 4.3.22), to "the foul womb of night" that the Chorus in *Henry IV* envisions (Act 4), to Cleopatra's image of "the memory of my womb" (3.13.363), to Iago's conception of "events in the womb of time" and the "monstrous birth" he "engenders" in Othello's unconscious (1.3.370, 403). A moment in *Antony and Cleopatra* neatly suggests the connection between projection and procreation: the Soothsayer is entertaining Cleopatra's attendants, and Charmian asks him to predict the number of her future children.

SOOTHSAYER

> If every of your wishes had a womb,
>
> And fertile every wish, a million.

CHARMIAN Out, fool, I forgive thee for a witch!

(1.2.38–40)

In *Macbeth,* the witch of wishing is both fertile and sterile.

Shakespeare's dramatic enactments of wishing—or of the struggle between fact and desire—call into question the status of imagination, and of imaginative revisions of the self. The place of fantasy in Shakespeare's historical world—in theater, politics, religion, alchemy, geography—involved questions that an inquisitive drama like Shakespeare's could powerfully raise and explore. In its challenge to imagine a world of simultaneous being and nonbeing, reality and fantasy, creativity and destruction, *Macbeth* offers its audience opportunities for momentary psychic disorientation. The play confronts our imaginations with a risky yet rewarding interrogation of the very assumptions of our worlds of experience and play. Lady Macbeth may scoff at "the eye of childhood / That fears a painted devil" (2.2.54–55), but even if adult vision may learn such a distinction, the existence of devils and witches was a real issue for Shakespeare's audience. (Seventeenth-century western Europe was zealously finding, trying, and killing witches.)[21] Moreover, what if a devil, painted or pure, were both there and not there—or both within, in psychological space, and without, in theatrical or theological space? Potentially more frightening than the existence of devils is the radical discontinuity of existence itself.

At an historical moment when theatricality was inextricably blended with representations of the self and the world ("All the world's a stage," says the poor player, strutting and fretting), the issue of imagination was seminal (Greenblatt 1981). For Shakespeare himself it may have been personally acute. As a poet whose imaginings were given local habitation, nomination, and enactment by players, he may have felt sharply the questions of private fantasy and public display. Commenting that Macbeth "cannot maintain the distinction between fantasy and action," so that "what he can imagine he must perform," Murray Schwartz speculates that "such a character expresses a central problem for a playwright, for any playwright must be concerned with the dynamic relationship between what can be imagined and what can be performed in word or deed" (1974:26; see also Michel 1976:56). *Macbeth* dramatizes the pathology of this dynamic relationship when it is short-circuited, when it lacks the buffer of a proper interim. (By contrast, *Hamlet* dramatizes the pathology of "all interim.") In every play, especially in the later tragedies and romances, Shakespeare plays with questions of fantasy and representability. *Macbeth* enacts extreme possibilities. *The Tempest* is Shakespeare's ultimate portrayal of the play-maker who has at his service "spirits, which by mine art / I have from their confines call'd to enact / My present fancies" (4.1.120–22). Prospero's fantasies are sometimes kindly (the Masque of Goddesses) but often cruel (the concluding antimasque of attacking dogs). Vengeance underlies the tempestuous anger that inaugurates and animates the play (Summers 1973; Abrams 1978). These fantasies of entertaining and punishing, involving spirits that enact present fantasies with no mediation (Prospero writes no script), represent an immediate translation of wish and fear into action. Such instant transmission of desire into deed is analogous to Macbeth's compulsive creativity ("Strange things I have in head, that will to hand, / Which must be acted, ere they may be scann'd"). A difference is that Prospero's fantasies have "confines" (he still threatens Ariel and Caliban with confinement). For Prospero, the demon of unconscious compulsion (the witch of wishing) is under guard, whereas for Macbeth she and her representatives are free, within and without. Prospero and Macbeth are reciprocal figures of the fantast: one is an image of the artist controlling his shaping fancy (though sometimes only barely), whereas the other is an image of the artist out of conscious control, compelled and ultimately victimized by his own unconscious projections.

At issue are the limits of imagining—a process dramatized in the words and acts of Shakespeare's characters, but potentially most fully developed in the thoughts and feelings of his audience. By arousing basic doubts about the psychological boundaries of theatrical play-space, a play like *Macbeth* may evoke responses beyond the conventional Aristotelian pity and terror. Even Francis Fergusson, in demonstrating that "Aristotle was right" by showing the unity of action in *Macbeth,* admits that the play "shows modes of the spirit's life undreamed of by Aristotle himself" (1957:125). To test the limits of our own potential spaces is a process not fully characterized by a term like *katharsis.*[22] Macbeth himself has passed beyond conventional responses. "The time has been," he muses,

> my senses would have cooled
> To hear a night-shriek, and my fell of hair
> Would at a dismal treatise rouse and stir
> As life were in't.
>
> (5.5.10–13)

He has moved from a conventional perspective in Act 1, when he confronted the alarming apparitions of the witches, to a radically new vision in which nothing finally can surprise him. His expectations, like Birnham Wood, have been uprooted. Trapped in a nightmare of compulsively enacted fantasies whose origins elude him, he succumbs. We, however, as privileged spectators to his plight, may be able to use Shakespeare's dislocations of theatrical experience to acknowledge and exercise our own capacities for fantasy, positive or negative. Nietzsche, in his critique of Aristotelian tragic theory, speculated fervently about such a possibility: "Not in order to escape from terror and pity, not to purify oneself of a dangerous passion by discharging it with vehemence—this is how Aristotle understood it—but to be far beyond terror and pity and to be the eternal lust of Becoming itself—that lust which also involves the lust of destruction" (1888:120). Not simply to release emotion but to enter a realm of desire in which "becoming" and "destruction," generativity and degeneration, *is* and *is not* all forge their disturbing coexistence: such is the potential experience of *Macbeth.*

NOTES

1. Quotations are from the Arden Edition of *Macbeth,* edited by Kenneth Muir (London: Methuen, 1962).

2. For a detailed review of psychoanalytic interpretations of the regicide as parricide, see Holland (1966:219–30). After 1964, see Vesny-Wagner (1968), Calef (1969), Bachmann (1978), and Watson (1984). For a useful account of the oedipal, patricidal interpretation, which also includes a Kleinian perspective of the jealous infant, see Roberts (1975:206–11). Noting that Macbeth decides to kill Duncan after the king chooses Malcolm as his heir, Norman Rabkin writes: "It is as if Macbeth decides to kill Duncan out of the rage of a

disappointed sibling" (1981:105–108). A Freudian reading of Fuseli's water-color illustration (1766) of the Macbeths just after the deed (based on Garrick's production) also finds the oedipal design, with Lady Macbeth in the role of mother: see Carr and Knapp (1981). Two important studies were published after this article was first in press: Adelman (1987) and Garber (1987b).

3. See *Hamlet*, 3.2.36off. ("Soft, now to my mother . . ."). For a provoc-ative paragraph on these fantasies in *Macbeth*, see Wheeler (1981:145–46). Another valuable essay is Biggins (1975). A critic of Polanski's film has noted the director's erotization of the regicide: see Wexman (1979–80). In an infor-mative essay on "Obstetrics and Gynecology in *Macbeth*," Alice Fox (1979) explicates the connotations of breech-birth in the description of Duncan's murder. See also Silling (1974).

4. Harry Berger (1980) finds Duncan "vaguely androgynous" as the source of paternal blood and maternal milk. In a paper delivered to the 1981 MLA Special Session on "Marriage and the Family in Shakespeare," David Sundel-son stressed the "horrifying fusion of sexes" that ideas of androgyny evoke in the tragedies (as opposed to the comedies), and remarked of the "new Gorgon" that is Duncan's corpse: "The father's ravaged body becomes the annihilating mother." See also Harding (1969), and Hunter (1980).

5. For further anatomical reconstruction of the castle, see Sacks (1980: 78ff.). The 1983 BBC television production filmed a blood-red sunset through half-open teethlike gates, just as Duncan and Banquo were describing the castle's pleasantries. The traditional image of the Hellmouth is of course re-lated.

6. Joan Klein finds this religious image in Macbeth's evocation of infant Pity (1981:242).

7. For a variety of insightful analyses of this event, see L. C. Knights, "How Many Children Had Lady Macbeth?" (1933), Calef (1969), Mack (1973), Schwartz (1980:28–29), and Berger (1980:27–28).

8. Fox discovers a language of nursing in Macbeth's final soliloquy about the player who "struts and frets his hour." She notes *OED* evidence that "strut" can mean to bulge, or swell (as with milk), and "fret" can mean to gnaw (1979:132, 140n18).

9. Commentators have noted the mirroring syntax in a variety of ways: most usefully, Laurence Michel (1976:52–53), Berger (1980), and Booth (1983:88–89). On doubling and rivalry, see Fineman (1980), Girard (1978), Kahn (1981), and Adelman (1980).

10. See Garber (1974:113–14), and Bayley (1981:188). Berger however, presents a good case for Banquo's implicit blame in the regicide (1980:29–30). In Holinshed, Banquo is Macbeth's accomplice.

11. Booth elaborates this claim, although he considers the Malcolm-Mac-duff scene a dramaturgical "irritation" (1983:105–11). Perhaps the most fer-vent assertion of our complicity with Macbeth came from Arthur Quiller-Couch, in *Shakespeare's Workmanship* (1918); quoted in Lerner (1963:175–78).

12. Stage productions confront a problem here. As Peter Hall said in an interview, "This is very difficult to do: it has to be absolutely real to Macbeth because he does see a dagger. The audience only see a dagger if he sees a dagger. That is a wonderful image" (1982:241). Modern film technology allows Polanski to solve this problem. When Macbeth (Jon Finch) looks at the dagger, it appears; when he looks away, it disappears. Its evident existence to the senses (Macbeth's sight and our own) is thus precisely contingent on Macbeth's "seeing" it.

13. Critics like Rosenberg (and A. C. Bradley) are not the only readers who seek after certainty. A British professor of mental health has diagnosed Macbeth's pathology: "On the International Classification of Diseases, Macbeth's illness would be classified as a psychogenic paranoid psychosis" (Davis 1982). The same expert suggests that timely therapeutic intervention might have saved the Macbeths' marriage (not to mention Duncan's life).

14. For a thoughtful and imaginative analysis of projected audience response to this anxiety of unanswerability, see Booth (1983).

15. Lawrence Danson makes a remark about the Jesuit doctrine of equivocation that is relevant here. "I think Shakespeare may have felt," he writes, that the doctrine "constituted an attack upon all the bases of rational discourse. For the doctrine, with its all-purpose escape clause about 'mental reservation,' perverts the nature of language, which must be public and exoteric, into something private and esoteric. . . . The doctrine gives a sort of metaphysical warrant to solipsism, and elevates individual fantasy to a status equal with public reality" (1974:133). I speculate that Shakespeare intended to attack the bases of rational discourse in *Macbeth*. Indeed, the notion of equality between individual fantasy and public reality states the dilemma and mystery of the play and our responses to it.

16. Bamber's book sympathetically yet critically revises Leslie Fiedler's (1972) concept of woman as Other.

17. The Arden editor, Kenneth Muir, gives *entrails* as the meaning of "chaudron," citing a Dekker play (the OED also gives this definition under "chaldron," an obsolete form of "chawdron"). However, the rhyming terms were synonyms as well (under "chaudron," the OED gives *cauldron,* from the French). Their cognation derives from the image of a container: either a container of viscera (a kettle of entrails) or a visceral container (entrails themselves). See also Barron (1960:269).

18. See Hunter (1980) for a development of these parallels. The larger theoretical issue I am treating here is openly discovered by Coppélia Kahn's (1982) review of feminist psychoanalytic theory.

19. I am using the definition of "isomorphism" provided by Douglas Hofstadter, who relates the mathematic idea to language and interpretation, and who considers the issue of isomorphism the key to the question of consciousness itself (1979:9, 49–50, 82).

20. I am not citing cognation, just hearing a pun. Shakespeare uses the

anatomical term ("pia mater") in *Love's Labour's Lost* (4.2.68) and *Troilus and Cressida* (2.1.77). Twice in *The Comedy of Errors* he uses "mated" in connection to madness (3.2.54, 5.1.282). The *OED* quotes the Doctor's line to illustrate one sense, derived from the Old French *"mater"*: "To put out of countenance; to render helpless by terror, shame, or discouragement; to daunt, abash; to stupefy." Under "mated," the *OED* gives "confounded, amazed"; most of these meanings relate to the position of "checkmate" in chess.

21. A good account of the "great witch-hunt" that obsessed western Europe from the late sixteenth through most of the seventeenth century is Cohn (1976). Although England was more legalistic and less severe than other countries (and preferred hanging to burning), Scotland seems to have been especially fierce in its persecution (253–55).

22. I am aware of the long-standing controversies over the psychological location and function of *katharsis* and do not wish to restrict its meaning to audience response. Indeed, the free-floating consanguinity between character's reaction and audience response is central to my theme. *Mimesis* can concern psychological "action" as well.

REFERENCES

Abrams, R. 1978. *"The Tempest* and the Concept of the Machiavellian Playwright." *English Literary Renaissance* 8:43–66.

Adelman, J. 1980. " 'Anger's My Meat': Feeding, Dependency, and Aggression in *Coriolanus*." In Schwartz and Kahn, eds, *Representing Shakespeare*, pp. 129–49.

———. 1987. " 'Born of Woman': Fantasies of Maternal Power in *Macbeth*." In Garber, ed., *Cannibals, Witches, and Divorce*, pp. 90–121.

Auden, W. H. 1964. *The Dyer's Hand*. New York: Random House.

Bachmann, S. 1978. "Daggers in Men's Smiles." *International Review of Psycho-Analysis* 5:97–104.

Bamber, L. 1982. *Comic Women, Tragic Men: A Study of Gender and Genre in Shakespeare*. Stanford: Stanford University Press.

Barron, D. 1970. "The Babe That Milks: An Organic Study of *Macbeth*." In Faber, *The Design Within*, pp. 251–79.

Bayley, J. 1981. *Shakespeare and Tragedy*. London: Routledge.

Berger, H. 1980. "The Early Scenes of *Macbeth*: Preface to a New Interpretation." *ELH* 47:1–31.

Biggins, D. 1975. "Sexuality, Witchcraft, and Violence in *Macbeth*." *Shakespeare Studies* 8:255–77.

Booth, S. 1983. *"King Lear," "Macbeth," Indefinition, and Tragedy*. New Haven: Yale University Press.

Bradley, A. C. [1904] 1955. *Shakespearean Tragedy*. New York: St. Martin's.

Brooke, N. 1980. "Language Most Shows a Man?: Language and Speaker in *Macbeth.*" In P. Edwards et al., eds., *Shakespeare's Styles: Essays in Honour of Kenneth Muir,* pp. 66–77. Cambridge: Cambridge University Press.

Brooks, C. 1947. "The Naked Babe and the Cloak of Manliness." In *The Well-Wrought Urn: Studies in the Structure of Poetry,* pp. 22–49 New York: Harcourt Brace Jovanovich.

Brown, J. R., ed. 1982. *Focus on "Macbeth."* London: Routledge.

Burton, R. [1628] 1932. *The Anatomy of Melancholy.* 3 vols. London: Everyman Library.

Calef, V. 1969. "Lady Macbeth and Infanticide." *Journal of the American Psychoanalytic Association* 17:528–48.

Carr, S. L., and P. Knapp. 1981. "Seeing through *Macbeth.*" *PMLA* 96:837–47.

Cartelli, T. 1983. "Banquo's Ghost: The Shared Vision." *Theatre Journal* 38:389–405.

Cavell, S. 1979. "Epistemology and Tragedy: A Reading of *Othello.*" *Daedalus* 108:27–43.

Cohn, N. 1976. *Europe's Inner Demons: An Enquiry Inspired by the Great Witch-Hunt.* New York: Dutton.

Danson, L. 1974. *Tragic Alphabet: Shakespeare's Drama of Language.* New Haven: Yale University Press.

Davis, D. R. 1982. "Hurt Minds." In Brown, ed., *Focus on "Macbeth,"* pp. 210–28.

Derrida, J. 1978. "The Theater of Cruelty." In *Writing and Difference, and the Closure of Representation.* Translated by Alan Bass, pp. 232–50. Chicago: University of Chicago Press.

Egan, R. 1968. "His Hour Upon the Stage: Role-Playing in *Macbeth.*" *Centennial Review* 22:327–45.

Faber, M. D., ed. 1970. *The Design Within: Psychoanalytic Approaches to Shakespeare.* New York: Science House.

Fergusson, F. 1957. "*Macbeth* and the Imitation of an Action." In *The Human Image in Dramatic Literature,* pp.115–25. Garden City, N.Y.: Doubleday.

Fiedler, L. 1972. *The Stranger in Shakespeare.* New York: Stein and Day.

Fineman, J. 1980. "Fratricide and Cuckoldry: Shakespeare's Doubles." In Schwartz and Kahn, eds., *Representing Shakespeare,* pp. 70–109.

Foucault, M. 1978. *The History of Sexuality.* Translated by Robert Hurley. New York: Random House.

Fox, A. 1979. "Obstetrics and Gynecology in *Macbeth.*" *Shakespeare Studies* 12:127–41.

Freedman, B. 1981. "Egon's Debt: Self-Division and Self-Redemption in *The Comedy of Errors.*" *English Literary Renaissance* 10:360–83.

Freud, S. 1916. "Some Character Types Met with in Psycho-Analytic Work." In vol. 14 of *The Standard Edition of the Complete Psychological Works of*

Sigmund Freud, pp. 316–31. Edited and translated by J. Strachey et al. 24 vols. London: Hogarth Press, 1954–76.

———. 1938. "The Splitting of the Ego in the Process of Defense." In vol. 23 of *The Standard Edition of the Complete Works,* pp. 271–78.

Garber, M. 1974. *Dream in Shakespeare.* New Haven: Yale University Press.

———, ed. 1987a. *Cannibals, Witches, and Divorce: Estranging the Renaissance.* Baltimore: Johns Hopkins University Press.

———. 1987b. "Macbeth: The Male Medusa." In *Shakespeare's Ghost Writers: Literature as Uncanny Causality.* New York: Routledge.

Girard, R. 1978. *Violence and the Sacred.* Baltimore: Johns Hopkins University Press.

Goldman, M. 1982 "Language and Action in *Macbeth.*" In Brown, ed., *Focus on "Macbeth,"* pp. 140–52.

Greenblatt, S. 1981. *Renaissance Self-Fashioning: From More to Shakespeare.* Chicago: University of Chicago Press.

Grove, R. 1982. "Multiplying Villainies of Nature." In Brown, ed., *Focus on "Macbeth,"* pp. 113–39.

Hall, P. 1982. "Directing *Macbeth.*" In Brown, ed., *Focus on "Macbeth,"* pp. 231–48.

Harding, D. W. 1969. "Woman's Fantasy of Manhood." *Shakespeare Quarterly* 20:245–53.

Hofstadter, D. 1979. *Gödel, Escher, Bach: An Eternal Golden Braid.* New York: Basic Books.

Holland, N. N. 1964. "*Macbeth.*" In *The Shakespearean Imagination: A Critical Introduction,* pp. 50–71. Bloomington: Indiana University Press.

———. 1966. *Psychoanalysis and Shakespeare.* New York: McGraw-Hill.

Hunter, D. 1980. "Shakespearian Myth-Making in *Macbeth:* Cultural Crisis and Return to Origins." In I. Reid, ed., *Myth and Shakespeare,* pp. 176–85. Victoria, Australia.

Ide, R. 1975. "The Theatre of the Mind: An Essay on *Macbeth.*" *ELH* 42:338–61.

Kahn, C. 1981. *Man's Estate: Masculine Identity in Shakespeare.* Berkeley: University of California Press.

———. 1982. "Excavating 'Those Dim Minoan Regions': Maternal Subtexts in Patriarchal Literature." *Diacritics* 12:37–41.

Klein, J. 1981. "Lady Macbeth 'Infirm of Purpose.' " In Lenz, Greene, and Neely, eds., *The Woman's Part,* pp. 240–55.

Knight, G. W. 1949. "*Macbeth* and the Metaphysic of Evil." In *The Wheel of Fire,* pp. 140–59. London: Methuen.

Knights, L. C. 1933. "How Many Children Had Lady Macbeth?" In *Explorations: Essays in Criticism, Mainly on the Literature of the Seventeenth Century,* pp. 13–50. New York: New York University Press.

Lenz, R., G. Greene, and C. Neely, eds. 1981. *The Woman's Part: Feminist Criticism of Shakespeare.* Urbana: University of Illinois Press.

Lerner, L., ed. 1963. *Shakespeare's Tragedies.* New York: Penguin.

Lesser, S. 1977. "*Macbeth:* Drama and Dream." In R. Noland and R. Sprich, eds., *The Whispered Meanings,* pp. 212–34. Amherst: University of Massachusetts Press.

Mack, M. 1973. *Killing the King: Three Studies in Shakespeare's Tragic Structure.* New Haven: Yale University Press.

Mahler, M. 1975. *The Psychological Birth of the Human Infant.* New York: Basic Books.

Michel, L. 1976. *The Thing Contained: Theory of the Tragic.* Bloomington: Indiana University Press.

Nietzsche, F. 1888. "Things I Owe to the Ancients." In *Twilight of the Idols.* Translated by A. M. Lodovici. In vol. 16, pp. 112–20, *Complete Works,* edited by O. Levy. 18 vols. New York: Macmillan, 1924.

Palmer, D. J. 1982. " 'A New Gorgon': Visual Effects in *Macbeth.*" In Brown, ed., *Focus on "Macbeth,"* pp. 54–69.

Rabkin, N. 1967. *Shakespeare and the Common Understanding.* New York: Free Press.

———. 1981. *Shakespeare and the Problem of Meaning.* Chicago: University of Chicago Press.

Ramsey, J. 1973. "The Perversion of Manliness in *Macbeth.*" *SEL: 1500–1900* 13:85–300.

Roberts, P. 1975. *The Psychology of Tragic Drama.* London: Routledge and Kegan Paul.

Rosenberg, M. 1970. *The Masks of Macbeth.* Berkeley: University of California Press.

Schnucker, R. V. 1974. "The English Puritans and Pregnancy, Delivery, and Breast-Feeding." *History of Childhood Quarterly* 1:637–58.

Schwartz, M. M. 1974. *A Thematic Introduction to Shakespeare.* New York: Empire State College Publications.

———. 1980. "Shakespeare Through Contemporary Psychoanalysis." In Schwartz and Kahn, eds., *Representing Shakespeare,* pp. 21–32.

Schwartz, M. M., and C. Kahn, eds. 1980. *Representing Shakespeare: New Psychoanalytic Essays.* Baltimore: Johns Hopkins University Press.

Silling, E. 1974. "Another Meaning for 'Breech'd.' " *Massachusetts Studies in English* 4:56.

Stallybrass, P. 1982. "*Macbeth* and Witchcraft." In Brown, ed., *Focus on "Macbeth,"* pp. 189–209.

Summers, J. H. 1973. "The Anger of Prospero." *Michigan Quarterly Review* 12:116–35.

Sundelson, D. 1981. Paper presented at session on Marriage and the Family in Shakespeare at the annual meeting of the Modern Language Association, New York, December, 1981.

Vesny-Wagner, L. 1968. *"Macbeth:* 'Fair is Foul and Foul is Fair.' " *American Imago* 25:242–57.

Watson, R. 1984. *Shakespeare and the Hazards of Ambition.* Cambridge, Mass.: Harvard University Press.

Wexman, V. W. 1979–80. *"Macbeth* and Polanski's Theme of Regression." *University of Dayton Review* 14:85–88.

Wheeler, R. 1981. *Shakespeare's Development and the Problem Comedies: Turn and Counter-Turn.* Berkeley: University of California Press.

Willbern, D. 1980. "Shakespeare's Nothing." In Schwartz and Kahn, eds., *Representing Shakespeare,* pp. 244–63.

Winnicott, D. W. 1953. "Transitional Objects and Transitional Phenomena." In Winnicott, *Playing and Reality,* pp. 1–25.

———. 1960. "The Theory of the Parent-Infant Relationship." In *The Maturational Processes and the Facilitating Environment: Studies in the Theory of Emotional Development,* pp. 37–55. New York: International Universities Press, 1965.

———. 1967. "Mirror-Role of Mother and Family in Child Development." In Winnicott, *Playing and Reality,* pp. 111–18.

———. 1971a. "The Location of Cultural Experience." In Winnicott, *Playing and Reality,* pp. 95–103.

———. 1971b. *Playing and Reality.* New York: Basic Books; London: Tavistock, 1984.

———. 1971c. "The Use of an Object and Relating Through Identifications." In Winnicott, *Playing and Reality,* pp. 86–94.

8

Thomas Traherne and the Poetics of Object Relations

ANTOINETTE B. DAUBER

I

Thomas Traherne's poetry is concerned with man's proper relation to objects. The manuscript his brother Philip edited comes down to us subtitled, "Divine Reflections on the Native Objects of An Infant-Ey" (1965).[1] As the title suggests, the proper relation is the infant's birthright, and the adult, who has lost his inheritance in the course of his development, can best regain it by reflecting on the babe and his objects. This is Traherne's central theme, and it implies a striking revision of the psychological assumptions underlying most seventeenth-century poetry.

I emphasize psychology and not religion advisedly. We are accustomed to analyzing theological and doctrinal differences among the religious poets. Barbara K. Lewalski, for example, in her formidable book on Protestant poetics, says of Traherne: "His most striking departure from the Protestant consensus is his ecstatic celebration of infant innocence, which all but denies original sin as an hereditary taint, ascribing its effects chiefly to corruption by the world as the infant matures" (1979:352). She attributes this departure mainly to the influence of neo-Platonic philosophy.[2] But religion and philosophy do not fully illuminate the poet's radical deviation from his contemporaries.

Lewalski's own formulation hints at the relevance of a developmental psychology that begins with infancy. In order to understand seventeenth-century poetry in general and Traherne's in particular, we must recognize that along with a religious consensus there existed a psychological consensus. In a body of poetry so preoccupied by the estate of childhood, it could hardly be otherwise.[3] I propose in this paper to outline the nature of the consensus, the changes Traherne wrought, and the specifically poetic implications of his view and the views he opposed.

At first glance, it may seem perverse to single out the importance of objects in Traherne's verse. Of all seventeenth-century poetry, his is the most empty of things. Nowhere do we find the familiar characters and settings, the houses and landscapes, furnishings and gardens, clothing and flowers that fill the verse of his contemporaries. Although Traherne may be best known for his so-called soaring imagination and telescopic vision (Nicolson 1960:196–204), we characterize his work more accurately by noting the absence of the mundane, the commonplace, the particular. And yet, despite this marked difference in texture, Traherne shared with the mainstream poets that grand goal of seventeenth-century poetry, to return to a sense of primal unity.

Objects play a significant role in this purpose, at least in the way that Traherne's great predecessors and contemporaries pursued it. For it was through the mediation of the particular that they caught a glimpse of blessedness. They saw eternity flicker in a cloud and heaven glimmer in a droplet. Paradoxically those very objects—clouds, droplets, flowers[4]—which anchored their poetry firmly in the mundane world, giving it, as I have said, a texture so different from Traherne's, became windows, as it were, opening onto a higher reality.

What is remarkable about such images is that they retain their capacity to excite a sense of at-oneness, even when the meditative or other devotional practices on which their power would seem to have depended no longer engage us. At a time when we can recover the discipline of meditation only through the reconstruction of brilliant scholars like Louis Martz (1962, 1964),[5] we continue to experience the unifying force of seventeenth-century poetry. Even without the scholarly aids, the poetry awakens feelings buried deep in our childhood. We must surmise, therefore, that devotional poetry drew its powers of integration from a deep, perhaps universal, human reality. Among the poets, Henry Vaughan, especially, and Traherne, despite his swerve from the consensus, gave expression to this felt reality through a tripartite myth of human development. Briefly, between original happiness (the perfect oneness with God enjoyed by the newborn soul) and the third period (the mature man's complete estrangement from his early bliss), there is a transitional interlude. Here, between infancy and manhood, the growing child sporadically recaptures the first oneness through the mediation of certain objects, and to this intermediate stage the seventeenth-century poets who dwelled on objects were drawn. Almost two centuries later, in the Immortality Ode, Wordsworth rehearsed a similar three-part view of human development, and, today, we again discern its outlines in the psychoanalytic theories of the object relations school,[6] if we allow for the displacement of God by the mother figure. The myth persists.

Traherne's infant enters the world with a perfect sense of at-oneness, environment undifferentiated from self. Indeed, the poet anticipates the modern label for this "oceanic" condition, when he describes his soul's original union with God: "He mine, and I the Ocean of his Pleasures" (48). As increased awareness brings with it the dawning realization of separateness, the initial unity threatens to break up. The potential rudeness of such an awakening, however, is forestalled by what modern psychology calls the transitional phase, when the formerly all-enveloping oneness is localized in a particular object or space. At this juncture, the child transfers his feelings of at-oneness from an increasingly alienated world incapable of sustaining the illusion to a treasured other, a plaything, perhaps, which now symbolically restores the waning wholeness.

In "The Retreate," Vaughan meticulously sets forth the phased decline from the blissful first unity, to the distinctly comforting transition, to the dark period when the soul is cut off entirely from its original happiness:

> Happy those early dayes! when I
> Shin'd in my Angell-infancy.
> Before I understood this place
> Appointed for my second race,
> Or taught my soul to fancy ought
> But a white, Celestiall thought,
> When yet I had not walkt above
> A mile, or two, from my first love,
> And looking back (at that short space,)

> Could see a glimpse of his bright-face;
> When on some *gilded Cloud,* or *flowre*
> My gazing soul would dwell an houre,
> And in those weaker glories spy
> Some shadows of eternity;
> Before I taught my tongue to wound
> My Conscience with a sinfull sound,
> Or had the black art to dispence
> A sev'rall sinne to ev'ry sence,
> But felt through all this fleshly dresse
> Bright *shootes* of everlastingnesse.
>
> (1957:491.1–20)

A mile or two from his heavenly home, the infant already experiences division and casts longing looks backward. As he moves too far away to catch even a glimpse, he concentrates his attention on a gilded cloud or flower, and through the mediation of these lesser objects ("weaker glories," he calls them), he feels flashes of well-being once more: "But felt through all this fleshly dresse / Bright *shootes* of everlastingnesse." If the transitional object is inevitably tinged with the melancholy colors of loss, if it represents a falling off from the pure whiteness of first thoughts, nonetheless, Vaughan implies, it compensates the child for the loss of the world.

It is on the value of such objects that Traherne differs most sharply. While he accepts the three-part structure of childhood development, the basis of what we earlier called the psychological consensus, he stands it on its head by reversing cause and effect. Unlike Vaughan, who gratefully receives the consolation of the transitional object as a divine gift, Traherne blames such attractive objects for the loss of the first bliss: they divide the young soul from God. Moreover, in their continuing hold on the psyche, he sees a stumbling block that must be removed, if man is ever to recover what he has lost. For, as the poet well understood, the transitional object is not simply outgrown. In its infantile form, to be sure—the magically soothing teddy bear or blanket to which the child is passionately attached—it will be cast aside soon enough. But even as he separates from his beloved possession, this first relationship with an object serves the child as a school for subsequent relationships. His ties to the object world now multiply rapidly.

Largely relinquishing his magical investment in the transitional object, he begins to assume a more objective relationship with the world. At the same time, he never lays aside the magic of the transitional object entirely: man's capacity to make symbols grows out of the intermediate space.

If we exclude Traherne for the moment, we may venture to translate the poetic aspirations of the seventeenth century into the prevailing psychological paradigm. It is becoming clear (and I suspect the criticism of the next few years will further demonstrate) that the poets of the seventeenth century sought to resurrect the satisfying illusion of the transitional phase (Marotti 1978; Barber 1978; Dauber 1976). Of course, one might argue that all poetry shares this project, given the ontogenesis of the symbol in the intermediate space. Support for this position may be found in recent psychoanalytic theory, which holds, even more sweepingly, that all creativity is prompted by this impulse: for the artist, the work is a transitional object through which he or she re-creates a former perfection (Kohut 1966:257–61). But whether or not one agrees that all poets are so motivated, the case I am making for the seventeenth century has nothing to do with possible unconscious motivation. Seventeenth-century poetry openly cultivates the intermediate space. Its favored objects are sparkling, iridescent, or filmy things that leap beyond their own boundaries and amaze our eyes. They are not just symbols, distant and sophisticated relatives of the transitional object; they are potential transitional objects themselves, with the capacity to carry us back to the very brink of at-oneness. The means of releasing this potential vary from poet to poet. Vaughan practices Augustinian meditation; Herrick, who loves small shiny trifles as much as Vaughan loves sparks and seeds, relies on distinctive forms of play.

Traherne, however, as the absence of objects from his work makes clear, is the radical exception. He insists on the perfection of the prior oceanic oneness with God and, with a conviction that his contemporaries lack, believes in its absolute recoverability. His extremism leads him utterly to reject the seductive comforts of the transitional stage. Objects, even the translucent objects that his peers put to such splendid use, remain opaque. In "Shadows in the Water," he sees another world within a puddle, but the "film" of water bars his entry. The liminal space, which a century of poets from Spenser to Marvell were exploiting for the sake of bridging the gap between self and other, stands here as a barrier to union. Only when "that thin Skin / Is broken" (130) can the speaker hope to be admitted into the watery world. Mediation and mediating objects are renounced in favor of the directness of piercing the skin. To Traherne, the particular is an obstacle, the material world a distraction from his true goal. Accordingly, he attacks those objects that are privileged in the poetry of his contemporaries, lumping together "The Ribbans, and the gaudy Wings / Of Birds, the Virtues, and the Sins" (138) as unworthy discriminations of a false experience. Shiny objects (and, for that matter, virtues and sins, the official counters of religious life) have no power to redeem. "Nay," he declares, "Things are dead, / And in themselvs are severed / From Souls" (139). Even more audaciously, he strikes at the transitional object itself, heaping his harshest abuse on tin soldiers and hobby horses.

Traherne scorns man's attachment to the world, and yet he could not be further from the traditional attitude of *contemptus mundi*. How ill the image of the ascetic, cramped by the rigor of renunciation, fits him! Traherne is optimistic; without railing, he attempts to change man's fixed ways at their inception, in the newborn psyche. Instead of trying to teach man to hate the world he cannot help loving, he attacks man's ingrained love of the world at its very foundations, in childhood, when the attachment is first formed. His poetry adumbrates the creation of a new child, one who is not tempted by tawdry objects. As he develops, his speech and attachments will not be founded on particularity, like those of ordinary men. Speech, for Traherne's new man, will be celebration; affections will be magnanimity.

The material world, we hasten to note, is not banished from Traherne's poetry. While the new man needs only his perfectly symbiotic relationship with God to insure his bliss, in practice God's lesser creatures, too, are admitted within the compass of their embrace. At the very least, as in "The Estate," man prizes the "Outward Objects" of the created world for the opportunity they offer him to praise God:

> Shall the fair and brave
> And great Endowments of my Soul lie Waste,
> Which ought to be a fountain, and a Womb
> Of Praises unto Thee?
> Shall there no Outward Objects be,
> For these to see and Taste?
> Not so, my God, for Outward Joys and Pleasures
> Are even the Things for which my Lims are Treasures.
>
> (78)

God, in turn, in "Amendment," values his creatures for the sacred love
that man bestows on them:

> O how doth Sacred Lov
>
> His Gifts refine, Exalt, Improve!
>
> Our Love to Creatures makes them be
>
> In thine Esteem above
>
> Themselvs to Thee!
>
> (156)

This minimal appreciation of the creatures expands as man approaches
redemption, especially in the poems of the "Thoughts" series. To ren-
ovated man, the essential divineness of all things is patent. But such an
exalted spiritual vision is not sustained in most of the poems. Traherne
permits himself to distinguish among things. Significantly, the criteria
by which he evaluates the created world derive neither from religion
nor from ethics. They are rooted instead in his new psychology. In
place of traditional hierarchies, such as the great chain of being, he
devises a new scale: at the positive pole lies oceanic fusion; at the
negative, ownership. Thus those objects that lend themselves to an
oceanic relationship, resisting physical possession, are most prized. The
vast elements are best suited to nurture the infant's illusion of union;
they, paradoxically, are most his:

> All mine! And seen so Easily! How Great, how Blest!
>
> How soon am I of all possest!
>
> My Infancie no Sooner Opes its Eys,
>
> But Straight the Spacious Earth
>
> Abounds with Joy Peace Glory Mirth
>
> And being Wise,
>
> The very Skies,
>
> And Stars do mine becom; being all possest
>
> Even in that Way that is the Best.
>
> (74)

Those elements that encourage possession in the "best" way, the poet
tells us again and again, are the seas, the skies, the stars, cosmic objects
unclaimed and unappreciated by fallen man because they elude his
grasp.

Occupying an intermediate position on the scale, and regarded ambivalently by the poet, is nature as it composes itself into a landscape of human proportions, the recreative *locus amoenus* of Renaissance poetry. Tempting though such a place may seem, it finally proves inadequate to the poet's imagination. While generalized trees and fountains may enchant, particular ones set in a habitable landscape disappoint. One of the rare poems in which the physical setting is designated describes the poet's desolation in a country field:

> How desolate!
> Ah! how forlorn, how sadly did I stand
> When in the field my woful State
> I felt!
>
> (98)

The landscape has no comfort to offer:

> The shady Trees,
> The Ev'ning dark, the humming Bees,
> The Chirping Birds, mute Springs and Fords, conspire,
> To giv no Answer unto my Desire.
>
> (99)

Lowest on the poet's scale are gold and gems, quintessential property, whose beauty, even whose naturalness, the poet questions. Most frequently they are dismissed in invidious comparisons:

> One Star
> Is better far
> Than many Precious Stones:
>
> (95)

and

> Shall I not then
> Delight in these most Sacred Treasures
> Which my Great Father gave,
> Far more then other Men
> Delight in Gold?
>
> (76)

Yet a more specific animus against gold also emerges:

> Only what Adam in his first Estate,
> > Did I behold;
> > Hard Silver and Drie Gold
> As yet lay under Ground.
>
> > > > (14)

and

> For Golden Chains and Bracelets are
> But Gilded Manicles.
>
> > > (78)

The marked hostility toward gold and gems gains its impetus neither from religion nor economics but from Traherne's view of object relations. Indeed in all the examples cited above, gold is a physical, tangible material, and not the abstraction of a moralized economics. Gold represents the power of the particular to bind man. Its sheen fixes his myopic vision on his own ringed finger, even while all the golden corn in the summer fields beckons to him ("The World"). The love it elicits is a perversion:

> But being, like his loved Gold,
> Stiff, barren, hard impenetrable; tho told
> He should be otherwise: He is
> Uncapable of any hev'nly Bliss.
> > His Gold and he
> > Do well agree;
> For he's a formal Hypocrite,
> Like *that* Unfruitful, yet on th' outside bright.
>
> > > (125–26)

As "Right Apprehension" implies, gold exerts a fascination more deeply rooted than the appeal of wealth or power. To possess gold is to relive the gratification of the early object relationship (Ferenczi 1914). Only the redeemed poet manages to escape its lure:

> No more shall Trunks & Dishes be my Store,
> Not Ropes of Pearl, nor Chains of Golden Ore;

> As if such Beings yet were not,
>   They all shall be forgot,
> No such in Eden did appear,
> No such in Heven: Heven here
>   Would be, were those remov'd;
>   The sons of Men
>   Liv in Jerusalem,
>   Had they not Baubles lov'd.
> These Clouds dispers'd, the Heavens clear I see.
> Wealth new-invented, *mine* shall never be.
>   (150)

But gold, as Traherne well knew, is merely a striking instance, not the origin of the problem. Lust for gold is but a sophistication of earlier love of childish toys. Herein lies the true enemy of man's happiness:

> All Blisse
> Consists in this,
> To do as Adam did:
> And not to know those Superficial Toys
> Which in the Garden once were hid.
> Those little new Invented Things.
> Cups, Saddles, Crowns are Childish Joys.
> So Ribbans are and Rings.
> Which all our Happiness destroys.
>   (171; cf. 96)

For Traherne, the love of silly trifles is the source of man's sorrow. At first, following the example of foolish men, he, too, succumbed to their appeal:

> But I,
> I knew not why,
> Did learn among them too
> At length; and when I once with blemisht Eys
> Began their Pence and Toys to view,
> Drown'd in their Customs, I became

> A Stranger to the Shining Skies,
>> Lost as a dying Flame;
> And Hobby-horses brought to prize.

>> (97)

It is thus the most harmless things that present the gravest threat. Yet because Taherne's analysis of man's spiritual decline is grounded in a sound psychology, it is remarkably supple. The furnishings of daily life are not inherently evil, after all. Were man's affections not easily led astray, things would not constitute a danger to his well-being. To the perfected psyche, all things of the world are equally wondrous. To the still untainted newborn, the world, though postlapsarian, is truly more marvelous in its variety than was Adam's:

> What Structures here among God's Works appear?
>> Such Wonders *Adam* ne'r did see
>> In Paradise among the Trees,
>>> No Works of Art like these,
> Nor Walls, nor Pinnacles, nor Houses were.
>> All these for me,
>> For me these Streets and Towers,
> These stately Temples, and these solid Bowers,
>> My Father rear'd:
>> For me I thought they thus appear'd.

>> (142–43)

Even those trifles expressly repudiated elsewhere have a place in the first oneness, as celebrated in "Wonder":

> Proprieties themselvs were mine,
>> And Hedges Ornaments;
> Walls, Boxes, Coffers, and their rich Contents
>> Did not Divide my Joys, but shine.
> Clothes, Ribbans, Jewels, Laces, I esteemd
>> My Joys by others worn;
>> For me they all to wear them seemd
>>> When I was born.

>> (10)

In the genuinely undivided world of infancy, nothing need be rejected; everything that exists participates in the initial oneness. But in Traherne's psychologically astute scheme of things, whatever is most prone to precipitate out of this glorious suspension—beginning with the transitional object—is most damaging to man's good.

II

So while Herrick and other seventeenth-century poets prize shiny baubles precisely because of their affinity to the transitional object, Traherne rejects them as the root of the problem. From this rejection flow major poetic consequences. For the aesthetic of the lyric, as it emerged in the seventeenth century, is, I believe, predicated on the transitional object. That is to say, the elusive features that we intuitively feel define the lyric poem originate in this early psychological space. The most salient feature of the lyric is the peculiar middle ground it charts for itself. Somewhere between "reality" and make-believe, it replicates the fusion of objectivity and subjectivity in the potential space (Schwartz 1975). Similarly, when we articulate the paradox that a poem is a supremely structured thing that is constantly poised against its own contradictory impulse to break out of that structure (McFarland 1973), we uncover the paradox of the transitional object, the original container of the uncontainable impulse. From the tension inherent in this paradox springs the capacity of lyric to recover the lost unity, for a surge of at-oneness is released when structure verges on dissolution. It is a nonformal feeling, a liberation—illusory, perhaps, in that it is always just a step outside the poem itself (Lawler 1979).

Traherne's rejection of objects, then, implies a rejection of lyric. His poems resemble contemporary lyrics, we have said, in their quest for spiritual at-oneness. Indeed the overtness of his quest serves as a gloss to the rest of seventeenth-century poetry: we understand Herrick and Vaughan better for understanding Traherne's doctrine of childhood. But their poetic requires that the poem itself be an artifact; to Traherne this is just one more distracting thing. And if, in a momentary flash, their artifact succeeds in approximating the perfect oneness, so much the worse. To Traherne, at-oneness is eternal, and it occurs only within the divine embrace. Accordingly, his poems, perhaps more openly dedicated to this goal than any ever written, neither approximate nor enact. They only describe.

We may as well own up to what students of Traherne criticism will have grasped at once: this argument updates the old charge that Traherne's poetry suffers from a disjunction between form and content. A. L. Clements cites a long list of readers who take this position (1969:3– 5). Louis Martz, for one, has observed that Traherne's poetry "too often consists primarily in versified statement, assertion, or exclamation" (1964:80). Fighting against the tide, Clements defends Traherne's sense of form by pointing to the care and craftsmanship he lavishes on his poems, their elaborate stanzaic patterns and rhyme schemes. Nonetheless, while we may admire their intricacy, we are never caught up in them. The craftsmanship is nonfunctional; the stanzas and rhymes do not add to our sense of the meaning of the poems. On the contrary, stanzas and rhymes seem arbitrary and interchangeable. This may be part of the poet's intention. He aspires, as far as possible, to an unbodied poetry. Traherne will not proffer a poetry of objects to an unredeemed readership. As aesthetic object, the poem is a trap for the unwary reader. Like a despised gem, its facets will captivate him (Krieger 1976:11ff.). Those poetic strategies, therefore, that conspire to fashion the statement into an object must be rejected. Two devices, in particular, give body to the poem: the corporeality of poetic language (Burckhardt 1968) and what Rosalie Colie has called the resources of kind (1973). They are both conspicuously absent from Traherne.

The project to prevent the poem from becoming a mediating object begins with language. Traherne seeks to unbody words in two ways. He attacks their referential function, breaking the connection between words and things, in order to undermine communication as the proper goal of speech. Simultaneously he resists the countermovement typical of the poetic function—the tendency to exaggerate the physicality of words—for the sake of creating a true medium. As we might expect, the assault on referentiality proceeds from the poet's psychology. Acquisition of speech inaugurates the fall from primal unity: "I *then my Bliss did, when my Silence, break*" (40). The rapture of being alone with the beauties of the world is shattered when human voices intrude. Through the medium of speech, men spread their moral infection:

> My Non-Intelligence of Human Words
> Ten thousand Pleasures unto me affords;
> For while I knew not what they to me said,
> Before their Souls were into mine conveyd,
> Before that Living Vehicle of Wind
> Could breath into me their infected Mind
> Before my Thoughts were levend with theirs, before

> There any Mixture was; the Holy Door,
> Or Gate of Souls was closd, and mine being One
> With in it self to me alone was Known.
>
> (40, 42)

Human discourse, as "Dumnesse" teaches, is tainted from the start. Even the noblest communications, "Administring of Justice, Preaching Peace" (46), for example, are speech acts occasioned by sin. In "Silence" the blessed speech of unfallen man, by contrast, takes praise, not communication, as its goal:

> The first and only Work he had to do,
> Was in himself to feel his Bliss, to view
> His Sacred Treasures, to admire, rejoyce
> Sing Praises with a Sweet and Heavnly voice,
> See, Prize, Give Thanks within, and Love
> Which is the High and only Work, above
> Them all. And this at first was mine.
>
> (46; cf. "Dumnesse," ll. 47–53)

Beyond the question of referentiality, the lines leave us uncertain whether or not Adam's songs of praise and thanksgiving were actually spoken and, for that matter, whether they were made up of words at all.

If we now turn to the poet's own usage as evidence, we are struck by the way in which his words tend to resist definition. They retain a virginal quality, appearing each time as if for the first time. No matter how frequently key terms like "pleasure," "treasure," or "joy" are repeated, they fail to accrue meaning, remaining instead abstract. The outlines of the things to which the words refer fail to emerge. This tendency to de-objectify language finds more open expression in an oddity noticed by Colie: in Traherne's vocabulary "words for qualities normally considered 'bad' become meritorious" (1966:164). That is, even the dictionary definitions of words, the bases of their exchange value, are sometimes subverted. The first stanza of "Desire" enacts this process:

> For giving me Desire,
> An Eager Thirst, a burning Ardent fire,
> A virgin Infant Flame,

A love with which into the World I came,
  An Inward Hidden Heavenly Love,
  Which in my Soul did Work and move,
    And ever ever me Enflame,
With restlesse longing Heavenly Avarice,
  That never could be satisfied,
That did incessantly a Paradice
Unknown suggest, and som thing undescried
  Discern, and bear me to it; be
  Thy Name for ever praisd by me.

(177)

"Desire" and "avarice" are gifts for which the poet praises God. He treats these words as if he were the first one to use them, so oblivious does he seem to their moral and theological connotations. "The Vision" exemplifies more dramatically the way in which Traherne cuts language off from ordinary expectations:

Even Trades them selvs seen in Celestial Light,
  And Cares and Sins and Woes are Bright.

(26)

While the paradox of *felix culpa* may enable us to see the happy side of sin, the potential brightness of cares and woes is more problematic. Finally, I believe, we cannot make sense of the line unless we subtly revise our usual understanding of these terms.

Traherne's famous lists are a related means whereby he frees words from the bondage of meaning. For his catalogues—strings of similar words—overwhelm precision in a flood of synonymity (Grant 1974:172). The reader quickly learns to bracket the list, as in these two typical examples:

The Sight
Is Deep and Infinit;
Ah me! tis all the Glory, Love, Light, Space
Joy Beauty and Varietie
That doth adorn the Godheads Dwelling Place.

(26)

and

>Whose Lov
>A Spring might prov
>Of Endless Glories, Honors, friendships, Pleasures,
>Joys, Praises, Beauties and Celestial Treasures!
>
>(168)

The mind wearies of seeking exact definition, and the multitude of abstract words falls back into the "Sight" and the "Lov" from whence they issued. The words partake of a diffused meaning and have few pretensions of their own. To Traherne, we might venture, even the simple meanings of words, the differences that define them, smack of a fussiness, a particularity, characteristic of the fallen world. Accordingly, he blends his words into lists, allowing meaning to suffuse the larger units.

Beyond disconnecting words from the things to which they presumably refer, Traherne works hard to prevent words from becoming things. In excess of the resources of ordinary language, poetry, in particular, has at its disposal a number of specialized methods for making words, its medium, palpable (Burckhardt 1968; Jakobson 1960:356). Foremost among these is the pun, the word flaunting its physical strength by binding two distinct meanings. Traherne does not entirely shun the pun, but he reserves it for "redeemed" uses. Like things, words may be redeemed, and when they are, the poet rejoices in them. Thus, he says, the parts of his body will become "Organs of thy Praise" (78), permitting the play on "organ" when his speech is engaged in its primary purpose, praise. More decisively, in "An Infant-Ey," the purely spiritual eye shines "in an hevenly Sence," a mild quibble on the two meanings of "sense." When the word reappears later in the poem in a fallen context, it is reduced to a single meaning: "So that my feeble and disabled Sense / Reacht only Near Things with its Influence" (87). The frequent I-eye pun, too, appears in moments of oneness:

>Then was my Soul my only All to me,
>A Living Endless Ey
>
>(20)

and

> . . . the Godheads Dwelling Place
> Tis all that Ey can see.
>
> (26)

For Traherne, perhaps, the pun reproduces union at the level of the word. Oceanic, it seamlessly joins two semantic definitions in one phonetic space.

Symbols and metaphors, on the other hand, are the progeny of the transitional phase. Like puns, they call attention to language as the physical medium of poetry. But instead of enacting oneness, they interpose a mediator between the poet and his dream of union. What oneness they do achieve is partial. In sophisticated versions of the transitional object, they substitute the temporary illusion of fusion for the real thing. The paucity of metaphors in Traherne's poetry has frequently been noted. Clements, however, has made a case for Traherne's use of symbols. He discerns seven clusters of "pneuma-revealing" symbols: eye, sphere, sun, mirror, king, dwelling place, fountain (1969:43–44). For the most part, however, "symbol" would appear to be a misnomer for Traherne's usage. Consider the sixth stanza of "The Vision," a major instance of fountain "symbolism":

> To see the *Fountain* is a Blessed Thing.
> It is to see the King
> Of Glory face to face: But yet the End,
> The Glorious Wondrous End is more;
> And yet the fountain there we Comprehend,
> The Spring we there adore.
> For in the End the Fountain best is Shewn,
> As by Effects the Caus is Known.
>
> (28; cf. 160)

This passage is almost incomprehensible if we read "fountain," here equated with the Divine presence, in the usual symbolic way. Pure waters flow nowhere in these lines. In order to read the stanza correctly, we must abandon our rich associations and understand "fountain" as simply a synonym for "source." We must insist, moreover, that our act of "letting go"—entertaining and then laying symbolism aside—stands emphatically outside the meaning of the poem. Nothing in this or in the previous stanzas warranted a symbolic reading. To add our error to our reading of the poem would, in this case, be unjustified.

The second major resource for shaping the poetic object is genre. Historically conceived, genre is a set of conventions, a more or less rough framework, within which the individual work plays itself out. Traherne, flatly refusing to fashion his poems into objects, largely eschews the historical genres that will give them ready-made shape. In passing, we may note that a poem takes its place in a poetic tradition through its conformity to historical kinds. Our predisposition to believe that we hear the voice of a new man in Traherne's poems, therefore, may owe something to this lack of kinds.

Traherne's practice, however, is more radical than the mere rejection of old forms (many of which were nearing exhaustion anyway) would indicate. He is so determined to keep his poems from assuming fixed shapes that he blocks new genres from emerging. Given the sameness of his poems, this is a feat. As Jonathan Culler has shown, genre functions as a contract between the writer and the reader: new genre, new contract (1975:147). One of the identifying marks of a genre, accordingly, is the characteristic relation it cultivates between writer and reader (Kennedy 1978). Traherne defeats genre by writing poems that bypass the rhetorical situation; they address no one, are spoken into space rather than at an audience. In "Shadows in the Water," the poet takes six stanzas to describe the water people who lie drowned within a puddle. "I call'd them oft, but call'd in vain," he reports, for they would not answer. Finally in stanza eight, he switches to direct address:

> O ye that stand upon the Brink,
> Whom I so near me, throu the Chink,
> With Wonder see: What Faces there,
> Whose Feet, whose Bodies, do ye wear?
>   I my Companions see
>   In You, another Me.
>
> (129)

No sooner does he invoke them as "ye," than it becomes clear to him that they are mirages, "another me." In the final lines of the stanza, therefore, he lapses from the second person into the third:

They seemed Others, but are We;

Our second Selvs those Shadows be.

(129)

In "An Infant-Ey," there is a rare direct exhortation—"O dy! dy unto all that draws thine Ey / From its first Objects . . . see thou carefully / Bid them adieu" (87). The reader, of course, may read this warning as if it were addressed to him or her. A few lines earlier, however, in a parenthetical statement, the speaker prepared for the final exhortation:

(I never can complain

Enough, till I am purged from my Sin

And made an Infant once again.)

(87)

His own sinful self is the primary subject of the speaker's warnings. With some exceptions, then, even when Traherne does explicitly identify an addressee, his identity tends quickly to fall back into the poet's own. This may recall the old charge of "solipsism," although I insist n its artistic motivation. Eliminating both fictive audience and real reader, it blocks the emergence of genre and so prevents the poem from becoming a thing. At the same time, the solipsistic stance is justified by the poet's psychology. By definition, the redeemed speaker is alone in the oceanic world he inherits. The laws of his psychology rule out a fictive addressee. It need hardly be noted that the speaker's singular presence fills the poems so completely that no corner remains from which the author might signal to the reader.

The striking exception is the prefatory piece, "The Author to the Critical Peruser," its very title specifying the rhetorical situation. Here and only here, Traherne speaks as an author trying to explain his poetic method to the reader. We might consider this poem an instance of metagenre, a poem whose purpose is to elucidate its own rhetorical and stylistic conventions. Perhaps it is intended to fill the gap left by the other poems. In any event, it violates practically every rule I have described. It portrays a world crammed full of objects, abounding with the proper names ordinarily absent. It gracefully takes its place in poetic tradition, alluding freely to Herbert's "Jordan (II)" and other poems. Despite its repudiation of curling metaphors, it is filled with figures of speech and figures of thought. Consider a typical passage, condemning those who slight God's work while they magnify their own:

> Their woven Silks and wel-made Suits they prize,
>
> Valu their Gems, but not their useful Eys:
>
> Their precious Hands, their Tongues and Lips divine,
>
> Their polisht Flesh where whitest Lillies join
>
> With blushing Roses and with saphire Veins.
>
> (3)

The last two lines, for the purpose of extolling the human body, adapt the sugary language with which countless poetical lovers have complimented countless fictive mistresses. The borrowing deepens the lines, underlining the poet's passionate admiration for God's creation. "The Person" provides an illuminating contrast:

> The Softer Lillies, and the Roses are
>
> > Less Ornaments to those that Wear
>
> The same, then are the Hands, and Lips, and Eys
>
> Of those who those fals Ornaments so prize.
>
> (76)

The idea is similar—an attack on the vulgar sensibility that prefers external ornament to the beauty of the body—but its expression is now typically extreme. Not just silks and suits and gems but even flowers are taken to be false ornaments. It follows that both the floral metaphor and the literary resonance of the first example must be abandoned. Lilies may not mingle with flesh; instead they separate from the flesh and become the very types of false ornament. "The Person" is typical of Traherne's work, while in several respects "The Author to the Critical Peruser" is the exception that proves the rule. Especially, however, in its direct appeal to the reader and its acceptance of the poetic consequences of this appeal, this poem makes us aware of the poet's general unwillingness to enter into contracts.

Further evidence of the poems' flight from genre lies in their unpredictability. We are often surprised by their endings (Smith 1968). "My

Spirit," one of the most admired pieces, begins with four stanzas on the original condition of the poet's soul. When a fifth, ejaculatory stanza follows, we expect an end, but instead a sixth stanza returns us to the manner of the first four. Stanza seven is another string of effusions, and so we stay on guard:

> O Wondrous Self! O Sphere of Light,
>> O Sphere of Joy most fair;
> O Act, O Power infinit;
> O Subtile, and unbounded Air!
>> O Living Orb of Sight!
> Thou which within me art, yet Me! Thou Ey,
> And Temple of his Whole Infinitie!
> O what a World art Thou! a World within!
>> All Things appear,
>> All Objects are
> Alive in thee! Supersubstancial, Rare,
>> Abov them selvs, and nigh of Kin
>>> To those pure Things we find
>>> In his Great Mind
> Who made the World! tho now Ecclypsd by Sin.
>> There they are Usefull and Divine,
>> Exalted there they ought to Shine.

$$(56)$$

The unexpected adversion to "sin," a new theme, in the antepenultimate line, may lead us to await further development. But belonging to no genre, Traherne's poems are under no compelling internal pressure. They are free to stop or continue. Furthermore, the grand cyclical myth—at-oneness, a fall, and the return—is equally available to every poem. How much of the myth any one poem will use often seems arbitrary. Thus here the poem ends after only the briefest mention of a fall.

Pieces not written in stanzas compound the uncertainty. "Silence," for example, achieves strong closure at lines 63–64:

> In that fair World one only was the Friend,
> One Golden Stream, one Spring, one only End.

$$(48)$$

"Love" closes with just this rhyme, but "Silence" continues. Line 68 and line 70 also seem like possible end points, but the couplets keep coming. Once again a satisfying closure is reached:

> Who tho he nothing said did always reign,
> And in Himself Eternitie contain.
>
> (ll. 79–80)

But the poem extends for six more lines. The actual ending is unusually limp:

> For so my Spirit was an Endless Sphere,
> Like God himself, and Heaven and Earth was there.
>
> (50)

Admittedly, the circularity of these lines makes them plausible as a conclusion, but had the poem continued, perhaps embroidering on the favorite sphere theme, we would not have been altogether surprised.

III

Although parts of the preceding argument may be reminiscent of attacks on the poet that have persisted since his poetry first came to light, I would like to conclude on a positive note. Traherne's work is important because it exposes some of the theoretical underpinnings of seventeenth-century verse. His doctrine of "thoughts" is the essential poetic of the age. The more brilliant poets consummate "thoughts" in their lyrics. They fix their gaze on mundane objects and permit the poetry to "reach to, shine on, quicken Things" (150). From the earthly, they extract the transcendent. The central paradox of Traherne is that he who is most deeply committed to a transfigured world, and who understands its psychological premises best, will not put his poetry to the service of achieving such luminous moments. Instead he analyzes "thoughts," and he praises them effusively:

> The Thought, or Joy Conceived is
> The inward Fabrick of my Standing Bliss.
> It is the Substance of my Mind
> Transformd, and with its Objects lind.

> The Quintessence, Elixar, Spirit, Cream.
> Tis Strange that Things unseen should be Supreme.
>
> (170)

Through thoughts, as the poet describes them most eloquently in "My Spirit," things become one with mind:

> And evry Object in my Soul a Thought
> Begot, or was; I could not tell,
> Whether the Things did there
> Themselvs appear,
> Which in my Spirit *truly* seemd to dwell;
> Or whether my conforming Mind
> Were not alone even all that shind.
>
> (52)

So Traherne recalls the moment of oneness and dissects it, but he will not bring it into being. It is, by definition, a direct apprehension; hence whatever at-oneness is achieved by poetry, the subtlest of mediators, is imperfect. His extremist position brooks no compromise, not even the original compromise reached by the transitional object and reenacted in much seventeenth-century poetry. Art always mediates, he insists in "The Person":

> The Naked Things
> Are most Sublime, and Brightest shew,
> When they alone are seen:
> Mens Hands then Angels Wings
> Are truer Wealth even here below:
> For those but seem.
> Their Worth they then do best reveal,
> When we all Metaphores remove,
> For Metaphores conceal,
> And only Vapours prove.
> They best are Blazond when we see
> The Anatomie,
> Survey the Skin, cut up the Flesh, the Veins

> Unfold: The Glory there remains,
> The Muscles, Fibres, Arteries and Bones
> Are better far then Crowns and precious Stones.
>
> (76)

Traherne forces us to remember what great poetry enables us to forget:
the poem is a medium, always standing between the subject and direct
thoughts. The demands of the poem conflict with the motives of poetry.
Not only do metaphors cloud the vision; form itself obstructs our view.

We need only compare this passage to Herrick's well-loved "The
Lilly in a Christal" to judge the distance between Traherne and his
contemporaries. Herrick puts his trust in good verses and raises the
poet's implicit faith in his art to a credo: mediation enhances. Short of
Herrick's basically secularist position, however, Traherne had the model
of Herbert, who valued poetry even as he exposed its limitations. His
poems, as Stanley Fish has shown, are self-consuming artifacts, en-
shrining the poetic object while simultaneously conspiring in its dissolution (1972:ch. 3). Were there any conflict in Traherne's mind between the mystical claims of "thoughts" and the claims of art, did
poetry exert any hold over him, we might have expected him to resort
to a similar solution. But Traherne owes no allegiance to poetry; he
will not allow his poem to become an artifact, even for the sake of
demonstrating its destruction.

And so Traherne's poetry resists form and avoids the sublime climax, which finally depends on form. Instead he strives for a formless
poetry, taking "thoughts" as his model:

> So Nimble and Volatile, unconfind,
> Illimited, to which no Form's assignd,
> So Changeable, Capacious, Easy, free,
> That wat it self doth pleas a Thought may be.
>
> (176)

Traherne's are poems to which "no Form's assignd." Precisely because
they will not compromise the poet's spiritual vision of the world, they
remain powerless to awaken a corresponding awareness in us. Instead
they are preparative, modestly trusting to powers greater than poetry
to achieve the wished-for oneness.

NOTES

1. All subsequent undocumented page references are from Traherne 1958.
2. See Grant (1974:ch. 6), who traces Traherne's views to the Pre-Nicene Father, Saint Irenaeus.
3. Marcus's book on childhood and seventeenth-century poetry (1978) stresses social history more than psychology.
4. In nondevotional poetry, we find jewels, veils, and other objects, not necessarily from the book of nature, serving similar mediating functions.
5. See, also, a lineal descendant like Anthony Low (1978).
6. In addition to Winnicott (1971), see Marotti (1978) for a useful bibliography.

REFERENCES

Barber, C. L. 1978. "Full to Overflowing." *New York Review of Books* (April 6):32–38.

Burckhardt, S. 1968. "The Poet as Fool and Priest: A Discourse on Method." In *Shakespearean Meanings,* ch. 2. Princeton: Princeton University Press.

Clements, A. L. 1969. *The Mystical Poetry of Thomas Traherne.* Cambridge: Harvard University Press.

Colie, R. 1966. *Paradoxia Epidemica: The Renaissance Tradition of Paradox.* Princeton: Princeton University Press.

———. 1973. *The Resources of Kind: Genre-Theory in the Renaissance.* Edited by B. K. Lewalski. Berkeley: University of California Press.

Culler, J. 1975. *Structuralist Poetics: Structuralism, Linguistics and the Study of Literature.* London: Routledge.

Dauber, A. B. 1976. "Herrick's Foul Epigrams." *Genre* 9:87–102.

Ferenczi, S. 1914. "The Ontogenesis of the Interest in Money." In *Sex in Psycho-Analysis,* pp. 269–79. Translated by E. Jones. New York: Dover.

Fish, S. 1972. *Self-Consuming Artifacts: The Experience of Seventeenth-Century Literature.* Berkeley: University of California Press.

Grant, P. 1974. *The Transformation of Sin: Studies in Donne, Herbert, Vaughan and Traherne.* Montreal: McGill-Queen's University Press.

Jakobson, R. 1960. "Concluding Statement: Linguistics and Poetics." In T. A. Sebeok, ed., *Style in Language,* pp. 350–57. Cambridge: MIT Press.

Kennedy, W. J. 1978. *Rhetorical Norms in Renaissance Literature.* New Haven: Yale University Press.

Kohut, H. 1966. "Forms and Transformations of Narcissism." *Journal of the American Psychoanalytic Association.* 14:243–72.

Krieger, M. 1976. *Theory of Criticism: A Tradition and Its System.* Baltimore: Johns Hopkins University Press.

Lawler, J. G. 1979. *Celestial Pantomime: Poetic Structures of Transcendence.* New Haven: Yale University Press.

Lewalski, B. K. 1979. *Protestant Poetics and the Seventeenth-Century Religious Lyric.* Princeton: Princeton University Press.

Low. A. 1978. *Love's Architecture: Devotional Modes in Seventeenth-Century English Poetry.* New York: New York University Press.

McFarland, T. 1973. "Poetry and the Poem: The Structure of Poetic Content." In F. Brady et al., eds., *Literary Theory and Structure: Essays in Honor of William K. Wimsatt,* pp. 81–113. New Haven: Yale University Press.

Marcus, L. S. 1978. *Childhood and Cultural Despair: A Theme and Variations in Seventeenth-Century Literature.* Pittsburgh: University of Pittsburgh Press.

Marotti, A. F. 1978. "Countertransference, the Communication Process, and the Dimensions of Psychoanalytic Criticism." *Critical Inquiry* 4:471–89.

Martz, L. 1962 (rev. ed.). *The Poetry of Meditation: A Study in English Religious Literature of the Seventeenth Century.* New Haven: Yale University Press.

———. 1964. *The Paradise Within: Studies in Vaughan, Traherne, and Milton.* New Haven: Yale University Press.

Nicolson, M. H. 1960 (rev. ed.). *The Breaking of the Circle: Studies in the Effect of the "New Science" upon Seventeenth-Century Poetry.* New York: Columbia University Press.

Schwartz, M. 1975. "Where is Literature?" *College English* 36:756–65.

Smith, B. H. 1968. *Poetical Closure: A Study of How Poems End.* Chicago: University of Chicago Press.

Traherne, T. 1958. *Centuries, Poems, and Thanksgivings.* Vol. 2. Edited by H. M. Margoliouth. 2 vols. Oxford: Clarendon Press.

———. 1965. *The Poetical Works of Thomas Traherne.* Edited by G. I. Wade. New York: Cooper Square Publishers.

Vaughan, H. 1957. *The Works of Henry Vaughan.* 2d ed. Edited by L. C. Martin. Oxford: Clarendon Press.

Winnicott, D. W. 1971. *Playing and Reality.* New York: Basic Books; London: Tavistock, 1984.

9

Wordsworth and Winnicott in the Area of Play

JOHN TURNER

Wordsworth's "Immortality Ode" and the Play of Paradox

The theme of Wordsworth's great "Ode: Intimations of Immortality from Recollections of Early Childhood" (*P.W.* 4:279–83) was summarized thus by Winnicott (1962): "The idea of eternity comes from the memory traces in each one of us of our infancy before time started" (34). But already here something has been lost. "Heaven lies about us in our infancy!" Thus the poetry. What is missing from the prose summary is Wordsworth's extravagance of expression, which embodies an important extravagance of feeling, a powerful access of wonder and gratitude that bursts through the gates of common sense and leads out into open fields where only the poetry of myth can guide us.

> Not in entire forgetfulness,
> And not in utter nakedness,
> But trailing clouds of glory do we come
> From God, who is our home.
>
> (ll. 62–65)

A note to the poem, added in 1843, seeks to guard the conventional reader against the presupposition that Wordsworth is appealing to the platonic myth of preexistence as to a literal article of his faith. "I think it right," he wrote, "to protest against a conclusion, which has given pain to some good and pious persons, that I meant to inculcate such a belief" (*P.W.* 4:464). But this disavowal removes one problem only to create another, perhaps more troubling still, the problem of the precise status of the images entertained by Wordsworth in his poem; and it is a problem that becomes even more acute as he turns to apostrophize the small child in some quite extraordinary lines:

> Thou, whose exterior semblance doth belie
>   Thy Soul's immensity;
> Thou best Philosopher, who yet dost keep
> Thy heritage, thou Eye among the blind,
> That, deaf and silent, read'st the eternal deep,
> Haunted for ever by the eternal mind,—
>   Mighty Prophet! Seer blest!
>   On whom those truths do rest,
> Which we are toiling all our lives to find.
> In darkness lost, the darkness of the grave;
> Thou, over whom thy Immortality
> Broods like the Day, a Master o'er a Slave,
> A Presence which is not to be put by;
> Thou little Child . . .
>
>   (ll. 109–22)

Even for Coleridge, Wordsworth's most sympathetic reader, these lines were too much. They were "*mental* bombast," containing "thoughts and images too great for the subject"—a fault that Coleridge attributed, it seems, to the excessive maleness of Wordsworth's genius, "the awkwardness and strength of Hercules with the distaff of Omphale" (1965:258). Coleridge's criticisms are sharp:

Now here, not to stop at the daring spirit of metaphor which connects the epithets "deaf and silent" with the apostrophized eye: or (if we are to refer it to the preceding word *philosopher*) the faulty and equivocal syntax of the passage; and without examining the propriety of making a "master *brood* o'er a slave," or the day brood at all; we will merely ask, what does all this mean? In what sense is a child of that age a philosopher? In what sense does he read "the eternal deep"? In what sense is he declared to be "for ever haunted" by the Supreme Being? or so inspired as to deserve the splendid titles of a mighty prophet, a blessed seer? By reflection? by knowledge? by conscious intuition? or by any form or modification of consciousness? These would be tidings indeed. (260)

It is the *paradoxicalness* of Wordsworth's writing at which Coleridge balks, as his conclusion makes clear:

> Thus it is with splendid paradoxes in general. If the words are taken in the common sense, they convey an absurdity; and if, in contempt of dictionaries and custom, they are so interpreted as to avoid the absurdity, the meaning dwindles into some bald truism. Thus you must at once understand the words contrary to their common import, in order to arrive at any sense; and according to their common import, if you are to receive from them any feeling of sublimity or admiration. (262)

To Coleridge, then, for reasons to which I shall return, Wordsworth's paradoxes were meretricious, empty of substance. But to me it is Coleridge's criticism that is empty beside the substantial poetry of the "Ode"; and so here is the first half of my subject, to describe the necessity for paradox to the kind of adventure upon which Wordsworth was embarked in the "Immortality Ode," to explore his need for a mythical apparatus that defies those categories of truths-to-be-believed or falsehoods-to-be-disbelieved into which Coleridge would confine it. We may recall, as we start, Keats's well-known definition of the great poet's characteristic gift: "I mean *Negative Capability,* that is when man is capable of being in uncertainties, Mysteries, doubts, without any irritable reaching after fact and reason"—a definition to which he added: "Coleridge, for instance, would let go by a fine isolated verisimilitude caught from the Penetralium of mystery, from being incapable of remaining Content with half knowledge" (1954:53).

From its epigraph onward, the "Immortality Ode" announces itself as paradoxical in manner. "The Child is father of the Man," we read, and the line might stand as an emblem of that great shift in consciousness which was to make possible a century later the development of psychoanalysis. A simple prose translation of Wordsworth's line might read, the quality of an adult life depends upon the quality of the child's life before it; and this is a translation that would encourage us to develop a linear causal understanding of the present in relation to the past, even to draw up predictive schemata to comprehend the future. It would encourage us, that is to say, to develop a science of the processes of human psychological development. Such a reading irons out the wrinkles of the paradox, as Stephen Prickett considers it proper to do: for "when Wordsworth writes 'The child is father of the man' he is (logically) only playing. He is using the shock-effect of the paradox to say something that is not really a paradox at all" (1970:129). The child is the precursor rather than the father of the man, we should say. Yet such a reading misses something too; for in speaking of the child as *father* of the man, Wordsworth *has* got something logically impossible into the meaning of his line, so that an apparently simple statement assumes complexities that transgress the boundaries of common sense and scientific method alike. What is more, this same paradoxicalness of manner, highlighted by the contrasting naturalism of stanza 7, shapes the whole central section of the poem from stanza 5 to stanza 8. What then was Wordsworth up to?

Let us go back to the first section of the poem (stanzas 1–4) with its tones of stately plangent regret for the lost habits of childhood perception.

> There was a time when meadow, grove, and stream.
> The earth, and every common sight,
>   To me did seem
>   Apparelled in celestial light,
> The glory and the freshness of a dream.
> It is not now as it hath been of yore;—
>   Turn wheresoe'er I may,
>   By night or day,
> The things which I have seen I now can see no more.
>
>   The Rainbow comes and goes,
>   And lovely is the Rose,
>   The Moon doth with delight
> Look round her when the heavens are bare;
>   Waters on a starry night
>   Are beautiful and fair;
>   The sunshine is a glorious birth;
>   But yet I know, where'er I go,
> That there hath past away a glory from the earth.
>
>   (ll. 1–18)

These two stanzas were written in the spring of 1802 when Wordsworth was almost thirty-two, together with the two following stanzas
where he vainly tried to cheer himself up with rhetoric—rhetoric being
here, as Yeats defined it, "the will trying to do the work of the imagination" (1903:215). But it is from their nostalgia that the poetry of
these opening stanzas derives, a nostalgia that belongs (in Winnicott's
words, from *Playing and Reality*) to "the precarious hold that a person
may have on the inner representation of a lost object" (1971:27). Here
the inner representation that concerns us is that of the poet's own
childhood self.

At this point the basis of an important distinction between Wordsworth and Coleridge suggests itself; for in writing the "Immortality
Ode," Wordsworth is reworking an earlier poem by Coleridge, called
"The Mad Monk," a Gothic ode in which a remorseful murderer
laments the killing of the woman he loved:

> "There was a time when earth, and sea, and skies,
>
>> The bright green vale, and forest's dark recess,
>
> With all things, lay before mine eyes
>
>> In steady loveliness:
>
> But now I feel, on earth's uneasy scene,
>
>> Such sorrows as will never cease;—
>
>> I only ask for peace;
>
> If I must live to know that such a time has been!"
>
> (ll. 9–16)

The poem is typical Coleridge, repeating the better-known pattern of
The Rime of the Ancient Mariner: each man must kill the thing he
loves, must (in Othello's phrase) put out the light, and then put out the
light. Whereas Wordsworth could, with difficulty, hold on to the inner
representation of a lost good object, the difficulty for Coleridge was
too great. Nostalgia for childhood in him turned out to be dead loss.
At best he could take vicarious pleasure in the continuities of the lives
of other people—such is the polarizing logic of depression that we find
in poems like "Frost at Midnight" or "Dejection: An Ode"—but at
worst nostalgia darkened into remorse and guilt, and fantasies of having killed the loved object.

The nostalgia of the "Immortality Ode," however, will prove itself
in time to be a creative nostalgia. Even in its first four stanzas, there is
much more going on than simple statement of regret for the glory that
has passed from the earth; for the lines are alert with a muted, unag-

gressive questioning into the paradoxical status of that glory. Wordsworth's theme, here as so often, is disillusion, the loss of that light that
bathes—or appears to bathe—the objects of the real world. The term
glory itself indicates the paradoxes with which he is grappling: for
while on the one hand it denotes "the splendour and bliss of heaven"
(OED), on the other hand it also denotes the halo that surrounds the
head of one's own gigantic shadow, cast by a low sun upon an opposing bank of clouds—the so-called Brocken-specter, of whose importance to Coleridge and Wordsworth Stephen Prickett has written so
well. Is the light the really real, the divine? Or is it merely illusion, a
kind of delusive overhead projection? Or is it somehow both of these
things together? The same questions gather around the other words
used by Wordsworth, alongside light and glory, to suggest the ambiguous status of the seeing that he has lost; for he speaks also of a *dream,*
or of a *visionary gleam,* weaving all these words together in a questioning that shows a mind active upon its own nostalgia but unable as yet
to find a fixed point from which to understand and accept it.

Here, irresolute at the end of the first four stanzas, the "Ode" stuck
for two years. It was not until 1804 that Wordsworth found himself
suddenly able both to develop his poem and to work through his
nostalgia, empowered by that extraordinary paradoxical vision of the
infant-philosopher in heaven upon the living-room floor. For with the
fifth stanza, the poem intensifies, its paradoxes deepen: the way forward is the way back. The platonic myth of preexistence enables
Wordsworth to do more than contemplate his own past self with the
self-envy of nostalgia; it enables him in gratitude to relive something of
its power as it survives within his adult consciousness, and thus to find
in his own memory a partial answer to that hanging question of two
years ago, "Where is it now, the glory and the dream?" (l. 57).

We may now begin to define the nature of Wordsworth's paradoxes
in the "Immortality Ode." Their form is that which Rosalie Colie calls,
in her book *Paradoxia Epidemica,* the "epistemological paradox, in
which the mind, by its own operation, attempts to say something about
its operation" (1966:6). Wordsworth's concern is with our sense of the
self in its relationship to time, as vouchsafed to us by our perception of
the objects of the real world; and the function of his paradoxes is to
explore the changes that befall that sense of the self, as we pass from
infancy through childhood into adulthood and old age. Traherne, writing in the mid-seventeenth century, had already noted the paradoxical
nature of these changes in the contemplation of his own childhood:
"All Time was Eternity, and a Perpetual Sabbath. Is it not Strange, that

an Infant should be Heir of the World, and see those Mysteries which the Books of the Learned never unfold?" (1958:111). But that which is strange and paradoxical, of course, lies not in the world but in our common understanding of it; and it is this common understanding that paradox would have us revalue. For, as Colie observes,

> a paradox generates the self-referential activity. Operating at the limits of discourse, redirecting thoughtful attention to the faulty or limited structures of thought, paradoxes play back and forth across terminal and categorical boundaries—that is, they play with human understanding, that most serious of all human activities. (1966:7)

The latency of those first four questioning stanzas of the "Ode" has yielded up a paradox both to sharpen the categorical boundary-line between infant and mature perception and also to initiate play across that boundary-line. We are made aware of a disjunction (namely, that the child may see and not know that he sees, that the adult may know what he has seen but may no longer see it) and also of a conjunction (namely, that these two states coexist separately within the adult mind, where they may either remain dissociated or interact creatively). Maybe behind the poem there lies a traditional religious sense of the human condition as necessarily paradoxical and of God as the ultimate *concordia discors*. For now we see through a glass, darkly; but then face to face. . . . Yet Wordsworth's emphasis falls not upon the reconciliations of theology but upon those paradoxes that characterize the development of human self-consciousness in time. Lionel Trilling, reading the poem as the record of a difficult struggle toward integration, seems to me in effect to ignore its paradoxes altogether:

> Inevitably we resist change and turn back with passionate nostalgia to the stage we are leaving. Still, we fulfil ourselves by choosing what is painful and difficult and necessary, and we develop by moving toward death. In short, organic development is a hard paradox. (1970:154)

But he means by this no more than that organic development is hard. The liberal humanist has lost touch with the true paradoxes of the seventeenth-century religious tradition, which Wordsworth was imitating—paradoxes that explore genuine contradictions in our common understanding of the Mysteries of the world. The function of paradox in the "Immortality Ode" is precisely to instigate a revaluation of those values upon which a liberal civilization rests.

The Child is father of the Man: there are three aspects to this paradox that concern me here. First, if the self is unitary, it is also from the very beginning multiple; and thus we must revalue our notion of what, in the inadequacies of everyday language, we call the individual. The child is in more than one way his own father; and as in his play he cons part after part (see stanza 7), no doubt including that of the father whose eyes are upon him, he shows himself from the first to be an inextricable tangle of innate potentialities and acquired characteristics, a bundle of many selves revealed only to himself and others through the relationships in which he is involved. Second, if the child's seeing is primitive, it is also primary; and thus we must revalue our notion of educational progress in the knowledge of the outside world. For we need a language not only of knowledge but of wisdom, counterbalancing mastery with wonder. Third, if self-understanding entails the grasp of those linear causalities that bind the present to the past, it also entails the capacity to relive the past as it survives in the present, to keep alive the child in the adult, together with their very different experiences of time. We need a language not only for self-knowledge but for what we might call grace, not only to understand the causal chains that bind the present to the past but also to facilitate the new potentialities of the future. Self, knowledge, and self-knowledge: the ordinary categories of our language, embodying truly our liberal utilitarian civilization, are inadequate to the complex relational structures that make up the self and to its multiple ways of perceiving both the world and itself. Wordsworth's use of paradox and myth, therefore, is designed to disturb those old familiar categories and facilitate the release of new mental power.

Power regenerated out of paradox: Wordsworth's own note to the poem proves this to have been his chief concern in the central section of the "Immortality Ode."

> Archimedes said that he could move the world if he had a point whereon to rest his machine. Who has not felt the same aspirations as regards the world of his own mind? Having to wield some of its elements when I was impelled to write this Poem on the "Immortality of the Soul," I took hold of the notion of preexistence as having sufficient foundation in humanity for authorizing me to make for my purpose the best use of it I could as a Poet. (*P.W.* 4:464)

By means of this paradoxical myth of preexistence, Wordsworth was enabled once more to lay firm hold upon the inner representation of that lost good object that was his own childhood; and so it is that the poem is freed to move toward the integration of its conclusion (stanzas 9 to 11), where the pain of nostalgia is accepted and the value of loss is discovered in the gain of an adult faith and wisdom.

> What though the radiance which was once so bright
> Be now for ever taken from my sight,
> Though nothing can bring back the hour
> Of splendour in the grass, of glory in the flower;
>   We will grieve not, rather find
>   Strength in what remains behind;
>   In the primal sympathy
>   Which having been must ever be;
>   In the soothing thoughts that spring
>   Out of human suffering;
>   In the faith that looks through death,
> In years that bring the philosophic mind.
>
> (ll. 176–87)

Yet there is something more than the integration of the self within time here, something more than the memory binding past, present, and future together. There is the copresence of the child's vision still active within the adult.

> Hence in a season of calm weather
> Though inland far we be,
> Our Souls have sight of that immortal sea
> Which brought us hither,
> Can in a moment travel thither,
> And see the Children sport upon the shore,
> And hear the mighty waters rolling evermore.
>
> (ll. 162–68)

This is the climax to the rich vein of paradoxical writing that has run right through the middle of the poem, and it recapitulates what the poem has already displayed: namely, that the man can still live the child's vision, transgressing the categories of time and space and thereby authenticating his perception and securing his wisdom against the

dreariness of endless self-repetition. The literary form of paradox reenacts for the reader the paradoxical nature of the poet's experience; it
initiates us into mystery, where new power may flow from the collision
of old categories. It leads us beyond nostalgia toward the poem's last
line and its unspecified "thoughts that do often lie too deep for tears"—
an openness in conclusion which reminds us that the creativity of the
thinking process is more important than the thoughts themselves, and
that our hope depends upon that continuing intercourse between the
articulate and the inarticulate, the known and the ineffable, which it is
particularly the business of paradox to stimulate.

Wordsworth and Paradox: The Cultural Context

I should like now to place the "Immortality Ode" within the wider
context of Wordsworth's own life and the cultural history of his time;
and I shall do this by means of a brief biography of his formative years,
which will then lead us back to reconsider his discovery of the use of
paradox, in the two senses of that word that concern me here: namely
(1) "a statement or tenet contrary to received opinion or belief," and
(2) "a statement seemingly self-contradictory or absurd, though possibly well-founded or essentially true" (OED).

Wordsworth was born in Cockermouth in 1770, the second son to
the law-agent of Lord Lonsdale, and thus began life among the privileges of the provincial professional classes. He was not, however, an
easy child, being possessed—as Mary Moorman notes, quoting his own
words—of "a stiff, moody and violent temper" (1957:13). The best
picture we have of him as a boy is the one he wrote himself in Home at
Grasmere:

> While yet an innocent little-one, a heart
> That doubtless wanted not its tender moods,
> I breathed (for this I better recollect)
> Among wild appetites and blind desires,
> Motions of savage instinct, my delight
> And exaltation. Nothing at that time
> So welcome, no temptation half so dear
> As that which [urged] me to a daring feat.
> Deep pools, tall trees, black chasms, and dizzy crags—
> I loved to look in them, to stand and read

> Their looks forbidding, read and disobey,
>
> Sometimes in act, and evermore in thought.

(ll. 910–21)

The perspective here, of course, is that of the adult remaking his past in the light of the present; and we may do no more than wonder how much of Wordsworth's unruliness predates or postdates the loss of his parents—his much-lamented mother when he was eight, and his rarely mentioned father (apparently a distant man immersed in his work), when he was thirteen. What is certain, however, is that Wordsworth's childhood rebelliousness was always sensed by him to be important to his vocation as a poet—and hence his cherishing of it here in *Home at Grasmere*, even as he tried to discipline it to the purposes of his revolutionary new poetic. David Ellis, in his book *Wordsworth, Freud and the Spots of Time*, guesses that Wordsworth, like so many sons in that patriarchal society, was never given the opportunity satisfactorily to work out his anger against his father (1985:17–34); and it may also be true that his future poetic decline was not unconnected with his inability to retain firm hold upon that unintegrated anger and the difficulties in which it had involved him. Be that as it may, the young orphan was then brought up by relatives, who had him educated at boarding-school in Hawkshead and at St. John's College, Cambridge, where he graduated early in 1791, having refused to sit the examination that would have won him a fellowship.

In short, in 1790 Wordsworth became what we should call today a dropout, under pressure from relatives to settle down in a career, but determined himself to be a poet and to make his own way in the world. He should have been such a man as Edmund Bertram in *Mansfield Park*; but instead he became a political radical who somehow resisted assimilation into those careers that bound the sons of professional people, Tory and Whig alike, into the political hegemony of eighteenth-century England—the church, the armed services, the law, education. After some time obscurely spent in London, he went to France to learn the language, apparently to equip himself to tutor a nobleman's son but perhaps more truly to avoid the ordination that his uncles were forcing upon him; and once in France he allied himself with the Girondin revolutionary cause and, in his newfound freedom, had an affair with a French girl, Annette Vallon, by whom he had an illegitimate daughter. He was compelled to return to England at the end of 1792 when his funds were cut off and, once there, he found himself irretrievably separated from France and Annette alike by the British declaration of war upon the revolutionary armies of France early in 1793. Here began what was to prove the most critical period of Wordsworth's life, a period in which he met the test that seems, to me at least, to have lain in waiting for him all his life—a test already anticipated in the loss of his parents and to be repeated many times during his life to come, most notably in the drowning of his brother John in 1805 and the deaths of two of his own children in 1812, but also in many other small moments of disappointment or disillusion, like those recorded in "Tintern Abbey" or the "Immortality Ode."

The test that Wordsworth experienced in 1793–94 is one that I should like to call the test by betrayal of central trust. Literary scholarship has made much of its discovery of the Annette Vallon affair, but my concern here is not with the unconscious or the concealed but with Wordsworth's freely given account of the origin of his sense of betrayal in the declaration of war by his own country upon the revolutionary armies of France. Here he was to find the great theme of his future poetry: hope betrayed in the very moment of its reaching out to extend its dearest relationships. Lest a young man's political hopes for the growth of the Liberty Tree appear in retrospect naive, let us remember their roots in the cultural life of his time—in religious hopes of universal brotherhood and radical hopes of the popular unity that would succeed upon the dissolution of the monarchy and aristocracy. Wordsworth's faith was in what Tom Paine called "the enlarging orb of reason, and the luminous revolutions of America and France" (1968:113): today America and France, tomorrow all the ancient monarchies of Europe. It was the light of this faith that was extinguished by the British declaration of war against France.

> All else was progress on the self-same path
> On which with a diversity of pace
> I had been travelling; this a stride at once
> Into another region.
>
> (*Prelude* 10.239–42)

The moment of disillusion, of transition from innocence to experience, was sharp. The world was not as he had thought, and the shock of that discovery caused "a conflict of sensations without name" (*Prelude* 10.266) in which he discovered that he too was not as he had thought. The painfulness of this betrayal, and the profound revaluations that accompanied Wordsworth's subsequent recovery, were to have momentous consequences for that development in the history of ideas that we now call Romanticism.

At the heart of Romanticism is a new perception of the importance of the culture of subjectivity; and commonly this is presented in literary discussion, drawing upon the essentially religious language of Coleridge, as the discovery—or alternatively as the rediscovery—of the imagination. Coleridge came to his conclusions as the result of a prolonged meditative process that had begun with his hearing Wordsworth's long poem *Salisbury Plain,* written out of the disillusion of 1793–94. Before that, Wordsworth's poetry had been descriptive in manner, bound by eighteenth-century mimetic doctrine; it had aimed at political change through the skillful use of rhetorical device. But despite the revolutions of America and France, despite the poet's exhortations, the rest of the world had remained unmoved; and in order fully to measure its abiding injustice, Wordsworth in *Salisbury Plain* had remade it in the image of his own horror—in the image, in fact, of the human sacrifice upon which the barbaric civilization associated with Druid Stonehenge had supposedly depended. It was in this capacity to remake the world, not only to measure its horror but also to draw out its potential beauty, that Coleridge and Wordsworth were to discover that power to which they gave the name of *imagination.* The revolutionary power to transform the world in idea was found among the ruins of the revolutionary program to transform it in fact.

But to celebrate the creativity of imagination, however appropriate it may be to Coleridge, is certainly inadequate to Wordsworth; for Wordsworth constantly keeps before our mind the formative power of those images that feed or famish imagination. Coleridge, exiled by dejection from the writing of poetry, turned for relief to philosophy, and his interest as a philosopher lay in the *faculty* of imagination; but Wordsworth's as a poet lay in its *relationships*—relationships, as it happened, chiefly with the nourishing images of the "natural" world, which he believed divine, rather than with the "artificial" works of man. The discovery of imagination, that is, was complemented by the discovery of nature, not simply as the creation of God but also as the creation of that whole process whereby the child's love for its mother is decathected and spread over the face of the world until its objects come to safeguard the child's sense of the goodness of life. In the poetry of 1798–99, most remarkably in the two-part *Prelude,* we find a fully developed version of what today we should call object relations psychology. Imagination *and* object relations: we remake the world but it is the world that we remake. It was in this relational interplay between mind and nature that Wordsworth explored the culture of subjectivity—an insight won with difficulty through a profound self-analysis of the processes of his own recovery from that bitter disillusion of 1793. "Nature never did betray / The heart that loved her," he was to write later in "Tintern Abbey" (*P.W.* 2:262); at each crisis of his life during his great years as a poet (1797–1807), the fear of betrayal was followed by deepening relationship. It was not a question of cheering himself up but of discovering that, all the while, unknown to himself, faith had been kept; and the *work* of the poetry was thus to secure that faith by laying firm hold upon those images that safeguarded his own sense of goodness and power and protected his imagination against deviance and sterility.

We may now begin to grasp the full force of Wordsworth's paradoxicalness and place such poetry as the "Immortality Ode" in its contemporary polemic. In its difficult attempt to sustain a relational understanding of self and other, the poetry is deliberately subversive of all those habits of scientific perception and reasoning which had come to characterize British cultural life since the middle of the seventeenth century. A typical eighteenth-century poem, Dr. Johnson's *The Vanity of Human Wishes*, began "Let observation with extensive view, / Survey mankind, from China to Peru": and in so doing, it embodied the common belief that observation benefits by separation from the idiosyncratic habits of the individual observer. Wordsworth, however, saw the need to enrich this impoverished view of human experience, and a sentence from the Preface to *Lyrical Ballads* declares a faith to which all the other Romantic poets who followed him would also have subscribed: "Poetry is the breath and finer spirit of all knowledge; it is the impassioned expression which is in the countenance of all Science" (*Prose* 1:141). Science, then, was to be complemented by Poetry—especially perhaps in political debate, since the rationalism characteristic of scientific method had flourished among those late-eighteenth-century radicals with whom Wordsworth had once made joint cause. Paine, for instance, in *Rights of Man* had celebrated the power of "the enlarging orb of reason" to disperse the mists cast by Burke's "paradoxical rhapsodies" (1968:96) in the *Reflections on the Revolution in France*. But reason had failed, and radicalism needed to be resited. A new relational understanding must be won in all the significant areas of our experience: in perception, where the object is mixed with its subjective, symbolic meaning; in psychology, where reason is mixed with the passionate images out of which it grows; in morality, where the question of duty is inseparable from the question of authenticity in its performance; and also in religion, where similarly the letter of dogma is rendered substantial only by the inner spirit of devotion. Despite the continuing universalism and the increasingly orthodox religious cast of his thinking, Wordsworth's emphasis upon the relational nevertheless represents a major cultural shift in the direction of a recognition of the essentially symbolic nature of thought; and so we may consider his poetry to be paradoxical in the one sense, that it worked "against received opinion or belief." Indeed, he carried through his personal revolutionary program, and the nature of poetry was changed—changed from an imitation of the outside world to a remaking of it, no longer aiming didactically at the reason to reform the world but attempting instead something sui generis, the reordering of time and space within time and space so as to furnish the sensibility with sane imagery and thus to enable it to evolve new and better habits of perception, feeling, and thought.

But Wordsworth's poetry was paradoxical in the other sense too, that it often dealt with matters "seemingly self-contradictory or absurd, though possibly well-founded or essentially true." What is interesting here is the tangential relationship between paradox and truth, and the power that is generated at the moment of their contact. The characteristic sentence structures of the eighteenth century are those of the epigram (as in Dr. Johnson's remark in chapter 26 of *Rasselas* that "Marriage has many pains, but celibacy has no pleasures") or the carefully balanced period, as for example that "he was neither x nor y but z" where z is a term that asserts the golden mean, the middle way between extremes (as in Pope's couplet from the end of the *Epistle to Dr Arbuthnot:* "Not proud, nor servile; Be one Poet's praise, / That, if he pleas'd, he pleas'd by manly ways"). Thus, when we come to sentences like the following of Blake's from *The Marriage of Heaven and Hell,* we sense the desire to subvert both epigram and period by paradox: "The tygers of wrath are wiser than the horses of instruction," or "Prudence is a rich ugly old maid courted by Incapacity," or "Those who restrain desire, do so because theirs is weak enough to be restrained." Such statements, though neither true nor false in themselves, nevertheless possess the cutting edge of truth; they are what Coleridge liked to call *truth-powers,* enabling the mind to sever the authentic from the inauthentic in its own experience at a single blow. Now Wordsworth does not explore paradox as aggressively as Blake; and yet, from 1798 onward, there is a paradoxical side to his work which surfaces, as we have seen, in the "Immortality Ode" and which

is repeatedly expressed in the unresolved juxtaposition of human opposites—old and young, educated and uneducated, sick and well, normal and abnormal—so that new meanings may be shaken free by their
collision. Some sparks may light on tinder. We are, that is to say, in the
presence of a newly *open* poetry, challenging received wisdom but
characteristically modern in its inability to image the future. Its great
theme—in the words of the aptly entitled *Prelude*—is with "something
evermore about to be" (6:542), with *hopefulness* for the future that is
grounded in the continuing life of the child within the adult. The Child
is father of the Man: Wordsworth's concern is not merely with truth
but also with power, not merely with self-knowledge and self-com-
mand but also with growth—with that imagery for growth whose
paradoxical, unpredictable life within the adult may either confirm or
overturn him in his chosen course of life. It is the peculiar business of
poetry to occupy itself with that imagery and its purification. "If from
the public way you turn your steps," begins one of Wordsworth's most
famous poems "Michael" (*P.W.* 2:80): and it is to poetry that he
would have us turn—to poetry as a place apart, a place engaged, a
place (if I may say so at last) of play. And with this I turn to the second
half of my subject.

Winnicott and the Play of Paradox

Here are some words from the introduction to Winnicott's last book,
Playing and Reality:

> I am drawing attention to the *paradox* involved in the use by the
> infant of what I have called the transitional object. My contribution
> is to ask for a paradox to be accepted and tolerated and respected,
> and for it not to be resolved. By flight to split-off intellectual func-
> tioning it is possible to resolve the paradox, but the price of this is
> the loss of the value of the paradox itself.
>
> This paradox, once accepted and tolerated, has value for every
> human individual who is not only alive and living in this world but
> is also capable of being infinitely enriched by exploitation of the
> cultural link with the past and with the future. (1971:xii)

The reader approaching *Playing and Reality* for the first time has his
appetite whetted by this early mention of paradox; but then he has to
wait for the tantalizing space of a hundred pages to discover what it is.
The experience of not-knowing-at-once is thus important to the nature
of the book; for Winnicott, aware that there are times when (in Words-

worth's words) "we murder to dissect" (*P.W.* 4:57), has structured his book in such a way as to frustrate what he calls split-off intellectual functioning. The book teases us with paradox and with paradox deferred; and it is this feature of Winnicott's *style* upon which, as a student of literature, I want to concentrate here—something that I feel emboldened to do since I have heard a number of analysts and lay-readers alike express in conversation a certain distaste for it. But *le style, c'est l'homme;* it is the mark of the individual, the observer's face materializing out of the one-way mirror of scientific observation. Especially do we need to make this point in the case of such a writer as Winnicott where, looking back over a career of forty years' writing, we can see the gradual evolution of a style that is the fit medium of the thought to be expressed. I have in mind here some words that De Quincey reported of Wordsworth:

> it is in the highest degree unphilosophic to call language or diction "the *dress* of thoughts." And what was it then that he would substitute? Why this: he would call it "the *incarnation* of thoughts." Never in one word was so profound a truth conveyed. (1890:230)

I take it too that, in drawing attention to the nature of Winnicott's prose as a fit subject of inquiry, I can do a little toward what Masud Khan recommended in his introduction to *Holding and Interpretation* (Winnicott 1986), comparing that book with an earlier paper of 1954 upon the same subject: "It is instructive to compare these accounts in their style, character and content" (1). We are witnessing a writer importantly coming into his own; and the question of style is, where Masud Khan puts it, in the place of *first* importance.

To overleap those hundred pages and come straight to the point: the paradox upon which *Playing and Reality* is styled is that "the baby creates the object, but the object was there waiting to be created and to become a cathected object" (1971:104). The nature of the child's play demands that we never challenge it with that most demoralizing of questions: "did you create that or did you find it?" I am reminded that Wordsworth (*P.W.* 5:4–5) described the mysterious wedding of the human mind to the visible universe as the "great consummation" to which all his poetry was to be the "spousal verse"; his sense of the relational, that is, drew him to what might be created *between* subject and object, an area for which he had no language and which he sought therefore to articulate by means of metaphor such as this of the marriage. Thus we might describe the challenge of which Winnicott speaks, and from which the child is to be protected, as one that effects a divorce between the mind and the world. It insists that the self identify itself in either the subjective world of fantasying or the objective world of fact, and it denies what might be created between them.

Of course, we might readily reduce Winnicott's paradox to prose summary, as we did Wordsworth's in the "Immortality Ode." We might for instance say, "In the interplay between subject and object, there is an area of illusion which it is important for the well-being of each infant, as well as of each adult, to respect." But what is it that is lost here? I should like to answer that question personally, as befits the discussion of a style like Winnicott's, from my own experience of reading *Playing and Reality* for the first time; for I well remember the mixture of irritation and curiosity with which I read the introduction to that book. Why should something evidently so well-written deliberately withhold its true subject-matter? I had come in a hurry to find a readily digestible theory of play, and what I found, page by page and chapter by chapter, was a book whose structure insisted that the way to truth lay in a winding stair. There was no short cut, no easy drop at the summit; and furthermore the entrance was protected by that sphinxlike figure of a paradox. The method, I need not add, is thoroughly typical of Winnicott; his essay "The Capacity to Be Alone," for instance, announces on its second page that "the basis of the capacity to be alone is a paradox; it is the experience of being alone while someone else is present" (1958:30). Such formulations as these are not to be explained away as tricks of style, or as the caprices of a psychoanalytic *enfant terrible;* for style is not to be separated from content, paradox is not to be disarmed by prose summary. The importance of paradox for Winnicott is that it safeguards that in-between space where the mind finds itself wedded to the world—that space which he calls, evoking the full paradoxical range of meanings in the word, the space of *illusion*—and that it does so by being itself a creature of that space, in ways that I shall now explore.

In the first place, simply enough, paradox stimulates curiosity in the reader—and curiosity, of course, originating in childhood, is one of the more important ways that subjectivity mixes itself with the objective world and creates the sense of the worthwhileness of life. In the second place, paradox insists upon the importance of difficulty in reaching understanding; and I am reminded here of Burke's attacks upon the simplicity so much admired by radicals like Paine. For the reader and writer alike, paradox gives poetic depth to experience, reminding us of the value of Keats's "uncertainties, Mysteries, doubts" and showing that there is more to acquaintance with the world than the accumulation of data about it: our knowledge can never match our experience. In the third place, as we have seen, the business of paradox is with those insights that confound the normal categories of our thought and the normal structures of our language. The meaning of "The Capacity to Be Alone" is not simply that loneliness is the state of having lost the present sense of things absent but that neither the objective category "solitude" nor the subjective category "loneliness" can, in their common usage, do justice to the relational nature of our experience as it has developed through time. Paradox, that is, reminds us that understanding is not just a matter of isolating fact but also of establishing connection, new and often difficult connection. Harold Searles has written of metaphors that "each of them kindles in us, momentarily a dim memory of the time when we lost the outer world—when we first realized that the outer world *is* outside, and we are unbridgeably apart from it, and alone" (1962:583). But this is too bleak, too elegiac: paradox and metaphor, like poetry itself and countless other absorbing cultural activities, re-create something of the time *before* we lost the outer world, of that experience of being alone while someone else is present that Winnicott has described so well, and *by so doing* they serve to extend our acquaintance. We do not ask the maker of a paradox or a metaphor "did you create that or did you find it?"; for the rules of the game, in its in-between play-area, inhibit such split-off intellectual functioning. Winnicott's paradoxes, if we accept and tolerate and respect them, work to keep alive the child within us, curious in the face of an inexhaustibly curious world; or, to put it perhaps more positively, in a phrase from Coleridge's *Biographia Literaria,* they work "to carry on the feelings of childhood into the powers of manhood" (1965:49).

Poetry is "the impassioned expression which is in the countenance of all Science": what I am trying to describe is the gradual materialization within Winnicott's prose of a poetic spirit that animates the traditions of his scientific inquiry. Take, for instance, these two sentences from *Playing and Reality,* where Winnicott is struggling against Lacan to present the infant's relationship with reality in terms of enablement rather than entrapment: "What does the baby see when he or she looks at the mother's face? I am suggesting that, ordinarily, what the baby sees is himself or herself" (131). Or take these three sentences from *The Child, The Family and the Outside World: "The thief is not looking for the object that he takes. He is looking for a person. He is looking for his own mother, only he does not know this"* (1964:163).

Or the most famous example of all, the sudden outburst at the Psychoanalytic Society, as related by Peter Fuller among others: "There is no such thing as a baby" (1983:237). Even the sentence with which I began has about it the poetry of paradox in response to Wordsworth's paradoxes in the "Immortality Ode": "The idea of eternity comes from the memory traces in each one of us of our infancy *before time started*" (italics added).

Each of these paradoxes surprises us into new relational thought by shocking the familiar categories of our understanding, and in each case their poetry ensures that the seat of this new thinking is not the intellect but the sympathetic imagination. The moment of understanding thus becomes initiation, initiation into the realities of a human community where what we misleadingly call the self is suddenly seen to be known only by its multiple relationships—mother and child, and all their countless derivatives, re-created by Winnicott in a prose that casts not only light but warmth. His paradoxes are powerful on behalf of the community they describe, they have a poetry that shows itself determined to lay fast hold upon the good; and thus, if it be true that we all fight hardest for those things that seem most under threat, either from within or without, we might ask against what forces Winnicott's style is mobilized. Why should he be so concerned for the unpredictable spontaneities of the creative spirit, for what each might make anew *of* time and space *within* time and space? Perhaps, in the difficult factional world of British psychoanalysis, torn between the traditions of Anna Freud and Melanie Klein, he felt on the one hand the threat of an excessively "scientific" determinism in considering the causalities of mental illness, on the other hand the threat of an excessively "theological" insistence upon the "original sin" of infantile aggression—both of them traditions that tended to belittle the creative possibilities of human interaction in the play-areas of nursery and therapy alike. Certainly the paradox in *Playing and Reality*—that "it is the *destructive* drive that *creates* the quality of externality" (1971:110; italics added), provided that the external world can *survive* its own *destruction*—operates against the rigors of both science and theology alike; and in this it is typical. Winnicott is celebrating the creative potential of destructiveness; and indeed the most characteristic pattern of his thought is a modern form of what used to be called theodicy—"a vindication of the divine attributes, especially justice and holiness, in respect to the existence of evil" *(OED)*, or translated into psychoanalytic parlance, a vindication of human creativity in respect to the destructiveness and perversity that should ideally confirm it.

Paradise Lost begins with the failing relationships of Satan, *Playing and Reality* with the failing relationships of the boy who played with string: in each case, in true platonic fashion, our reason is called into play not to combat the dangerous destructiveness of the perverse but to contemplate its insubstantiality, its failure to realize the world and thus to attain those common ends of relationship upon which we all of us are set. For life at its best is not the dour battle of ego against id and superego that has been so often portrayed in the pages of Freud and his followers. It is *play,* to which even the sad rituals of the perverse aspire; and it is the *poetry* of the human mind at play that provided Winnicott the scientist with his great theme, celebrated in a prose style that aimed both to retain that poetry for himself and to communicate it to others.

Conclusion: Wordsworth and Winnicott, Connections and Reservations

In the middle of *Playing and Reality,* we suddenly find this important passage:

> In some way or other our theory includes a belief that living cre-
> atively is a healthy state, and that compliance is a sick basis for life.
> There is little doubt that the general attitude of our society and the
> philosophic atmosphere of the age in which we happen to live con-
> tribute to this view, the view that we hold here and that we hold at
> the present time. We might not have held this view elsewhere and in
> another age. (1971:76)

Here, suggestively brief, are the beginnings of an anthropologist's perspective upon the here and now, the first few steps down that path which in philosophy and literature has been called deconstruction: that is, the inquiry in which the grounds of our discourse, even as we speak, are examined both for the speech they enable and the silence they enforce. Here are the beginnings of a serious historical enterprise, needing especially to be undertaken in a discipline like psychoanalysis where knowledge slides imperceptibly into value systems, to be elucidated fully only with reference to the culture and the language in which they are embedded. But it is the beginning only that we find in Winnicott, and commonly in the British psychoanalytic tradition: the boundaries that hedge in the professional field are rarely crossed. Writers such as Masud Khan and Bruno Bettelheim have recently argued, against Freud himself, that, in Khan's words, "the vision, intention, and contents of Freud's discoveries and genius derive more from the humanistic tradition of the European cultures than its scientific one" (1972:126–27). A similar argument needs to be made in the case of Winnicott as well, to explore the hints he gave about "the philosophic atmosphere of the age in which we happen to live" and thus to complete the task he left undone: the extension of subjectivity from the poetry of the prose into that psychoanalytic practice and theory whose true relationship to one another he had once described, surely inadequately, as "an applied science based on a science" (1961:13).

For my part, an account of the prehistory of Winnicott's "third area"—the area of play, culture, illusion, whichever of these very different words we choose—would begin where this paper began: with the work of Wordsworth and Coleridge, and of Burke before them; with the work of their Victorian descendants, especially with Matthew Arnold's *Culture and Anarchy;* and with the subsequent work of the Bloomsbury group at the start of this century, professing what Raymond Williams has called "the supreme value of the civilized *individual,* whose pluralization, as more and more civilized individuals, was itself the only accepted social direction" (1980:165). James Strachey, of course, provides us with one direct link between Winnicott and—in Strachey's own words—that "middle-class, professional, cultured, later Victorian, box" (1963:228) which we now know as Bloomsbury; but the indirect links, those connections that belong to the Zeitgeist, are even more suggestive still. From Joseph Conrad's *Nostromo* to Virginia Woolf's *To The Lighthouse* and E. M. Forster's *A Passage to India,* the language of illusion was widely invoked by the bourgeois avant-garde to explore the frailty and the solipsism of those civilized individual values to which they were devoted. A history of Winnicott's "third area" would thus involve us in a social as well as an intellectual history of the idea of illusion from the Romantic age onward—a history forming part of that larger history of the antithetical relationship between culture and society, which Raymond Williams has given so much time to tracing. "We live, as we dream—alone," wrote Conrad in *Heart of Darkness* (1982:57): writers since the Romantic age, feeling themselves increasingly marginalized within their own class, had come more and more to believe that culture was being increasingly encroached upon by capital. The creative basis for shared authentic living seemed to them increasingly endangered by the lie of an inauthentic compliance forced upon them by the demands of a mechanical civilization that wholly disregarded the inner life; and thus our history of illusion, from Wordsworth's "light that never was, on sea or land" (*P.W.* 4:259) to Forster's imprisoned reflections of matchlight in the walls of the Marabar caves, would be a history that charted intensifying alienation. The distinctive contribution of Winnicott to this history was that, adopting the widespread language of illusion, he turned it to such positive, nonpositivistic account. He was able by his paradoxes to rehabilitate a word charged with the poet's alienation and the scientist's disdain because (and it is here that he reminds me most closely of Wordsworth) he had the rare personal capacity to find *substantial* hope in the future of an *illusion*. Like F. R. Leavis, the Arnoldian literary critic whose affinities to Winnicott have been noticed by John Fielding, he put his faith in that " 'third realm' to which all that makes us human belongs" (1985:60); and unlike Leavis, the generosity and confidence of that faith increasingly irradiated his work.

Yet despite the distinctive contribution of Winnicott's thought in *Playing and Reality* to our present-day appreciation of that *"potential space"* (1971:126) between subject and object in which we play, we must not lose sight of the fact that he was working within a broad Romantic tradition whose characteristic strengths and weaknesses he shares. He was drawing upon an understanding of culture that valorized the creative above the compliant by celebrating the "natural" inner life above the "artificial" life imposed upon us from without. Raymond Williams has described the progress of this characteristic Romantic antithesis as follows:

> The primary effect of this alternative was to associate culture with religion, art, the family, and personal life, as distinct from or actually opposed to "civilization" or "society" in its new abstract and general sense. It was from this sense, though not always with its full implications, that "culture" as a general process of "inner" development was extended to include a descriptive sense of the means and works of such development: that is, "culture" as a general classification of "the arts," religion, and the institutions and practices of meanings and values. Its relations with "society" were then problematic, for these were evidently "social" institutions and practices but were seen as distinct from the aggregate of general and "external" institutions and practices now commonly called "society." The difficulty was ordinarily negotiated by relating "culture," even where it was evidently social in practice, to the "inner life" in its most accessible, secular forms: "subjectivity," "the imagination," and in these terms "the individual." (1977:14–15)

In this process of the dissociation of culture from society, psychoanalysis with its concern for the inner life of the individual enjoys an ambiguous status; for it is at once a symptom that offers itself as a cure. It seems to me that when Winnicott writes in *Playing and Reality* that *"the work done by the therapist is directed towards bringing the patient from a state of not being able to play into a state of being able to play"* (1971:44), he is asking of the psychotherapist what Wordsworth had already asked of the poet over a hundred years before: that, within a place apart, he might rectify the sensibility in those areas where it had gone wrong, so that the inner life might once again begin to reengage creatively with the outer. Thus from the very beginning, the third area of play and culture has always been defined not only by what it is but also by what it (only apparently) excludes, namely, the daily realities of our social, economic, and political life—and to understand this, we need to grasp the political purpose that the idea of culture has always served for the bourgeoisie.

At each decisive point of our recent history, in the 1790s, the 1830s, the 1860s, and the years after the First World War, the idea of culture has generally been invoked as an antirevolutionary principle, setting against the immediate imperatives of Reason or Right the necessity for the slow cultivation of good habit. Burke began it; Coleridge kept it up; and so too did Wordsworth, even during that period that saw his best poetry born out of the attempt to adapt the conservative thrust of Burke's antirevolutionary arguments to radical ends of liberty, fraternity, and equality. This broad cultural tradition, bourgeois as it always was, progressive with regard to the aspirations of its own class but reactionary with regard to those of the working class, survived powerfully into the twentieth century; and despite the fragmentation of the class base upon which the coherence of Bloomsbury had rested, it continues alive today in those professional and commercial enclaves that see themselves still as the custodians of culture in a philistine world. To the strengths and weaknesses of this tradition, Winnicott seems to me to have been remarkably true—to its strengths, which have lain in a certain tenderness toward things as they are, seeking out their goodness and indulging their frailty, and also to its weaknesses, which have lain in an undervaluation of anger at injustice, of that political passion whose aim is precisely to transform things as they are. The business of this paper has primarily been with Winnicott's strengths, with his search for the springs of creative living in those relationships established by what he called, marvelously well, "good-enough mothering." My business here however, briefly, is with his weaknesses; for if we turn to his occasional pieces, to the often deliberately provocative essays on feminism, democracy, the family, or the monarchy, it seems to me that those of us who are looking for a language with which to explore injustice will look in vain. This is not to say that the psychotherapist has nothing to say in these areas. Far from it: the essays are interesting and to be reckoned with. It is, however, to say that social, economic, and political affairs cannot be wholly collapsed back into psychology, since they involve both the realities of property, wealth, and power and also the principles of a morality that is sui generis. The mistake is to exclude these matters from our idea of culture, as Winnicott so notably does in *Playing and Reality*. For here too, in the language of our social, economic, and political relations, in the language with which again and again we rewrite our history, is the genuine sphere of subjectivity. We need to extend our relational thinking to include not only culture but also politics and psychoanalysis itself; we need, that is, to turn to positive account what is merely positivistic in Freud's question, "Must not the assumptions that determine our political regulations be called illusions as well?" (1927:34); and to help us here, we need to understand Winnicott's delimitation of the arena of play in terms of that bourgeois antirevolutionary tradition that dates back to the 1790s and the start of the Romantic movement.

In the recovery of that history, it seems to me that the poetry and the paradoxes of Wordsworth might play an important part. Charles Rycroft, pursuing his belief that "psychoanalysis could be regarded as a semantic bridge between science and biology on the one hand and religion and the humanities on the other" (1966:21), has attempted recently in *The Innocence of Dreams* "to marry Coleridge's Theory of the Poetic Imagination and Freud's theory of dreams" (1979:167). What I wish to add to his argument is simply told. We should remember that, although Coleridge evolved his theory of the imagination out of a reading of Wordsworth's early poetry, its actual formulation in *Biographia Literaria* belongs to his middle age when he was engaged in distancing himself from the radicalism of his youth; and the definition itself, in the wider context of Coleridge's discussions of criticism, literature, and philosophy, is colored by the interest of the conservative intellectual in those cultural activities that distinguish him above ordinary men. Hence, in part, the great success of the book in academic circles. Wordsworth certainly shared Coleridge's high evaluation of imagination; but he never restricted its work so simply to cultural artifact and, more importantly, his interest in imagination was always complemented by an interest in the imagery upon which it fed. As I said above, while Coleridge's preoccupations as an intellectual lay with the faculties of the mind, Wordsworth's as a poet lay with its relation-

ships; and hence his peculiar impatience with the abstractions of theoretical writing.

> I know no book or system of moral philosophy written with suffi-
> cient power to melt into our affection[?s], to incorporate itself with
> the blood & vital juices of our minds ... these bald & naked
> reasonings are impotent over our habits, they cannot form them;
> from the same cause they are equally powerless in regulating our
> judgments concerning the value of men & things. They contain no
> picture of human life; they *describe* nothing. (*Prose* 1:103)

It is, of course, wrong to disparage theory in this way, for we need it to
organize understanding and to guard against the persuasiveness of our
own pet images; and yet Wordsworth's poetry has an inclusiveness of
inner and outer reference that seems to me to highlight the poverty of
mere theory. His paradoxes, as in the "Immortality Ode," shake us
free from old categories of thought and reach out with openness toward
more comprehensive understandings; and although those understandings may be as yet unattained, the imagery of his poetry—striving to
integrate the different areas of experience that we falsely categorize as
psychological, social, political, and so on—sets out to discipline our
sensibility so as to safeguard the nature of all future intellectual ad-
vance.

For in the end it is our imagery that counts, not our imagination.
Imagination grows and is able to know itself only by its images, the
faculty by its relationships; and hence my interest here in the poetry of
Wordsworth rather than the theory of Coleridge. It is not simply that I
prefer a radical perspective grounded in the perception that "we have
all of us one human heart" (*P.W.* 4:239) over a conservative privileging
of those cultural attainments that distinguish us one above another
(although I do). It is rather that, of all the poetry of the last two
centuries, it is still the poetry of Wordsworth that has been most
comprehensive in its attempt to integrate the variety of our experience,
to explore the symbolic origins of our thinking, to educate our subjectivity, and to cultivate the poetry at the heart of our science. And hence
the power that I claim for it here: the power to challenge that tradition
of object relations psychoanalysis whose interest also lies in paradox,
metaphor, and symbol, and to safeguard it against the split-off intellectual functioning of scientism. Psyche and soma, self and other, poetry
and science, woven inseparably together, the line lost that divides them:
still Wordsworth's struggle is exemplary, reminding us of the business
of paradox and metaphor to break open and to extend the categories

of our thought. For still we need to remake our language as part of the long process of remaking our world.

REFERENCES

Coleridge, S. T. [1817] 1965. *Biographia Literaria*. London: Everyman's Library.

Colie, R. L. 1966. *Paradoxia Epidemica: The Renaissance Tradition of Paradox*. Princeton: Princeton University Press.

Conrad, J. [1902] 1982. *Heart of Darkness*. London: Penguin Books.

De Quincey, T. [1840] 1890. "Style." In vol. 10 of *The Collected Writings of Thomas de Quincey*. 14 vols. Edited by D. Masson. Edinburgh: Adam and Charles Black.

Ellis, D. 1985. *Wordsworth, Freud and the Spots of Time*. Cambridge: Cambridge University Press.

Fielding, J. 1985. " 'To Be or Not to Be': Hamlet, Culture and Winnicott." *Winnicott Studies* 1 (Spring 1985):58–67.

Freud, S. 1927. *The Future of an Illusion*. In vol. 21 of *The Standard Edition of the Complete Psychological Works*, pp5–56. Edited and translated by J. Strachey et al. 24 vols. London: Hogarth Press, 1953–74.

Fuller, P. 1983. *The Naked Artist*. London: Writers and Readers Publishing Cooperative.

Keats, J. 1954. *Letters of John Keats*. Selected by F. Page. World's Classics Editions. London: Oxford University Press.

Khan, M. M. R. 1972. "The Becoming of a Psychoanalyst." In *The Privacy of the Self*, pp. 112–28. London: Hogarth Press, 1974.

Moorman, M. 1957. *William Wordsworth: A Biography*. Vol. 1, *The Early Years 1770–1803*. London: Oxford University Press.

Paine, T. [1791–92] 1968. *Rights of Man*. London: Pelican Books.

Prickett, S. 1970. *Coleridge and Wordsworth: The Poetry of Growth*. Cambridge: Cambridge University Press.

Rycroft, C. 1966. "Introduction: Causes and Meanings." In *Psychoanalysis Observed*. London: Penguin, 1968.

———. 1979. *The Innocence of Dreams*. London: Hogarth Press.

Searles, H. F. 1962. "The Differentiation Between Concrete and Metaphorical Thinking in the Recovering Schizophrenic Patient." In *Collected Papers on Schizophrenia and Related Subjects*, pp. 560–83. New York: International Universities Press.

Strachey, J. 1963. "Joan Rivière: Obituary." *International Journal of Psycho-Analysis* 44:228–30.

Traherne, T. 1958. *Centuries, Poems, and Thanksgivings.* Vol. 1, *Introduction and Centuries.* Edited by H. M. Margoliouth. Oxford: Clarendon Press.

Trilling, L. 1970. *The Liberal Imagination.* London: Penguin.

Turner, J. 1986. *Wordsworth: Play and Politics.* London: Macmillan.

Williams, R. 1977. *Marxism and Literature.* London: Oxford University Press.

———. 1980. *Problems in Materialism and Culture.* London: Verso Editions.

Winnicott, D. W. 1958. "The Capacity to Be Alone." In *The Maturational Processes and the Facilitating Environment,* pp. 29–36. New York: International Universities Press, 1965; London: Hogarth Press, 1965.

———. 1961. "Psychoanalysis and Science: Friends or Relations?" In *Home Is Where We Start From,* pp. 13–18. London: Penguin, 1986.

———. 1962. "The Five-Year-Old." In *The Family and Individual Development,* pp. 34–39. London: Tavistock, 1965.

———. 1964. *The Child, the Family and the Outside World.* London: Penguin.

———. 1971. *Playing and Reality.* New York: Basic Books; London: Pelican Books, 1974; London: Tavistock, 1984.

———. 1986. *Holding and Interpretation: Fragment of an Analysis.* London: Hogarth Press.

Wordsworth, W. 1940–49. *(P.W.) The Poetical Works of William Wordsworth.* Edited by E. de Selincourt and H. Darbishire. 5 vols. London: Oxford University Press.

———. [1805] 1958. *(Prelude) The Prelude.* Edited by E. de Selincourt. 2d ed., revised by H. Darbishire. London: Oxford University Press.

———. 1974. *(Prose) The Prose Works of William Wordsworth.* Edited by W. J. B. Owen and J. W. Smyser. 3 vols. London: Oxford University Press.

———. 1977. *Home at Grasmere* (MS B). Edited by B. Darlington. Ithaca, N.Y.: Cornell University Press.

Yeats, W. B. [1903] 1961. "Emotion of Multitude." In *Essays and Introductions.* London: Macmillan.

10

Lawrence's False Solution

DAVID HOLBROOK

Then I saw that there was a way to hell, even from the gates of heaven, as well as from the City of Destruction! —John Bunyan, *The Pilgrim's Progress*

As everybody in England now knows, *Lady Chatterley's Lover* (1928; first complete text, 1960) is the story in novel form of a young titled married woman who falls in love with her husband's gamekeeper, Oliver Mellors, and has a clandestine, passionate affair with him in the grounds of her home, Wragby Hall, in the Industrial Midlands, in the 1920s or thereabouts. The story recounts the pains and joys of their sexual life together, and their progress toward "a measure of equanimity" (1960:217). In the end Mellors is working away on a farm and writes to Lady Chatterley that "what I live for now is for you and me to live together." She is pregnant, and there is desire on the part of both, apparently, to marry, after having divorced their respective spouses. The story has been called by some a definition of marriage. It is the first story to be published at a popular price in English which gives full accounts of sexual intercourse in all its details, using the Anglo-Saxon words that many people privately use but that are publicly taboo for the act of coition and for the private parts of the body, without substitution or inhibition. The book has sold several million copies.

Its release has been acclaimed as a triumph of enlightenment, and no doubt in a sense it was. It was also a *succés de scandale* that arose from a publisher's business acumen in the first instance. The question of what contribution this work makes to our culture has been too little examined. The question is not whether Anglo-Saxon words of direct sexual meaning should be printed in books, or whether descriptions of sexual intercourse should be available to all who want to read them, but, fundamentally, an artistic one.[1] Is this a good novel? We know it to be by a sensitive artist. But are the possessed values it may give, in the end, good ones, leading us forth—as Lawrence would have consciously wished to lead us forth—toward more adequate, more truly civilized, fuller living? Will it, as a work of art, enrich and develop the concepts of those who read it?

The question of the popular influence of such a great imaginative artist and his effect on attitudes to life is crucial today. As Lawrence himself declared, the intuitive aspects of the whole being in us, linked as they are with fantasy and imagination, are suffering from starvation. In consequence our reality sense and our power to find meaning in life are weak. Rich imaginative nourishment is scarce and so our concepts—as of values in human relationship—are impoverished. What a Lawrence can offer to the popular mind and to the mind of the intellectual minority counts a great deal, because we have so little of the truly creative and positive today in popular and minority culture.

Our concepts and attitudes to life, and our capacities to employ them more or less effectively in living, as in sustaining the free flow of feeling in love and family life, depend to a degree on cultural influences, including books. As culture has become so generally trivial, our life nowadays seems to suffer from the absence of what may be called spiritual challenge, the pursuit of constructive aims and values in contest with our inward nature and the nature of external reality. Lawrence was the last great English writer to offer us such a contest in which to engage ourselves. Our culture since the war seems to have abrogated this positive concern, and many of our works of literature and entertainment picture human beings as helpless victims of a hostile environment, depressively. Meanwhile entertainment culture offers fantasy, which has no relation to reality at all, except to disguise it or defend us against it, like a drug. Yet our fantasy life is crucial to the growth of our capacities to deal with reality: without fantasy there is no effective consciousness. The conscious exercise of the imagination, metaphorically, to come to terms with the painful aspects of reality—with our mortality and our aspiration to transcend it—may be called "spiritual discipline."

England had before this century a popular tradition of spiritual discipline. In Bunyan, who was from about 1650 to 1850 England's greatest popular writer (after 1850 he shares the honor with Dickens), we can see the process of this search for something "beyond" us, greater than, "outside" the individual. Bunyan's Christian cries that the City of Destruction is doomed: he must fly! Life! Eternal Life! The implication of his work may be taken in nonreligious as well as religious terms: as a recognition that our mere existence merely dies—to live well we need to achieve a perception of something that does not die with us. Even if not believers, we may, like Bunyan, still accept that there are values and truths greater than the individual such as may be found in love and personal relationship, or in a sense of life's continuity that transcends mere personal existence, as Shakespeare portrayed these in his work. Christian in *Pilgrim's Progress* (1678) progresses through all manner of spiritual challenge. He seeks the wicket-gate of Christ's grace—nowadays in modern terms we might consider this experience as one of undergoing a progress of personal integration—coming to terms with inner and outer reality. Such a process moves from infant to adult, toward toleration of the reality of human existence and toward acceptance of the mortal condition of human life, in search for values, a perception of "good" and a belief in life's continuity, that transcend the mere reality. Acceptance of such truths must be a real acceptance. The false acceptance is indicated by Bunyan by the fate of Ignorance, who seems to have run the course, but who is seized and thrust into a fiery hill, even from the Gates of Heaven—because his self-discovery is not complete, and so his access to Grace is not complete either. He attains only a false solution. He comes, at the end of his quest, only to destruction. This is a perception in Bunyan's art of the need continually to discipline ourselves to come closer to accepting the reality of our predicament: we never come through. This is the true quest, and it can bring self-fulfillment. We may perhaps accept that equally in creativity, in study, in devotional disciplines, or in psychoanalysis, the quest for insight and understanding must be unflinching if we are to find peace in a profound sense of felt order in life, and of meaning in the individual life. In the long contest we must continually seek to combat distortions and falsifications—as of By-Ends and Mr. Worldly Wiseman—as Bunyan did.

Christian, the protagonist of this poetic projection of Bunyan's own spiritual quest, enters the heavenly gates at last. Because of the successful outcome of his ordeal, in the second part of *Pilgrim's Progress* (1684) the artist is able to offer the world a benign compassionate humanity, a power of succor in living, a tender, triumphant awareness of life's perplexity, even unto death—in the end an earnest of how the human spirit may triumph over death. There is a release from the stern egocentricity in Part One, to a warm sense of community life in Part Two. The people—*all* the people—pass over the River singing, and even the Daughter of Mr. Despondency goes through the river singing, though "none could understand what she said" (1965:370). It is a deeply moving passage, rendering a compassionate vision of the shared spiritual experience of humanity that can triumph over death itself. All are portrayed, at the end, in the sympathetic light of an apprehension of the universality of human experience. This escape from isolation into compassionate at-oneness Bunyan discovered through the solitary spiritual torment that he describes in *Grace Abounding* (1666). He attains a compassion springing from the achieved assurance of something beyond the self, found in the common vitality of humanity, as a great manifestation of life. It is a truly democratic vision, because Bunyan portrays *all* as able to make access to grace.

In the second part of *Pilgrim's Progress,* Puritan life in the community is depicted as warm and humane—it is in the bath scene even virtually erotic: "When they were returned out of the garden from the bath, the Interpreter took them, and looked upon them, and said unto them, Fair as the moon" (1965:256). Mercy, humanly weak, womanly weak, is granted even the indulgences fit for a young pregnant girl:

> But Mercy being a young and breeding woman, longed for something that she saw there, but was afraid to ask . . . so they called her and said to her, Mercy, what is that thing thou wouldst have? Then she blushed, and said, The great glass that hangs up in the dining room. So Sincere ran and fetched it, and, with a joyful consent, it was given her. (346)

This is the essence of English Puritanism, that first the solitary individual must set out alone, sternly to fight the personal battle of self-discovery, driven by conscience, listening to the voice of God, speaking to him alone. *Pilgrim's Progress* is the poetic rendering of the quest described in *Grace Abounding* for peace in the soul. No one can complete the quest for self-awareness for another by proxy, so each one goes alone. And, then, when "Grace Abounding" is found, the self is released to a fulfilled recognition of the beauty of creation, and not least of the beauty of physical life and human love: the solitary Puritan, after his grim ordeal, becomes benign and tolerant. Bunyan's own affection for his wife and children tenderly and beautifully colors the second part of *Pilgrim's Progress*. But the essence of the devotion, the humanity, the happiness, the great spiritual elation and satisfaction conveyed in *Pilgrim's Progress* as a whole depends upon Christian's earlier lonely struggle against Appolyon, Doubt, Despair, and the Valley of the Shadow, in the first part, to find his personal reality, the true voice of God in his soul, his inward reality and the tragic truth of man's state on earth. In *Pilgrim's Progress* we see how the Puritan tradition has affinities with the deep stoical attitudes, born of suffering, in English folksong: these express with gravity a commitment to life as a whole, especially to the experience of the heart. Whether Christian or stoical, spiritual discipline obliges each first to seek to understand himself, and gain his sense of significance in finding how much he belongs to the human family: then he may understand and succor others. Only then can he *afford* to do so, wholly.

The Puritan tradition has decayed, and among the disciplines lost has been this kind of contest with experience in the quest for truth— the struggle to find something beyond ourselves, the wicket-gate, of triumphant values, of Christ's mercy, if we are believers; or of the truth of ourselves and the world whether we are or not. *Pilgrim's Progress* corresponds closely with the process of self-discovery, escape from obsessions and delusions, the overcoming of the falsifications of manic defence, and effective release to the world, in the psychoanalytic patient. Bunyan made his quest first in *Grace Abounding* by expressing, ordering, and analyzing his own spiritual conflicts, and then gave a metaphorical account of this process in *Pilgrim's Progress*. Interestingly enough, he was able to effect this development of his soul because to him words had a forcible, actual, felt existence in the reality of human life: "That sentence lay like a mill-post at my back." For him the creative quest in words affected the depths of his being and wrought changes there. So Bunyan exemplifies the value in English life of the vital, metaphorical richness of the English language, its poetic power to enable us to come at our inner truth, and that of the world. Bunyan's language is the rich language of the old English rural community, with all its cadences of gravity. As in folksong, issues of the deeper psyche are enacted out in metaphor, by a "carrying across" from inner to outer reality. This traditional verbal power and its effectiveness has been weakened in our own time by an uncreative education, by the loss of vernacular idiom, by superficial forms of communication and entertainment, by the prostitution of words, images, and emotion in advertising and other media. The word "love," for instance, is polluted now by meretricious use in the language of advertising ("People love Players"): so it is less possible to use it well in our relationship with God or in significant relationships between man and woman. Because we can only use the word "love" in its lessened way, we are that much less able to come to explore reality through love. We are consequently the less able to reach, as Bunyan did, our personal truth, because we have not the good words. Because we cannot find this ourselves, we are less able to attain the release to community, to give out succor and compassion. But a Lawrence can help to refine language again, and so help refine our thought and feeling.

In this situation it is crucial to consider the work of such a distinguished and influential artist as Lawrence—a clear, vivid writer, whose background gave him affinities with the same Puritan conscience that produced Bunyan. Lawrence was such a creative and deeply religious man, albeit he was an agnostic, that he was driven to seek into the heart of things.

Lawrence's last book, *Lady Chatterley's Lover,* is now one of the most widely read novels in the English language. In terms of sales it is second only to the Authorized Version of the Bible. It is having as much influence as any imaginative work can have in an illiterate world, of trivial culture. What effect will this have, if any?

In a way the book is very much like *Pilgrim's Progress:* it is an imaginative search of a kind for insight into personal reality and understanding of the author's own behavior, by analogy. Lawrence himself was in the Puritan tradition and touched the world of Bunyan from the world of the working-class chapel that was his inheritance. He wished to explore his own personal reality, to discover something beyond the self which could give life significance and meaning, even in our industrial and mechanical age, even though he was agnostic: he sought this in love. He experienced—albeit at a distance—the destructive cataclysm of the Great War. He could see the final disintegration and loss of an England that had existed for several hundreds of years, and saw the population being made by commerce into money-conscious "money-boys and money-girls" (1960:108), devoted to a meaningless pursuit of material possessions, to making things "go" simply for the sake of the "go," in an acquisitive society. What was lacking? To Lawrence it was wholeness of being, of spontaneous-creative being, of the flowing of the intuitive faculties. He took as the central index of this lack the relationship in love between man and woman. To every man his parents' relationship is crucial in forming his own capacities to love, and his attitudes to love. In his own life Lawrence had experienced as a child, as he records in *Sons and Lovers* (1913), a deeply disturbing awareness that this relationship, over his own stripling head, had broken down. His own mother and father had not had a rich relationship in marriage. That he perceived this we know from several places in his work. In *Sons and Lovers* Paul Morel's mother says to him, "I've never had a husband, Paul, not really" (221). In *Odour of Chrysanthemums* (1934) the woman protagonist realizes the same thing. In life Mrs. Lawrence, it would seem, came to relate to her son almost as a lover, turning to him the polarity due to her husband. In trying to cherish his mother, to whom he became the son-as-lover, Lawrence comes to attribute the failing in her sexual life (which affected him in consequence deeply) to the effects of the industrial society which had degraded men to toilers in the pit—the pit to which his father wanted to send *him*. Obviously this connection established itself powerfully in his mind. His father would have committed him in subjection to industry: his mother prevented this and strove to see that he was educated. So his mother represented "civilization": she becomes in his work a symbol of the best in English social life, and in her is the inspiration of Lawrence's zeal. He wanted to restore "England" and the countryside as reparation to the mother. Of the woman of the English Midlands he says:

> Looking out, as she must, from the front of the house towards the activity of man in the world at large, whilst her husband looked out to the back at sky and harvest and beast and land, she strained her eyes to see what man had done in fighting outwards to knowledge. . . . She also wanted to know, and be of the fighting host. . . . It was this, this education, this higher form of being, that the mother wished to give her children, so that they too could live the supreme life on earth. (1949:9)

The women, in industrial England, as Lawrence pointed out in *The Rainbow,* kept up the civilized values in the working-class life, degraded as it was by bad living conditions, hideous conditions of work, and the meanness of industrial wage rates. They struggled amid laissez-faire justifications of the inhumanity of utilitarian attitudes. They saw the English countryside being made hideous. They felt the indifference to social welfare and social order of the industrial magnates. The women were oppressed by the meaningless trashiness of commercial provision-mongering—as nowadays they still are, in a different and more affluent way.

> The car ploughed uphill through the long squalid straggle of Tevershall, the blackened brick dwellings, the black slate roofs, glistening their sharp edges, the mud black with coal-dust, the pave-

ments wet and black. It was as if dismalness had soaked through and through everything. The utter negation of natural beauty, the utter negation of the gladness of life, the utter absence of the instinct for shapely beauty which every bird and beast had, the utter death of the human intuitive faculty was appalling. The stacks of soap in the grocers' shops, the rhubarb and lemons in the greengrocers! the awful hats in the milliners' all went by ugly, ugly, ugly, followed by the plaster and gilt horror of the cinema with its wet picture announcements, "A Woman's Love!," and the new big primitive chapel, primitive enough in its stark brick and big panes of greenish and raspberry glass in the windows. (1960:158)

There is, of course, an unfair exaggeration in the passage—industrialization can hardly be blamed for lemons and rhubarb, stacks of which can surely sometimes restore a little beauty to the urban scene? But the scene is evocative of Connie Chatterley's feeling—which was Lawrence's—that the deadness of her own life is reflected in the ugly industrial world. The personal life had been made squalid by circumstances, especially for women, who wanted beauty. Lawrence feels this because he wanted to make the world beautiful for his mother. The ugliness and oppression extended, Lawrence suggests, to the sexual lives of the women in industrial society—indeed to the intuitive life of the body in all of us.

We must accept the deep and relevant truth in Lawrence's analysis of this aspect of modern life. There *is* an intuitive failure in us, and it has something to do with the industrial revolution, the dissociations it brought about in family life, and the makeup of English people (Thompson 1962). But the problem with Lawrence comes when the life-seeking impulse turns, as it does in *Lady Chatterley*, to an utter rejection of the modern world, and to something approaching malevolence: the industrial workers in this book are, in the end, described as "half-corpses" (1960:159). How did Lawrence's impulse come to be reversed?

There is as we know the Luddite side of Lawrence. He writes in the poem "Work": "And so it will be again, men will smash the machines" (1964:450). There is a Lawrence who is hysterically offensive about procreation: "Children from such men! Oh God, oh God!" (1960:166). He is quoted in the same vein in Catherine Carswell's *The Savage Pilgrimage*: "There are plenty of children, and no hope . . . even the mice increase, they cannot help it. What is this highest, this procreation? It is a lapsing back to the primal origins, the brink of oblivion.

... There are many enceinte widows with a cup of death in their wombs" (1932:60).

This Lawrence is one with no belief in the continuity of life and who restricts education: "Never teach the mass of the population to read and write. Never!" Allowing for occasional extravagances, we must still admit that Lawrence often wrote savagely not only bombast or nonsense, but with a disturbingly destructive misanthropy. These elements culminate in *Lady Chatterley's Lover*.

This negative and destructive side of Lawrence we need to reject. To do so we must try to discover why he became so negative. The reasons are deep—so deep and complex that we can no longer fully unravel them, since Lawrence himself is dead, and we cannot examine his mind. But from his writings we may piece together a number of symptoms of a fundamentally disturbed attitude to experience—against which he strove himself courageously. Yet he could not overcome these distortions, and so his attitude to life contains dangerous elements, which lead to falsifications, and to disastrous social and political attitudes. The root of these is in the fear of woman, which has something to do with Lawrence's too-close attachment to his mother. He himself records the possessiveness of his mother and her will to dominate him in *Sons and Lovers*: this he must have experienced in reality, and more deeply, as infant and child. The effect of this overmothering seems to have been that he came, as an adult, to find it impossible ever to tolerate, much less to cherish, the mother-child relationship.

How the fear of woman and woman's domination became a deeply implanted fear in Lawrence we cannot tell because such a deep fear must surely have very early origins. It would obviously be wrong to judge only from his own autobiographical account of his relationship with his mother, since that is a biased narrative from later stages in his life. But we need to note that nowhere in Lawrence's work does a normative love-relationship culminate in family life—except perhaps for episodes in *The Rainbow*. The typical situation is one in which the man flees family life, as in *Aaron's Rod* (1922), or the children seem apart from the love-relationship, or the protagonists devote themselves to chastity (as in *St Mawr*, 1925).

The relationship between mother and child, and its importance in human life and society, are truths so evident that we tend to take them for granted and so fail to give them sufficient emphasis. In Tolstoy, of course, we may see this truth of human experience made central in a way it certainly is not in Lawrence. In European art it is symbolized in the innumerable depictions of the Virgin and Child. But nowadays it is sadly possible for large numbers of people to protest that they can only "fulfil" themselves, and their love-relationships, *without* children. No doubt there always were such people who were prepared to rationalize so their own incapacities in living: what disturbs one about the manifestation is the degree of fear of life it manifests. Children are, for these people, feared as representing the unknown quantities, the unbiddable and uncontrollable elements that may at any moment emerge from the flux of their living. They must be in control, and so they cannot give themselves up to life: at some time or other, inevitably, one feels, these people's capacities to deal with life must break down, because the unknown and unavoidable cannot be so controlled, and to try so to live is unreal. That is, the degree of procreative failure in our society marks a failure to accept certain primary aspects of reality. This fear of reality perhaps centers on that "primary maternal preoccupation" (Winnicott 1956), which is a psychic "illness," necessary for the infant's growth but too disturbing for those whose intuitive life is inhibited or suppressed.

Acceptance of sexual creativity is necessary to our relationship with the life in us, and the natural world in which we have our being, even if we have no children. This is no condemnation of the selfishness of those who don't have children. What we must be concerned with is concepts and *attitudes* to love and procreation in human life. In these must be included, for the whole truth, an adequate appreciation of the creativity of love and the importance of the mother-child relationship to human society. To deny this may involve an inability to accept reality, and this may have its roots in a fear of or denial of woman.

Some of the relevant connections between the fear of woman, her creativity, and politics, are made by D. W. Winnicott in "The Mother's Contribution to Society," an essay in his *The Child and the Family* (1957). Here he links fear of woman's dominance and the refusal to recognize the mother's role to the impulse to dominate. He urges us to recognize "the immense contribution to the individual and to society which the ordinary good mother with her husband in support makes at the beginning, and which she does simply through being devoted to her infant." He speaks of the "infinite debt" any sane person owes to a woman. "At a time when this person knew nothing about dependence, there was absolute dependence." To accept this, he says, should not give rise to "gratitude or even praise" but "a lessening in ourselves of a fear" (142).

Lawrence could not accept the immense importance of the mother-child relationship, at times and in part of him. Of course, elsewhere,

Lawrence is marvelous, both about children, birth, pregnancy, and the baby (see the poem, "As a drenched, drowned bee;) 1964: 73). But the impression one has of his work is never associated with the kind of happy and rich relationship between mother and child, such as we gain from Tolstoy, in his portrayal of Kitty and her baby, for instance. On the contrary, much of Lawrence's work manifests a deep fear of woman and her creativity.

Winnicott goes on (significantly when we think of the Lawrence of *Lady Chatterley's Lover*, *The Plumed Serpent* [1926], and *Aaron's Rod*):

> If there is no true recognition of the mother's part, then there must remain a vague fear of dependence. This fear will sometimes take the form of a fear of woman, or fear of a woman, and at other times will take less easily recognized forms, always including the fear of domination. Unfortunately the fear of domination does not lead groups of people to avoid being dominated; on the contrary it draws them towards a specific or chosen domination. Indeed, were the psychology of a dictator studied one would expect to find that, amongst other things, he in his own personal struggle is trying to *control* the woman whose domination he unconsciously fears, *trying to control her by encompassing her, acting for her, and in turn demanding total subjection and "love."* (1957:142–43; italics added)

Lawrence fears the woman's domination, as we know from many places in his work. In return he demands that she accept the man's domination. Much of his bad work is given to enlist us in this attempt—to act out the encompassing, controlling, and "acting for" the woman—and in *Lady Chatterley* he does this with intensity. These astute observations by Winnicott suggest a link between the woman-fearing and the Lawrence who wanted a man-controlled dictatorship, with all his dangerous urges toward such dictatorship, as in *The Plumed Serpent*, *The Woman Who Rode Away* (1928), and *Kangaroo* (1923).

Yet the origins of Lawrence's fears of woman are inseparable from the springs of his more creative impulses. They have roots in the powerful unconscious feelings Lawrence has about the relationship between his father and mother, and their function in the community of industrial society. These unconscious feelings are symbolized by this artist in various forms. Industry is to be rejected, for instance, because of Lawrence's hatred of his father and the father's ill-treatment of the mother. Yet because he loved his father, industry is also to be hated for what it did to his father, too, reducing him to a slave of the machine, and lessening his capacity to be a good husband to the mother. Yet while Lawrence wants to give his mother a "good" husband, he is at the same time so much still in love with his mother that he enters into the person of the fantasy-father (such as Mellors who has escaped from the pit and, indeed, from all connection with industrial life, reality and time—and is "temporizing"). In consequence of this incestuous impulse he fears retribution. The retribution seems to gather from the same industrial "Thing" that also symbolizes the father and has "blotted out" the countryside, which, again, Lawrence associates with the mother (and so he makes Connie Chatterley—who is in a sense an image of his ideal mother—a *landed* aristocrat).

The extended analysis of the book in these terms would run something like this:

Lawrence's mother was "in love with him," to an extent that left no room for the father and was too much the intense expression of a personal need. She could not, that is, give her sensitive and acutely perceptive son a good-enough environment. In the early stage, as W. R. D. Fairbairn emphasizes, the mother's role is to convince the infant that she is loving him in his own right as a person. Because of some failure here in his early environment Lawrence found, as a man, huge impediments in himself to the formation of adequate object-relationships—as we know from *Sons and Lovers* and autobiographical material. Of course, because he is a great artist and a courageous soul, he wrests his oeuvre from the struggle to overcome the weaknesses of his psyche. But the truth is that in his own makeup there remained strong elements of infantile attitudes to relationship and love, because his too-close relationship with his mother had inhibited his maturation.

My theory here is that Lawrence failed in *Lady Chatterley* to approach adult relationship at all, and loses his way altogether. He depicts a picture of neurotic genitality, conditioned by infantile oral aggressiveness: thus, both the book and its direction are virtually an act of infantile oral sadism. A quotation from Harry Guntrip is relevant here: "Neurotic genitality, which is compulsive, expresses oral sadistic rather than truly genital attitudes. . . . Truly genital relationships by contrast, represent the co-operative mutuality and giving of two equal partners" (1961:291). I shall try to demonstrate how Lawrence cannot attain a picture of "truly genital . . . co-operative" relationships, involving equal partners, and how his conception of genitality remains infantile. Infantile too, I consider, is the oral-verbal assault, which the book, with its explicitness and its "direct" language, is.

Another failure in the artistic elements of the book, and the direction it takes, with origins in the failure to leave behind infantile concepts, is in its concentration, as we shall see, on sensuality. Lawrence cannot discover here that "the ultimate goal of the libido is the object" (Fairbairn 1952:162). He tries to solve the problem of love in terms of erotic pleasure merely. To quote Guntrip again, this false quest is inevitably doomed, since man's chief need is in mutual and equal relationship, and not in libidinal expression in sensual pleasure:

> If one switches attention away from the object to the pleasure of the object-relationship experience, the object is lost sight of, the experience of a satisfying object-relationship is lost, and the pleasure soon evaporates. Those who seek pleasure only find the unpleasurable kind of excitement of the continuing tension of a never satisfied quest. (1961:288)

This is a description of both Lawrence's doom in this novel and our response in reading it: "The pleasure soon evaporates," as it never does from a book that gives us the essence of problems of object-relationships, such as *Sense and Sensibility*, *King Lear*, or *Odour of Chrysanthemums*.

The infantile modes pervade the whole of the story. In presenting the coition between Connie and Mellors the art seems to be satisfying an unconscious need in Lawrence to fantasize his own unconsciously desired coition between himself in the place of his father with his mother. (I call the composite hero-author figure Morelorence.) Because of the degree of identification and projection in the fantasy, this is virtually a narcissistic coition with himself, and reality is thus totally evaded by short-circuit. In this relationship there must be no child—it would be rival to the son's demand on the mother or her projection: so there can be no real acceptance of a child in the love-story. Again, since the book is an act of control over the feared woman, there can be no child, for it is the woman's creativity that is essentially subject to destructive attack.

At the outset Connie's urge is related to the chicks in Mellors' care, as a symbol of the natural desire to procreate. But after this episode the procreative theme is suppressed in favor of mere sexual docility on her part, and moves toward a denial of her separate existence, and of her creativity as woman. Lawrence unconsciously seemed not to be able to tolerate the creation of a child: he cloaks his reasons under comments on the state of the world. But the hostility to creativeness lies deeper than that. So his portrayal of love inevitably becomes distorted, limited, and the reverse of life-promoting, while reality is increasingly denied.

The sex between the protagonists in *Lady Chatterley's Lover* becomes a mere "rather awful sensuality" (259), anxious and even perverted, leading not toward a sense of significance, to the security of the rainbow, which triumphs over death and time, or a hope in continuity, achieved by love and generation, but instead toward a haunting sense of doom and strangulation. The book ends in a splenetic denial of the best in human nature, a pharisaical attitude to industrial society and the people in it. It conveys a deathly attitude to the unborn child, a vacillating attitude to marriage, and a failure to accept that mutual regard in equal right, in "disquality," between man and woman—though such concepts of identity and separateness are so crucial to our future. A "measure of equanimity" is achieved (as in the poems, from which the phrase comes): but the novel implicitly denies the values in his best work. The sensual love culminates not in the creative vulva but, symbolically, in the anus, a parallel to Birkin's urge to have a relationship with a man, at the end of *Women in Love*.

Lawrence's very agonies of trying to escape from his own toils, because he is a brave, sincere, sensitive artist, are in themselves of major interest and value, because he was a genius. Such portrayal of tenderness as he does achieve, such escape from the self, in the discovery of love and reality is marvelous. But in this work it is blocked, and *Lady Chatterley's Lover* is an embracement of the self: it is narcissistic, self-enclosed, and denies reality. Lawrence falsifies the world and sex. The book becomes a barrier to understanding and insight, rather than an illumination: falsification rather than truth.

There is a sense in which any work of writing is a narcissistic work, and even an exhibitionist acts in narcissistic ways—any writer experiences uncertain pleasures and agonies in seeing his name or work in print, and in exposing his private suffering to public view. He obtains relief and satisfaction from the very act of narcissistic exhibitionism and oral aggressiveness that writing is, because he is sharing it with others, and taking the world into his mouth, as it were, as a baby wants to do. All the creatures in any man's work, including Shakespeare's, are spun out of himself, part of himself. How much he succeeds, of course, depends, as T. S. Eliot has said, on how far he "separates the man who suffers and the mind which creates" (1923:18): how much he translates his private agony into terms by which it can be apprehended as universal experience, seen afresh, and seen in its place as an aspect of our shared compassionate humanity, so that we may gain insight and understanding, feeling, "Ah, yes, I recognize this experi-

ence, that I too have had." But in this book the narcissism is a prison—
a *huis clos*—from which Lawrence does not escape.

We may begin looking for proof of the overpersonal nature of the
novel even in the names of the characters. Here the imaginative processes are perhaps similar to the ways dreams are used by patients in
psychoanalysis, to discuss emanations from the psyche which can only
emerge in metaphorical and cryptographic disguise: in this, wordplay
often plays a major part. So it does in imaginative creation.

Lawrence perhaps began to compose his names thus. From the cry
for life maybe comes the name OLIVER (O-live-er) for the hero. But
certainly MELLORS is an anagram of MOREL, the name Lawrence
used for his father in *Sons and Lovers*. MELLORS also contains the
syllable LOR having the same sound as the "Law" in Lawrence.[2]
Where is the rest of Lawrence's own name concealed? It is in ConstANCE. I suppose it might be possible that in the sensitive verbalizing
activity of Lawrence's mind "Constance" also echoes alliteratively "Jo-
casta," and there is some significance in Mellors' christian name beginning with an "O"—Lawrence could not disguise from his unconscious
mind or even his aware intelligence that he was writing an oedipal
tragedy. Clifford is Laius: but his name also contains the L O R
syllable, albeit divided up. There is also the distant echo of Lawrence's
aristocratic confidante Lady O. Morrell, to whom he wrote to tell her
that she needed his kind of verbal aggression.

The most important aspect of these verbal-anagram clues seems to
me that which suggests that when Mellors is making love to Constance
there is an aspect of Lawrence making love to himself, and this draws
our attention to the narcissism of the book. Lawrence is, as it were,
ravishing himself with words: and though Constance is perhaps called
Constance because the one *constant* love in Lawrence's life was his
mother, she is also *him*. Lawrence in this was embracing himself, and
ends by making an anal possession of himself, in final oral-anal aggressive verbal sensuality. This process of intense identification with his
heroine would explain why throughout Lawrence's work he is so
preoccupied by the female experience; concerned, too, to demolish the
female self since he wants to take the woman's place; and why in this
book there is a continual concern with Connie's feelings in sexual
union and orgasm, and much less with Mellors'. Lawrence wants the
woman to have "good" sex (because his mother "never had a husband
really"). Yet it is to himself he wants to make sex good—the self that
has suffered from the mother's sexual inadequacy (she was not properly polarized toward the father). This egocentric preoccupation is so

monistic and unwilling to encompass reality that any actual woman he wants to destroy, because he fears her reality. Mellors the actual lover is thus preoccupied, on the other hand, largely with his feelings of doom, fear, mistrust, with his sloganizing, and the preservation of his integrity.

This self-ravishment—more and more prevalent in modern literature among Lawrence's imitators, particularly in American novels concerned with sexual reality—is done in words. The verbal aggression is itself a defense against reality—an attempt to throw the closed-circuit hallucination over it. It is done "chatterly"—talkatively, wordily. This explains the name in the title—for *Lady Chatterley's Lover* is virtually a symbolic dream-statement of self-ravishment by words—the very thing Lawrence makes a scapegoat in the castrated Laius-self of Clifford, the thing that he himself fears to become, the ball-"less" verbalizer who cannot escape into creation from his own will-driven millwheel of words, and who cannot engage with experience potently. *Lady's Chatterley Lover, Lady's Lover Chatterley*—the talkative (or word-) lover of Her Ladyship: but yet Lady Jane and John Thomas are both aspects of the one creature, in the writing, for a man can only describe his own experience. Lawr*ence,* who has much in him of wanting to be a woman, perhaps so that he could "warm-heartedly fuck" (1960:215) himself, merges into Con*stance,* and the book *Lady Chatterley's Lover* is a verbal act of self-embracement, *Lover Verbally Loving Himself.* The whole is a projection of narcissistic fantasies that touch reality at no point. In this lies the contradiction that Lawrence should so much condemn the word-mill and the mind-mill in sex, yet offer us, even to the point of a national scandal, the "four-letter words" scandal, a great quantity of tedious verbalizing of what should never have been described in words and of what *cannot* be described in words. Ironically, we have at the end of this story of ideal, idyllic sex, his hero *verbalizing about his own satisfactions* at the moment when his seed springs forth in the "creative act that is far more than procreative." At the point when, in the arms of his beloved, he should have been in forgetfulness of the world within and without he *thinks in words,* "I stand for the touch of bodily awareness" (1960:292). And we are left with a mental-verbal conscious anxiety (as to whether we have good sex) instead of enriched intuitive awareness.

This negative translation of a personal psychic agon into a cultural act of narcissistic exhibitionism explains the insistent, overinsistent tedium of much of the story. It explains the sense we are left with afterward that the indescribable should not have been described. It explains the strange sterility of the book. It leaves us in no way with our life flowing in new discriminative sympathy, with no renewed sense of the act of sex being more valid and precious. It leaves us disconcerted, less able to bear our own reality. The qualitative failure of the book goes with its quantitative success now: the millions of popular readers do not read, mark, and learn in a compassionate mood; they read for that tittilation that satisfies anxiety—many only read, in fact, the "good bits" and the "rude words." The result is an increased inhibiting mentality about sex, if anything. As with Freud, the world has exaggerated Lawrence's bad rather than his best side.

Lawrence could not conquer his psychic Appolyon. Perhaps the point where he meets his Arch Enemy is the explicit discussion through Mellors of his own unfortunate experiences with women. Mellors could not find access to grace at the wicket-gate of Connie's body, because Lawrence was not able, in his whole psyche, to accept the conception in the woman's womb, nor was he able to accept the essential equality—or "disquality"—of woman. Lawrence can record, in Mellors, his striving toward accepting his own yielding to woman—something that Mellors fears as deeply as Lawrence did. Lawrence explores Connie's yielding as a woman to a man. But, right at the end, Mellors retains his mental separation, his willed domination over the woman, his denial of female reality, by preserving his egocentric "integrity" ("Thank God I've got a woman"; 1960:292)—*and Lawrence applauds*. The hero ends in loving "the chastity now that it flows between us" (317). And, as in other books by Lawrence (at the end of *St Mawr*, for instance), there is a strange preoccupation with chastity rather than the glad acceptance of the established rhythms of a love relationship. From this we may deduce that it was Lawrence himself who found physical sex and the reality of love intolerable, and found in them no gateway to a belief in continuity, through procreation. At a less deep level we will find some faults in the book arising from the fact that for Lawrence the sexual act may well have been something of an offense to the female because he resented his father's relationship with his mother. He loved his mother and wanted to make love to her himself, Oedipus-wise, unconsciously—remaining in the infantile attitude. This would have been shameful and taboo, because it was incestuous, and the mother must not, of course, enjoy such a shameful thing. Also, the infant mind finds it intolerable to allow the mother to be in any way imperfect, and for her to enjoy such a guilt-laden thing as sex cannot be allowed. Again, the son would fear the father's vengeance for incest, and this vengeance may come from within the woman. Certainly for such reasons—common manifestations but exacerbated in him by his deeper fears—for Lawrence the sexual act with any woman seems to have been filled with trouble, as it always is to some degree for all men.

He may have been impelled to write most of his books unconsciously to seek to overcome this trouble, and did so with great courage. His characters seem at times to be seeking to prove their normal potency as Lawrence must have needed to do himself. But the sense of doom and shame inherent in sex never leaves him, even though he seeks to exorcize it by words that are often almost incantatory.

Lawrence sets out to resurrect for his ladyship mother a creative sex his own mother did not have. For the reasons I have suggested he sets out to prove himself, in Morelorence, sexually, a "proper" man, a better man than the usurped father.

Here Lawrence falls into the humiliating situation we all experience in our love and marriage situations—he repeats for unconscious reasons the mistakes of his own parents and, being unable to gain insight into them or recognize their bad aspects, endorses them. Here, obviously, for one thing, his oedipal feelings for his father link with his class feelings. Lawrence, in the person of Mellors, feels humiliated to think he has working-class origins: he will not be kept by a lady; he will not be a mere "my lady's fucker" (1960:289). But, Mellors reflects, you don't lose your integrity as a man by going into a woman. And moreover—so implies the sexual experience as delineated in the book—you can *humiliate* her into the bargain, even, really, destroy her. Lawrence, as I have argued, is unconsciously having sexual intercourse with his mother, the aristocrat of his family, the cultured one, the "her ladyship" of the Bottoms. But of course, he has related feelings about his own wife who was an aristocrat too. He enters her ladyship by entering the person of his father, and the consequent guilt, in which he seems to fear the retributions of impotence, castration, humiliation, links with his feelings of possible retribution for this from the Industrial scene on which he has projected his feelings about his father. Or he fears that the aristocratic woman (i.e., the one above, as is the mother) will laugh at him, humiliate him, possibly hurt or attack him from within. Thus he invents a woman who will not laugh (the book is unbearably solemn), and who will *submit* and be controlled. She must be humiliated to see how much "mummy" will endure—if she will endure all, then the infant son is truly loved and his fears of retribution or separation—and death—can be at last allayed. Her body must be exorcized of its inner threats, including the anus. In Mellors Lawrence invents a superpotent working-class man who will "burn out all" the "shames," in the deepest places, by force of sensuality (though the sensuality is really verbal), by sheer aggression.

But this dominant exorcizing male becomes in fact, in the process, worse than the brutal and unrefined Morel! He becomes, *with Lawrence's full endorsement,* a creature whose impulsive domineering is not far from that of the drunken miner come home to his comforts— "a real man!"—sodomizing his woman:

> He jerked his head swiftly . . . she took it obediently . . . it was a night of sensual passion. And how in fear, she had hated it. But how she had really wanted it! At the bottom of her soul. . . . To find a man who dared to do it. . . .
>
> What liars poets, and everybody were! They made one think one wanted sentiment. What one supremely wanted was this piercing, consuming rather awful sensuality. . . . How rare a thing a man is. (1960:259)

How far we are here from the recognition of "disquality in equality," such as Lawrence explores between Birkin and Ursula! The old working-class brutality is strangely vindicated in Mellors—the brutality of the man driven into untenderness by the circumstances of the wretched life of industrial poverty—children coming, the wife worn-out, tired, unable to live the life of the mind. Hopeless, the husband tries to be tender for a time, then exerts his will on her: sexual relationship becomes a matter of humiliating rape. But it is this very failure to achieve mutual genitality that Lawrence virtually *vindicates* in Connie and Mellors; and Connie does not even complain—she "really wanted it!" He is a *man!*

The whole book, therefore, is a disastrous projection of Lawrence's own psychic difficulties. These are projected over the face of reality, so that the nature of things may be blamed for his own troubles. Outer reality is blamed for troubles of his inner reality. The distortions enable him to find an external cause in industrial society for the unacceptable inward truths that he finds too painful for acceptance.

So energetic and persuasive is Lawrence in defense of his distortions that only by working very hard to unravel his tangles can we protect ourselves and expose his untruths, in order to come better at his truths. It is important to do so, because Lawrence is often recommended as healthy and creative in his attitudes to love and sex. I think this belief is a very dangerous one. Lawrence often seeks to involve us in neurotic and perverted attitudes. One central aspect of this process is the cunning distortion of sexual truth he weaves in *Lady Chatterley's Lover*. What we may first accept, perhaps, from evidence in his work, is that, in confirmation of my analysis of his symbolism above, whenever he gave himself to a woman, Lawrence, like Mellors, was seized with a sense of impending retribution and doom, sometimes in terms of strangulation, sometimes in terms of a threat of mutilation from within the woman (see the beaklike clitoris, 210–11). Sometimes this threat associates with "money-getting" (as are Mellors' "white hands") that threaten strangulation to anyone who tries to "live beyond money"—so possibly this manifests the memory of a childish fear that the father wanted to send the son out to work in the industrial machine, and thereby "squeeze the life" (315) out of him. Another underlying reason for this fear is perhaps in the unconscious intense incestuousness of Lawrence's feelings for his mother: even on his honeymoon Lawrence wrote love poems to his mother wishing she could be having his experiences through his eyes. These are couched in intense phallic imagery ("I am a naked candle *burning* on your grave"; 1964:233). Such incestuous urges, as they accompanied Lawrence's sexual activity (as we can tell from his poems), would naturally be followed by guilt and fears of retribution.

What is not true is Lawrence's explanation of this fear in terms of it being a consequence of that will in man to make things go that produced industrial society, and that industry threatens man. This is a projection over outer reality, and a paranoiac projection of his fears of retribution from the industrial father.

These unrealities both perhaps associate with a reality problem over love. The clue here is in Lawrence's postcoital woe. The melancholy frequently expressed by Lawrence as following sexual satisfaction, and his desire to have the mother present in his honeymoon experience, suggest that for him sexual desire, the image of the loved one, and the rhythms of sexual relationship were deeply informed with feelings that were nostalgic—in the sense that they were commingled (as they tend to be in all of us) with a desire to return to an impossible state of bliss such as the infant hallucinates. He writes in "Song of a Man Who Is Loved":

> So I hope I shall spend eternity
> With my face down buried between her breasts.
>
> (1964:249)

This may be linked with failures of the reality sense and the sense of continuity. In a man who has limitations on his capacity to accept the reality of adult love—who finds it hard to accept mutual genitality and to recognize his own and his partner's separate identities in together-ness—his confusion of infant states of relationship with adult states may prove disastrous. It may confuse his dealings with the other—because the realities of both the self and the other are confused by projected images, and by identification and introjection. Even desire and satisfaction then become tormented because adult modes are im-bued with the aggressions and fears of the infant.

In discussing how the baby "creates" the mother's breast when he is hungry, Winnicott speaks of the other faculty in the baby of "making the breast disappear when not wanted":

> This last is most terrifying and is the only true annihilation. To not want, as a result of satisfaction, is to annihilate the object. This is one reason why infants are not always happy and contented after a satisfactory feed. One patient of mine carried this fear right on to adult life and only grew up from it in analysis, a man who had an extremely good early experience with his mother and his home. *His chief fear was of satisfaction.* (1945:153–54; emphasis added)

In a footnote Winnicott adds: "I will just mention another reason why an infant is not satisfied with satisfaction. He feels fobbed off. He intended, one might say, to make a cannibalistic attack and he has been put off by an opiate, the feed. At best he can postpone the attack" (154).

These two aspects of satisfaction, in their relation to adult sexuality, will be found to be most significant when we turn back to Lawrence and his preoccupation with the gloom and anxiety that, in him and his protagonists, follows even the most successful coition. The anxious comparisons are a symptom of this fear of satisfaction, and anxiety as to whether states of flop will prove bearable. The satisfaction brought by coition may even bring a threat of ceasing to exist.

In the sequence of poems *Look! We Have Come Through!* we can find expressed some of these moods in coital experience, as of a man reexperiencing in an intense love relationship problems related to those of infancy. Lawrence, being a terrifyingly honest man, records fits of violence, fear, rage, and depression associated with sexual satisfaction. No doubt one of our most disturbing experiences is to find that even our happiest sexual experiences can leave us with a sense of anxiety, anger, depression, restlessness, and even hostility, and to find that these associate with a whole reality-problem.

How can these things be overcome? Here lies the crux of the prob-lem that Lawrence tackles in *Lady Chatterley's Lover*. Briefly and crudely it may be said that in this work Lawrence sought to overcome the postcoital anxiety he knew from his own experience, by insisting on sensuality—on deepening the erotic experience. His attention, we must note here, is totally given to *erotic impulses,* and the *desire to put them right:* if they could be put right, then everything else (i.e., the rest of reality) would follow. This is to invert the truth. The roots of the anxiety are not in the erotic impulses at all, since these have been satisfied, by sexual gratification, as by a feed in the baby. The anxiety is a matter of our *whole reality sense.* The anxiety has its roots in the fear that one has "annihilated the object"—that is, in the difficulty of holding on to a sense of the reality of one's self and the reality of the beloved when all desire is gone. This has to do, obviously, with one's sense of the reality of one's love and being, to things that belong to *other areas than the erotic.* The problem is one of our dealings with reality altogether, and with love, not simply the reality of sex. Again, another source of the anxiety is in the frustration of aggressive and destructive impulses, which were directed, as in the baby, at "eating" the beloved. Of course, in normal adult sexual intercourse, these impulses are present as slight sadism—biting, and aggressive movements in coition. But inevitably, since one cannot devour the beloved any more than the baby can devour the breast, some aggression and destructiveness may remain polarized, postponed but not resolved. This may well become associated with all our other many fears connected with sex—of incestuous feelings, retribution for these, fears of harmful things inside the partner, and so forth. But certainly, we may note, again—these are problems of *finding the object* in mutual relationship. They have to do with problems of our inner reality, in terms of unresolved aggressive impulses. The solution of these has to do with our capacities to make reparation, capacities developed at the "stage of concern." (Winnicott 1950:206–7).

Anxiety over sexual relationships, then, has its origins in a complex combination of impulses—erotic, aggressive, destructive—and to do with one's whole hold on reality. Lawrence's error was in supposing he could exorcize the anxiety by *concentrating on the sensual alone,* and by aggressive verbal-oral *accounts* of the erotic. He preoccupies himself, that is, too exclusively with sex and sex-talk—and forgets all those complexities and realities that belong to love. But because the anxieties are not caused by the sex, rather by the other aspects of the realities of self and of love, he was inevitably doomed to failure and to error.

Nor is aggressiveness, oral or sexual, a way out. The way out of such anxieties is by restoring a whole reality sense: "In early stages [of an infant's life or of a psychoanalysis that is following the pattern of the child's early development], when the *Me* and the *Not-me* are being established, it is the aggressive component that more surely drives the individual to a need for a *Not-me* or an object that is felt to be *external"* (Winnicott 1950:215).

In the love relationship this seems to me to imply that the way to overcome the torments and unresolved anxieties of loving is by seeking to become more aware of the reality of the partner—of her "separate being," of her "MYSTIC NOW" (1964:266, 268)—to use Lawrence's own terms. As the mother's continuing existence, love, and care help the child through torment and trial after torment and trial, so that he or she can gain experience of triumph over difficulty and knowledge of constructive whole experiences, toward wholeness and balance, so in the adult lover, to develop a respect for the other existence of the partner is the means to survive and triumph over the torments and trials of love. Winnicott goes on:

> The erotic experience can be completed while the object is subjectively conceived or personally created, or while the individual is near to the narcissistic state of primary identification of earlier date.
> The erotic experience can be completed by anything that brings relief to the erotic instinctual drive, and that allows of fore-pleasure, rising tension of general and local excitement, climax and detumescence or its equivalent, followed by a period of lack of desire (which may itself produce anxiety because of the temporary annihilation of the subjective object created through desire). *On the other hand, the aggressive impulses do not give any satisfactory experience unless there is opposition. The opposition comes from the environment, from the NOT-ME which gradually comes to be distinguished from the ME.* (1950:215; italics added)

Although Winnicott is here describing a progress in psychoanalysis, which follows a progress in the baby's mind, he might well also be describing the progress of a love relationship. The important point is that which draws attention to the need for opposition, so that aggressive impulses can be *satisfied:* for opposition, we may read "touch with reality"—the reality of another person, and his or her existence in the real world. In *Lady Chatterley,* Lawrence provides himself, in his ideal relationship, with a partner who is neither real nor exists in a real world—and provides no opposition. All is still "subjectively conceived" and narcissistic. Lawrence's novel is too much enclosed in the monistic *Me*—and so is the attitude to sexual relationships he recommends by implication. Even Connie, the created love object, has no opposition to offer—as Ursula offers in *Women in Love,* and as Frieda eminently did, as a real woman, who threw pots at his head.

The sense of continuity in a love relationship that can transcend periods of anxiety and deadness depends upon a complexity of shared elements between the partners that belong to the civilized plane. A love relationship that was solely erotic, such as Lawrence tries to postulate here, would find periods in which desire was allayed, with the love-object "annihilated," to be intolerable—one has to learn, as it were, to let things "die" for a time, without fearing death or loss because of it. Related to this is the energetically idealizing title of the poem-sequence *Look! We Have Come Through!* Nobody has ever come through, and no one ever will. We all need to go on contesting, seeking, and re-creating—coming through, yes, but never come through. To cry, "Look! We have come through!" is to court disaster, because it is implicitly to make impossible demands on life and insist that it *must* be good now, at will. Of course, a confidence in a relationship can grow, but even so, here, the very insistent note of that "Look!" suggests a lack of confidence against which Lawrence is exerting a destructively idealizing urge.

What Lawrence is unable to do in *Lady Chatterley* is to find the clue to continuity—by allowing the sexual and erotic to fall into place in the larger complex of relationship and love. This larger complex includes the aggressive, the destructive, and the sense of the external *Not-Me*—and civilized values by which conflict and setbacks can be resolved and transcended. In these civilized areas are to be found possibilities of continuity and survival: the lover who relies solely on the erotic is doomed to fear from time to time, because he has allayed desire and thus destroyed the object of his love for the time. To quote Guntrip again, "the object is lost sight of" and "the pleasure soon evaporates." We all know this kind of deep anxiety from our honeymoon days—and *Lady Chatterley's Lover* fails because it never develops beyond the honeymoon stages of touch to a mutuality that enables us to transcend moments of separation, anxiety, the subsidence of passion, and the fear of ceasing to exist.

Winnicott's final paragraph is illuminating here: "In adult and mature sexual intercourse, it is perhaps true that it is not the purely erotic satisfactions that need a specific object. It is the aggressive or destructive impulse in the fused impulse that fixes the object and determines the need that is felt for the partner's actual presence, satisfaction, and survival" (1950:218).

Here we have, in the language of modern psychology, an expression of that need for mutual regard, in freedom and separate togetherness such as Chaucer and Shakespeare explore in the quest for love, and such as we know Lawrence to have explored in his best work.

Lawrence's error, in this bad work, was to concentrate too exclusively on the erotic, at the expense of the need to find the actuality of the partner in love, in the world out there—in those areas where aggressive and destructive impulses find opposition, and can be fused and brought to civilized association. In one sense the partner given Mellors is annihilated by him; in another sense Lawrence is enclosed in his narcissism like a fetus—and has annihilated everything except himself. He makes the world as monistic as it is for the newborn baby. In this his work becomes as far from reality as it is possible to get.

Until we devise more effective modes of discussing these deeper aspects of an author's psychology, however, we cannot hope to continue literary analysis at such a level. We should, however, remember and try to recognize the deeper elements that belong to areas of Lawrence's consciousness formed in his primitive early relationship with his mother—at the time of feeding and weaning—and long before the later time of son-lover-to-the-mother whose experience he records in *Sons and Lovers*. Everything we examine of, say, Lawrence's oedipal impulses toward his father and mother has earlier concomitants, in which were formed his very capacities to utter images at all, and to explore experience in fantasy as he does in his writings. The very nature of his sexual fantasy, as I have suggested here, is inevitably closely linked with intense feelings for the mother—and so, inevitably, she and every heroine merge. But the sons-and-lovers problem is but an extension of a much deeper dissociation caused by traumatic experience, or failures of the maternal environment, in Lawrence's earliest infancy.

Certainly we shall have no difficulty in accepting that sex for Lawrence was full of trouble. He makes it so for Mellors, and so, in many of his books he seeks to allay this trouble and, by coming to the root of it, to exorcize it. The trouble, however, was so deep (and Lawrence was, we are forced to say, so neurotic) that in fact, despite all his brave, creative, and supreme efforts, he could never overcome his sense of doom, following on the sexual expression of love. In personal love he could but attain the "measure of equanimity" such as is reached by Mellors and Connie, and the protagonists of *Look! We Have Come Through!*

Possibly, as we would consider now, psychoanalysis might have helped Lawrence personally to overcome this difficulty in his living.

But it is because he could not overcome these problems as an artist, despite his genius, that he became in the end malevolent and destructive. He could not redeem his inner reality and its agonized distortions; so he protected himself by projecting the distortions on to external reality—on to the industrial world, and to England, and, in the end, over human nature.

NOTES

1. One unfortunate effect of the book's release was of course an increased tolerance of pornography such as that of Henry Miller and other writers without even his pretensions. Publishers have been quick to take commercial advantage of this. No one can pretend the impulse to market *Fanny Hill* or Frank Harris is a "literary" one.

2. This clue suggests also an identification by the letter-code AWR with St MAWR of *St Mawr,* with the Stallion for whom Lou (with whom Lawrence identifies) has such affection.

REFERENCES

Bunyan, J. [1678 / 1684] 1965. *Pilgrim's Progress.* London: Penguin.

Carswell, C. 1932. *The Savage Pilgrimage: A Narrative of D. H. Lawrence.* London: Chatto and Windus.

Eliot, T. S. 1923. "The Function of Criticism." In *Selected Essays,* pp. 12–22. London: Faber and Faber, 1932.

E. T. (Jessie Chambers). 1936. *D. H. Lawrence: A Personal Record.* London: Cape.

Fairbairn, W. R. D. 1952. *Psychoanalytic Studies of the Personality.* London: Tavistock.

Guntrip, H. 1961. *Personality Structure and Human Interaction.* London: Hogarth.

Lawrence, D. H. 1913. *Sons and Lovers.* London: Heinemann.

———. [1915] 1949. *The Rainbow.* London: Methuen.

———. [1928] 1960. *Lady Chatterley's Lover.* London: Penguin.

———. 1964. *Complete Poems.* Edited by V. de S. Pinto and W. Roberts. London: Heinemann.

Thompson, E. P. 1962. *The Making of the English Working Class.* London: Gollancz.

Winnicott, D. W. 1945. "Primitive Emotional Development." In Winnicott, *Collected Papers,* pp. 145–56.

————. 1950. "Aggression in Relation to Emotional Development." In Winnicott, *Collected Papers*, pp. 204–18.

————. 1956. "Primary Maternal Preoccupation." In Winnicott, *Collected Papers*, pp. 300–5.

————. 1957. *The Child and the Family*. London: Tavistock.

————. 1958. *Collected Papers: Through Paediatrics to Psycho-Analysis*. London: Tavistock.

11

Frost, Winnicott, Burke

RICHARD POIRIER

Frost was among the first to be openly skeptical of the modernist complaint that the twentieth century was a uniquely terrible one, and his skepticism was understandably directed toward his compatriots and competitors, Pound and especially Eliot. In Eliot's case—though Frost never quite puts it this way—the effort to give the appearance of cultural necessity to modernist literary practices was compelled, especially in the early poems, by problems and necessities altogether more personal. Allusive densities, stylistic and formal intricacies were the results, so we were asked to think, of the author's preoccupation with what Frost sardonically calls "the larger excruciations." Eliot's "The Metaphysical Poets" offered, in 1921, one of the more pretentious apologias for this position, even to the pretend-tentative tones, as of a man reluctantly transmitting a vision of poetic vocation reluctantly accepted as a cultural burden. "We can only say," he wrote,

> that it appears likely that poets in our civilization, as it exists at present, must be *difficult*. Our civilization comprehends great variety and complexity, and this variety and complexity, playing upon a refined sensibility, must produce various and complex results. The

poet must become more and more comprehensive, more allusive, more indirect, in order to force, to dislocate if necessary, language into his meaning.

Modernist literature, that is, is obliged by the conditions under which it is written to be "difficult" and "complex," "comprehensive," "allusive," and dislocating.

If, to take exception, it were asked when poets could be or ever have been anything other than "difficult," "complex," etc., Eliot would say that "our civilization" requires them to be more so, indeed "more and more" so. Presumably if the poet were not "difficult"—and Frost was manifestly not "difficult" in Eliot's sense—then this was evidence (and there would surely be more) that he was not "in our civilization" and that he was not of "a refined sensibility." Eliot was telling literary criticism where and how it should go fishing for the Big Ones in deep water. Obediently and subserviently, literary criticism, which has not even yet sufficiently challenged some of Eliot's self-serving critical dicta or his confusions of personal aridities with cultural wastelands, did just what he wanted them to do. Frost was left, so it seemed, in the shallows, admired of a Sunday by ladies and old men peering off country bridges. In my view, however, he maneuvered himself into depths beyond any of the hooks criticism has so far put out to catch him.

This is still another, a renewed effort to find out where he is, and I am calling for assistance on three writers remarkable in their own right: the indispensable Emerson; Kenneth Burke, in his own Emersonian moods; and the British psychoanalyst D. W. Winnicott. About Winnicott it is not possible to say here as much as I would like, but my rehearsal of certain of his better-known psychoanalytic theories will immediately suggest affinities to the literary theories of Emerson, Burke, and Frost, and thus to Frost's poetry, which is itself a species of literary theory. My initial emphasis will be on the term "transitional objects," which Winnicott first discussed in his paper "Transitional Objects and Transitional Phenomena" (1953), and which figures throughout his book *Playing and Reality* (published in the year of his death, 1971) and in a number of essays, some of which are collected in *The Maturational Processes*.

The term *transitional objects* is at first a little tricky because Winnicott is primarily concerned not with objects so much as with transitional states in the infant. He traces the process by which the infant's allegiances change from one object to other objects. There is a question of whether or not, in such cases, we should even refer to "objects," so great is the infant's subjective and creative investment in the transitions. The essential transitions are these: the infant has at first a sense of being merged with its mother; it then attaches itself to an external object, usually the breast, which is felt by the infant still to be part of itself; it then moves from this to an object even more external, any soft fondleable doll, a piece of blanket, a toy, which is thereby endowed with some of the associations attached to the breast. At all stages, including the last, the infant, though in transition from internal to external objects, may and should be given a sense of omnipotence and of magical control. Winnicott will later emphasize, as he does in the essay entitled "Communicating and Not Communicating" (1963), that by magical control he means something more general—"the creative aspect of experience," as he calls it. These are of course the infant's illusions, but the mother, if she is smart about her own future as well as the child's, will assist in the illusion of the infant's omnipotence and control. Such illusions (of omnipotence, control, and of magical creativity) are not, as we know from reading *King Lear* and *Moby-Dick*, signs of healthy adulthood. But according to Winnicott, and it is easy to be persuaded, there is no productive or safe way to *dis*illusion the child without first allowing it these illusions. Otherwise the desires for omnipotence and magical control go unsatisfied. They persist into adult ambition, along with a refusal to recognize their illusionary and dangerous nature. You end up, that is, with a Captain Ahab around the house instead of a Robert Frost, who, not incidentally, was raised almost entirely by women (his often absent father died when Robert was eleven), and fairly indulgent ones at that. The infant who feels omnipotent, confirmed in its illusion that it creates the object of its desire, has the best chance to find its way to a more neutral kind of contact with the ever-increasing number of outside things that call for its attention.

Here—and this is especially important to this inquiry and to certain theories of language—the infant enters an intermediate area of experience. What Winnicott writes about this intermediate area in *Playing and Reality* will, I trust, make his relevance to Frost's poetry a bit clearer than it may have seemed up to now: "This intermediate area of experience, unchallenged in respect of its belonging to inner or external (shared) reality, constitutes the greater part of the infant's experience, and throughout life is retained in the intense experiencing that belongs to the arts and to religion and to imaginative living, and to creative scientific work." Think for a moment what happens to "things," to "objects," in this "intermediate area of experience." It is an area "unchallenged," you will note, in respect "of its belonging to inner or to external (shared) reality." It is precisely in this area, first created by the infant, that adult creation also takes place.

For Winnicott, cultural life generally is made possible by an adult equivalent of the transitional phenomena he observed in his clinical work with infants. The central point is that for the child, as well as for the artist, communication manages to evade the issue of whether or not the objects involved are either subjective or objectively perceived. The precursor of poetry is, in that sense, the infant's creative work with transitional objects; the precursor of the poet is the child "lost in play." Winnicott's special genius shows most persuasively, and is of greatest use to literary theory, in his rejection of the workings of an American ego psychology. American ego psychology tends to put its emphasis on structure and structuring, and it tends to identify internal conflicts as conflicts with the Real, rather than as conflicts of self-identification, which are most acutely felt in the child. Lawrance Thompson's official biography of Frost (1966; 1970; Thompson and Winnick 1976) is an example of the adaptation to literary study of American ego psychology in its most rudimentary forms, and it is notably prejudicial in dealing with a poet who, by my estimates, was throughout his life an old seventeen, which is nonetheless older than many of us ever get. The view of language befitting Thompson's practices as biographer and reader is one that finds it necessary to rigidify and literalize Frost's voice and Frost's metaphors, whether these are found in his lectures, his letters, his conversation, or in his poetry. Playfulness thereby becomes a way merely of hiding or disguising a true line of intent which, for Thompson, is seldom a very pleasant one. How astonished, how appalled people were when it turned out, if they believed Thompson, that Frost was not the dear but cagey old thing of legend and public relations. How could he write those beautiful poems and be such a son of a bitch? And how all the more unpardonable that he was a son of a bitch not in London, like Eliot, or Dublin, like Yeats, or Venice, like Pound, against suitably glamorous and shadowy backdrops—but in places like Ripton, Vermont, where, instead of giving radio broadcasts for the Fascists, you showed your true colors by cheating neighbors in the egg business.

Obviously we need to find some other way to look at him. We need to understand him, as we probably need to understand most men and women of genius, in the aspect of childhood. That is where Winnicott may be helpful. His work intersects that of Jacques Lacan, to whom he refers (long before it was stylish to do so) in an appreciative way, especially when it comes to identifying the meaning of objects to the infant child. For Lacan, as for Winnicott, the particular object used by the child for comfort or play or security is not, in itself, a matter of consequence. Substitute objects are not symbols; they are not representational. The child could express itself with anything at all. What the child creates at play, as it chooses and manipulates objects, is a species of language; the language may (but need not) include words, and it constitutes a text that can be read and interpreted. Winnicott therefore takes a very positive and excited view of the deviousness essential to play and to poetic expression. This is consistent with his account of the intermediate realm where objects have no clear or stable identity. "In the artist of all kinds," he writes in the essay "Communicating and Not Communicating," "I think I can detect an inherent dilemma, which belongs to the co-existence of the two trends, the urgent need to communicate and the still more urgent need not to be found. This might account for the fact"—and he is here offering what is to me a crucial perception—"that we cannot conceive of an artist's coming to the end of the task that occupies his whole nature." Obviously he is talking of a great artist, one whose work constitutes not a mere accumulation of works but which emerges as a shape, an arc, let us say, compelled less by prior, conscious intention than by some productive necessity of being. I call his perception crucial, however, not because it intelligently queries the mystery of artistic creation. Its greater importance is that it encourages us to think of the task of the poet as one that "occupies his whole nature," as it would the nature, again, of a child "lost in play." The poet, like the child, is fully immersed in, obsessionally possessed by objects whose status, whether subjective or objective, is never wholly verifiable.

I turn now to a second and related text, an essay by Kenneth Burke called "What Are the Signs of What?," subtitled "A Theory of 'Entitlement' " (1962). (It is reprinted in *Language as Symbolic Action* [1966].) Burke offers his argument with a tentativeness that makes it sound almost hazardously original. And it is, even though its origins are to be found conspicuously in Emerson, about whom Burke has written so wonderfully. In this instance, however, he refers only, and rather vaguely, to the long essay "Nature," and does not mention the centrally appropriate text, the essay called "The Poet" (1844). There, still at this point speaking positively of Swedenborg, Emerson says, and I italicize, *"I do not know the man in history to whom things stood so uniformly for words."* Emerson means words in the "vehicular and transitive" sense, having written in the previous paragraph that "all language is vehicular and transitive, and is good, as ferries and horses are, for conveyance, not as farms and houses are, for homestead." In twenty dense but always exciting pages Burke affirms the same idea about "things" and "words" and uses the same phrasing: "In this sense things would be the signs of words." If one were to make a more thorough tracing of the line from Emerson to Burke, it would include Charles Pierce in the middle and Jacques Derrida at the end. Remarking, in *Of Grammatology* (1967), that "Pierce goes very far in the direction that I have called deconstruction of the transcendental signified," Derrida further observes that for Pierce "the thing itself is a sign . . . manifestation itself does not reveal a presence, it makes a sign."

From among these writers I have chosen Burke for particular notice because his articulation of the position is the most developed and the most clear. Briefly, he wants to reverse the usual, commonsense view that "words are the signs of things." He explains this commonsense view to mean that "various things in our way of living are thought to be singled out by words that stand for them; and in this sense the words are said to be the 'signs' of those corresponding things." Take, for example, Frost's "Spring Pools":

> These pools that, though in forests, still reflect
> The total sky almost without defect,
> And like the flowers beside them, chill and shiver,
> Will like the flowers beside them soon be gone,
> And yet not out by any brook or river,
> But up by roots to bring dark foliage on.
>
> The trees that have it in their pent-up buds
> To darken nature and be summer woods—
> Let them think twice before they use their powers
> To blot out and drink up and sweep away
> These flowery waters and these watery flowers
> From snow that melted only yesterday.

Note particularly the first two lines: "These pools that, though in forests, still reflect / The total sky almost without defect." In a commonsense view, the word "pools" would be a "sign" of small bodies of water, deeper than a puddle and fed recurrently from outside, especially by melting snow, the best New England has to offer; the word "forests" would refer to any gathering of trees on a large tract of land. Surely some of us have seen such things. Or have we? We can at least picture such things. But can we? If you want to settle for the possibility that all he means is that you can see pools like these in lots of forests, what then do you do with "total sky"? The commonsense view by which "words are the signs of things" does not appear to answer the case here. Because while you might see pools in *a* forest, how, except in a reconnaissance aircraft, do you see pools in "forests"? If you want to find these pools, then you will have to look for them someplace else. One likely spot, as David Bromwich and William Keach have shown me, is in Shelley's "To Jane: The Invitation" and "To Jane: The Recollection." (It is in these same poems, incidentally, that Frost probably found "objects" for still other poems: Shelley's "An atmosphere without a breath" insinuates itself into a poem called "Atmosphere"; and Shelley's "Blots one dear image out" is transmitted both to "Spring Pools" and to "For Once, Then, Something.")

To read Frost as if "words are the signs of things" gets you into trouble, and more trouble merely than the location of "pools" in "forests." It is necessary, therefore, to wonder with Burke and with Winnicott about the peculiar status of "things" or "objects" in his poetry and of the inadequacy, when it comes to accounting for that status, of the commonsense idea of the relation of words to objects. As I have indicated, Burke proposes, "if only as a *tour de force*," that we invert the usual view that "words are the signs of things" and instead try to uphold the proposition that "things are the signs of words." If we did so, might it not be discovered, he asks, that words

> possess a "spirit" peculiar to their nature as words? And might *the things of experience then become in effect the materialization of such spirit,* the manifestation of this spirit in visible tangible bodies. . . . Thereby the things of the world become material exemplars of the values which the tribal idiom [or Shelley, or infant desire] has placed upon them. . . . Things become the signs of the genius that resides in words [so that] for man nature is emblematic of the spirit imposed upon it by man's linguistic genius. (italics added)

This is, of course, pure Emerson. Emerson, Burke, Winnicott—the implication in all three is that "things" or "objects" become endowed with magic and with meaning. Because of this, "things" or "objects" then entitle us to speak in all kinds of ways that would be plain silly if language had to do with the object only in a merely referential way.

This is not to say that the "things" or "objects" do not exist. It is to say, rather, that for a child or a poet they exist in a form of verbal and creative opportunity. Poetry is in a sense the area of performance where a residue of the infant's sense of omnipotence, the infant's illusion of totally creative power over "things" and "objects," confronts and must negotiate with the so-called reality principle.

Frost, in his concept of metaphor, more or less subscribes to this view. For him metaphor is a challenge initially laid down, the testing out of and effort to appropriate a thing or an object to some subjective use or to what he would call "enthusiasm." In the progress of the poem, you discover the limits of the metaphor. The discovery constitutes your "Education by Poetry" (1931), as Frost titled one of his lectures:

> Unless you are at home in the metaphor, unless you've had your proper poetical education in the metaphor, you are not safe anywhere. Because you are not at ease with figurative values: you don't know the metaphor in its strength and weakness. You don't know how far you can expect to ride it and when it may break down with you. You are not safe in science; you are not safe in history.

Good advice, but think how dull a poetry would be that proceeded quite so judiciously. In practice, Frost continually defies, by his own intrusive urgency of voice, precisely the "education" offered by the working out of a given metaphor. If the poems are about the play of metaphor, the testing out of possibilities in metaphoric language, then the test, with its predictably conservative outcome, is very often subverted by the action of voice. That is, voice can choose to collaborate with the positions arrived at by arbitrations going on within the metaphors of the poem, or it can choose to reject them. Where then is Frost? Is he in the voice? Is he in the metaphoric process? Where? For example, at the end of line one of "Spring Pools"—"These pools that, though in forests, still reflect"—he obviously wants the Miltonic enjambment to tease us with the sentimental notion that "pools" can think and share human consciousness. The notion is immediately dropped by, and into, the next line—they "reflect," it turns out, "The total sky almost without defect." Here is a little example of how we are educated by metaphor, if we need to be. Only eight lines later, however, he is insisting, quite angrily, that even if pools do *not* think, trees really *do*: "Let them think twice before they use their powers / To blot out and drink up and sweep away / These flowery waters and these watery flowers / From snow that melted only yesterday." Perhaps, as Frank Lentricchia (1975) says, the poem is "as much about shifting subjective states which are touched off by changes in the objective world as it is about nature itself." And yet the voice here, in making demands upon "nature itself" or "the objective world" (whatever those can be said to be), does not refer us for justification to any definable "subjective state," unless to something so baggy and banal as the passing of time and the threat of death. We are left suspended, and the suspension is a result of voice which creates rather than resolves the problem of identity.

Voice in Frost depends heavily on words like "maybe," or "perhaps," or "it seems," or "as if." As Margery Sabin shows, "Once by the Pacific" is a poem in which voice quite obviously scrambles the message, no matter what you take the message to be, but where it is obvious too that Frost wants to make fun of the vision of apocalypse much as he does elsewhere in his writing. In the process, the voice can deliver with firm, unruffled regularity a line that has no less than four disclaimers: "you could not tell . . . and yet . . . it looked . . . as if / The shore was lucky in being backed by cliff / The cliff in being backed by continent." And while he is is saying that "you could not tell" (in the idiomatic sense of "you couldn't know for sure") he is in another sense going right ahead and "telling" you, as if what he is not sure of is probably the case. "You get more credit for thinking," he wrote to Louis Untermeyer in 1917,

> if you restate formulae or cite cases that fall in easily under formulate, but all the fun is outside, saying things that suggest formulae that won't formulate—that almost but don't quite formulate. I should like to be so subtle at this game as to seem to the casual person altogether obvious. The casual person would assume that I meant nothing or else I came near enough meaning something he was familiar with to mean it for all practical purposes.

What I am getting round to saying is that with respect to "things" and "objects" Frost was no less schizophrenic than he was with respect to his readers or to his own career, as at once a massively popular poet and, he claimed, the greatest craftsman of the age. In his poems of hiding, or in his poems of retreat or admitted deception, in his repeated confession that he is a trickster and a deceiver, he is at the same time— and by these very admissions—pretending to be outrageously truthful and available. The availability, the admission of disguise, is the ultimate mask of a permanently hidden Frost. Forget about some break-in artist finding an open window. His voice sounds familiar precisely when he is being most hidden. To return, for brevity, to Winnicott, in "Communicating and Not Communicating":

> I suggest that in health there is a core of personality that corresponds to the true self of the split personality; I suggest that this core never communicates with the world of perceived objects, and that the individual person knows that it must never be communicated with or be influenced by external reality. This is my main point, and the point of thought which is the center of an intellectual world. . . . Although healthy persons communicate and enjoy communicating, the other fact is equally true, that *each individual is an isolate, permanently non-communicating, permanently unknown, in fact unfound.*

I am proposing, then, the following: the emphasis on voice in Frost's poetry and in his statements about poetry is not in fact an indication of his enjoyment of communication, of his being *with* and *of* the voices he uses. Quite the opposite. It is his way (and ours?) of enjoying his extraordinary capacity for *not* communicating. He takes enormous pleasure in knowing all the ways in which the messages received by his readers are in fact never sent, never delivered, constantly detoured, interrupted, readdressed, returned unopened, or, especially, returned because of insufficient postage. In the voice is not the *found* but the *unfound* and *unknown* Frost.

Frost writing directly about disguise and deception, Frost pursuing the unfindable, Frost by conscious error naming the unnameable, Frost evoking a big buck and then saying "that was all," Frost walking out alone and getting lost so that he can (or can he?) find himself—an anthology could be made for each of these. He is so inordinately proud of his candor on the subject of evasiveness that most people have been dissuaded from recognizing that he is not being candid at all. The admissions of an elusive self are meant to defeat our discovery that in fact there is in his poetry a true absence of self.

I want to focus more directly now on voice as a form not of revelation but of deception, on the admission of deception and on the technique of deception, on disguise as an evidence that Frost is essentially unknowable and unfindable. And I want to do this while also insisting on the evidence that Frost is often a radically nonreferential poet. It is less true, to repeat, that words are the signs of "things" in Frost than that "things" are the signs of words. "Things" entitle words, and do so because, as if left behind by the children in "Directive," "things" have been made magical and creative. Speechless in themselves, they are nonetheless waiting to be read and talked about.

How and why, you may ask, should we connect these aspects of Frost? That is, why attempt to show that the voice, as a form of self-disguise instead of self-disclosure, is intimately related to the notion of "things as the signs of words"? I can answer most economically by pointing to a characteristic turn that Frost shares with Thoreau. One of the ways Frost achieves the illusion of vernacular familiarity is by his use of the word "thing" and variants of "thing" like "anything," "nothing," "something." His poetic voice rides, in such instances, on one of the inevitable, inescapable, trusting words of ordinary speech, especially when we talk without expectation of challenge about matters that do not admit of proof. In other words, within the most vernacular usages there hides the deepest mysteries—the mystery of "things." Here is a small sampling, and any reader of Frost can easily add to it:

> "Something there is that doesn't love a wall." ("Mending Wall")

> "He did not notice in that smooth coal
> The one thing palpable besides the soul" ("Star in a Stone Boat")

> "For once, then, something." ("For Once, Then, Something")

> "With no expression, nothing to express." ("Desert Places")

> "Perhaps it was something about the heat of the sun,
> Something, perhaps, about the lack of sound—" ("Mowing")

> "One had to be versed in country things
> Not to believe the phoebes wept" ("The Need of Being Versed
> in Country Things")

> "Something sinister in the tone
> Told me my secret must be known." ("Bereft")

> "We love the things we love for what they are." ("Hyla Brook")

Many of Frost's poems of nature are written as if by someone who suspects that someone else has been there before him, working the same turf, leaving "something" for him to find. These are also, usually, his great mythological poems, like "A Tuft of Flowers," "Mowing," or "Putting in the Seed," like "Mending Wall," "After Apple-Picking," or

"Directive." The leavings, the tracings of others, as in "Never Again Would Birds' Song Be the Same," where Eve's voice is crossed upon the voices of birds in "the garden" or "a wood"—it is never possible to know *what* it is that has been left in the "things" seen or heard, in flowers, pools, the wind in the trees, in bundles of logs, in bird song. Indeed it may be "nothing." But if it is imaginably "nothing" then it is also possible that it is "something" or "anything."

As in the poem "The Census-Taker," Frost goes into a place where others have been in order to count things. He may find nothing to count, and yet there is nonetheless the prospect, promise, directive to make a count and an estimate. Sometimes, as in "Desert Places," he is himself "too absent-spirited to count." What does it mean in these circumstances to be "absent-spirited" unless it means, in part, not being able to find any other familiar, companionable, confirming spirit there—not even the odd little bird of "The Wood-Pile"; and what does it mean "to count"? For a poet it can mean to hold to his meter and to his syllables. In the absence of familiar or prior spirits (all of them blanked out by the snow) he cannot "count," cannot write verse, though of course he is writing the poem that all the while intimates this. He cannot write because he is prevented from reading. Snow, by covering things, obliterates any signs, any traces of other, of previous human presences. That, generally speaking, is the significance of Frost's obsession with snowfall. Snow is not a blank on which he tries to *write;* it is a blank that threatens his capacity to *read:* "A blanker whiteness of benighted snow / With no expression, nothing to express." Snow does not allow, say, the "hay to make" (in "Mowing"); it does not allow pools to "reflect," or oven birds to ask "what to make of a diminished thing"—it doesn't, that is, let us see how "things" may *make* poetry.

The fear of snow, the fascination with "snow" in Frost—most brilliantly and completely explored in the long and neglected poem called "Snow" (1916)—is that it covers the entitlements that allow him to ask if perhaps there is "something," "anything," or "nothing" left for him out there. In this preoccupation he precedes, and by a number of years, Wallace Stevens, whose "The Snow Man" first appeared in 1921. Snow, like death, threatens Frost's capacity to live in that intermediate stage where "things" carry entitlements from the past which he can try to read and play with. To return to Burke, and the eloquent conclusion of his essay: "if the things of nature are, for man, the visible signs of their verbal entitlements, then nature gleams secretly with a most fantastic shimmer of words and social relationships. And quite as men's views of the supernatural embody the forms of language and society in recognized ways, so their views of the natural would embody these same forms, however furtively." "Furtively" is for my purposes exactly the right word. Nature, the nature of "things," entitles Frost to read and to speak and, above all, to speak in a voice that hides him. He is, I am beginning to think, the Hawthorne of American poetry.

REFERENCES

Burke, K. 1962. "What Are the Signs of What? (A Theory of 'Entitlement')." In *Language as Symbolic Action: Essays on Life, Literature, and Method*. Berkeley: University of California Press, 1966.

Derrida, J. 1967. *Of Grammatology*. Translated by G. C. Spivak. Baltimore: Johns Hopkins University Press, 1976.

Emerson, R. W. [1844] 1983. "The Poet." In *Essays and Lectures*. Edited by J. Porte. New York: Library of America.

Eliot, T. S. [1921] 1964. "The Metaphysical Poets." In *Selected Essays*. New York: Harcourt, Brace and World.

Frost, R. [1931] 1966. "Education by Poetry." In *Selected Prose*. Edited by E. C. Latham and L. Thompson. New York: Collier.

Lathem, E. C., ed. 1969. *The Poetry of Robert Frost*. New York: Holt, Rinehart and Winston.

Lentricchia, F. 1975. *Robert Frost: Modern Poetics and the Landscapes of Self*. Durham, N.C.: Duke University Press.

Thompson, L. 1966. *Robert Frost: The Early Years, 1874–1915*. New York: Holt, Rinehart and Winston.

———. 1970. *Robert Frost: The Years of Triumph, 1915–1938*. New York: Holt, Rinehart and Winston.

Thompson, L., and R. H. Winnick. 1976. *Robert Frost: The Later Years, 1938–1963*. New York: Holt, Rinehart and Winston.

Untermeyer, L., ed. 1963. *The Letters of Robert Frost to Louis Untermeyer*. New York: Holt, Rinehart and Winston.

Winnicott, D. W. 1963. "Communicating and Not Communicating Leading to a Study of Certain Opposites." In *The Maturational Processes and the Facilitating Environment: Studies in the Theory of Emotional Development*. New York: International Universities Press, 1966.

———. 1971. *Playing and Reality*. New York: Basic Books; London: Tavistock, 1984.

12

Samuel Beckett's Relationship to His Mother-Tongue

PATRICK J. CASEMENT

Beckett's writings abound with allusions to mothers, and many of these allusions are contemptuous. In Deirdre Bair's extensive biography of Beckett[1] (1978) we also find frequent references to Beckett's complicated relationship with his mother. This appears to have continued to be full of conflict until his mother died.

It would be simplistic to assume direct biographical links between Beckett's external relationship to his mother and the "mother" in his writings. Equally it should not be assumed that it is merely an expression of his internal relationship to his mother that we find in what he writes.

I wish to suggest that Beckett uses his writing, and in particular his writing in French, as a "potential space" (Winnicott 1971) in which he is able to play out something of his own unresolved internal relationship to his mother alongside the new phenomenon of the "re-created" mother of his literary art. I do not here wish to be specific as to the interconnections between these three mother-relationships (the internal, the external, and the re-created). I have preferred to let Beckett's text speak for itself, to let it pose questions that may invite further investigation rather than to offer premature answers myself in the limited brief of this paper. I should add that I have concentrated on Beckett's novels, not his plays.

There have been various reasons offered to explain Beckett's use of French as his primary literary language, adopted by him, so it is said, in order to escape the richness of the Irish speech rhythms. When asked about this Beckett is quoted as once saying that it was easier to write in French "without style" (149).

When Herbert Blau (codirector of the San Francisco Acting Workshop) asked Beckett about this use of two languages, and suggested that by writing in French he was avoiding one part of himself, he replied that there were a few things about himself he didn't like and French had the right "weakening effect" (516).

When writing in French Beckett certainly took great care that no sign of his English origins should be evident in his French. However, in addition to any question of literary style there is evidence quoted in the biography which suggests that Beckett's careful elimination of any trace of his mother-tongue may also have expressed his need to escape from his turbulent relationship with his mother. He had spent the first twenty-nine years of his life, until his break with his mother in 1937, in trying to free himself from her hold upon him. This had bound him to her almost as much from afar as when in her presence, and it seems that his mother's influence intruded into him so relentlessly it began to make him ill. It also threatened to make him unable to write, a problem that Beckett referred to as his "verbal constipation" (94). He tried to suppress his problems. Perhaps he also tried to seek refuge in forgetting.

> Memories are killing. So you must not think of certain things, of those that are dear to you, or rather you must think of them, for if you don't there is the danger of finding them, in your mind, little by little. That is to say, you must think of them for a while, a good while, every day several times a day, until they sink forever in the mud. That's an order. (*The Expelled,* in *Four Novellas,* p. 33)

If this can be taken as an allusion to Beckett's own thinking, what was he trying to forget? What was he trying to avoid? From the biography we learn that from an early age Beckett and his mother were at loggerheads. Her stubborn wish to rule, and overrule, was equaled only by his determination not to be possessed by her (194, 259ff.). From this backdrop to his adult life Beckett's sole ambition to be a writer emerged, precluding thought of any other meaningful use of his life. But to become a writer he needed time, he needed room to breathe and the chance to wait upon his reluctant Muse (159ff.). Over against this were his mother's constant attempts to have him brought to heel, if possible to enter the family business like his elder brother, or at least to be settled (if necessary to be crushed) into a "normal job" (154, 157, 214). For Beckett this would have been a fate worse than life, to be trapped forever in a place devoid of meaning, waiting for death—or perhaps for Godot.

Of his childhood Beckett offered the enigmatic comment "you might say I had a happy childhood . . . although I had little talent for happiness. . . . My father did not beat me, nor did my mother run away from home" (14). In the biography we find that it was his mother who beat him and his father who was absent (15ff.). The manner of this absence included his father's failure to stand up to this strong woman who used her explosive rages, as well as her clutch at the purse strings, to bend her children to her will (137, 250). His father, whom he loved, would secretly give him financial help beyond the allowance officially limited by his mother (142). But this clandestine support, behind his mother's back to keep the peace, was not enough to rescue Beckett from her overriding influence.

Beckett paid a dear price for this kind of peace. Among his psycho-somatic ailments he suffered from physical sensations of suffocation and choking (136). In addition he was frequently laid low by cysts and boils, which in their way would erupt with the suppressed venom of his feelings for which he had not yet found other forms of expression. It was as if his mother's attempts to control him threatened to kill the only seed of meaning to his life that he had discovered. To survive at all he may at times have brooded upon her death. If so he was later able to express this venom, better than his boils, by allowing the characters of his novels to speak out his own unthinkable thoughts: "I'm looking for my mother to kill her, I should have thought of that a bit earlier, before being born" (*The Unnamable*, p. 395). Elsewhere he has Molloy wonder hopefully whether his mother might be "already dead . . . ? I mean enough to bury" (*Molloy*, p. 7).

After his father's death in 1933, Beckett's elder brother Frank was the only remaining ally in his embattled relationship with his mother. It was to Frank he would cling for protection from the night terrors which then began to plague him. He tried to avoid sleeping because he was afraid to dream (174–75). He seemed to be close to a nervous breakdown. He was becoming unable to find any escape even in writing. Visits abroad always led ultimately back home. Drinking offered only temporary oblivion. And on his blackest days, it is said, he would enclose himself in his room curled up in a fetal position, with face to the wall, allowing no one near him (135). However, he maintained such lifelines as he had in his intimate correspondence with Thomas McGreevy (159, 169) and in long discussions of his problems with the late Dr. Geoffrey Thompson, his long-standing friend from Trinity College Dublin (169–70).

It was Geoffrey Thompson, himself later to become a psychoanalyst, who recommended that Beckett should receive psychoanalytic treatment to relieve him of these increasingly crippling ailments. Eventually he went to London where he was treated by Dr. W. R. Bion, who was then working at the Tavistock Clinic (177ff.). This at least clarified the problem, that Beckett was gripped by a fiercely ambivalent attachment to his mother. He could neither be with her nor could he, for any long period, keep himself away (202). If analysis were to have been able to release him from this pathological attachment to her, it would have taken longer than Beckett felt he could afford. Time as well as money were pressing issues for him. His conflict was constantly with him. Is Beckett again speaking of himself in *Molloy?* It certainly seems possible.

> And of myself, all my life, I think I had been going to my mother, with the purpose of establishing our relations on a less precarious footing. And when I was with her, and often I succeeded, I left her without having done anything. And when I was no longer with her I was again on my way to her, hoping to do better the next time. And when I appeared to give up and busy myself with something else, or with nothing at all any more, in reality I was hatching my plans and seeking the way to her house. (*Molloy,* p. 87)

When after two years Beckett left his analysis he told Bion that he was returning home to Dublin and that this was because he "owed" so much of himself to his mother (212). His attachment to her still remained complex and deep, and again there seem to be echoes of this in *Molloy.*

> I took her money, but I didn't come for that. My mother. I don't think too harshly of her. I know she did all she could not to have me, except of course the one thing, and if she never succeeded in getting me unstuck, it was that fate had earmarked me for less compassionate sewers. But it was well-meant and that's enough for me. No it's

not enough for me, but I give her credit, though she is my mother, for what she tried to do for me. (*Molloy*, p. 19)

Without his mother's money Beckett could not support himself while he remained unacknowledged by publishers and public alike. (His first novel, *Murphy,* had not sold well and his second novel, *Watt,* was rejected forty-four times before being accepted for publication.) But with his mother's money he was still her captive. And yet either way his own ambivalence held him to her just as strongly.

For in me there have always been two fools, among others, one asking nothing better than to stay where he is and the other imagining that life might be slightly less horrible a little further on. So that I was never disappointed, so to speak, whatever I did, in this domain. And these inseparable fools I indulged turn about, that they might understand their foolishness. (*Molloy*, p. 48)

Elsewhere in *Molloy* we seem to be offered a further glimpse of Beckett's struggle to resist the lure of this fated hated tie to his mother. Could anyone have held him back?

Could a woman have stopped me as I swept towards my mother? Probably. Better still, was such an encounter possible, I mean between me and a woman? . . . I once rubbed up against one. I don't mean my mother. I did more than rub up against her. And if you don't mind we'll leave my mother out of this. (*Molloy*, p. 56)

Something occurred in the autumn of 1937 about which Beckett remains silent (262). Its significance can be estimated from the fact that it enabled him to make the break with his mother that previously had seemed impossible. Again he went to France, this time to stay; and, as if to reinforce his need for separation, he turned to French and disowned his mother-tongue. Simultaneously then, from this newfound distance, he could allow himself to be surprised by moments of unsuspected affection for his mother which formerly he had kept hidden even from himself (280, 292ff.). The two sets of feeling for her could be allowed to emerge and to coexist. In *Molloy* too we find:

I called her Mag, when I had to call her something. And I called her Mag because for me, without my knowing why, the letter g abolished the syllable Ma, and as it were spat on it, better than any other letter would have done. And at the same time I satisfied a deep and

doubtless unacknowledged need, the need to have a Ma, that is a
mother, and to proclaim it, audibly. For before you say mag, you say
ma, inevitably. And da, in my part of the world, means father.
(*Molloy*, p. 17)

Beckett here plays with the syllable "Ma". In his wish to hide the
allusion to his mother he chooses the letter *g* as "better than any
other"; and it is better by far than *y*, which would instantly have
revealed his mother by name, for her name was May.

In the same passage Beckett makes a passing reference to his father,
as if to remind us that it was to the land and language of his Huguenot
forefathers he turned to escape from the siren call that had so frequently threatened to wreck him. Was he seeking there the paternal
influence that his father, in life, had been unable to provide for him?

From his refuge in France, and in French, Beckett could begin to
achieve the separateness and freedom from his mother's "savage loving" (263), which nothing else had made possible. He could then
succeed through language where other attempts had failed.

In the Addenda to the novel *Watt*, his last novel for many years to
be written directly into English, Beckett writes: "The maddened prize-
man . . . for all the good that frequent departures out of Ireland had
done for him, he might just as well have stayed there" (*Watt*, 248). But
in *Molloy* we find the following:

Perhaps they haven't buried her yet. In any case I have her room. I
sleep in her bed. I piss in her pot. I have taken her place. I must
resemble her more and more. All I need now is a son. Perhaps I have
one somewhere. But I think not. He would be old now, nearly as old
as myself. (*Molloy*, pp. 7–8)

As in so much of Beckett this piece of writing is filled with the *unlogical
logic* that dreams are made of. If then we think of Beckett as the
dreamer of this (and he was after all the writer of it), I think we may
sense an unconscious hopefulness that some life could conceivably exist
for him beyond the still-to-be-fathomed deep that lay ahead in the
writing of the *Trilogy;* beyond the despair, the death, and the dying of
it.

At the time of writing *Molloy* Beckett was already self-exiled in
France and into French. By leaving his motherland, and by finding
another language, he had found freedom enough to write. Yet strangely
it was only upon his later return to that once abandoned mother-
tongue that he seems to have been able to lay to rest the suffocating

influence on him of his mother who had so dominated his life in hers. Paradoxically too it was only when Beckett allowed his own language once again to resemble that of his mother that he could establish himself as separate from her, and himself most fully alive. I believe that here, even in the French, we can foresee the time when Beckett would find his own mother's son—the son who was that Self which for most of his life until then he had not been able to be.

To be able to write Beckett needed psychological space. Without this his creativity remained inhibited, along with his suppressed anger. In 1932 he had forlornly hoped that his Muse might erupt, that he might be able to excavate a poem "one of these dies diarrhoeae" (155). But, unable to vent his anger, and without the space he needed to become free in himself, he seems to have turned in upon himself to a point of impasse.

The Unnamable says of himself:

> I must have got embroiled in a kind of inverted spiral, I mean one the coils of which, instead of widening more and more, grew narrower and narrower and finally, given the kind of space in which I was supposed to evolve, would come to an end for lack of room. Faced then with the material impossibility of going any further I should no doubt have had to stop, unless of course I elected to set off again at once in the opposite direction, to unscrew myself as it were, after having screwed myself to a standstill. (*The Unnamable*, pp. 318–19)

As so often in his writing Beckett may be describing himself here by proxy. He had intimately known this strangulation of his creativity from which there was no way on but back. He could not write while there was no room for creative play, and yet it was particularly in the ability to play with words, and with language, that his genius ultimately lay.

Let us examine this area of creativity *in statu nascendi*. To be free to enter into imaginative and creative play a child needs there to be a space between himself and the mother, over which he has the autonomous rights of initiative. Given this space, which has been described by Winnicott (1958) as "being alone in the presence of the mother," the child then begins to explore the creative potential of this space. But this requires of the mother a sensitive reluctance to enter into this play area uninvited. If all goes well the playing child can put into this the products of his own imagination—being free to "include" her into, or out of, his play. He can use the mother's "absent" presence or her "present" absence as the warp and woof of his play. He can "create" or "uncreate" her at will, and thereby enjoy the magic of playing God and King over his own playrealm. The seeds of later creativity are sown and nurtured here. Of this Winnicott writes "It is in playing and only in playing that the individual child or adult is able to be creative and to use the whole personality, and it is only in being creative that the individual discovers the self" (1971:54). So, to be deprived here is no simple deprivation as it threatens the very essence of the child's creative potential. For Beckett it was to be suffocated and choked in a central part of the self to the point of inwardly "dying." And if the inner life be dead why should the body tarry so? In this light we may be able to understand Beckett's preoccupation with death as a wished-for state. He had near-glimpsed this, and had longed for the other kind of dying. He has Malone say: "I shall soon be quite dead at last in spite of all" (*Malone Dies*, p. 179).

Thus, when all is not well for a child he may not be able to play because the potential play area has become a sterile or persecutory world. This may occur if the mother is too long absent, leaving the child too depressed or too preoccupied to be free to play. Or, nearer to Beckett's experience, the space may be so dominated and intruded upon as to be affectively unavailable to the child. Faced by this threat a healthy child will resist his mother's invasion of his mental space, to preserve his own essential aliveness. The less vital child may collapse into a capitulation to these pressures, and in this compliance he abandons the inner stirrings of his own creativity. This was Beckett's particular dilemma. He had to fight back, to preserve from suffocation his essential creative ability, for to give in to these pressures upon him would have been to succumb to the worst kind of death for him. He would have become dead in himself, entombed within a body that had the perverse audacity to go limping on through "life" until a some-other-time death which never seemed to come. It was touch and go who would come out on top, he or his mother's misguided determination to act in Beckett's assumed best interests: "and when you cease to want, then life begins to ram her fish and chips down your gullet until you puke, and then the puke down your gullet until you puke the puke, and then the puked puke until you begin to like it" (*Watt*, p. 43).

At times it must have seemed much easier to capitulate, to give up any aspirations of becoming or being a writer. Without access to the necessary mental space, within which to play with the tools of his genius, Beckett felt that he had screwed himself to a standstill. He alludes to this sense of sterility in a playfully irreligious question in

Molloy: "What was God doing with himself before the creation?" (*Molloy*, p. 168).

Beckett had earlier begun to use his writing to prove that though it may be "hard to kick against the pricks" it was not impossible, choosing the title of his first collection of stories to proclaim this—*More Pricks than Kicks*. He seems to use this book to give an account of his experience of purgatory in life, and it is no accident that he gives the hero of this book the name Belacqua, which Beckett takes straight out of Dante's *Purgatorio*. His opening words are: "It was morning and Belacqua was stuck in the first of the canti in the moon. He was so bogged that he could move neither backward nor forward" (*More Pricks than Kicks*, p. 9).

In *Murphy,* which Beckett worked on from 1934 until it was accepted for publication in 1937, his hero begins and ends strapped into his rocking chair in which he escapes from the world by rocking himself into an orgasmic ecstasy.

> He sat in his chair in this way because it gave him pleasure! First it gave his body pleasure, it appeased his body. Then it set him free in his mind. For it was not until his body was appeased that he could come alive in his mind. . . . And life in his mind gave him pleasure, such pleasure that pleasure was not the word. (*Murphy*, p. 6)

In the mad patient, Mr. Endon, Murphy meets another who sought escape from the world and has found it more successfully than he can: "The relation between Mr. Murphy and Mr. Endon could not have been better summed up than by the former's sorrow at seeing himself in the latter's immunity from seeing anything but himself" (*Murphy*, p. 171). He envies Mr. Endon's *impenetrable insanity,* the perfect mental state—beyond the reach of anyone. But, unable to forgo his own sanity, Murphy sees himself as a failure and returns to his room to rock himself into a final explosive oblivion (*Murphy*, p. 172ff.).

Watt was Beckett's next novel, his first written after leaving Ireland, which he wrote in France during the war. He spoke of the writing of it as "only a game, a means of staying sane, a way to keep my hand in" (327).

In psychoanalysis we are familiar with the way in which a prolonged experience of an intrusive relationship can come to be internalized as a "persecutory object." This internal persecution, if succumbed to, can lead to mental illness or it can be resisted and expelled. In Beckett's subsequent writing in French he increasingly developed this theme of expulsion and of spitting out all that belonged to this former invasion of him, and he calls one of his short stories "The Expelled."

Beckett's part in the war, in France, may also have given him relief from his internal battle and offered him some diversion and hope. Having joined the Resistance, he had a chance to deal with those other invaders and to survive, and for his work in this he was later to receive the Croix de Guerre.

It was during the war that he began writing exclusively in French, and in this adopted language Beckett could start the purgation of his more hidden thoughts. He could thus begin to achieve in writing what his body had expressed symptomatically. L. Janvier, cotranslator of *Watt,* said "the 'dark he had struggled to keep under' was ultimately to become the source of his creative inspiration" (351). This seems true throughout his writings. "Look at Mammy. What rid me of her, in the end? I sometimes wonder. Perhaps they buried her alive, it wouldn't surprise me" (*Molloy,* p. 81). Now with the new freedom of his French, Beckett could be more hopeful, and his words could vent the suppressed "pus" of his feelings. "The truth about me will boil forth at last" (*The Unnamable,* p. 352).

The former crippling ambivalence, which had so bound him to his mother, Beckett was now able to allow into the open.

> I forgive her for having jostled me a little in the first months and spoiled the only endurable, just endurable, period of my enormous history. And I also give her credit for not having done it again, thanks to me, or for having stopped in time, when she did. And if ever I'm reduced to looking for a meaning in my life, you never can tell, it's in that old mess I'll stick my nose to begin with. (*Molloy,* p. 19)

And later in the *Trilogy,* while Malone is eagerly anticipating death, he remarks: "Let me say before I go any further that I forgive nobody. I wish them all an atrocious life and then the fires and ice of hell" (*Malone Dies,* p. 180).

Within this new language Beckett could contemplate the circularity of his life and possible exit from its engulfment. In *Molloy* he writes:

> And having heard, or more probably read somewhere in the days when I thought I would be well advised to educate myself, or amuse myself, or stupify myself, or kill time, that when a man in a forest thinks he's going forward in a straight line, in reality he is going in a circle, I did my best to go in a circle, hoping in this way to go in a straight line. For I stopped being half-witted and became sly, when-

ever I took the trouble. . . . And if I did not go in a rigorously straight line, with my system of going in a circle, at least I did not go in a circle, and that was something. And by going on doing this, day after day, and night after night, I looked forward to getting out of the forest some day. (*Molloy*, p. 85)

Typically, here, Molloy is trying to find his way back to his mother. We know that Beckett would often do this too. Equally we get the impression that his relationship to his mother was circular and encircling, as was the forest to Molloy. So maybe this could offer to be for Beckett his way out of that maze. By doing his best to go in a circle he could hope to be able to find something that would not be a circle, "and that would be something." Thus, in the course of this circular way of proceeding Beckett found in France, and later in French, the asylum that he looked for where at last he could begin to be free in himself and in his writing.

How close Beckett may have felt he came to inner annihilation we can perhaps judge from his description of near-extinction in *The Unnamable:*

perhaps that's what I feel, an outside and an inside and me in the middle, perhaps that's what I am, the thing that divides the world in two, on the one side the outside, on the other the inside. . . . I'm in the middle. I'm the partition, I've two surfaces and no thickness, perhaps that's what I feel, myself vibrating. I'm the tympanum, on the one hand the mind, on the other the world, I don't belong to either. (*The Unnamable,* p. 386)

In 1950 Beckett's mother died, he having done what he could to establish a more amicable relationship with her, but he took no possessions of hers with him when he returned to France. He seems to have preferred to remain unencumbered by further links or by associative ties (406).

I don't believe it was by chance that Beckett began to translate his French writings, as it were "back" into English, only after his mother had died. It is as if a taboo upon his mother-tongue had been exorcized with her death.

The process of translation seems always to have been difficult, Beckett at first using a translator to work with him. Later he began to translate his own work without this assistance. Of this process Seaver remarked, when cotranslating *The End* with Beckett, "what we ended up with was not a translation but a complete re-doing of the original.

And yet, even though it was completely different, he was totally faithful to the French. It was a completely new creation" (438). Bowles, cotranslator of *Molloy,* similarly recalled that Beckett had stressed "it shouldn't be merely translated; we should write a new book in the new language" (439).

Why such care to create a new work upon his return to using the once abandoned English? Of course the literary artist in Beckett required of him as much care to avoid traces of French style remaining in the English as in the reverse when working in French. But if, as the translator Janvier had intimated, there were dark elements of himself concealed in the French, then these would have had to be faced by Beckett when beginning to relinquish the defensive aspect of his initial flight from English. A further clue to this is indicated when Beckett turned on his artist friend Pierre Schneider who, I think, got too near to the truth for comfort when he had suggested that for Beckett writing in French was not so much an evasion as an attempt to state his darkest thoughts without actually confronting the inner sphere in which these thoughts were located (516). When Beckett had begun writing in French this may well have been true. He had needed to deaden that in himself which had been deadening him. Maybe then the work of translation included working at this delayed confrontation with himself.

If we compare the French and the English, some remarkable things emerge. The French is often bland whereas the English by comparison reveals a freshness and a new liveliness of language that seems absent in the original text. It has been suggested that Beckett may be a different person, or a different kind of writer, in one language from how he is in the other. Is it due to the years that had elapsed between the French and the English? Or does it reflect second thoughts on his writing, not necessarily dependent upon the passage of time? May it be due to differences endemic in the two languages? All of these are possibilities, but I would like to explore yet another.

Let us go back to a passage already referred to and compare this with the French: "The truth about me will boil forth at last, scalding, provided of course they don't start stuttering again" (*The Unnamable,* p. 352). In the French we find "D'une seule coulée la vérité enfin sur moi me ravagera" (Les Editions de Minuit, 1953:127). Although this clearly suggests the ravage that such an outpouring of self-truth may entail, the French falls short of the allusive fullness of the English version. There we find that Beckett chooses the phrase "will boil forth," which links immediately to his own years-long trouble with boils. He then moves on from "boil forth" to "scalding" (cf. the French "la coulée"). But it would also be entirely like Beckett to sense here a play upon the phonetic link between "scalding" and "scolding," with its reminders of childhood correction from a hotly correcting parent. It is typical of his translation that this short sentence alone is able to evoke such a plethoral image of internal turmoil. We get a glimpse of long-suppressed feelings that half-hopefully look forward to a someday cathartic outpouring. Alongside this we can see the caution of habitual doubt that anything so fulsome could be achieved, with the pessimistic fear that instead it might result in nothing more than an impotent stuttering which would continue to hold back just as violently as it strains to speak out.

We find a similar filling out with associative nuances in my next example: "Ah the old bitch, a nice dose she gave me, she and her lousy unconquerable genes. Bristling with boils ever since I was a brat, a fat lot of good that ever did me" (*Molloy*, p. 81). In the English we again find reference to boils, whereas in the French Beckett uses the word for "pimples" (boutons) instead of using "furoncle" (boil) or "clou" (carbuncle), either of which in the French would have been nearer to a description of his own troubles. This might be because Beckett chooses in the French to write "away" from himself, and this would be consistent with what we know about his need to get away from his past while writing in French. It is only upon translating this that Beckett allows more of himself to emerge into the English text.

We find a similar associative richness around his choice of the word "dose," which is absent in the French: "Ah elle me les a bien passées, la vache, ses indéfectibles saloperies de chromosomes. Que je sois hérissé de boutons, depuis l'âge le plus tendre, la belle affaire!" (Les Editions de Minuit, 1951:107). In the English there is a double entendre with Beckett's use of the English slang for "V.D.," which is further supported by this use of the word "lousy." The French "saloperies" with its allusion to "salope" (trollop or slut) has a similar connotation, which Beckett typically extends in the translation. Having given us to sense the risks of contamination from too close an intimacy, this idea is then left to argue with the contrary thought that Molloy's troubles were inherited from his mother. We are thus left with the impression that either way there was no escape, for what was to be gained by avoiding contact if the fateful effects of being the son of your mother follow you still just as inevitably?

Before leaving this example we may wonder whether there might be an implied sarcastic reference to a "dose" of medicine that is supposed to be good for you. Much of the unchangeable attitude of Beckett's mother toward him had been intended by her to be for his own good, as envisaged by her for him. A fat lot of good it had ever done Beckett to have had his mother's unconquerable good intentions for him or, for that matter, to have had his own boils bristling with the boiling of his own inner resentment against this. Either way there had seemed to be no winning or any escape.

When Beckett did find release from that which had bound him it is much more than just the release of his suppressed resentment that follows. He discovers a new freedom of expression in his writing.

> Personally I have no bone to pick with graveyards, I take the air there willingly perhaps more willingly than elsewhere, when take the air I must. The smell of corpses, distinctly perceptible under those of grass and humus mingled, I do not find unpleasant. (*First Love*, p. 8; cf. Les Editions de Minuit, 1970:8)

> a pair of venerable trees, more than venerable, dead, at either end of the bench. It was no doubt these trees one fine day, aripple with all their foliage, that had sown the idea of a bench, in someone's fancy. (*First Love*, p. 14; cf. Les Editions de Minuit, 1970:18.)[2]

In these examples we find a playfulness that is absent in the original. I shall indicate only a part of what is evident here: (1) The associative allusion to a boneyard and "I have no bone to pick with graveyards" is entirely absent in the French: ("Personellement je n'ai rien contre les cimetières, je m'y promène assez volontiers . . . quand je suis obligé de sortir"); (2) the play on the word "must," sliding into its other English meaning as it leads onto "the smell of corpses," is also absent in the French; (3) again a new fertility of thought is introduced when the trees "one fine day, aripple with all their foliage . . . had sown the idea of a bench." The French has only "qui avaient suggéré . . . l'idée du banc."

We can see a reemergence in Beckett's translation of that capacity for self-expression, and for creative play in writing, which I believe had been formerly inhibited and nearly destroyed.

Let us look at how Beckett speaks of this in what he writes. For instance he has Malone think upon death as providing him at least with an opportunity for play: "Now it is a game, I am going to play. I never knew how to play, till now. I longed to, but I knew it was impossible. And yet I often tried to" (*Malone Dies*, p. 180). Frequently, in the translating into English, we find Beckett playing with language, playing with words, bringing familiar words into new conjunctions;

infusing a fresh vitality into metaphor, phrase, and cliché, which in English had been long since dead without a proper burial. Beckett, who seems to have regarded himself as one who had "never been properly born" (*Watt*, p. 248), breathes new life into them. Through this return to his mother-tongue, which now he can use afresh as his own, Beckett is able to pass beyond his own unnamable death into a new aliveness.

In this escape from a half-life choked by his own mother-tongue, via his sojourn in another land and another language, with his eventual "translation" of himself "back" into English, we find what Winnicott speaks of as the essential need to recover a capacity to play. Winnicott regarded this as a central part to any successful analysis, and of this he says: "The person we are trying to help needs a new experience in a specialized setting. The experience is one of a non-purposive state, as one might say a sort of ticking over of the unintegrated personality" (1971:55). Compare this with Beckett writing in *Watt:* "Having oscillated all his life between the torments of a superficial loitering and the horrors of disinterested endeavour, he finds himself at last in a situation where to do nothing exclusively would be an act of the highest value, and significance" (*Watt*, p. 39).

As if to echo this, Winnicott continues: "There are patients who at times need the therapist to note the nonsense that belongs to the mental state of the individual at rest without the need even for the patient to communicate this nonsense, that is to say, without the need for the patient to organize nonsense. Organized nonsense is already a defence, just as organized chaos is a denial of chaos" (1971:56). Thus an opportunity for creative rest is missed if the therapist needs to find sense where nonsense is. This recalls how Beckett ends his novel *Watt:* "No symbols where none intended" (*Watt*, p. 255).

So we come, like Beckett, full circle. It is as if the French text emerged as a dream does within the dreamer. The French seems to be thrown up from the unconscious, disguised and overdetermined, often hiding as much as it reveals and yet containing the seeds of that which later can be revealed by interpretation. Beckett then works on his own text in much the same associative way as occurs in the work on a dream in an analytic session. At first Beckett needed a translator to work with him in this, for there was much "interpretive" work to be negotiated between the original text and the resultant richness of the new works brought finally to birth into English. Once freed from his mother Beckett becomes "mother" to himself, his return to English being so much more than to that which he had discarded. His circle does not bring him back to where he was before but to where before he couldn't be. So, with French en route, his formerly deadened Self "dies" as it were into life.[3]

I think it appropriate to end with words from Beckett himself, words given by him to Moran in the closing passage of *Molloy:*

> I have spoken of a voice telling me things. I was getting to know it better now, to understand what it wanted. It did not use the words that Moran had been taught when he was little and that he in his turn had taught to his little one. So that at first I did not know what it wanted. But in the end I understood this language. I understood it, I understand it, all wrong perhaps. That is not what matters. It told me to write the report. Does this mean I am freer than I was? I do not know. I shall learn. (*Molloy*, p. 176)

NOTES

1. All undated page numbers in the text refer to this biography.

2. I am indebted to Professor Christopher Ricks for drawing my attention to the last two of these examples of Beckett's translation from the French.

3. On this A. Alvarez comments: "His [Beckett's] move into French is also part of that spirit of negation he has so persistently explored. It involves a cat's cradle of complications which Watt might have been proud of: an Irishman living in Paris, writing in French about Irishmen, then translating himself triumphantly back into English. And genuinely transforming himself in the process: through his translations from his own French he has emerged as a master of English prose, which he certainly was not when he wrote only in English. In other words, even his creativity begins with a refusal, a denial of everything he had been up until that moment at the beginning of middle age when he began to write in a foreign language" (1973:47).

REFERENCES

Alvarez, A. 1973. *Beckett.* London: Collins / Fontana, 1978.
Bair, D. 1978. *Samuel Beckett: A Biography.* London: Jonathan Cape.
Beckett, S. 1934. *More Pricks than Kicks.* London: Pan Books.
———. 1969. *Murphy.* Juniper Book edition. London: Calder Books.
———. 1976. *Watt.* Calderbook edition. London: John Calder.
———. 1976. *Molloy; Malone Dies; The Unnamable.* London: John Calder.
———. 1977. *Four Novellas.* London: John Calder.

Winnicott, D. W. 1958. "The Capacity to Be Alone." In *The Maturational Processes and the Facilitating Environment: Studies in the Theory of Emotional Development*, pp. 29–36. New York: International Universities Press, 1965; London: Hogarth Press, 1965.

———. 1971. "Playing: Creative Activity and the Search for the Self." In *Playing and Reality*, New York: Basic Books; London: Tavistock.

Part Three

CULTURAL
FIELDS

13

Jesus and Object-Use: A Winnicottian Account of the Resurrection Myth

BROOKE HOPKINS

"The key to the reading of the gospels is that it is necessary to project in order to receive."
—Dolto and Severin, *The Jesus of Psychoanalysis*

No one will deny the centrality of the myth of the resurrection to Christian theology. To be sure, accounts of Christianity are as various as the spectrum, but if Christians can be said to be united in anything, it is in the belief that Jesus of Nazareth was crucified, died, buried, and rose again in the flesh, both to forgive men for the sins they had committed and to proclaim his eternal love.[1] This is the central event in Christian history, an event that is commemorated and reenacted in an endless variety of communal and private contexts by Christians throughout the world. Regardless of the objective truth of this account, it would be hard to deny its deep emotional and psychological appeal for millions of believers. That appeal, however, has never been adequately explained in emotional and psychological terms, and this is what I would like to try to do.

The purpose of this essay, then, will be to offer an account of the resurrection myth. The terms of the account will be psychoanalytic, largely Winnicottian, in character. This is not only because Winnicott's work tends to be far more sympathetic to the role played by cultural and religious phenomena in human development than Freud's does (Meissner 1984). It is also because Winnicott's writing, particularly his writing on the paradoxical role of aggressive and destructive impulses in human development, sheds direct light on the processes dramatized by the myth itself—specifically, the destructiveness embodied by the act of crucifixion and the central fact of Jesus' reappearance, his acceptance of the world that tried to destroy him. These seem to reflect developmental processes Winnicott describes as leading to the capacity to "use" objects (1969:86), that is, the capacity to experience them as separate from oneself, as reliable and constant despite their separateness. Of course, Winnicott's own work does not stand wholly outside the circle of cultural influence. And, while he tends to disapprove of many aspects of conventional Christian morality, particularly that which "continues to create and re-create God as a place to put that which is good in [man] himself, and which he might spoil if he kept it in himself along with all the hate and destructiveness which is also to be found there" (1963a:94), it might be the case that his underlying conception of infant and adult relationships is formed and influenced by, perhaps even drawn out of, a tradition in which destructiveness, rejection, aggression, and yet survival and forgiveness are the central themes. If so, this is simply another version of the hermeneutic circle. But we will leave such ultimately unanswerable questions aside for the time being in order to pursue our goal; let us first look briefly at the central features of the myth itself.

Two things stand out in the account: the destructiveness of Jesus' death on the cross and the miracle of his survival, the fact that he continues to love despite the terrible offence committed against his body in the act of crucifixion. The former, of course, serves to represent the Christian concept of sin in its starkest and most uncompromising form, the murder of the Messiah, the God/man who came to bring peace into the world. One has only to think of the vivid depictions of Jesus' crucifixion to recall the physical violence of the act—the scourged flesh, the nailed hands and feet, the spear-pierced side, the crown of thorns, the agony of the last moments, and the callousness of those who inflicted the pain. Suffering is almost an understatement. The latter aspects of the account, Jesus' miraculous survival of the murderous acts committed against his person, serve to represent the Christian concept of redemption, redemption through love; they offer the promise of salvation for the individual and for mankind as a whole. Jesus' resurrection serves as definitive proof for believers of his godhood and the promise of eternal life, while Jesus' forgiveness of those who caused his suffering likewise serves as proof of the permanent and complete nature of his divine love. These, then, are the two central features of

Jesus' story: the subjection to destructive attacks and the survival of those attacks, the ability to accept remorse, to continue to love those who inflicted them. Destructiveness and continuing love are the salient features of the central event of Christian history, the event that lies at the heart of Christian doctrine.

Like all "cultural objects" (Kuhns 1983:21), objects that inhabit that "potential space" (Winnicott 1967:103) in which individuals and groups do their most creative living, the story of Jesus' death and resurrection mirrors fundamental developmental processes. In this case, I want to argue, the processes are those whereby the infant and, later, the adult, comes to acknowledge his or her own destructive impulses and, as a consequence of that acknowledgment, comes to discover the otherness, the reality of the object whose destruction was desired. In the case of the myth, and the historical events upon which it is based, of course, those desires are actually acted out. Jesus *is* crucified. But that is precisely what renders the myth such a powerful reflection of the processes it embodies, the processes whereby the survival of the object and its lack of retaliation for the destructive impulses directed against it are what transforms it into a *genuine* object of love.

According to Winnicott (1963b), the original object in human experience is the mother or, more precisely, the mother's breast. This is the original object of the infant's love. Paradoxically, however, this is also the original object of its aggression and destructiveness as well, the fantasized "attack and destruction" that inevitably accompanies "full-blooded id-drives," particularly in the act of feeding (76). From the infant's perspective, to take nourishment from the mother, to swallow the contents of her body, is inseparable in fantasy from destroying her. Furthermore, since "the instinct-driven episodes . . . have acquired the full force of fantasies of oral sadism and other results of fusion," the infant's acts in feeding are genuinely aggressive in nature. But this aggression is transformed in its very occurrence and is in the end productive. The key to the successful outcome of this process, according to Winnicott, is the mother's capacity to survive the attacks directed against her, "to continue to be herself, to be empathic towards her infant, to be there to receive the spontaneous gesture, and to be pleased." This is what "makes the infant able to hold the anxiety" it inevitably feels, and "the anxiety held in this way becomes altered in quality and becomes a sense of guilt" (77). The process here is a transitional one. In the course of it the infant comes to feel guilt or, even more favorably, to transform latent guilt feelings for destructive fantasies into constructive, reparative behavior. Thus the infant achieves a new sense of the other—the mother—and of the reliability of her love. This results in what Winnicott calls "the development of the capacity for concern," a capacity that can only develop in the infant with the mother's survival of its attacks. Winnicott calls this a "benign cycle," a cycle that somehow makes constructive, positive use of destructiveness in the infant's discovery of the world.[2]

The process described above occurs at the earliest stages of development. According to Winnicott, however, it also repeats itself in later relationships involving various forms of transference: projection, idealization, and destructive fantasies. In his seminal paper, "The Use of an Object and Relating Through Identifications" (1969), Winnicott describes the process whereby what he calls the "subject" comes to relate to the "object" (in the sense in which that term is used in object relations theory) as something external, as fundamentally different from itself and as something that can be loved; this is to be able to *use* it. (By "use," it should be stressed, Winnicott does not mean manipulate or exploit; he means simply experience as something external, *different* from oneself.) These adult relationships also involve destructiveness, the subject's fantasized destruction of the object and, if the object survives, a new appreciation for its otherness, for what its survival has meant in terms of the subject's growth.

The first stage in this adult process of coming to use objects Winnicott calls "object-relating." That is when the subject relates to the object as "a bundle of projections," as part of, an extension of, itself, just as the infant did at the earliest stages of its relationship with the mother, the mother's breast, before its destructive fantasies and attendant changes in perception made her real (1969:88). The transition between "object-relating" and "object-use" Winnicott describes as "the most difficult thing, perhaps, in human development." What it involves is "the subject's placing of the object outside the area [of its] omnipotent control . . . the subject's perception of the object as an external phenomenon, not as a projective entity . . . recognition of it as an entity in its own right" (89). This comes about through the subject's fantasized destruction of the object. The process here is an essentially dialectical one. Destruction of the object in fantasy leads to the discovery of the object's reality, its otherness, and vice versa: "the subject is being destroyed in fantasy as fantasy and is felt as real because of this, at the same time its realness makes *fantasy* destructiveness possible" (Eigen 1981:417). This results eventually in the creation of a new space, no longer a "potential space," but what Michael Eigen calls an "area of faith," an area in which the subject can relate to the object as "in some basic way outside [its] boundaries, [as] 'wholly other.' " This, Eigen goes on,

> opens the way for a new kind of freedom, one *because* there is radical otherness, a new realness of self-feeling exactly because the other is now felt as real as well. The core sense of creativeness that permeates transitional experiencing is reborn on a new level, in so far as genuine not-me nutriment becomes available for personal use. The subject can *use* otherness for true growth purposes and, through the risk of difference as such, gains access to the genuinely new. (415)

By this process, according to Winnicott, the subject comes "to live a life in a world of objects," always keeping in mind that "the price has to be paid in acceptance of the on-going destruction in unconscious fantasy relative to object-relating" (1969:90). The key word here is "acceptance"; this is the measure of the subject's growth.

In both the infant and adult developmental processes, the crucial factor in the scenario is the object's survival, its lack of retaliation against the subject for the subject's destructive fantasies. This provides the context for *both* the subject's rediscovery of the object as separate from, as external to, itself *and* its recognition of the destructive nature of its fantasies, its recognition of fantasy generally. Winnicott captures this moment in the following passage:

> After "subject relates to object" comes "subject destroys object" (as it becomes external); and then may come "*object survives* destruction by the subject." But there may or may not be survival. A new feature thus arrives in the theory of object relating. The subject says to the object: "I destroyed you," and the object is there to receive the communication. From now on the subject says: "Hullo object," "I destroyed you." "I love you." "You have value for me because of your survival of my destruction of you." "While I am loving you I am all the time destroying you in (unconscious) *fantasy*." (90)

The importance of this moment in the Winnicottian scheme of things cannot be overestimated. It represents a kind of rebirth for the subject in the recognition of the object's reality. The object's survival of destructiveness, its lack of retaliation, its being "there to receive the communication" are everything here. For these characteristics of the object are what enable the subject to experience love in the genuine sense of that word, love for another *as* other and not the product of one's "projective mental mechanisms." This is what enables the object to "contribute-in to the subject, according to its own properties" (90). It is what enables the object to be *used*.

There is, as is not uncommon in Winnicott, a genuine paradox here. Fantasized destruction, "the quality of 'always being destroyed,' " is what contributes (from the subject's point of view) to the reality of the object, its "object-constancy" and its ability to "feed back other-than-me substance into the subject" (93–94). At the same time, this nurturing in turn contributes to "the subject's sense [of its own] aliveness" (Eigen 1981:415), to its ability to see *itself* as an object, as (presumably) something that could be of use as well. "In this way," Winnicott writes, "a world of shared reality is created," a "world of objects" each of which is separate and unique. Again, survival is everything. It is the object's survival of, its lack of retaliation for, the subject's destructive fantasies that alone enables the subject to grow, and to be able to regard both the object and itself as independent entities.

How, then, does the myth of the resurrection mirror this process? Let us step back for a moment and view the Gospels from a distance. They were written, of course, in a variety of different contexts and for a variety of different audiences (Perrin 1977). At the core of each of them, however, lies the passion and death of Jesus and, with the probable exception of Mark, his return, his reappearance. Like all narratives, these invite participation in the story. They invite identification on the part of their readers with the main figures and situations, both with those who betrayed and murdered Jesus and with Jesus himself—that is, both with those who acted out their destructive fantasies and with the object they destroyed. Thus, the narrative gives its audience the opportunity to reenact one of the most basic developmental patterns, the destruction/survival/rebirth pattern we have been examining. It does this by inviting the reader to experience the destructive drives that contribute to human development both from the point of view of those who act them out and from the point of view of their object, from both points of view at once.

That object, of course, is depicted in the Gospels as a figure who attracted both devotion and animosity, a highly cathected figure and therefore one vulnerable to "radical decathexis" (Green 1978:184).[3] The Gospels stress, among other things, Jesus' patience, his mildness, his remarkable capacity to heal. Above all, Jesus is depicted as good, as loving, as kind, especially to those considered socially unacceptable and to children, and his teachings are depicted as capable, if followed, of bringing about the reign of universal love. As they are represented, his betrayal and crucifixion constitute destructive acts of the most basic and primitive sort, the acting out in reality of unconscious destructive fantasies that serve to threaten this love.

But the Gospels also depict Jesus' resurrection, his survival of those destructive attacks. History, the "facts," are of little relevance here. What matters is what Jesus' resurrection meant to those who believed it and what it symbolizes for those who continue to do so. And, as it is depicted, that survival of, that lack of retaliation for, destructive impulses represents Jesus' capacity to love, even more importantly, to "be there to receive" love when it comes, even from those who attempted to destroy him or those who acquiesced in that attempt. Thus the resurrection story provides a clear analogue to Winnicott's account of the destruction/survival paradigm. Like the mother whom the infant believes it has destroyed but who is always there, continuing to love, like the object of the subject's destructive fantasies which remains constant despite them, Jesus is depicted as harboring no urge to retaliate, no urge to pay back those who betrayed or even murdered him. His attitude is one of infinite forgiveness, just the sort of forgiveness that makes possible "the explosion of the introjection-projection circle" (Eigen 1981:415) dramatized above: " 'Hullo object!' 'I destroyed you.' 'I love you.' 'You have value for me *because* of your survival of my destruction of you' " (italics added). It is Jesus' "quality of 'always being destroyed' " that makes him an object, in Winnicott's terms, that can be *used,* that is, experienced as something external, something independent, "wholly other." Because Jesus is not only always being destroyed (in fantasy) but also always surviving that destruction, he stands, so to speak "outside the area of omnipotent control," outside "the area of objects set up by . . . projective mental mechanisms" (1969:94). He is, in fact, completely autonomous. What is crucial about this quality of externality in the account, however, is the way it frees those who believe in Jesus' survival of the (their unconscious) attacks upon him to "live in a world of objects . . . a world of shared reality." This is because, being external, being experienced against "a backcloth of unconscious destruction," Jesus has now achieved "object-constancy," has become an object of trust and, having become an object of trust, can "feed back other-than-me substance," especially love, into those who trust in him. But there is a price. The experience of Jesus' independent reality and continuing love is possible only with the "acceptance of the ongoing destruction in unconscious fantasy relative to object relating" (90), that is, only if the believer is able to acknowledge the permanence of his destructive impulses, or what Christianity calls sin.

The theologian Rowan Williams has argued that the essence of the resurrection doctrine is "the invitation to *recognize one's victim as one's hope*" (1982:11), and that "to recognize my victim as my hope involves the recognition of the fact that I victimize, and of the identity of my victim" (19). This involves, Williams says, both self-discovery and discovery of the other, in this case, Jesus, "the symbolic figure who transcends the order of human violence, a figure first to be identified with my victim and then with myself, in a continuing process of meditation and reinterpretation" (25). What Williams does not recognize is that part of that "continuing process" involves the continuing reenactment of processes outlined by Winnicott, not only the acknowledgment of one's own destructive impulses but "the development of the capacity for concern" for the other and for what the other has come to represent, and the eventual transition from object-relating to object-use that produces "a world of shared reality." Jesus' symbolic, transcendent status is a measure of the "object-constancy" believers grant him in this process. He has become, quite literally, the symbol of trust.

From this Winnicottian reading of the resurrection story I think it is possible to see why the account would have such (relatively) lasting appeal, as a "symbol," as "a vehicle of human self-interpretation and a challenge to human self-interpretation" (Williams 1982:26). The figure of Jesus is, on some level, a maternal imago, or at least one who, in our culture at least, represents certain strikingly (albeit stereotypically) feminized qualities: patience, nurturance, the ability to love. (He represents other qualities, of course, but they are not so relevant here.) And Jesus' murder embodies, on some level, the infant's fantasized destruction of the mother, as well as the adult subject's fantasized destruction of the loved object, its radical decathexis. The violence of the act, the assault on Jesus' body, his hands, his feet, his side, is fundamental here. The crucifixion (as it is represented) is an essentially corporeal act. As a representation of destructive drives, it could not be more brutally honest. Jesus *is* the body in pain, the pain human beings inflict, in fantasy or in reality, upon one another from infancy on. This is Jesus' "quality of 'always being destroyed,' " the correlate of the Christian sense of sin. Yet if Jesus, as an analogue of the mother or of the loved object, is "always being destroyed," he is also *always surviving*, always *not retaliating* against those who, in their "sinfulness," destroy him; rather, he is always waiting for and accepting their love. He is, in fact, in his survival of destructive impulses and in his refusal to retaliate, the embodiment of "object-constancy," of trust and love.

These elements are at least part of what accounts for the tremendous potency of the myth of the resurrection for those who believe in it, the way it *simultaneously* reenacts the destruction of the loved object *and* its survival, the possibility of continued love. Two essential things are acknowledged by the account—destructiveness, which, according to Winnicott, "creates the quality of externality" in things, and the survival of that destructiveness, which makes it possible for the object "to feed back other-than-me substance into the subject" (1971:93). A doctrine, a "symbol" that acknowledged less to its believers would tell only part of the story. This one manages, for those who are able to accept its full consequences, a good deal more, feeds "back other-than-me substance into" them as well.

It might now be possible to see why a sacrament like that of the eucharist has such appeal. Winnicott had already made a few observations on the symbolic function of the sacrament for Catholics and Protestants in his paper on transitional objects. "For the Roman Catholic community," he observes, the wafer "*is* the body [of Christ], and for the Protestant community it is a *substitute,* a reminder, and is essentially not, in fact, actually the body itself" (1953:6). This points to differences in the ways the two communities experience potential space, how much illusion, how much play is tolerated. But in both traditions the body, or the wafer that symbolizes the body, is *eaten;* it is incorporated, in a way that reenacts the infant's incorporation of the mother, her breast, the nourishment from her body. In both the infant's interaction with the mother and in the religious rite, something disappears, is destroyed.

In both cases, the mouth is the vehicle of that disappearance, that destruction. Yet in both cases, something survives. In the case of the infant, what survives is the mother, who remains as she was despite the "id-drives" directed against her body and who can begin to become, on account of her survival and lack of retaliation, a symbol of object-constancy (the way other transferential objects will in later life, under analogous circumstances). In the case of the sacrament, it is Jesus himself who survives, even though the wafer, his body, is eaten; he survives both bodily *and* symbolically—that is, both in his physical (or spiritual) body, represented by the bread and wine, and in the spiritual body represented in Christian doctrine by the community, in the spirit of love between its members. Every time the believer takes the sacrament, he must acknowledge his own destructiveness (in eating the wafer, the symbol of the body, or the actual body itself) and his own faith that the love-object survives and continues to love. Thus, the sacrament, like the account of the resurrection, involves destructiveness, yet involves it as something that can become, under the right circumstances, ultimately creative of a world of shared reality which can be used by those who share it.

We have been talking about symbols, and the developmental origins of their potency and appeal. There should be, I hope, nothing reductive in this. In fact, our account should only render those aspects of the Christian myth and practice of which we have been exploring the psychological roots all the more noteworthy. After all, this account gives us a way of seeing them in a new, and perhaps more deeply human, light, as arising "out of human nature" and not imposed "from outside" (Winnicott 1968:143). Read, as we have been reading them, in a Winnicottian context, they are representations of some of the most basic human drives and impulses—destructiveness and the painfully achieved capacity for "object-constancy" and trust. For, and this is where Winnicott differs so profoundly from Freud, symbolic and therefore cultural representations of the sort we have been examining here are not necessarily expressions of the human impulse to *escape* or *avoid* painful "reality." They can be powerful ways of *facing,* indeed of creating, reality, of continuing a process begun nearly at birth, a process of making things, including both transitional and cultural objects, that render experience a bit more comprehensible. This is called "reality-testing." It takes place in the "intermediate area of *experiencing*" (Winnicott 1953:2), where we have just been.

NOTES

1. I am treating the resurrection story as myth here not in its pejorative sense but to describe a story that appeals on a "primordial" level to some of the most basic human impulses and needs and that "provides the structure of identity and cohesion of particular human groups and ways of life" (Wilder 1976:73–74). I am aware, of course, that the Gospels contain separate and at times contradictory accounts of the resurrection story and that the differences between those accounts are profoundly revealing in themselves of the different intentions and audiences of their authors. But that is not my concern here. My concern is with the general account of the resurrection that can be gathered from all of them and that serves as the object of Christian belief: that Jesus suffered, died, and rose again. For a good summary of differences and some of the reasons for them, see Perrin (1977).

2. Cf. Melanie Klein: "Here is a benign circle, for in the first place we gain trust and love in relation to our parents, next we take them, with this love and

trust, as it were, into ourselves; and then we can give from this wealth of loving feelings to the outer world again" (1937:115).

3. Green uses this term to clarify what he takes Winnicott to mean by destructiveness in "The Use of an Object." "Hence," Green writes, "what we are concerned with is a succession of libidinal or aggressive cathexes and of decathexes which abolish the preceding cathexes and the objects linked to them. When carried to an extreme, such decathexes lead to psychic death." This could be said to be the fate of Judas.

REFERENCES

Dolto, F., and G. Severin. 1969. *The Jesus of Psychoanalysis: A Freudian Interpretation of the Gospel.* Translated by H. R. Lane. Garden City, N.Y.: Doubleday.

Eigen, M. 1981. "The Area of Faith in Winnicott, Lacan and Bion." *International Journal of Psycho-Analysis* 62:413–33.

Green, A. 1978. "The Object in the Setting." In S. A. Grolnick and L. Barkin, eds., *Between Reality and Fantasy: Transitional Objects and Phenomena,* pp. 169–89. New York: Jason Aronson.

Klein, M. 1937. "Love, Guilt and Reparation." In M. Klein and J. Rivière, *Love, Hate and Reparation,* pp. 57–119. New York: Norton, 1964.

Kuhns, R. 1983. *Psychoanalytic Theory of Art: A Philosophy of Art on Developmental Principles.* New York: Columbia University Press.

Meissner, W. W. 1984. *Psychoanalysis and Religious Experience.* New Haven: Yale University Press.

Perrin, N. 1977. *The Resurrection According to Matthew, Mark, and Luke.* Philadelphia: Fortress Press.

Wilder, A. 1976. *Theopoetic: Theology and the Religious Imagination.* Philadelphia: Fortress Press.

Williams, R. 1982. *Resurrection: An Easter Meditation.* London: Darton, Longman, and Todd.

Winnicott, D. W. 1953. "Transitional Objects and Transitional Phenomena." In Winnicott, *Playing and Reality,* pp. 1–25.

——. 1963a. "Morals and Education." In Winnicott *The Maturational Processes,* pp. 93–105.

——. 1963b. "The Development of the Capacity for Concern." In Winnicott, *The Maturational Processes,* pp. 73–82.

——. 1965. *The Maturational Processes and the Facilitating Environment: Studies in the Theory of Emotional Development.* New York: International Universities Press; London: Hogarth Press.

——. 1967. "The Location of Cultural Experience." In Winnicott, *Playing and Reality,* pp. 95–103.

————. 1968. "Children Learning." In *Home Is Where We Start From*, pp. 142–49. New York: Norton, 1986.

————. 1969. "The Use of an Object and Relating Through Identifications." In Winnicott, *Playing and Reality*, pp. 86–94.

————. 1971. *Playing and Reality*. New York: Basic Books; London: Tavistock, 1984.

14

Picturing the Child's Inner World of Fantasy: On the Dialectic Between Image and Word *

ELLEN HANDLER SPITZ

> "[Play is characterized by] the precariousness of magic itself, magic that arises in intimacy, in a relationship that is being found to be reliable."
>
> —D. W. Winnicott, *Playing and Reality*

I

Contemporary interdisciplinary literature in the humanities abounds with fascination for the analysis of signs and sign systems. In particular, there is a resurgence of interest in the distinguishing characteristics of, and relations between, words and images. When these issues are discussed by philosophers, the discourse often turns on questions of representation. Is representation achieved by resemblance or analogy (the modes usually postulated of imagery), by contiguity or convention (the modes associated with language), or by causal connec-

* Since drafts of this essay have been presented in many venues, I wish to acknowledge all my gracious audiences as well as the following colleagues: Gannit Ankori, David Kittron, Amnon Toledano, Michal Grossman, Yosef Hayim Yerushalmi, Peter Jelavich, and especially Bettina Stronach, whose student essay in a course I taught in the mid-eighties on psychoanalytic theory and the arts was especially helpful. To her, to my other students, and to the many who have shared their parental and childhood experiences with me, I extend my warmest appreciation.

tion (as in demonstration)? Functional distinctions such as the density of the image versus the differentiation of the linguistic sign have been noted (Goodman 1976). Efforts have been made (Gombrich 1956, 1963, 1981) to tease apart the relative contribution to both verbal and pictorial signs of biology (nature) and convention (culture). Speculation on the effect of experiential differences between the categories of time (associated with words) and space (associated with images) has been linked with the differential reliability attributed to the evidence of the eye (as witness) versus that of ear (hearsay). Such philosophical discourse, with its venerable tradition extending back into the pages of Platonic dialogue, reveals recrudescent efforts—both subtle and crude—to foster the hegemony, the preeminence, the superiority of one type of sign (normally the linguistic, either spoken or written) over the other. However, as W. J. T. Mitchell (1986) has pointed out, the terms of the discourse are not innocent. A "war-torn" border lies between image and text, between picture and word.

My essay offers a modest contribution to this discourse by taking a psychoanalytic developmental perspective on a picturebook for young children. Picturebooks, equally neglected in the literature of art, psychoanalysis, and philosophy, are fascinating precisely because they are intended to span this "war-torn" border just at the juncture in the lifespan when such bridges are being constructed. Picturebooks are artifacts expressly made for use during those unheralded but cataclysmic moments in childhood when gaps between the world of image and verbal language are being negotiated.

Rather than discuss picturebooks in general, I have chosen here to examine in detail just one extraordinary example—*Where the Wild Things Are,* written and illustrated by Maurice Sendak (1963). This slender volume, which boasts nineteen double unnumbered pages, not only won the coveted Caldecott Medal (awarded to the most distinguished picturebook of the year) but has been translated into many languages; though published over a quarter of a century ago, it has remained a cherished favorite among young children in the intervening years—so much so that recently, in the United States, soft toy replicas of its characters, in various sizes, have been placed on the market, and it has been used as a basis for children's theater as well as re-created as an opera (with score by Oliver Knussen).

My effort here will be to show that in this picturebook word and image reinforce each other to create crosscurrents that simultaneously affirm the need for regressive fantasy while gently moving in the direction of more adaptive, integrative function. My claim is that the constituent roles played here by picture and text, their collaborative function, their interdependent shares in this extraordinary evocation of, and direct pipeline to, the inner fantasy life of young children, may contribute, at least tangentially, to the philosophical discourse.

Where the Wild Things Are works actively to deconstruct the dichotomies inherent in this discourse while at the same time creating a continuity between words and images that preserves their differences. The picturebook reveals that the tendency of art (Mitchell 1986) and play (Winnicott 1971) is not only to breach the supposed boundaries between the spatial and the temporal, natural and cultural, inside and outside, self and other, but also and importantly to subtend and elaborate these very dichotomies. In this example, the verbal and pictorial signs serve varying functions with respect to each other: while refusing stereotypy, they maintain their differences, thus enabling the child to move toward reality testing but without renouncing fantasy and imagination.

II

Unlike the simplest picturebooks, which juxtapose an image with its name or, as in alphabet primers, an image with the initial letter of its name, *Where the Wild Things Are* is a picture story in which the images are narrativized and the narrative pictorially represented. Briefly, the narrative concerns a little boy named Max who, after performing "mischief of one kind and another," is called a "WILD THING" by his mother (to whom he retorts, "I'LL EAT YOU UP!") and is sent off to bed without his supper. A forest grows in his bedroom, and Max sails off on an ocean in a "private boat" to "where the wild things are." There he tames the wild things by magic (staring into their eyes) and then participates with them in a "wild rumpus." After making them "stop!" and sending *them* off to bed without *their* supper, Max suddenly feels lonely and wants "to be where someone loved him best of all." He resists the appeal of the wild things (who urge him to stay by protesting that they love him so much they could eat him up) by saying "No!" to them, and finally he sails back "into the night of his very own room," where he finds his supper waiting for him, "and it was still hot."

Addressed to children of about three to five years of age, the book is meant, significantly, to be read *to* them rather than *by* them. It creates a potential space (Winnicott 1971) between fantasy and reality, which is exquisitely appropriate in that children of this age actually inhabit a universe of shifting realms in which the boundaries between fantasy and reality are not as yet firmly established (Fraiberg 1959).

Through its acceptance and exploration of the interpenetration of these realms, this work distinguishes itself from more superficial picturebooks designed for the same age child that focus on premature adaptation to selected aspects of external reality. *Where the Wild Things Are* openly acknowledges (and in fact dramatizes) a child's subjective state: responsively, it supports needs for regressive fantasy, while unobtrusively it reassures that there will be a safe return to reality. In doing so, it functions vis-à-vis its child spectator/audience as do all major works of art on both the highest and deepest levels. And, in parallel with masterpieces of art created for adults, the picturebook depends crucially on the working of convention to secure positive and meaningful experience. Because of the performancelike aspect of the genre (in that it is read *to* the child), its effect depends in large part upon the qualities (self-acceptance, emotional equilibrium, sense of humor, and dramatic flair) of the reading adult—whose presence and engagement must serve, like that perhaps of the conductor and/or performer of a musical score, to contain, guide, and modify the child's experience. Whereas the images of the picturebook are seen essentially without the mediation (are "autographic"), its words are both seen and heard, spoken through the voice of another ("allographic") (Goodman 1976).

Winnicott has given us the evocative and deceptively simple notion of "holding environment," in which mother (and, by analogy, analyst) serves the role of safe and dependable container for the infant's (patient's) fantasies, fears, and hostile impulses. Crucial for the establishment of secure self-object differentiation, reality testing, and therapeutic success is the parent's survival of the infant's aggression. In the arts, various aspects of form and convention serve parallel roles as containers—the frame of a painting; the language, meter, rhyme scheme, and diction of a poem; the established spatial limits, including stage, curtain, lights, and fixed temporal range of a given theatrical performance. When these holding environments are unstable or transgressed, uneasiness and displeasure may ensue: life may invade art, therapeutic milieus collapse, and painted monsters emerge from the pages of books to terrorize young minds.

Where the Wild Things Are instantiates a holding environment on several levels. First, in reading it to the child, the mother or mother-surrogate provides a safe and nurturing context for the experience. We can imagine that, quite concretely, in many cases, the child is actually being physically held while read to. Second, the design of the book itself (which I shall discuss in detail) creates a sensitive milieu for both fostering and containing the unfolding of the child-listener's own (private) fantasies. On a third level, looking beyond form to content, we perceive another trace, an echo—an invisible character, the off-stage mother of Max, who (in parallel with the reader of the story) provides an attentive, responsive, and dependable medium for the protagonist's play and fantasy. This good-enough mother (Winnicott 1971) is also a true-to-form Kleinian mother in that she is out of sight, visible only through the perceptions and distortions of her child's psyche. Her voice is heard just once, but she is never seen. Of significance too is the space in which the story unfolds: the child's bedroom, his most familiar and private external space, which is here transformed by fantasy into an arena for the enactment of inner drama.

Freud (1900) spoke about the regressive transformation of thoughts, ideas, and words into pictures. By means of its extraordinary design, *Where the Wild Things Are* almost literally illustrates this concept while simultaneously moving in the opposite direction, that is to say, encouraging its youthful "reader" to progress from the world of the imaginary to the world of the symbolic. The book begins with verbal language—that is, with ordinary communication, as the child-listener hears his or her mother's reading voice. Words and pictures form coequal partners in conveying the story. Page by page, however, the words (and mother's voice) gradually diminish, and the pictures grow in size relative to the printed text—until, finally, when Max (and the child-listener) are fully transported into their own fantasy worlds, the pictures expand to fill all available space. Fantasy completely overtakes reality. Mother's voice is no longer heard.

Just as Max has been transported into the world of wild things in a "private boat" (signed in both verbal and pictorial registers), so the child listening is permitted now to fuse with the magical power of fantasy and image. And because these transitions are effected so gradually, almost imperceptibly, the child is not overwhelmed by the world of imagination. Furthermore, since (even at the climax of Max's orgy with the wild things) child and mother are still together, turning the pages of the book, we can conceive the child as experiencing optimally that auspicious state characterized as "being alone in the presence of another" (Winnicott 1958). Later, as fantasy subsides, the pictures diminish in size. The world of words reasserts itself. With Max, the child-listener returns to consensually validated, intersubjective reality—to the comforting presence of the mother's reading voice, which, like Max's supper, has retained its warmth.

Thus, the very design of the book constitutes a dialectic between image and word, creating what Winnicott has called a facilitating environment. We might also point to the stylistic quality of its drawings. Sendak's style is characteristically linear and precise. His clear, carefully executed graphics convey subtly to the viewer that he is in control—of his medium, surely, and if that, then perhaps by implication of his message as well. As with other artists whose fantasies are figured with intense linearity (e.g., Bosch, Blake, Dali, Magritte), this quality functions doubly to endow the imagery with a sense of hyperreality while simultaneously marking it as, at least in part, consciously controlled. It is also worthwhile to note that the wild things themselves, the monsters, even in their largest, most frenzied, orgiastic incarnations, are not entirely frightening but also silly, humorous, even strangely lovable—rather like parents who become, evanescently, monsters, or children (like Max) who don bestial costumes. A propos, Sendak (1991) has stated that his inspiration for the wild things came from the Eastern European Jewish relatives who, visiting his Brooklyn home on weekends when he was a child, proceeded to eat everything in sight and then to pinch his cheeks (he being the youngest in the family), and to tell him that he too was good enough to eat! With regard to the verbal signs, *Where the Wild Things Are* narrates its plot in the past tense so that implicitly Max has already survived these events—as will, by identification, the child who is listening and looking.

III

The story begins with Max wearing his "wolf suit" and making mischief. We see Max in an enactment of aggression in several registers, and here the images elaborate the verbal text, enriching it, filling it out, offering to it a repleteness (Goodman 1976), while the words themselves serve mainly as instructions to us for the focus of our gaze. As a costume, Max's wolf suit possesses exaggerated phallic appendages—pointed ears, claws, and an enormous bushy tail—thus reminding us that the symbol of the wolf is redolent of oedipal as well as preoedipal themes, not only threats of devouring and being devoured (the "I'll eat you up" of "The Three Little Pigs" and of "Little Red Riding Hood") but also the notion of wolf as seducer. The costume, identified via both sign systems, condenses oedipal genitality with preoedipal oral sadism. The pictorial image works doubly, both to deny and to extend the verbal signifier, in that Max's suit looks suspiciously like a baby suit, a sleeper or pajama, thus mitigating its alleged hostility and revealing the child's aggressiveness to be, in part, an outgrowth of infantile smallness and helplessness.

From the beginning, we can see that the dialectic of word and image functions to forge complex links between preoedipal and oedipal themes, to counterpose and reintegrate them by introducing them into the representational field, even occasionally by distorting, excluding, exaggerating, or foregrounding one over the other. Since the child to whom the picturebook is addressed is on the cusp between these developmental curves, the dual registration matches with exquisite fitness his or her own intrapsychic imperatives.

What is the mischief here? Max has strung up a small animal doll, symbolic perhaps of younger siblings or envied babies. He messes up the house. He ignores the verbal content of two books by stepping on them, thus proclaiming his emancipation from the rule of language, law, and order. With an enormous hammer, he bangs a nail into the wall. From a Kleinian perspective, it is possible to see the house as signifying the mother, the aggression in general as an attack upon the mother's body in consequence of the child's envy of it as powerful provider (and withholder) of good things. Although from the parental point of view Max's behavior is destructive, we are given pictorial clues that his activities are from his own viewpoint constructive as well. While messing things up inside his mother's house, he seems at the same time to be building himself a sort of tent—a private space, as it were—that will be replicated later in fantasy in terms both of his "private boat" and of the royal tent under which he sits forlornly when he becomes "king of where the wild things are."

On the next page, the mischief continues. Here, in addition to the symbolic attack on the envied body of the mother, we observe an attack with a fork (both oral and phallic) against a little white dog who might almost be taken, at this moment, as a double for Max himself. This dog, incidentally, is a representation of Sendak's beloved Sealyham terrier, Jennie, whom he memorialized in a number of his books and to whom he dedicated *Higglety Pigglety Pop!* (1967).

The doubling of the image suggests a further biographical association that is irresistible. Sendak, in choosing "Max" as the name of his naughty protagonist, links this name to his own, Maurice, which is a cognate for the German "Moritz," thus inviting an association to the two devilish young pranksters of the "Max und Moritz" cartoons by Wilhelm Busch—the comic strip being a form closely related to the picturebook, in which word and image, temporal and spatial models, are coupled. A propos, Sendak not only knew "Max und Moritz" but has actually acknowledged his indebtedness to another famous cartoon strip, "Little Nemo" by Winsor McCay, which he imitated quite directly in the initial pages of his 1970 work, *In the Night Kitchen* (Lanes 1980). In one 1865 "Max und Moritz" drawing especially relevant to *Where the Wild Things Are* (Robinson 1974), a peasant woman, smiling in anticipation of her dinner, washes a plate in the basement of her house, while on the hearth above, a panful of little game hens are roasting. A small white dog, not unlike Sendak's, barks; the two naughty boys on the roof, Max and Moritz, gleefully dance around the chimney while, with a fishing rod, they clandestinely extricate the woman's dinner (through the chimney), one roast hen at a time. Thus, the themes of oral aggression, reversal of deprivation, and secret triumph over the mother are here anticipated.

In the second drawing of *Where the Wild Things Are,* oedipal rivalry is adumbrated by the grasping gesture of the child toward the dog's erect tail, and we might remark the understated presence of the shadowy stairway, associated by Freud (1900) with mounting tension and sexual excitement in the oneiric lexicon. Max's mischief, then, by dramatizing both oedipal and preoedipal themes, exquisitely taps the developmental imperatives of the child who experiences the story. On the wall hangs a drawing by (and, by implication, a self-representation of) Max as an oral-sadistic monster, bisexual, with plenty of teeth and hair (including a beard), eyes like breasts, and a horn as a displaced phallus. Gleefully, the child's aggression is fused with his polymorphous sexuality and exuberant narcissism. In the background, unseen, the mother in a double sense as reader (performer) and character allows, permits, continues (goes on being; Winnicott 1958), unthreatened.

On the third page, however, Max's aggression calls forth a response. He has, as it were, projected his own badness into the offstage mother, and now he must experience her counteraggression. As mentioned, it is significant that the mother never appears visually in the book, that she lives entirely through the experience of the child, again, in the double sense—both for Max and for the child-listener. In a classic dramatization of projective identification, the child, having done mischief and provoked the mother into calling him a "wild thing," now feels the need to incorporate her orally—to eat her up (as he says quite literally). Incidentally, the notion of "wild thing" and the phrase itself may well be inspired by (and a free translation of) the Yiddish expression "wilde chaye," which Sendak undoubtedly heard during his childhood years in Brooklyn, since it is a term used by mothers toward children who exhibit particularly trying behaviors.

The principal dynamic here, projective identification, has been described as the forceful entry into an external object which is then
compelled to acquire unacceptable characteristics. Subsequently, as the
external object becomes threatening and persecutory, a need arises to
control and (orally) destroy the now-threatening object (Segal 1964).
Max is bad (implicitly, to the mother); mother is bad (to Max). Max
wishes to devour and destroy her (i.e., to destroy the consequences of
his own aggression).

But now, Max *loses* her. He loses food, and food equals mother. In
the picture, the expression on Max's face conveys more clearly than
words the response he is making to this painful consequence of his own
hostility. His face proclaims: "I'll show you!" To avoid pain and
anxiety, he must deny the loss. Through the medium of Sendak's
graphics, we can almost see him resorting unconsciously to the defense
of splitting—as he prepares to triumph in fantasy over this "bad"
mother who has sent him to his room and refused him supper. Here
the image does not illustrate or expand upon the text but rather responds to it in a kind of counterpoint: word contra image (child versus
mother).

In the fourth picture, we witness the proliferation of fantasy, as Max
magically transgresses the boundary set by the mother. As the forest
grows in his bedroom, we see, marvelously portrayed in Max's face
and pose, his triumph over any feelings of anxiety and loss. Again,
words and image form a contrapuntal ensemble, as in the next duo of
pages where Max's covering of his mouth with the paw to hide his
smile betokens and betrays the secret sadism of his victory. Finally, his
room completely disappears, and the forest takes over. In this next
picture (the sixth), the many-treed forest may be read as emblematic
not only of mystery and the feminine (as in "The Sleeping Beauty" and
"Hansel and Gretel," for example) but, more deeply, as the forbidden
inside of the mother's body, with all its treasures, including the phallic
treasure, multiply represented. It is also interesting to note the presence
and changing shape, size, and position of the moon in each of the
pictures in which it appears, beginning with Max's banishment and
loss therefore of his mother. Here, for example, the moon is ambiguously both crescent and full, and Max prances directly under it. It is
hard to resist interpreting these ever-changing, omnipresent moons as
displacements, fantasy evocations of the absent yet ever-present maternal object.

This interpretation of the moon is borne out by the repetitive representation of it as a symbol in other picturebooks for young children,
two of the most famous of which (both antecedents of *Where the Wild*

Things Are and neither of which could have been unknown to Sendak) are *Goodnight Moon* (Brown and Hurd 1947) and *Many Moons* (Thurber 1943). In another context (Spitz 1989), I have pointed out that the moon may figure as a maternal signifier not only because of its roundness (suggestive of the breast) but perhaps also because of its cycles: like the mother, the moon disappears gradually and predictably reappears—changing shape but always recognizable. Illuminating the darkness, it (again like the mother) serves as a beacon in the frightening realm of the unknown. Associated by the child with time for bed and thus separation, its predictable presence stands as a constant, a bulwark against the fear of strangeness and boundlessness that loss of parental objects betokens. In this sense, the moon shining on the page of the picturebook may be seen as a pictorial representation of the very "holding environment" instantiated by the reading of the picturebook itself in the company of the caretaking adult.

As fantasy overtakes reality in this sixth picture, only Max's back is shown. Thus, the child can supply and project his or her own affect and expression, for, as possibilities for reading-in multiply, so the potential for identification increases. Max assumes the posture of a necromancer, a shaman casting a spell.

Having created and entered an alternative world, Max in the seventh picture faces fully toward us and smiles with a pose and expression unmistakably smug and self-satisfied. He sails on an ocean of rhythmical waves—soothing, womblike perhaps, betokening new birth as well as return to the place of no loss and without boundaries. This is the first time in the book that the illustration exceeds its limits, transgressing the space previously reserved for written text. From this point on, image will increasingly encroach upon the domain of words until, at the height of fantasy, printed words are crowded out altogether.

It is significant that Max is provided with a "private" boat, since a focal aspect of his fantasy is his denial of dependence on the "bad," withholding mother. Here, with sails rigged, floating independently in his private sailboat, he is free—captain, literally, of his fate. The notion of privacy is also relevant, as I have indicated, to the relationship between the child-listener and the reader of the story, in that it gives license, so to speak, for a certain kind of independence as well—encouraging the child to create his or her own private fantasies while listening to the story.

As image gradually gains hegemony over word, space prevails over linear temporality. Max travels "in and out of weeks and almost over a year"—an evocation of the timelessness of the unconscious. As loss is denied, with the transcendence of both temporal and spatial boundaries and the increasing invasion of the world of words by pictorial image, it is possible to interpret a confluence of narrative and intrapsychic time, so that the fantasy of the wild things, narrativized by the text, is taken as occurring simultaneously with the mischief-making. In other words, the dialectic of signs makes possible a reading that privileges synchronic rather than diachronic time—subjective over historic or narrative time. According to this alternative reading, Max does not do mischief and *then* fantasize the wild things; rather, Max does mischief and simultaneously fantasizes his journey and his return.

Now, however, in the eighth and ninth pictures, Max must meet the persecutory objects he has introjected—creatures of his own (disowned) aggression. In terms of the cyclical syndrome described by Klein, these persecutory introjects are now reexperienced and appear as monsters—"wild things." Just as Max's mother called *him* a "wild thing," so he projects his wild thing-ness into these fanciful creatures.

Interestingly, there are several wild things and not just one. Bion (1967) has developed a notion of what he has called "bizarre objects," which refers to just such a maneuver, namely, the secondary splitting of persecutory objects for defensive purposes. The strategy, a variation on the theme of "divide and conquer," splits the enemy into fragments; like the brooms of the sorceror's apprentice, these become multiple potential persecutors which then need, of course, all the more urgently to be controlled.

The monsters themselves are marvelous illustrations of the fantasy of the combined parental imago. They possess secondary sexual characteristics of both sexes and represent at the same time a warding off of castration anxiety by their superabundance of phallic appendages, including horns, claws, teeth, tails, and hair. That they resemble in these details Max's portrait at the beginning of the story betokens an underlying identification of the child with them. As the parents become increasingly differentiated for the child at the oedipal stage, and their sexual intercourse arouses both envy and jealousy, he or she may regress to a fantasy of the combined parental imago, which both denies their coveted and exclusive partnership while at the same time providing a vehicle for the expression of aggression against them. Max's wild things thus serve as exquisitely elaborated instances of the rather typical monsters dreamed up by children on the cusp of preoedipal and oedipal development.

In the tenth picture, Max tames the wild things. By this time, image has literally superseded text, the latter being placed here (as on the preceding page), not insignificantly, beneath it. Max defends against his persecutory objects by a counterphobic omnipotent act of mastery and control. By this act, he instantaneously reverses the young child's helplessness with respect both to his drives and to his parental objects. Bypassing the slower, more difficult path of true reparation, which acknowledges loss and guilt, Max secures his omnipotence by means of magic—the act of magic being that he stares into the monsters' eyes.

In a classic paper on the symbolism of the eye, Ferenczi (1913) pointed out that, because of their extreme sensitivity, vulnerability, movability, changeability of size, and the extraordinarily high value which we accord to them, the eyes serve as apt symbols for the genitals. We also note the frequency of equations in verbal language of the visual with the oral ("he devoured her with his eyes"), so that the magical staring may be related both to notions of oral incorporation and of phallic attack. Staring may betoken a potential violent intimacy—a condensation, as with the wolf suit, of oral sadism and genital rape.

It is extremely important that Max *does* triumph over his wild things—that, even in fantasy, the child is not destroyed by his monsters. From an object relations perspective, the survival of this (fictional) child despite his ravaging introjects is indicative of the abiding virtual presence of the good maternal object who is perhaps figured, as mentioned above, in the various new, half, crescent, and waning moons.

As, in the eleventh picture, Max becomes king, gaining crown and scepter (and, to use the classical psychoanalytic terminology, ego achieves supremacy over id), we see that Max does not have any further need to squelch or destroy his introjects. Instead, he can now permit himself to *enjoy* them! Because his ego is intact, and he is in control, he can afford to take pleasure in regression. In a vibrant illustration of the notion of regression in the service of the ego (Kris 1952), Max gives his permission for frenzied frolic, crying, "And now, let the wild rumpus start!"

The next three pages form the centerpiece of the book. With Max, pictorial signs now reign triumphant. Narrative sequencing is suspended. Transported into the realm of pure play, pure daydream, pure wish fulfillment, words fall away. Words are, for a child, at a greater remove from drive than images. Therefore, these scariest moments of the storybook are experienced by the child in silence purely through imagery, as he or she is permitted to be alone with private fantasies. At the height of the orgy, however, Max is still king; the pages of the book itself provide a tangible boundary, and, as suggested above, the child is alone *within* a holding environment jointly created by imagery, text, reader's presence, and the contribution of his or her own psyche—alone now in Winnicott's sense, as an achievement—alone securely in the presence of another.

Some parents, however, have reported that, during this wordless middle section of *Where the Wild Things Are,* they do not merely sit still turning pages. With a gleam in the eye, they confess that they actually get up with their child to whoop, stomp, prance, hoot, whirl, and cavort about the room, thus enacting their own rumpuses to accompany Max and his monsters! Such moments of shared parent/child playing can create, I suggest, precisely the sort of magic to which Winnicott alludes in the epigraph to this essay—namely, the magic that occurs in those effervescent instants when inner and outer reality suddenly converge.

Another reading of Max's voyage to the isle of the wild things places this picturebook on the continuum of a centuries' old tradition in Western literature in which tales are told of civilizing conquerors who sail off to cannibal islands and tame the native savages they find there—often, in fact, by magic, as is the case here, where little Max stares into the eyes of his hirsute, scaley, animal-like monsters. This cultural reading blends with the psychoanalytic in that it casts Max as a plucky victor over the primitive forces of instinct and aggression.

On the fifteenth page, a major shift occurs. The silence is broken as Max tells the wild things to "stop!" In sending them off to bed without their supper, he does precisely to them what was done to him by his mother. He not only turns passive into active but identifies with the maternal object. In replicating her (speech) act, he reinvokes her in her absence. Having attacked and banished his persecutory objects, he feels depleted and begins to experience loneliness. The wild, frenzied activity, the imaginative projection, has left him empty, yearning for the love object—whose loss he only now begins to suffer. His oral dependent needs reassert themselves: he smells food.

As he allows himself for the first time to experience sadness and separation, he is shown sitting, pondering, wondering whether perhaps—as a consequence of his own aggression—he has in fact destroyed his beloved mother. As the pictorial sign figures little Max, still crowned, pining, at the door of his regal tent (a fantasy fulfillment and visual quotation of the abortive efforts made on page one), it is hard to avoid associations to images of the biblical Saul (1 Sam. 16) who, like Max, is tormented by evil spirits and for whom, by analogy, the sweet sounds of David's lyre might be likened to the soothing sounds of the mother's voice. In silence, the evil spirits may terrify, but with the return of a gentle voice, melancholy ensues.

Accepting his need and his lack, Max gives up being king of where the wild things are. He relinquishes the fantasy of omnipotence and complete independence. He begins to go back. Verbal language reasserts itself, and the pictures begin to recede.

The wild things, however, will not let him go so easily. By repeating to Max exactly what he had said to his mother ("we'll eat you up"), they inadvertently betray the double entendre of this expression. The desire to incorporate the loved object in order to possess it and the desire to destroy the loved object in order to possess it both stem from the paradigm of the infant feeding at the breast: both betoken a denial of the independent existence of the beloved.

Max, however, says "No!" Here, the child's negative constitutes a powerful positive assertion of self. As René Spitz (1965) points out, the child must learn to say no to him- or herself, and the negative therefore possesses enormous power in defining the boundaries of self. By saying "No!" Max returns to the realm of boundaries—he moves toward reality and away from fantasy. Winnicott would stress that it is the very presence of a good internal object that renders the child capable of saying no. We see in this picture (number sixteen) the reintroduction of Max's boat. Going back, interestingly, it does not present the side marked with his name—an indication, possibly, that the boat no longer needs to be quite so "private." As the pictures diminish in size and the domain of verbal language reasserts itself, the young child is borne along on its waves, traveling onward, developmentally, from the land of private image to the realm of public word. We also see the child's strength and pleasure in his capacity to say no and to stop his play, and not only to stop but even to wave good-bye, and to do so with a smile.

As Max slowly and gradually sails back through the timeless land of make-believe, the child-listener also is eased back; in the eighteenth and next-to-last picture, the safe boundaries of Max's bedroom are reinstated. We notice that his wolf's hat is beginning to slip off his head. The picture is a replication of page three; familiarity has been restored. And, best of all, his supper is waiting for him. The invisible mother has survived his assaults. She still loves him; she is still feeding him. And Max too, and the child who has heard and seen the story, have lived through it and survived. Visually, it is interesting to note that the table, bowl, and moon in this image may for the child-spectator explicitly evoke another picturebook (*Goodnight Moon,* mentioned above), which is addressed to a slightly younger child and tenderly deals with the issue of bedtime separation. Parenthetically, *Goodnight Moon* also addresses with unusual sensitivity the child's developmental dialectic between image and word as the magical recurrence of its images is mirrored by the rhymes of its verbal text.

On the last page of *Where the Wild Things Are* there is no picture. The child listening to the story hears his mother utter the final words, "and it was still hot." Love is ongoing and warm; it occurs in the intersubjective realm of language and consensual reality. As the child has experienced, through the vehicle of this deeply empathic and exquisitely constructed work, the vicarious enactment of splitting, projective identification, manic triumph, omnipotence, and, finally, loss and separation, he may take steps toward gradually learning that both he and his objects can and will survive the ravages of his destructive impulses. It probably takes, however, a mother who is quite comfortable with her own wild things to be able to read this story again and again and enjoy it fully with her child.

IV

My effort has been to demonstrate, by the analysis of just one picturebook, the treasure trove constituted by this genre, not only for our understanding of the fantasy life and developmental imperatives of young children but for the philosophical discourse on word and image. Because the child of picturebook age is not yet fully assimilated into the realm of verbal language, spoken or written, this genre functions on the boundary, the divide, between two great sign systems. It must travel, as we have seen, dialectically between them, sometimes translating verbal into visual signs and vice versa, sometimes supplementing one code with the other, at other times employing the different modes as opposing voices in a dialogue. For the child, at least two major agendas are operant—the push toward language and socialization, toward acceptance of differentiation, limit, loss, diachronic time, and *pari passu* the pull toward image, wish, and fantasy.

From a psychoanalytic perspective, the border zone here is better described as criss-crossed in highly complex paths than as "war-torn," for although the developmental trajectory leads ineluctably toward the mastery and refinement of verbal language, it does not lead away from image. The wizened ideology of mother/earth/space/picture versus father/time/story/name is partially deconstructed by a genre that is impelled by the naïveté of its clientele to play freely with both sign systems in unorthodox, highly original ways. Representation is achieved via all three modes—analogy, contiguity, and indexicality (the last largely through its performance aspect). What Sendak's beautiful book and others like it demonstrate is the awesome power of images to inform as well as to deform, to inspire as well as derail, the inevitable trajectory.

REFERENCES

Bion, W. R. 1927. *Second Thoughts.* London: Heinemann.

Brown, M. W., and C. Hurd. 1947. *Goodnight Moon.* New York: Harper and Row.

Ferenczi, S. [1913] 1952. "On Eye Symbolism." *First Contributions to Psychoanalysis,* pp. 270–76. New York: Brunner/Mazel.

Fraiberg, S. 1959. *The Magic Years.* New York: Scribner and Sons.

Freud, S. 1900. *The Interpretation of Dreams.* In vols. 4 and 5, *The Standard Edition of the Complete Psychological Works.* Edited and translated by J. Strachey et al. 24 vols. London: Hogarth Press, 1953–74.

———. 1907. *Delusions and Dreams in Jensen's "Gradiva."* In Vol. 9, *The Standard Edition of the Complete Psychological Works,* pp. 3–95.

———. 1908. "Creative Writers and Daydreaming." In Vol. 9, *The Standard Edition of the Complete Psychological Works,* pp. 143–53.

Gombrich, E. H. 1956. *Art and Illusion.* Princeton: Princeton University Press.

———.1963. *Meditations on a Hobby Horse and Other Essays on the Theory of Art.* New York: Phaidon Press.

———. 1981. "Image and Code." In W. Steiner, ed., *Image and Code,* pp. Ann Arbor: University of Michigan Studies in the Humanities, no.

2. Goodman, N. 1976. *Languages of Art.* Indianapolis and Cambridge: Hackett.

Klein, M. 1957. "Envy and Gratitude." In *Envy and Gratitude and Other Works, 1946–1963.* New York: Delacorte Press/Seymour Lawrence, 1975.

Kris, E. 1952. *Psychoanalytic Explorations in Art.* New York: International Universities Press.

Lanes, S. G. 1980. *The Art of Maurice Sendak.* New York: Abrams.

Mitchell, W. J. T. 1986. *Iconology.* Chicago and London: University of Chicago Press.

Robinson, J. 1974. *The Comics.* New York: Berkeley Windhover.

Segal, H. 1964. *Introduction to the Work of Melanie Klein.* New York: Basic Books.

Sendak, M. 1963. *Where the Wild Things Are.* New York: Harper and Row.

———. 1967. *Higglety Pigglety Pop!* New York: Harper and Row.

————. 1970. *In the Night Kitchen*. New York: Harper and Row.

————. 1991. Lecture at the West Side YMCA, November 15, 1991, sponsored by "The Writer's Voice."

Spitz, E. H. 1989. "Primary Art Objects: Psychoanalytic Reflections on Picturebooks for Children." *The Psychoanalytic Study of the Child* 44:351–68.

Spitz, R. A. 1957. *No and Yes*. New York: International Universities Press.

Thurber, J. [1943] 1971. *Many Moons*. San Diego: Harcourt, Brace, Jovanovich.

Winnicott, D. W. 1958. "The Capacity to Be Alone." In *The Maturational Processes and the Facilitating Environment: Studies in the Theory of Emotional Development*, pp. 29–36. New York: International Universities Press, 1965; London: Hogarth Press, 1965.

————. 1971. *Playing and Reality*. New York: Basic Books; London: Tavistock, 1984.

15

Gender and Voice in Transitional Phenomena

CLAIRE KAHANE

One of the most fruitful concepts of British object relations theory for literary studies has been D. W. Winnicott's twofold formulation of transitional phenomena: *potential space,* that intermediate area between the subjective and objective, in which all creative and spontaneous gestures are initiated, and the *transitional object* that resides within it, an unchallengeable first possession "between the thumb and teddy bear, between oral eroticism and the true object relationship" (1953:2). For Winnicott, the transitional object arises before subject-object differentiation, and thus presumably before gender. Sexual differentiation comes into being after the transitional object turns into an actual object, an outcome made manifest by the girl's subsequent preference for soft toys and the boy's for hard ones. The transitional object, on the other hand, is purportedly indeterminate and, like the work of art in cultural space, can be appropriated as a subjective object by both sexes. In this essay I want to explore Winnicott's assumption that sexual difference has no place in transitional phenomena and its antecedent mirror relations.

The most important presence in the field of transitional phenomena is Winnicott's "good-enough mother," a protectively hovering spirit who, always striving to adapt to her infant's needs, provides a holding environment in which the infant is contained. Her perceptions mirror the infant, who utilizes this mirroring to organize its own perceptions. As Winnicott points out, functionally there is no baby but only the mother-infant dyad, which produces a subjectivity (the baby's) that is a consequence of their interrelations. If Winnicott's description of the almost perfect complementarity between mother and infant at times seems a fantasmatic ideal, it remains an ideal that Winnicott's object relations theory assigns to the mother in the real world. She alone bears the responsibility for the dyadic relation: she must sustain the infant's illusion of omnipotence by providing the object of its need so promptly and so sensitively that the infant experiences no disturbing hiatus between desire and gratification. She must support the illusion that her breast is under the magical control of the infant, for only when omnipotence is a fact of infantile experience, when the infant has been under the illusion that external reality corresponds to its own capacity to create, can it make creative use of the world. Furthermore, the devotion that allows this sensitive manipulation of the dyadic relation is presented by Winnicott as an instinctive maternal response to the infant's rhythms, a response based on her biological attunement. After having instilled the capacity for illusion, the good-enough mother *naturally* knows when and how to undermine this hallucinatory omnipotence by a gradual failure of adaptation, a weaning from the breast which allows the infant to realize separation and to enter that intermediate area between me and not-me, the potential space that is the matrix of imagination.

This tendency in Winnicott's text to privilege biology as the self-evident ground of truth and to ignore the way in which culture mediates, if not constructs, our perception of the "natural" has disturbing ramifications for feminists. Not only does the biological mother become the implicit standard for good-enough mothering, but Winnicott's ubiquitous invocation of the word "breast" as a constitutive term tends to reify that biological standard as a cultural imperative. Certainly, as Winnicott asserts in the following footnote, "the breast" can signify the technique of nurturant mothering:

> When it is said that the first object is the breast, the word "breast" is used, *I believe,* to stand for the technique of mothering as well as for the actual flesh. It is not impossible for a mother to be a good-enough mother (in my way of putting it) with a bottle for the actual feeding. (1953:11n 1; italics added)

Not impossible, but as the passive voice and negative syntax suggest, perhaps not easy? Certainly the power of metaphor to construct as well as reveal meaning is not negligible; the pervasive valorization of the signifier "breast" in object relations theory would seem itself sufficiently intimidating so that no adoptive mother, let alone father, could feel easily adequate to it. But Winnicott's disclaimer is further undermined by the persistent slippage in his discourse between "the breast" as metaphor of nurturance and as biological object. Although Winnicott allows in principle that people other than the biological mother can be good-enough nurturers, in fact, "the breast," like "the good-enough mother," routinely refers to the biological object, as, for example, when Winnicott describes the creation of illusion—"The mother places the actual breast just there where the infant is ready to create, and at the right moment" (1953:11)—or when he discusses the mother's handling of infantile aggression in terms of her ability to withstand the infant's biting of her breast (1969:92).

Without question, Winnicott's formulations have richly contributed to our understanding of the constitution of subjectivity and its relation to cultural representations. Christopher Bollas's "The Aesthetic Moment and the Search for Transformation" (1978), which depicts the aesthetic experience as a reexperience of maternal holding, Evelyn Fox Keller's *Reflections on Gender and Science* (1985), which uses the concept of potential space to explore a relation between gender and creativity, and Jean Wyatt's *Reconstructing Desire* (1990), which looks to the symbiotic mother-daughter dyad for a model of reading that can have radical social effects, are only three of the valuable interdisciplinary extrapolations of Winnicott's clinical work with mothers and children. Moreover, by promoting the shift in psychoanalysis from the Freudian focus on the father and castration to the mother-infant dyad, Winnicott has encouraged new feminist theorizations of the psychic effects of primary mothering in the construction of gender identity.[1] Nevertheless, Winnicott's formulations remain deeply problematic. By neglecting the effects of the larger cultural environment in which the mother-infant dyad functions, Winnicott ignores the ways in which that environment not only holds but *captures* both mother and infant within its prevailing symbolic network of representations constructed according to the norms of a masculine subject. As a writer, he ignores the way in which his own discourse participates in this gendered network and perpetuates its assumptions.

Although language in its broadest sense can be described as a system of signification that organizes inchoate experience and makes it meaning-full, women often experience the symbolic order of language as a tyranny, an alien structure more repressive than expressive, as Virginia Woolf first affirmed in *A Room of One's Own* (1929). Of course, both sexes suffer from the gap between felt experience and the constraints of representation, but as feminist linguists have convincingly argued, women are placed in a particularly disadvantageous relation to language.[2] That handicap can be readily located in our Indo-European symbolic order, which, from its monological insistence on "man" as the generalized signifier of both men and women to its gendered dualisms grounded in the pervasive dichotomy that links masculinity to doing and femininity to being, establishes man as the normative active subject and woman as object.

In "Creativity and Its Origins" (1971a), Winnicott defines sexual difference in terms of this patriarchal opposition. Regarding instinct or drive as male in contrast to the experience of pure being, which he designates as female, Winnicott distinguishes between the breast that does, which he calls a "male element breast," and the breast that is, a "female element" with which all infants need to be able to identify in order to experience pure being (81–82). Although Winnicott distinguishes these male and female psychic elements from actual male and female persons and proposes like Freud a ubiquitous psychic bisexuality, nevertheless that bisexuality is fundamentally dichotomized. In declaring that "some boys and girls are doomed to grow up with a lopsided bisexuality, loaded on the *wrong* side of their biological provision" (83; italics added), Winnicott again privileges biology as the basis of a normative definition of sexual difference in which "doing" is male and "being" female.

Freud also invoked the conventions of gender dichotomy, employing masculine and feminine as analogous to active and passive, but he complained that this was a linguistic constraint to which he submitted for the sake of exposition.

> It is essential to realize that the concepts of "masculine" and "feminine," whose meaning seems so unambiguous to ordinary people, are among the most confused that occur in science. . . . "Masculine" and "feminine" are used sometimes in the sense of activity and passivity . . . [the sense] the most serviceable in psychoanalysis. (1905:219–20; note added 1915)

Some fifteen years later, he reiterated: "For psychology the contrast between the sexes fades away into one between activity and passivity, in which we far too readily identify activity with maleness and passivity with femaleness, a view which is by no means universally confirmed in the animal kingdom" (1930:105–106).

Winnicott, however, not only reifies "doing" and "being" as "pure male" and "pure female" but also fails to question the transferential effects of these definitions on his role as mirroring therapist.[3] Nor does he consider the influence of such cultural codes on maternal perception more generally. If the mirror reflecting the infant to itself is, like a double exposure, already contaminated by a relation to preexisting images of sexual difference, then, since there is no baby but only the mother-infant dyad, the subjectivity of the infant assimilates the effects of that binary logic on the maternal mirror.

Interestingly, in this essay Winnicott does present a clinical case in which the mirror has a distinct effect on gender identity, that of a male patient who, having been seen first as "a girl-baby" by his mother, suffered from gender confusion (1971a:72–75).[4] Although Winnicott elaborates on the pathogenic effects of this particular mother's distorting reflection of her son—which resulted in a dissociation between male and female parts of the self—the possibility that the sexual dichotomizing of normative mirroring also might have pathogenic effects is not considered. Certainly Winnicott recognizes how much depends upon external factors, which he here calls "environmental provision":

> Either individuals live creatively and feel that life is worth living or else they cannot live creatively and are doubtful about the value of living. This variable in human beings is directly related to the quality and quantity of environmental provision at the beginning of each baby's experience. (1971a:71)

Yet his text does not include the way in which cultural meanings impinge on, and are part of, that environmental provision. In excluding the cultural constitution of sexual difference, Winnicott's texts reflect another, more theoretically innocent time, when male and female, doing and being, were terms that could circulate unproblematically as essential categories.

To take another example, in the well-known "Mirror-role of Mother and Family in Child Development," he writes of a woman who "married and brought up three fine male children" (1967b:113); the word "fine" in this context is weighted with a special applause difficult to transfer to a similar statement about female children. He then relates her depression to her position as the only woman in a family of men and, recognizing her need for a mirroring confirmation of her gender identity, writes that "the woman had to be her own mother. If she had had a daughter she would have found great relief" (114). Yet merely to have had a mother's or a daughter's reflection of her feminine identity would not by itself solve the patient's problem of finding adequate mirrors. If the maternal mirror is inevitably mediated by a system of valuation that privileges the phallus, the presence of the maternal mirror and its constructed reflections might be just as problematic for the female child as its absence.

Moreover, Winnicott again confines his perception of the patient's need for adequate mirroring to a particular family constellation and does not take into account that the same situation has obtained for women generally in the culture at large. As feminist analyses of the visual field have demonstrated, women are ubiquitously surrounded by alienating cultural mirrors of subjectivity constructed from an Imaginary the normative gaze of which is masculine. Indeed, Winnicott's case implicitly tells us something about why the high incidence of depression among women exceeds any familial etiology; it suggests that depression among women is in great part a consequence of alienating cultural representations, all the more insidious for being unconsciously imbibed, as it were, with mother's milk.

One can see this kind of alienating representation at work in Winnicott's own description of a woman patient of "striking appearance," who experienced being looked at as an undoing. Winnicott, on the other hand, thinks she should exploit her position as attractive object, writing that "if she were able to use herself she could be the central figure in any group" (115). If in Winnicott's view her striking appearance gives her the power to compel the gaze of others, she nevertheless seems to shrink from that gaze, as if it were an assault. Discussing her reticence at appearing at a coffee bar, Winnicott writes: "I asked: 'Did anyone look at you?' She was able to go over to the idea that she did in fact draw some of the fire" (115). In remarking that "she did draw some of the fire," Winnicott's very metaphor unwittingly unveils the implicit violence of the gaze that makes being seen so problematic for women, an experience of disintegration rather than confirmation. Is it surprising then that she has a "desire to be seen in a way that would make her feel she existed," to be seen "for what she in fact is" (115)? Where is the mirror that would gratify that desire when even the analyst succumbs to the tyranny of the Symbolic order?

In spite of these blind spots, "Mirror-role of Mother and Family in Child Development" is an important essay for feminist theorists. Not only does Winnicott's text bring into focus the indubitable phenomenon that "what characterizes so many women [is] an interest in the face" (115), but it also suggests reasons for the pervasive dissemination of the female visage as a cultural object of fascination. In this context, it is especially illuminating to consider the overdetermined relation to the woman's face in the photographs of Cindy Sherman. For over a decade, Sherman has used her body to represent woman in our culture—or rather women, for in each photograph she appears as a different recognizable image derived from popular media such as film, advertising, and scandal sheets. Indeed, Sherman's photographic mutations of herself into these simulacra suggest that there is no "herself," no other, ontologically privileged identity under the face; the media image is all there is.

Although Sherman's repetitive use of herself confirms the emptiness beneath the face, by her very production of the face-as-mask, her photographs also evince, like Winnicott's patient, a generalized female desire "to be seen in a way that would make her feel she existed." One might recall here another patient of Winnicott's, a woman for whom the only real thing was the gap (1953). For this patient, the absence of an object was more real than its presence, in part, Winnicott suggests, because what her mother symbolized was perceived as untrue. Describing her realization that her mother lied, Winnicott writes:

> Here was the picture of a child and the child had transitional objects, and there were transitional phenomena that were evident, and all of these were symbolical of something and were real for the child; but gradually, or perhaps frequently for a little while, she had to doubt the reality of the thing that they were symbolizing. That is to say, if they were symbolical of her mother's devotion and reliability they remained real in themselves but what they stood for was not real. The mother's devotion and reliability were unreal. (1953:24)

Like Cindy Sherman's photographs, this patient's reality suggests that even when the mother's face *is* physically there, what it represents can seem unreal, empty. If it is true, as Winnicott theorizes, that when the face of the mother does not reflect the baby, a false self is constructed in "compliance with environmental demands" (1960:147), female children are more encouraged to construct that empty image of accommodation that Joan Rivière delineates in "Womanliness as Masquerade" (1929).

In short, it is not merely Winnicott's position as transferential mirror that is infected with patriarchal gender representations, but every mother's. The mother is not the pure origin of the perception her face reflects to the infant. Rather, the mother's face participates in a cultural dynamic of refraction and representation which has systematically devalued women as subjects. Consequently, women have been inhibited in their creative use of what Winnicott has called the potential space, "between the individual and the environment (originally the object)," in which cultural experience takes place (1967a:100). As Winnicott points out, only when the infant feels a confidence based on the dependability of the mother-figure or environmental elements can it experience potential space; failure of dependability leads to loss of the play area and of meaningful symbols.[5] Only recently have the cultural effects of negative mirroring on women been mitigated by feminist interventions, promoting a new consciousness of the countertransferential implications of theory.[6] Precisely because Winnicott's texts remain so influential and useful for both clinicians and literary critics, we need to attend to the effects of their assumptions about gender.

To supplement Winnicott's ideas I want to turn now from the visual to the acoustic mirror, and to the role of the maternal voice within the field of infantile phenomena. Most psychoanalytic considerations of the mother's voice have maintained that it is identified by the baby long before her physical appearance, and thus precedes the mirror-stage in the constitution of the subject. As Michel Chion writes:

> For the child after birth, the Mother is more an olfactory and vocal continuum than an image. One can imagine the voice of the Mother, which is woven around the child, and which originates from all points in space as her form enters and leaves the visual field, as a matrix of places to which we are tempted to give the name "umbilical net." (1982:57)

In terms reminiscent of Winnicott's transitional phenomena, Guy Rosolato describes the maternal voice as a blanket of sound, a sonorous envelope that surrounds and sustains (1974:81); Didier Anzieu refers to "a bath of sounds" (1976:173). But as these and other psychoanalysts have remarked, that heterogeneous field of the voice very quickly takes on the discriminations and differentiations that mark its relation to language.[7] Thus, unlike Winnicott's representation of the visual mirror as a continuous reflection to the infant of what the mother sees, the acoustic mirror gives rise to a primary split in both the speaking voice and its infant auditor that is a consequence of its communicating both sound and sense.

Among those who have explored the ambiguities of the maternal voice, Julia Kristeva, both a linguist and a psychoanalyst, has given feminist critics a powerful conceptual framework for theorizing the relation of the mother's voice to the construction of subjectivity. In particular, her concept of the semiotic, a register of language that encompasses prelinguistic modalities of psychic inscription, has appealed to feminists concerned with finding a site of representation outside the patriarchal order.[8] Utilizing psycholinguistic research about the mental operations that precede the acquisition of language, Kristeva describes a preverbal functional state, "the semiotic chora," dominated by oral and anal drives that govern the connections between the body, objects, and family figures (1984).[9] As a "receptacle of as yet unorganized clusters of desires," the chora is similar to Winnicott's holding environment, binding the infant to the mother in an amorphous continuum comprising auditory as well as other drive-oriented infantile experiences of the body. Detected in the first mimetic utterances of infants as "rhythms and intonations anterior to the first phonemes, morphemes, lexemes, and sentences" (1980:133), this semiotic chora is analogous to vocal and kinetic rhythms that underlie figuration. Thus Kristeva posits that while syntactical language with its rules and boundaries ruptures this amorphous anteriority to constitute a separate subject—the "I" who speaks—the semiotic continues to function as a primary process modality of language, evoking a drive-oriented relation to the maternal body. This modality, moreover, is privileged by avant garde writers and feminists alike since its phonemic and rhythmic evocations undermine the rigidities of symbolic codes and logical syntax.

Although the concept of the semiotic chora seems to be grounded in a mother-infant dyad not unlike Winnicott's, Kristeva nevertheless adds a third term to that dyadic relation by positing through the infant's experience of the maternal voice an imaginary, preoedipal father as well as mother from the beginning. For Kristeva, Lacan's mirror stage itself emerges from a *preoedipal* triangulation necessary for perception and the initiation into object relations. In Kristeva's complex theory of the infant's relation to the maternal voice, even before there is an apprehension of a maternal object, through oral assimilation, the infant identifies with a maternal voice as a pattern, an organization of sound that is the paternal precursor of its language. Describing the process of the subject's relation to speech, she writes:

When the object that I incorporate is the speech of the other, precisely a non-object, a pattern, a model, I bind myself to him in a
primary fusion, communion, unification. . . . In being able to receive
the other's words, to assimilate, repeat and reproduce them, I become
like him: One: a subject of enunciation. (1985:244)

Although from Winnicott's point of view this assimilation of language
would seem to indicate a fusion with the speaking mother, in using the
pronoun "him," Kristeva designates this primary fusion with "a non-
object, a pattern, a model" as constituting a masculine subject of
enunciation. That masculine designation is implicitly theorized by her
reference to Freud's concept of "primary identification—a 'direct and
immediate transference' of the nascent ego—to the 'father of individual
prehistory,' who . . . possessed the sexual characteristics and functions
of both parents." For Kristeva, this father of prehistory is not a person,
but an archaic disposition preceding the mirror stage (1985:250).
Claiming that this "father of prehistory" functions as a "magnet of
identification" for the infant's narcissism, Kristeva theorizes that identification with "this form, structure, or agency (rather than person)
helps to bring about primary stabilization of the subject" (1987:25).
Although "*empirically,* the first affections, the first imitations and the
first vocalizations are directed toward the mother . . . pointing to the
father as the magnet for primary love, primary identification, is tenable
only if one conceives of *identification* as being always already within
the symbolic orbit, under the sway of language" (1985:245). Under the
sway of language, the maternal voice is an acoustic bridge not only to
the maternal body but to an ordering of speech already constituted
within the maternal unconscious.

   In sum, in the process of becoming an ego, a speaking subject, the
infant moves from a primary maternal vortex of corporeal needs and
pleasures toward an idealizing primary identification with the Other,
an imaginary site of power and desire located elsewhere, beyond the
mother. As Kristeva writes, the voice is an "ideal signifier, a sound on
the fringe of my being, which transfers me to the place of the Other,
astray, beyond meaning, out of sight" (253). It is to this Other that
the mother also turns when she holds up her infant for the admiration
of an invisible gaze, indicating an off-stage spectator without whom
mother and child would be locked in psychotic fusion. Whatever "other"
the mother unconsciously addresses when she exhibits the child for
approval or judgment—whether we call this the ego ideal, the superego, the Name of the Father, or even her actual parents—that ideal

"Other" has a phallic valence in the maternal unconscious and in language.

From my reading of Kristeva and of Winnicott, it follows that in the move from the semiotic to the symbolic, from the mirror stage through transitional phenomena, infant girls become doubly alienated: from an identification with the mother who is objectified by language as the breast that *is* rather than the breast that *does,* and from a symbolic discourse that disavows feminine subjectivity. Because women subjects nonetheless exist, their sense of self is often marked by a hysterical, bewildering division between identification with the maternal as bearer of the semiotic voice, privileged only as a sensual, nonrational body, and a paternal identification with a symbolic discourse that represents her, and by which she represents herself, as either an inauthentic subject or an object.

Can we negotiate new terms within this closed circle? In Winnicottian parlance, how can the infant bring something of herself that is new to potential space? Whatever answer we may imagine, a consciousness of the effects of language and the systems of representation that constitute our cultural experience must be involved. Thus far the response of feminists has been either to call for an "écriture feminine," in the overworked phrase of Hélène Cixous, that will celebrate a preoedipal modality of interrelating, or to parody and mimic existing symbolic discourses, as Cindy Sherman does in her photographs, unveiling the illusory basis of their authority. The latter makes strategic use of symbolic mirrors in a postmodern mockery that is meant to crack them. The former calls for a discursive violation of the symbolic oedipal contract, flirting with fragmentation and regression in an effort to reorder language and the unconscious.

André Green has provocatively remarked that "the unconscious creates its own structure only by way of the Imaginary" (1972:294). Insofar as literature privileges the Imaginary by encouraging an identification with the fantasy patterns of the text, and insofar as it can promote a regression analogous to Ernst Kris's "regression in the service of the ego" (1964), it has the potential to modify the reader's unconscious structures and effect what Kristeva calls a "revolution in poetic language" (1984). At this juncture, one thing seems clear: no change is possible without alterations at the level of symbolic representations; even in the field of transitional phenomena and their antecedent mirroring relations, pure being is pure nostalgia.

NOTES

1. See for example Nancy Chodorow's influential *Reproduction of Mothering* (1978) and Jessica Benjamin's "A Desire of One's Own: Psychoanalytic Feminism and Intersubjective Space" (1986). My own "Gothic Mirrors and Feminine Identity" (1980) is likewise greatly indebted to Winnicott's "Mirror-role of Mother and Family in Child Development" (1967b), which describes with deceptive simplicity the visual basis of the experience of identity.

2. See McConnell (1980) for essays that elaborate the effects of patriarchal language on women's subjectivity. Lacanians argue that language per se assumes a masculine subject, which is a position in language and not synonymous with an actual male person. For an elucidation of this theoretical stance, see Jacqueline Rose's introduction to the collection of Lacan's essays, *Feminine Sexuality* (1985), and Kate Linker's "Sexuality and Representation" (1984).

3. In another disclaiming footnote, Winnicott writes: "I shall continue to use this terminology (male and female elements) for the time being, since I know of no other suitable descriptive terms. Certainly 'active' and 'passive' are not correct terms, and I must continue the argument using the terms that are available" (1971a:76). Yet how else can we understand "doing" and "being" but as a version of the active/passive dichotomy?

4. This case of a second son suggests a relation between sibling position and gender construction. The mother's view of her second son as a girl may be part of a more general family dynamic regarding second sons who are reflected as "not-man," because the place of the man is already occupied by the first son. I would speculate that especially within mother-dominated households the position of second sons is often characterized by mother-son identification rather than oedipal desire, a dynamic delineated in D. H. Lawrence's *Sons and Lovers*, in which Paul Morel identifies with his mother in great part because she has already chosen her first son as the desirable male other.

5. Winnicott describes cultural productions as a mature kind of play "in a potential space between the individual and the environment (originally the object). . . . The use of this space is determined by *life experiences* that take place at the early stages of the individual's existence" (1967a:100).

6. Of course, my remarks about the consequences of negative mirroring also are relevant to other nonhegemonic groups who are represented in the dominant culture as symbols of otherness; Toni Morrison's novel, *The Bluest Eye*, is a powerful representation of that negative mirroring communicated most destructively by a black mother to her vulnerable daughter.

7. See, for example, Lecourt's discussion of the musico-verbal envelope, comprising two indissociable faces of the sonorous envelope: "The verbal face, more linear (in time), univocal and a visible thread in the texture, is turned toward the outside. The musical face, in thickness, woven of voices (in space as in time) and plurivocal, is turned more towards the inside. . . . One sounds,

sings, vibrates . . . the other is articulatory and more abstract. One is 'us', the other is 'I' " (1990:225).

8. Thus for example, Jean Wyatt's *Reconstructing Desire* (1990) tries to meld Winnicott and Kristeva by theorizing that certain texts, in promoting preoedipal fantasies and transitional phenomena, can alter unconscious structures.

9. Kristeva takes this meaning from "the Greek *semeion:* trace, mark, distinctive feature. At the very beginning of philosophy, before thought was constricted by the notion that language must reflect ideas, Plato, recalling the work of the atomists, spoke in the *Timeaeus* of the *chora,* an ancient, mobile, unstable receptacle, prior to the One, to the father, and even to the syllable, metaphorically suggesting something nourishing and maternal" (1987:5).

REFERENCES

Anzieu, D. 1976. "L'enveloppe sonore du soi." *Nouvelle revue de psychanalyse* 13:173.

Benjamin, J. 1986. "A Desire of One's Own: Psychoanalytic Feminism and Intersubjective Space." In T. de Lauretis, ed., *Feminist Studies/Critical Studies,* pp. 78–101. Bloomington: Indiana University Press.

Bollas, C. 1978. "The Aesthetic Moment and the Search for Transformation." *Annual of Psychoanalysis* 6:385–94.

Chion, M. 1982. *Le voix du cinema.* Paris: Editions de L'Étoile.

Chodorow, N. 1978. *The Reproduction of Mothering.* Berkeley: University of California Press.

Freud, S. 1905. *Three Essays on the Theory of Sexuality.* In vol. 7 of *The Standard Edition of the Complete Psychological Works,* pp. 123–243. Edited by J. Strachey et al. 24 vols. London: Hogarth Press, 1953–74.

——. 1930. *Civilization and Its Discontents.* In vol. 21 of *The Standard Edition of the Complete Psychological Works,* pp. 64–145.

Green, A. 1972. "Potential Space in Psychoanalysis." In *On Private Madness,* pp. 277–96. Madison, Conn.: International Universities Press, 1986.

Kahane, C. 1980. "Gothic Mirrors and Feminine Identity." In S. Garner, C. Kahane, and M. Sprengnether, eds., *The M/Other Tongue: Essays in Feminist Psychoanalytic Criticism,* pp. 334–51. Ithaca: Cornell University Press, 1985.

Keller, E. F. 1985. *Reflections on Gender and Science.* New Haven: Yale University Press.

Kris, E. 1964. *Psychoanalytic Explorations in Art.* New York: Schocken.

Kristeva, J. 1980. *Desire in Language.* Edited by L. S. Roudiez. New York: Columbia University Press.

——. 1984. "Revolution in Poetic Language." In Kristeva, *The Kristeva Reader,* pp. 89–136.

————. 1985a. "Freud and Love: Treatment and Its Discontents." In Kristeva, *The Kristeva Reader*, pp. 240–71.

————. 1985b. *The Kristeva Reader*. Edited by T. Moi. New York: Columbia University Press.

————. 1987. *In the Beginning Was Love*. New York: Columbia University Press.

Lacan, J. 1985. *Feminine Sexuality*. Edited by J. Mitchell and J. Rose. New York and London: Norton.

Lecourt, E. 1990. "The Musical Envelope." In D. Anzieu, ed., *Psychic Envelopes*, pp. 211–29. London: Karnac Books.

Linker, K. 1984 . "Sexuality and Representation." In B. Wallis, ed., *Art After Modernism*, pp. 391–416. Boston: Godine.

McConnell, S. G. 1980. *Women and Language in Literature and Society*. New York: Praeger.

Riviere, Joan. 1929. "Womanliness as Masquerade." In V. Burgin, J. Donald, and C. Kaplan, eds., *Formations of Fantasy*, pp. 35–44. New York and London: Methuen, 1986.

Rosolato, Guy. 1974. "La voix: entre corps et langage." *Revue francaise de psychanalyse*, vol. 37.

Winnicott, D. W. 1953. "Transitional Objects and Transitional Phenomena." In Winnicott 1971, *Playing and Reality*, pp. 1–25.

————. 1960. "Ego Distortion in Terms of True and False Self." In *The Maturational Processes and the Facilitating Environment: Studies in the Theory of Emotional Development*, pp. 140–52. New York: International Universities Press, 1965; London: Hogarth Press, 1965.

————. 1967a. "The Location of Cultural Experience." In Winnicott, *Playing and Reality*, pp. 95–103.

————. 1967b. "Mirror-role of Mother and Family in Child Development." In Winnicott, *Playing and Reality*, pp. 111–18.

————. 1969. "The Use of an Object and Relating through Identifications." In Winnicott, *Playing and Reality*, pp. 86–94.

————. 1971a. "Creativity and Its Origins." In Winnicott, *Playing and Reality*, pp. 65–85.

————. 1971b. *Playing and Reality*. New York: Basic Books; London: Tavistock, 1984.

Woolf, V. 1929. *A Room of One's Own*. New York and London: Harcourt Brace.

Wyatt, J. 1990. *Reconstructing Desire*. Chapel Hill and London: University of North Carolina Press.

16

*From the Clinic to the Classroom: D. W. Winnicott, James Britton, and the Revolution in Writing Theory**

ANNE M. WYATT-BROWN

Contemporary literary theorists and those interested in class-room behavior have not ignored psychoanalysis. They have, however, focused primarily on the theories of Freud, Lacan, and, in rhetoric, Carl Rogers (Brent 1991). As a result, when *College English* devoted two issues to psychoanalysis and pedagogy, not one author mentioned Donald Winnicott (Brooke 1987; Con Davis 1987a, 1987b; Donahue and Quandahl 1987; Johnson and Garber 1987; Ulmer 1987). Even in a recent symposium in honor of James Britton, who was Winnicott's brother-in-law and one of the foremost writing theorists of his genera-tion, Winnicott's name never appeared (Tirrell et al. 1990). Nor did Jane Tompkins (1990) discern that her "pedagogy of the distressed," with its call for emphasizing the coaching aspect of teaching over the performative, owes a great deal to Winnicott's techniques.

*I am much indebted to Dixie Goswami of Clemson University and The Bread Loaf School of English, who read an early version of this paper, offered useful suggestions, and at my request sent a copy of it to James Britton. Britton himself has kindly com-mented upon the paper, sent me copies of his early text, *English on the Anvil* (1934), as well as a more recent essay (1977) in which he cites Winnicott, and given me permission to quote from his letters.

Still, A. S. Byatt's knowing reference to the " 'transitional area,' in Winnicott's terms" in her prize-winning academic novel *Possession* (1990:362) suggests that his star is rising in the literary world. Within psychoanalysis his ideas have influenced innumerable leading figures, including Marion Milner (1987), who examines the connection between art and mental behavior, and Daniel Stern, whose research on infancy combines psychoanalysis and developmental psychology (1985). Winnicott's theory of the "intermediate space" has also been fruitfully connected to language (Schwartz 1978) and to creativity and aging (Schwab 1986; Schwartz 1986; Woodward 1991). Among those interested in the theory of writing, only Summerfield and Summerfield (1986) and I (1991) have recognized the impact of these ideas and their bearing on the behavior of teachers. Clearly it is time to examine how Winnicott's formulations of the creative process and his low-keyed clinical attitudes can alter the teacher's role in the writing class, even at the graduate level in a university English as a Second Language (ESL) program.

Winnicott's early papers show respect for children and their families, as well as considerable skepticism about the role that physicians play in healing their young patients. Direct observation of mothers and babies along with careful history-taking taught him that most mothers provide their infants with an emotionally healthy environment, but that they themselves need the support necessary to "find their feelings," what he calls "support-without-interference" (1948:162). In addition, he learned how much it means to mothers to be able to meet their infant's needs, to become the "ordinary good mother" who creates "a *good-enough* environment" for her child (1949:245).

External circumstances in the psychiatric community affected the evolution of Winnicott's ideas. For example, the shortage of trained analysts in the 1930s and 1940s limited the number of children who could receive analytic treatment, but fortunately some families rose to the challenge and provided the safe surroundings their children needed. Reasonably successful outcomes convinced Winnicott that patients could sometimes forgo psychiatric treatment. If parents were offered some intelligent support from the psychoanalytic community, many were able to cooperate with social workers and school authorities to supply the necessary holding environment (Winnicott 1953, 1955).[1] This success led Winnicott to notice that the behavior of doctors at a clinic can determine the parents' later reactions. If the doctors treated them as intelligent adults, they often shouldered the responsibility for the child rather than "anxiously" abdicating to the professionals. In his judgment, it is best for parents to stay in charge, especially when analysis is not possible (1942:71).

Of course, Winnicott believed in the therapeutic usefulness of psychoanalysis. He himself was analyzed by both James Strachey and Joan Rivière, and his second wife by Melanie Klein (Phillips 1988:36, 47). Once he declared that no other treatment is "in any way comparable with analysis," but rarely is it "both applicable and available" (Winnicott 1942:81, 83). When analysis had to be ruled out for some practical reason, he advised not even mentioning it to families as an option. On one occasion when confronted with a hypochondriacal mother, he discouraged any further therapy. The child needed to be spared further intrusion, and analysis was impractical (80–81). No intervention was better than an inappropriate one.

At the same time, Winnicott never hesitated to deplore the ignorance that many physicians showed about the way feelings can affect symptom production. In his clinical practice he saw many children who had been consigned to bed for supposed chorea, a treatment that exacerbated their nervousness. The misdiagnoses, he determined, came from the doctors' disregard of the children's psychology. Therefore he urged pediatricians to resist medical interventions and to develop a wait-and-see approach with their patients (1931a, 1931b). He also argued that there are times when psychological illness can be a normal, if painful, part of human development. For example, when the birth of a sibling causes acute jealousy and ensuing symptoms, he urged the pediatrician to act as a friendly observer, "a sympathetic witness to the child's distress" (Phillips 1988:52). In Winnicott's opinion, we all must learn to experience frustration, and "surely, a most important aim of education should be to enable the child to manage life unaided" (Winnicott 1931a:4).[2] In sum, he found children to be more resourceful than many experts in his time seemed to think. According to Adam Phillips, Winnicott "tends to look, not for what is remotely unconscious, the esoteric unknown, but for what there is in a person 'waiting for acknowledgement' " (1988:52–53).

Winnicott's confidence in his patients and his methods of detached observation with minimal interference have had an important influence on the thinking of James Britton, who in turn has inspired a generation of Anglo-American researchers and educators. The question of influence is an extremely difficult matter to determine. Most imaginative thinkers are inspired by a variety of people, ideas, and circumstances, and Britton is no exception. Moreover, World War II itself had an enduring effect on British society and its educational system. During the war the difficulty of relocating children who had been evacuated from London challenged the accepted principles of educators, physicians, and other professionals (Phillips 1988). At that time Britton's sister, Clare, worked with Winnicott to assist the evacuees and their caretakers, and in 1947 they described some of their innovative solutions in an article that Britton still has in his possession (personal communication, October 29, 1991). When the Labour government gained power in 1945, many called for reforms in the classbound British educational system so that working-class children would have a greater chance of success. All these factors influenced Britton's thinking in the postwar period.[3]

From the beginning of his career, Britton observed how children learn, and he valued the importance of fantasy in their lives, an aspect neglected by more traditional educators. Thus, he found Winnicott's ideas congenial. Although one finds only a few references to his brother-in-law in Britton's essays (1970, 1977), Winnicott's confidence in children and their families reinforced Britton's own predispositions. Indeed the remnants of traditional educational assumptions that appear in Britton's *English on the Anvil* (1934) indicate by contrast the extent of Winnicott's later influence. Britton wrote the textbook in 1934, six years before his sister Clare first met Winnicott (Phillips 1988:62–63).

In 1934 Britton's primary mentor was his former tutor, Professor Percy Gurrey of the London Day Training College. Throughout the book Britton uses literary excerpts from a variety of sources to stimulate children's fantasies, which he sees as an important but often untapped source of creativity. The same literary passages become the basis for imaginative grammar exercises, a practice that underscores the interaction of reading and grammar. Britton also recommends encouraging children as young as eleven to write essays, rather than "working composition exercises," the expected task of the English classroom in the 1930s (1934:10).

The material in *English on the Anvil* reflects Britton's lifelong commitment to poetry and language structure as "complementary interests" (personal communication, November 11, 1991). The author talks directly to the children in an engaging and respectful fashion that must have made the book irresistible. At the same time he does not hesitate to issue occasional instructions. When writing compositions Britton declares, "Here you *must* pick and choose very carefully, and you must *not* be content with the nearest word,—the one which you think of first" (1934:51).

At that time Britton, like his mentor Gurrey, believed that young children needed to be instructed in the grammatical structures of their language to be fully literate. The exercises in the text are challenging, and less well-read pupils might feel slightly daunted by the sophisticated literary excerpts that provide the basis of the writing assignments. Gurrey himself encouraged students "to try out their own hunches" and supported their efforts to do so (Britton, personal communication, November 11, 1991). Most important, neither Gurrey nor Britton subscribed to the notion that teachers have the " 'single right answer' in matters of language usage" (Britton, personal communication, January 23, 1992). One can imagine that other teachers might not have implemented the text in quite so enlightened a fashion. Britton reports quickly abandoning the idea of explicitly teaching grammar to young children. He discovered that they are capable of absorbing what they need more naturally by reading, writing, and listening. At the time he wrote the text, however, he still believed that some direct instruction was necessary.

The war provided an important turning point in Britton's career and his attitudes toward education. A severe paper shortage meant that he could not return to his prewar job as an education editor for John Murray, Publishers. Therefore he began a Master's degree in educational psychology, which he was awarded in June 1952. In the autumn of 1946, Britton, together with Gurrey and Nancy Martin, founded the London Association for the Teaching of English (personal communication, February 17, 1992).[4] Their intention was to stimulate classroom-based research. By that means they would discover how children actually learn to "speak, write, read, and listen" (Macrorie 1984:246). They developed new qualitative research methods, innovations that Britton with characteristic understatement calls "a quiet form of research" (1983:13).

Consequently by the time Britton wrote *Language and Learning* (1970), a book that is still regarded as a seminal study of children's development of language (Martin 1988:xv), he no longer viewed the teacher as a culture-bearer. Instead he and his colleagues obviously shared Winnicott's fundamental assumptions about the collaborative nature of learning. Although at no point in his career has Britton ever denigrated the importance of good pedagogy (nor has he lost his regard for Gurrey's inspired teaching), he now puts even more faith in the innate creativity of children and in their ability to learn their language in the home. He has consistently sought to challenge traditional methods of teaching writing rather than merely conclude that some children are too deprived or too stupid to learn to write. While other educators have deplored children's poor home environments and their lack of preparation for schooling, Britton continues to assume that most children long to express themselves to an interested audience, but that teachers too often ignore subjects about which children have considerable prior knowledge. He argues that the curriculum should allow pupils to "tap the resources gathered in *speaking*" and should draw on their already extensive knowledge of narrative through exposure to fairy stories (Britton et al. 1975:16).

Thinking like a clinician, Britton began the investigations of his midlife by observing carefully how British children learned or failed to learn to write. Throughout his active career—in recent years he has retired but is still busy writing—he has visited many schools, read students' essays, and written case histories. The most extended of these is of "Clare" (Britton 1970), who was actually Britton's daughter Celia (Britton, personal communication, February 17, 1992). Like Winnicott in his case histories, Britton charts Clare's developing skills both as a writer and an interpreter of her psychic experiences. In general, Britton shares Winnicott's predilection for regarding the child as a "collaborator rather than an antagonist" and in employing methods that are "minimal and unobtrusive" (Phillips 1988:52, 54). Rather than impose an academic model of writing on children, Britton consistently argues that most have the capacity to learn to express themselves provided that they are allowed to develop their own style.

Britton also has attributed some of his faith in the creativity of children to the influence of art educators such as Sir Herbert Read, who "emphasized each child as artist in his or her characteristic and un-adult fashion." Observing fellow teachers at a college of art led Britton to realize early in his career that English departments were inclined to treat literature as "something *that other people had done*" (Tirrell et al. 1990:175). English professors, he notes, persist in acting as if children had no innate creativity. In Britton's view, such traditional teaching inhibits students from developing their distinctive style. He urges teachers, particularly at the elementary level, to refrain initially from correcting all the errors. Moreover, they should allow their pupils to write about subjects of intrinsic importance to them. Such freedom would allow more children to master the conventions of writing better than if they were forced too early into the straightjacket of academic prose (Britton et al. 1975; Martin 1983).

Thanks in part to Britton's influence, a new generation of researcher-scholars in England, Canada, Australia, and the United States have borrowed Winnicott's techniques of friendly but detached observation in their work with children learning to write.[5] In America two prominent allies are Donald Graves (1983; Graves and Stuart 1985) and Lucy Calkins (1983, 1986; Calkins with Harwayne 1991), both of whose studies of elementary classroom writing have reached a wide audience of teachers and educators of teachers. Like Britton, Graves and Calkins have also stressed the connection between early artistic development and creativity in writing.[6] All three have argued persuasively for giving children space and time to develop their individual voices and sense of urgency in writing. Each of them has also made effective use of the classroom-based research method first developed by Britton and his London research team shortly after World War II and as a result have been part of an effort to dramatically alter traditional attitudes toward pedagogy.

Britton's contributions to research and teaching have not always been given adequate recognition, even when clear evidence of indebtedness exists. Strange breaks appear in the intellectual genealogy. For instance, Graves immediately realized his affinity for Britton's methods; the two men briefly worked together some years ago in England (Britton, personal communication, October 29, 1991). Both researchers respect one another and regularly cite each other's work. In turn, Graves helped train Calkins in research methodology. He encouraged her to leave full-time school teaching for his research project (Calkins 1983:5–6). Yet for some reason, Calkins has never named Britton in any of the three books cited above, preferring instead to acknowledge Graves and other influences. Despite Calkins's reticence, her intellectual debt to Britton, and through him to Winnicott, is worth exploring.

Lessons from a Child (1983), Lucy Calkins's account of her two years as a participant observer in a New Hampshire classroom, suggests how intertwined the achievements of all these important researchers have been. Her primary focus is on the development of a third grader named Susie, who, like Britton's daughter, became a confident writer over the course of two years almost without any direct help from her teachers, or for that matter from the researcher. Calkins's study provides a remarkable example of Winnicott's techniques at work, although she is apparently unaware of her indirect connection to the psychoanalyst. Instead Calkins is conscious of her debt to several other clinicians. For example, she acknowledges that Piaget's description of the process of internalization that children go through in middle childhood helped her understand Susie's mental growth over the two years of observation (1983:62). She also felt that she benefited from Vygotsky's notion that the teacher should collaborate with students until they are able to work on their own (1983:60). Furthermore, she applied Jerome Bruner's concept of scaffolding both to her observations of Susie and to her own writing. For example, Calkins noticed that when faced with a difficult task, Susie found ways of creating "a concrete scaffolding," a system of organization that simplified her task (1983:63). In a similar way Calkins, like a good teacher in the classroom, explains her terminology, introduces key words somewhat slowly, and searches for analogies that will clarify meaning. Finally, Calkins followed Piaget's lead in being unwilling artificially to hasten a child's progress. According to Bruner, Piaget categorized all inquiries about how one might speed up mental development as "la question americaine" (Bruner 1986:141). Following Piaget's lead, Calkins developed the patience to allow Susie to learn on her own.

Although Winnicott goes unmentioned by Calkins, his ideas about infancy can be fruitfully connected in various ways to the clinical findings she admires. Once again the observations of several theorists reinforce each other's findings. Winnicott asserts that an individual learns to be alone, *"as an infant and small child, in the presence of mother"* (1958:30). Under benign circumstances children use such moments for imaginative play, which leads to a discovery of their inner lives and sense of authentic self. If all goes well, children learn to respect their play and their thoughts.[7] Young children develop elaborate monologues, which Piaget suggests allow them to express themselves, but show no sign of wishing to affect the behavior of those around them. He argues that children make little effort to clarify their speech because they assume that listeners already understand; indeed they fear that adults can even read their minds (1959:116). Vygotsky's clinical studies, however, demonstrate that this egocentric speech becomes internalized later in life and remains part of our repertoire for solving problems (1934:30–31). This explains why Calkins observed Susie talking out loud as she selected words for her essay and created other forms of "concrete scaffolding" to help her complete the job (1983:63).

The concept of scaffolding, Bruner's (1981, 1985) term for Susie's behavior, is also remarkably similar to Winnicott's observation that "a mother's job" is "to go on steadily providing the simplified bit of the world which the infant, through her, comes to know" (1945:153).[8] As a result, Bruner's research projects extend Winnicott's informal findings, as well as those of Vygotsky, by demonstrating that mothers use baby talk and analogies from the child's own world to simplify their language and recontextualize what the child wants to learn in an accessible fashion (Bruner 1981, 1985).

Furthermore, Winnicott's insights about creativity and learning also suggest that Susie's classroom situation was more psychologically complex than Calkins realized. Susie, like the students described by Robert Brooke (1987), developed a sort of transference relationship with her teachers and with the researcher herself. Brooke analyzes the process in Lacanian terms, suggesting that the students regard the teacher as "the Subject Who Is Supposed to Know" (1987:680), but the validity of his observations can be reinforced by Winnicott's clinical narratives. Brooke argues that "non-directive feedback helps facilitate this process of projection and response." When the teacher avoids stating her opinions, then the learner projects her own notion of what the teacher thinks and thereby discovers her own meaning (681). In Susie's case, "nondirective" feedback from classmates and teacher conferences, amplified by the gratifying attention of the researcher herself, contributed to the child's remarkable development. As Brooke points out, students learn from a "plurality" of responses (686), both from themselves and from other readers, and especially from what Winnicott called the "preliminary chaos" that precedes artistic creation (Milner 1987:247).

Winnicott's accounts of the varied ways he assisted families clarifies Calkins's role in the classroom even further. Her presence gave the teacher, Pat Howard, nondirective support. By refraining from telling the teacher how to revamp her classroom, Calkins allowed Howard to make changes on her own. Like the children in her own and other similarly constructed classrooms, Howard also engaged in "a joint exploration" (Dombey 1988:78). Gradually Howard found it easier to show that she was taking her students seriously as individuals; her talk demonstrated her good will. Indeed, Winnicott explicitly emphasized the need for discretion in making interpretations. In some cases, he would interpret the unconscious (1942:73, 75–77); in others, the surface behavior. Occasionally he had to fight the tendency to "intrude myself" and "to avoid giving understanding in relation to the repressed unconscious" (1953:114). Yet when he limited his interpretations, his patients would gain insight from "the application of knowledge gained by me in psycho-analytic work" (108). In keeping with Winnicott's principles, Calkins provided the necessary support for the teacher to explore and change the holding environment that she offered the students. As a result, Susie took charge of her writing process. Calkins might have appeared to be on the sidelines, but her knowledge provided a new resource for the teacher and the students.

The implications of all these ideas for a writing teacher are obvious. Students should be encouraged to use their egocentric speech for making plans but at the same time to talk about their ideas with other students and the teacher. For if, as Piaget contends, the child learns from the educational process to imagine that an audience consists either of potential collaborators or opponents (1959:59), then a writing teacher's job is to encourage cooperation rather than confrontation through such methods as peer review. I have found that even advanced writing ESL programs at the university level can benefit from the techniques Winnicott initiated and Calkins carried out in the third grade classroom in New Hampshire. For example, few graduate students make oral presentations except when their writing is finished— after they have written a proposal or a dissertation. Students, however, can learn much from making a series of oral presentations of work in progress—ranging from the informal to the more elaborate. Early in the semester they introduce the audience to their key words, begin to define the problems they face, and learn to use speech as a way of planning, a rehearsal for writing. To that end, response sheets encourage good critical listening. If students must answer some questions, they cannot ignore the speaker and think their own private thoughts. The informed questions from fellow students can illuminate procedural problems before the students have committed themselves to one particular approach. They often discover for themselves how to solve problems or change direction without explicitly being advised to do so.

The teacher can point out what individual students have already accomplished. Shy international students may not recognize their own strengths. Yet many of them have had much experience creating visual aids. Getting a chance to exhibit their expertise can bolster morale, a necessary ingredient in the difficult task of improving one's writing. When individuals come to respect their own knowledge, they are more apt to persevere. As Winnicott remarked, the mother feels rewarded for her hard work in piecing together the narrative of her child's emotional history when the analyst acknowledges her achievement (1942:82). In the classroom, teachers and fellow students can provide the same recognition.

In sum, it becomes obvious that Britton in a direct way and Calkins indirectly through Britton and Graves have benefited from the example of a great clinician, albeit one heretofore slighted by literary theorists and writing experts. Not only have they conducted their research along the lines proposed by Winnicott by playing the role of the friendly but unobtrusive observer, but they have shared his enthusiasm for the self-discoveries of their students. Recognizing that the children need large blocks of time to make their experiments, they have encouraged a new generation of teachers to revolutionize the schedule, as well as the goals, of the elementary school classroom. As a result of their work, Winnicott's convictions about the nature of research and therapy are receiving a new testing ground. One hopes that by examining the principles of his thinking and the circumstances necessary for an adequate professional holding environment, we may be able to improve the odds that his attitudes will survive in the writing classroom at all levels.

NOTES

1. Taking a parallel course, Peter Elbow in *Writing Without Teachers* (1973) argues not so much for a teacherless classroom as a collaborative one, in which the teacher shares responsibility for learning with the students.

2. In writing the same situation arises when the student struggles to find a topic. In the long run it is better not to intervene. Once students have made their choice, their commitment tends to be much greater.

3. Don Rutledge reports that Britton introduced other teachers and scholars to the writings of Vygotsky, Luria, Piaget, Kelly, Polanyi, Langer, Sapir, and Chomsky, "the theoretical giants on whom he draws to produce his rich synthesis" (1988:228).

Burton A. Melnick (personal communication, December 1, 1991) reminded me of the ferment in education in postwar Britain.

Britton served as an officer in the Royal Air Force Volunteer Reserve, stationed first in the Middle East and then in Italy during the war. Hence he did not learn the details of his sister's wartime work with Winnicott until the postwar period (personal communication, February 17, 1992).

4. Britton reports that he and his colleagues had no knowledge of Winnicott's work when they founded LATE. He first met Winnicott on April 5, 1952, and subsequently Winnicott and his wife Clare assisted their organization on various occasions. Britton recalls using Winnicott's work in the academic year 1953–54, but has no record of the details (personal communication, February 17, 1992).

5. Excellent collections of essays by practitioners who have been influenced

by Britton include Goswami and Stillman (1987) and Lightfoot and Martin (1988).

6. Graves describes the writing process as often beginning with drawing; the teacher's job is to respond "to the specifics" of what children have written, to "let them know their scribbles come through" (1983:18).

7. Britton extended Winnicott's finding by collecting rich linguistic data during moments when his daughter "Clare" was playing alone in his presence (1971:88–89), thus enriching Winnicott's description of the child developing a sense of "his own personal life" from being alone "in the presence of someone" (Winnicott 1958:34).

8. Britton still has a copy of "Primitive Emotional Development" (1945), the paper in which Winnicott described this important mother-infant interaction (personal communication, October 29, 1991).

REFERENCES

Brent, D. 1991. "Young, Becker and Pike's 'Rogerian' Rhetoric: A Twenty-Year Reassessment." *College English* 53:452–66.

Britton, J. N. [1934] 1963. *English on the Anvil: A Language and Composition Course for Secondary Schools.* London: John Murray.

———. 1970. *Language and Learning.* London: Penguin.

———. 1971. "Language and Representation." In G. M. Pradl, ed., *Prospect and Retrospect: Selected Essays of James Britton,* pp. 88–93. London: Heinemann, 1982.

———. 1977. "The Third Area Where We Are More Ourselves." In M. Meek et al., eds., *The Cool Web,* pp. 40–47. London: Bodley Head.

———. 1983. "A Quiet Form of Research." In Goswami and Stillman eds., *Reclaiming the Classroom,* pp. 13–19.

Britton, J. et al. 1975. *The Development of Writing Abilities (11–18).* Houndmills: Macmillan Education.

Brooke, R. 1987. "Lacan, Transference, and Writing Instruction." *College English* 49:679–91.

Bruner, J. 1981. "The Social Context of Language Acquisition." *Language and Communication* 1:155–78.

———. 1985. "Vygotsky: A Historical and Conceptual Perspective." In J. V. Wertsch, ed., *Culture, Communication, and Cognition: Vygotskian Perspectives,* pp. 21–34. Cambridge: Cambridge University Press.

———. 1986. *Actual Minds, Possible Worlds.* Cambridge, Mass.: Harvard University Press.

Byatt, A. S. 1990. *Possession: A Romance.* New York: Random House.

Calkins, L. McC. 1983. *Lessons from a Child: On the Teaching and Learning of Writing.* Portsmouth, N.H.: Heinemann.

———. 1986. *The Art of Teaching Writing.* Portsmouth, N.H.: Heinemann.

Calkins, L. McC., with S. Harwayne. 1991. *Living Between the Lines*. Portsmouth, N.H.: Heinemann.

Con Davis, R. 1987a. "Freud's Resistance to Reading and Teaching." *College English* 49:621–27.

———. 1987b. "Pedagogy, Lacan, and the Freudian Subject." *College English* 49:749–55.

Dombey, H. 1988. "Stories at Home and at School." In Lightfoot and Martin, eds., *The Word for Teaching is Learning*, pp. 70–81.

Donahue, P. and E. Quandahl. 1987. "Freud and the Teaching of Interpretation." *College English* 49:641–49.

Elbow, P. 1973. *Writing Without Teachers*. New York: Oxford University Press.

Goswami, D., and P. R. Stillman, eds. 1987. *Reclaiming the Classroom: Teacher Research as an Agency for Change*. Portsmouth, N.H.: Heinemann.

Graves, D. H. 1983. *Writing: Teachers and Children at Work*. Portsmouth, N.H.: Heinemann.

Graves, D. and V. Stuart. 1985. *Write from the Start: Tapping Your Child's Natural Writing Ability*. New York: New American Library.

Johnson, B., and M. Garber. 1987. "Secret Sharing: Reading Conrad Psychoanalytically." *College English* 49:628–40.

Lightfoot, M. and N. Martin, eds. 1988. *The Word for Teaching Is Learning: Language and Learning Today: Essays for James Britton*. London: Heinemann.

Macrorie, K. 1984. *Twenty Teachers*. New York: Oxford University Press.

Martin, N. 1983. *Mostly about Writing: Selected Essays*. Upper Montclair, N.J.: Boynton/Cook.

———. 1988. Introduction. In Lightfoot and Martin, eds., *The Word for Teaching is Learning*, pp. ix–xvii.

Milner, M. 1987. *The Suppressed Madness of Sane Men: Forty-four Years of Exploring Psychoanalysis*. London: Tavistock.

Piaget, J. 1959. *The Language and Thought of the Child*. Translated by M. Gabain. New York: New American Library, 1974.

Phillips, A. 1988. *Winnicott*. Cambridge: Harvard University Press.

Rutledge, D. 1988. "Institutionalizing Change: The Problem of System Belief." In Lightfoot and Martin, eds., *The Word for Teaching is Learning*, pp. 219–30.

Schwab, G. 1986. "The Intermediate Area Between Life and Death: On Samuel Beckett's *The Unnamable*." In Woodward and Schwartz, *Memory and Desire*, pp. 205–17.

Schwartz, M. M. 1978. "Critic, Define Thyself." In G. H. Hartman, ed., *Psychoanalysis and the Question of the Text*, pp. 1–17. Baltimore: Johns Hopkins University Press.

———. 1986. Introduction. In Woodward and Schwartz, eds., *Memory and Desire*, pp. 1–12.

Stern, D. N. 1985. *The Interpersonal World of the Infant: A View from Psychoanalysis and Developmental Psychology.* New York: Basic Books.

Summerfield, J., and G. Summerfield. 1986. *Texts and Contexts: A Contribution to the Theory and Practice of Teaching Composition.* New York: Random House.

Tirrell, M. K. et al. 1990. "Re-presenting James Britton: A Symposium." *College Composition and Communication* 41:166–86.

Tompkins, J. 1990. "Pedagogy of the Distressed." *College English* 52:653–60.

Ulmer, G. L. 1987. "Textshop for Psychoanalysis: On Deprogramming Freshmen Platonists." *College English* 49:756–69.

Vygotsky, L. [1934] 1986. *Thought and Language.* Translated by A. Kozulin. Cambridge: MIT Press.

Winnicott, D. W. 1931a. "A Note on Normality and Anxiety." In Winnicott, *Through Paediatrics to Psycho-Analysis,* pp. 3–21.

———. 1931b. "Fidgetiness." In Winnicott, *Through Paediatrics to Psycho-Analysis,* pp. 22–30.

———. 1942. "Child Department Consultations." In Winnicott, *Through Paediatrics to Psycho-Analysis,* pp. 70–84.

———. 1945. "Primitive Emotional Development." In Winnicott, *Through Paediatrics to Psycho-Analysis,* pp. 145–56.

———. 1948. "Paediatrics and Psychiatry." In Winnicott, *Through Paediatrics to Psycho-Analysis,* pp. 157–73.

———. 1949. "Mind and Its Relation to the Psyche-soma." In Winnicott, *Through Paediatrics to Psycho-Analysis,* pp. 243–54.

———. 1953. "Symptom Tolerance in Paediatrics: A Case History." In Winnicott, *Through Paediatrics to Psycho-Analysis,* pp. 101–17.

———. 1955. "A Case Managed at Home." In Winnicott, *Through Paediatrics to Psycho-Analysis,* pp. 118–26.

———. 1958. "The Capacity to Be Alone." In *The Maturational Processes and the Facilitating Environment: Studies in the Theory of Emotional Development,* pp. 29–36. New York: International Universities Press, 1965; London: Hogarth Press, 1965.

———. 1975. *Through Paediatrics to Psycho-Analysis,* New York: Basic Books.

Winnicott, D. W., and C. Britton. 1947. "Residential Management as Treatment for Difficult Children." In D. W. Winnicott, *Deprivation and Delinquency,* pp. 54–72. Edited by C. Winnicott, R. Shepherd, and M. Davis. London: Tavistock, 1984.

Woodward, K. 1991. *Aging and Its Discontents: Freud and Other Fictions.* Bloomington: Indiana University Press.

Woodward, K. and M. M. Schwartz, eds. 1986. *Memory and Desire: Aging—Literature—Psychoanalysis.* Bloomington: Indiana University Press.

Wyatt-Brown, A. M. 1991. "Life After Graduate School: Skill Development for International Scholarship." Gainesville, Fla.: University of Florida. (ERIC Document Reproduction Service No. ED 319 241.)

Contributors

CHRISTOPHER BOLLAS is a member of the British Psycho-Analytical Society in private practice in London. He is the author of *The Shadow of the Object, Forces of Destiny,* and *Being a Character.*

PATRICK J. CASEMENT is a training analyst in the British Psycho-Analytical Society and practices in London. His first book, *On Learning from the Patient,* has been published in twelve languages; its sequel, *Further Learning from the Patient,* in four.

ANTOINETTE BUTLER DAUBER has taught at Hebrew University in Jerusalem and published essays on a number of sixteenth- and seventeenth-century English poets. She currently works as a marketing executive.

DAVID HOLBROOK is emeritus fellow of English at Downing College, Cambridge, and the author of over forty books of poetry, fiction, pedagogy, and criticism, including *English for the Rejected* and *Flesh Wounds,* a war novel. He has recently published *Images of Woman in*

Literature, The Skeleton in the Wardrobe, a study of the fantasies of C. S. Lewis, and *Where D. H. Lawrence Was Wrong About Women,* where the views expressed in his contribution to this volume are expanded and modified.

BROOKE HOPKINS is associate professor of English at the University of Utah, where he specializes in British Romanticism, Shakespeare, and psychoanalytic criticism. His recent essays include "Keats and the Uncanny" and "Representing Robespierre."

ALBERT D. HUTTER is an associate professor of English and comparative literature at UCLA and a psychoanalyst in part-time private practice in Los Angeles. The author of numerous essays on literature and psychology, he is currently working on a book, *Writing Bridged and Writing Blocked.* He has also published short fiction and a novel and is a member of the Screenwriter's Guild. He recently completed his second novel, *The Other Side of Silence.*

CLAIRE KAHANE teaches in the English department and directs the graduate program in literature and psychology at SUNY Buffalo. She has published articles in feminist theory, psychoanalysis, and modern literature, and coedited the anthologies *The (M)other Tongue* and *In Dora's Case.* She is currently at work on a book on the hysterical narrative voice in modern British fiction.

MARION MILNER is a retired member of the British Psycho-Analytical Society living in London. Her books include *On Not Being Able to Paint, A Life of One's Own, The Hands of the Living God,* and *The Suppressed Madness of Sane Men.*

RICHARD POIRIER is Marious Bewley Professor of English at Rutgers University, the editor of *Raritan Quarterly,* and a founder and chairman of The Library of America. His latest book is *Poetry and Pragmatism.* A longer version of his piece in this volume appears as the Afterword to the paperback version of *Robert Frost: The Work of Knowing,* published by Stanford University Press.

PETER L. RUDNYTSKY is associate professor of English and director of the Institute for Psychological Study of the Arts at the University of Florida. He is the author of *Freud and Oedipus* and *The Psychoanalytic Vocation: Rank, Winnicott, and the Legacy of Freud.*

MURRAY M. SCHWARTZ is Vice President for Academic Affairs and Dean of Faculty at The Claremont Graduate School in Claremont, California. He is coeditor of *Representing Shakespeare* and *Memory and Desire: Aging, Literature, Psychoanalysis*. He has written many essays on Shakespeare, psychoanalysis, and literature and psychology.

ELLEN HANDLER SPITZ is visiting lecturer of aesthetics in psychiatry at Cornell University Medical College. A Getty scholar in 1989–90, she is the author of *Art and Psyche* and *Image and Insight*.

MADELON SPRENGNETHER is professor of English at the University of Minnesota, where she teaches both critical and creative writing. She is the author of *The Spectral Mother: Freud, Feminism, and Psychoanalysis* and a coeditor of *The (M)other Tongue*. She has published a collection of poems, *The Normal Heart*, and one of personal essays, *Rivers, Stories, Houses, Dreams*, in addition to coediting *The House of Via Gombito: Writing by North American Women Abroad*.

JOHN TURNER is lecturer in English at University College, Swansea. He is the author of *Wordsworth, Play and Politics* and coauthor of *Shakespeare: The Play of History* and *Shakespeare: Out of Court*. He has also published a guide to *Macbeth* for the Open University and articles on Shakespeare, Wordsworth, and D. H. Lawrence.

DAVID WILLBERN is associate professor of English at SUNY Buffalo, on the faculty of the Center for the Study of Psychoanalysis and Culture, and author of essays on Shakespeare, Renaissance drama, Freud, and psychoanalytic criticism. He is currently completing a book, *Poetic Will: Shakespeare and the Play of Language*.

D. W. WINNICOTT was president of the British Psycho-Analytical Society from 1956 to 1959 and from 1965 to 1968. His books include *Through Pediatrics to Psycho-Analysis*, *The Maturational Processes and the Facilitating Environment*, *Playing and Reality*, *The Piggle*, and *Psycho-Analytic Explorations*.

ANNE M. WYATT-BROWN is assistant professor in the linguistics program at the University of Florida. She is the author of *Barbara Pym: A Critical Biography*, coeditor of *Aging and Gender in Literature: Studies in Creativity*, and has published articles and review essays in gerontological, literary, and psychoanalytic journals.

Index

Designer: Susan Clark
Text: 10/12 Sabon
Compositor: Maple-Vail
Printer: Maple-Vail
Binder: Maple-Vail